POULTRY SCIENCE
AND
PRODUCTION

Robert E. Moreng and John S. Avens

Department of Animal Sciences
Colorado State University
Fort Collins, Colorado

RESTON PUBLISHING COMPANY, INC.
A Prentice-Hall Company
Reston, Virginia

Library of Congress Cataloging in Publication Data

Moreng, Robert E.
    Poultry science and production.

    Includes index.
    1. Poultry. 2. Poultry industry. I. Avens, John S.
II. Title.
SF487.M84 1985   636.5   84–6853
ISBN 0–8359–5559–1

*Editorial/production supervision and
interior design by Norma M. Karlin*

10 9 8 7 6 5 4 3 2 1

PRINTED IN THE UNITED STATES OF AMERICA

DEDICATION

This book is dedicated to past, present, and future students of poultry science and the men and women of the poultry industry who have, over the many years, provided the basis for this text on the science and business of poultry production. The successes and the failures experienced as the poultry industry developed have contributed to our knowledge. We look forward to a bright future for all involved in poultry science and production; a future that will provide the student with an exciting career challenge and will provide the poultry industry well-educated graduates who can be the basis for continued success.

This book is personally dedicated to each individual student of Professors Bob Moreng and Jack Avens. You have been an essential part of our long and enjoyable careers as your teachers because we have been affected by each of you. It is our hope that you continue, as we, to be life-long learners and teachers, whether it be in the classroom or somewhere else.

REM and JSA

CONTENTS

Preface   ix

Acknowledgments   x

Chapter 1   **THE COMMERCIAL POULTRY INDUSTRY RELATED TO AGRICULTURAL FOOD PRODUCTION   1**

Poultry Development as an Industry, 1
Poultry as an American Agricultural Enterprise, 8

Chapter 2   **CLASSIFICATION, NOMENCLATURE, AND SHOWING OF POULTRY   15**

Domestication and Development of Breeds, 16
Breed Identification and Classification, 21
Terminology, 33
Showing, 40

Chapter 3   **AVIAN ANATOMY AND PHYSIOLOGY   47**

Feathers and Skin, 48
Skeletal System, 52

Muscular System, 56
Digestive System, 60
Urinary System, 64
Cardiorespiratory Systems, 65
Reproductive System and the Egg, 70
Endocrine and Nervous Systems, 79

Chapter 4   **GENETICS, BREEDING, AND CULLING AND
SELECTION   85**

Genetic Inheritance, 86
Breeding Practices, 100
Culling and Selection, 107

Chapter 5   **REPRODUCTION, EMBRYONIC DEVELOPMENT,
AND INCUBATION   115**

Reproduction, 115
Embryology, 134
Incubation, 146

Chapter 6   **BROODING, REARING, HOUSING AND EQUIPMENT,
AND PRODUCTION OF POULTRY   163**

Brooding and Rearing, 165
Housing and Equipment, 174
Ventilation Systems and Environment, 187
Waste Disposal and Utilization, 190
Poultry Production, 192

Chapter 7   **NUTRITION AND FEEDING   203**

Poultry Nutrition, 204
Feeding Poultry, 228

Chapter 8   **MANAGEMENT FOR DISEASE CONTROL   235**

Diseases, 236
Miscellaneous Disease Problems, 245
Other Abnormal Conditions, 247
Disease Prevention and Control, 248

Chapter 9   **FOOD EGGS AND EGG PRODUCTS**   **257**

     Egg Quality, 259
     Egg Products and Marketing, 276

Chapter 10   **POULTRY MEAT AND MEAT PRODUCTS**   **285**

     Processing Poultry Meat, 288
     Government Regulation of Poultry Processing, 315
     Further Processing, 325
     Purchase, Preparation, and Consumption of Poultry Meat, 335

Chapter 11   **AGRICULTURAL ANIMAL WELFARE**   **345**

     Animal Care, 346
     Animal Rights, 348

Chapter 12   **PLANNING AND MANAGING A POULTRY ENTERPRISE**   **357**

     Hatchery Operation Management and Design, 357
     Planning, 364
     Management, 369

Appendix 1   **CHICKEN BREEDS AND VARIETIES**   **373**

     Breeds, Varieties, and Strains, 373
     American Class, 374
     Asiatic Class, 380
     English Class, 383
     Mediterranean Class, 388
     Games Class, 392
     Continental Class, 393
     French Class, 394
     Hamburg Class, 396
     Oriental Class, 397
     Polish Class, 398
     Miscellaneous Varieties, 399
     Bantams, 401

Appendix 2   **PREPARING A SKELETON**   **403**

Appendix 3   **MEASURING SPECIFIC GRAVITY OF EGGS   407**

Appendix 4   **POULTRY FEED INGREDIENT ANALYSIS TABLE   409**

Appendix 5   **TYPICAL POULTRY RATIONS   417**

Chick Starter and Developer Rations, 417
Layer Rations, 418
Turkey Rations, 419

Appendix 6   **CUTTING A POULTRY CARCASS   421**

Appendix 7   **DEBONING A POULTRY CARCASS   425**

Glossary   **429**

Index   **433**

PREFACE

This book has been prepared to provide the student and poultry producer with pertinent information concerning the many aspects of poultry science and production. The poultry industry has excelled in the application of innovative ideas and new techniques to the efficient production of nutritious food products for humans. We have found the task of relating this story by adequately uncovering all aspects involved to be a challenge. We have attempted to approach the topics with sufficient detail in avian science to provide an adequate basis for meaningfully studying the interesting applications to production. We realize we have not told the complete story in the detail an entire volume on each topic could provide. However, it is our intention that the book will provide a comprehensive text for an introductory course on the application of science to the business of food production through poultry.

Writing this book has involved much work, but has been an intellectually stimulating and, therefore, rewarding experience. Our mutual appreciation for how the avian species has always provided the human senses a source of visual and audio pleasure, as well as taste satisfaction, provided our stimulus to start writing. The excitement we have both experienced over many combined years of telling this story verbally to hundreds of students provided the incentive to continue writing. We are excited to explore with you one of the successful attempts of humans to supply their increasing demand for food. Let us tell you now the exciting story about chickens, turkeys, ducks, and geese; truly fascinating creatures, as you will see.

ACKNOWLEDGMENTS

The authors wish to acknowledge the many people who have indirectly contributed to the information contained in this text: former students, teachers, scientists, and industry personnel. Specifically, we are grateful to the typists who diligently prepared the manuscripts, to the reviewers of the manuscript for useful suggestions, and to the publisher who has provided the opportunity to make this book possible. Specific acknowledgment should go to Dr. John Skinner, University of Wisconsin, for information and materials on chicken breeds and varieties; Marty Traynor for many of the photographs; Longmont Foods Company and Morning-Fresh Farms for opening their doors to our photographer; and Susan Gruhlke for cartoon caricatures. Dian Webster, an avian scientist and biological illustrator, created most of the drawings to illustrate much of the text of this book. She very capably has visualized and illustrated what otherwise would have been merely verbal descriptions.

CHAPTER 1

THE COMMERCIAL POULTRY INDUSTRY RELATED TO AGRICULTURAL FOOD PRODUCTION

A wholesome, nutritious, inexpensive, and versatile source of nutrients has become available to humans at most income levels. A barnyard poultry enterprise has developed through advances in efficiency and uniformity of production, enhanced by a philosophy of innovation in technology and management, to become a dynamic multibillion dollar poultry industry. The application of poultry to the science of food production exemplifies a major phase in the total agricultural success story.

POULTRY DEVELOPMENT AS AN INDUSTRY

The poultry industry began to take shape in the mid-1930s with an interesting pattern of independent development. The word *industry* may be misleading in terms of pure industrial development. Although the term industry may project the image of large commercial units, the early development involved the combination of small production flocks that led to larger integrated commercial chicken and turkey units. These units produced a valuable food commodity and consumed manufactured products and feed ingredients, thus creating new supplier and marketing enterprises providing new sources of income to a substantial segment of the population. The global economic impact of this commodity group has

1

certainly been significant in terms of total world food production. Many countries throughout the world have followed the same basic developmental pattern of integrating family unit production, which in many instances has helped stablize the rural economy. The relatively small financial investment required to start a poultry enterprise and the relative flexibility in facilities utilization provide an excellent base for poultry development in areas of the world with largely rural economies. The commercial investor enjoys the rapid turnover of capital as flocks are marketed between 7 and 25 weeks, depending on the type.

During the years 1929–1936, when the United States suffered from economic depression, severe drought, and dust storms, many rural families survived on the products and income of the family chicken flock. The basic poultry unit, even after 1936, provided the foundation for the family farm and added economic stability, especially during periods of financial stress. The ability of chickens to produce valuable food products with a minimal investment in time and money placed poultry production within the means of every rural family. These production advantages have allowed poultry to consistently provide a source of nutritious food for families with limited resources, an important factor in developing countries throughout the world.

Although chickens are a primary source of poultry meat throughout the world, other forms of poultry provide a substantial source of food and income in specific areas. Ducks are widely produced in both small and large units in the Orient where the meat and eggs become part of a varied diet that may otherwise be deficient in animal protein. Pigeons (squab), guinea fowl, and geese are produced commercially in many parts of the world, but are not a major part of the poultry industry in the United States. Although the turkey is of commercial importance in the United States, Canada, Israel, and some areas of Europe, few are raised as small farm fowl in any country. The turkey (Figure 1–1), native to the North American continent, was hunted by the natives and its bones and feathers were utilized in ritualistic costumes. However, there is little evidence that turkeys were widely utilized by the American Indians as a food source.

Development of the commercial poultry industry began in the early 1940s as the world became involved in World War II. In the United States the industry grew independent of government programs, thus maintaining a competitive edge by striving for efficiency of production in a highly competitive market. Without the yoke of rationing and other restrictions during World War II, the production of poultry meat and eggs progressed rapidly. Technical developments based upon achievements of scientific research provided the momentum for rapid industry expansion. These research results, ultimately applied to production management and technology, provided meat for almost everyone regardless of economic status.

FIGURE 1–1
The wild turkey has proven to be the forerunner of a basic segment of the United States poultry industry; it was utilized by the American Indian and "discovered" by European explorers as one of the products of the new world.

The chicken changed from a holiday or Sunday dinner treat to an anyday meal item. In a span of 20 years, 1940–1960, the broiler chicken changed from a bird marketed at 16 weeks of age to one marketed at 8 weeks, weighing 3–3½ pounds and converting at the rate of three pounds of feed per pound of gain. This amounted to a savings of close to 100% in production cost. This rapid improvement in production efficiency provided the consumer and producer a great economic advantage over other food commodities in a period of rising production costs. The retail price of broilers dropped substantially so that chicken meat that sold for 65 cents per pound in 1940 was available for 29 cents per pound in 1960, with a concurrent increase in quality and wholesomeness. With this success as an impetus, the poultry industry has experienced continued rapid advancement since 1960. This advance has been based on a philosophy of innovation and dynamic change that was unique in animal agriculture (Figure 1–2). Per-capita consumption of broiler chicken meat reached 48.6 pounds in 1981 in the United States. Per-capita consumption of all poultry meat in the United States has reached a total of 64 pounds. Growth of the broiler industry has been predicted to increase at a rate of 2%–3% a year, to reach a "destiny" by 1990 when broilers would be the number-one meat by volume sold in the United States.

    The egg industry did not exhibit the same growth pattern as broilers, as per-capita egg consumption has steadily decreased since 1944. In 1981, per-capita consumption of eggs in the United States was 265 per person. As American life-styles changed and the postwar standard of living increased, the consumer became very diet conscious and convenience oriented. Large breakfasts built around eggs were replaced with pastry and coffee or dry cereal for the busy working family. While chicken and turkey benefited from advertising "Low in fat, high in protein," eggs suffered from a "cholesterol scare." In spite of the high total nutritional value of

FIGURE 1–2
Improved management, nutrition, genetics, disease control, and business innovations have made possible the brooding and rearing of large numbers of birds together, thus providing the consumer with a wholesome and inexpensive source of animal protein.

eggs, the consumer restricted egg use in order to reduce dietary cholesterol. It has only been in the last few years that the cause-effect relationship associating dietary intake of cholesterol to heart disease has been seriously questioned. The facts that eggs are versatile and provide an inexpensive source of high quality protein and many other essential nutrients provide a potential for gradual expansion of the egg industry. However, appropriately applied marketing skills are essential if per-capita consumption of eggs is to increase significantly.

The turkey industry has developed at a slower pace than the broiler industry. However, the traditional holiday bird has recently been developed into a variety of convenient and available food items. The United States per-capita consumption of turkey meat in 1981 was 10.7 pounds, up from 6.1 pounds in 1960. The industry has turned from "turkey" production to "meat" production and is much more extensively converting the whole turkey carcass meat into specialized processed meats. Cooked boneless roasts and sausage, ham, ground meat, bologna, hot dogs, and smoked specialty meats are a few of the turkey meat products now widely used in our daily diet at breakfast, lunch, and dinner. The truly competitive nature of these familiar meat products made from economically produced turkey has placed the turkey industry at an economic advantage to gain a substantial share of the processed meat market. The very fact that this potential is being realized in the United States places turkey on the horizon for future product development in selected other areas of the world.

If animal protein is to play a part in human nutrition, poultry meat and eggs certainly have the potential to be a primary protein source because of their economic advantages and relatively few religious or cultural restrictions. Developing nations seek knowledge of poultry meat and egg production to provide relatively low cost, highly nutritious food for large populations. Commercial expansion of established poultry companies has occurred recently in some areas of Africa and South America. This has provided a demand for products from American and European manufacturers as well as for technically trained personnel. One of the more rapid areas of development has been in South America, with Brazil a major poultry exporting country. Lack of available local feed supplies appears to be one of the major limiting factors to poultry development in some areas of the world. Competition for grain consumed by humans also restricts poultry development. However, conversion of relatively unpalatable feedstuffs to more nutritious poultry meat and eggs provides a very promising potential.

The poultry industry in the United States started on family farms in the Midwestern states where grain production was concentrated. Broilers were grown in small flocks and eggs were produced from small flocks providing a substantial source of "grocery money" to the woman of the household. Every Midwest town developed a hatchery, feed store, and poultry processing facility. Collection and distribution centers connected the widely dispersed poultry industry with consumer markets. Producers of seed corn found their systems of genetics and hybrid breeding could be applied to breeding chickens, and thus a new bird was developed that would provide a basis for greatly improved production efficiency to follow. This new, scientifically developed chicken proliferated in the Midwest. As its competitive advantages became apparent, it became widely accepted in what would emerge as the nation's poultry industry. Broiler and egg flocks began to prosper and grow on the East coast, particularly in Maine and Delmarva Peninsula, and in Indiana and Illinois, and in California. Other areas failed to develop significantly because of the apparent competitive advantage realized in the Southeastern states. The South, recovering from the ravages of the Civil War, had developed intense tobacco and cotton production, which depleted many nutrients from the soil. A vast pool of labor, inexpensive housing, a mild climate, and a feed source close enough to production provided a necessary competitive edge on which the broiler industry was to develop and grow. Thus began a success story never equaled in animal agriculture, as a poultry "enterprise" was transformed into a poultry industry. Feed was shipped south from the Midwest, and the family poultry business, which once supplied grocery money on farms throughout the nation, also went south. Poultry soon took a prominent place on the grocery shelf, as it became less costly to buy broiler meat and eggs at the store than to keep chickens in small flocks.

Integrated broiler production units (Figure 1–2) with birds grown under contract with processors developed a partnership of many relatively small independent producers. Integrating provided the advantages of consistent supplies at least cost and a predetermined market. Financing and production incentives were offered growers for improved livability and efficient feed conversion. Refrigerated trucking to all parts of the country assured the consumer fresh poultry. Locally produced chicken no longer could obtain the premium price required to meet production costs of small inefficient production units. The states of Arkansas, Georgia, Alabama, North Carolina, and Mississippi now supply a large portion of the broilers consumed in the United States.

Growth of the egg industry was slower than that of the broiler industry. As per-capita egg consumption declined, total egg consumption remained quite steady as the population grew. Small poultry flocks began to disappear from farms as economic units, and large firms specialized in the production, processing, and packaging of only eggs. (Figure 1–3). Although the large egg production "ranches" shipped eggs to distant markets, smaller flocks consisting of 35,000 to 100,000 hens could, with careful management, compete by promoting the advantages of freshly laid, locally produced eggs. Eggs have the advantage of relatively simple processing requirements compared to broilers, allowing more flexibility in movement of product through various marketing channels. Egg production established its foothold in California and in the Southeastern states. States that now lead in egg production are California, Georgia, Pennsylvania, Indiana, and Arkansas, followed closely by Texas, Alabama, and North Carolina. Centers of egg production are scattered throughout the nation, keeping production from being as highly concentrated as production of broilers and turkeys. The interregional shifts that have occurred in egg production since 1930 reveal moves into the Pacific, South Atlantic, and South Central states that now comprise over half of the total United States egg production.

North Carolina, Minnesota, and California have lead the nation in production of turkeys, with Arkansas, Missouri, and Virginia currently holding the next three positions. Changes have occurred in the geographical concentration of turkey production. Areas that once thrived on production of the festive Thanksgiving bird have found seasonal production to be inefficient. Following World War I, turkeys were produced throughout the nation on many small farm units of 100 to 1,000 birds. Central processing plants, usually not over 50–100 miles from the production farms, processed these birds into a form called "New York Dressed,"

FIGURE 1–3
Eggs from flocks of laying hens under controlled environmental conditions assure the consumer of a highly nutritious, attractive product. (Photograph by Marty Traynor.)

with blood and feathers removed, but head, feet and entrails remaining. These birds were packed in ice in wooden barrels and shipped by railroad to the large city markets. By World War II complete carcass processing was initiated to improve shelf-life and consumer acceptability. At this time the pattern of the commercial turkey industry emerged forcing the small flock producer to become larger (Figure 1–4) or to contract with a processing and marketing business able to provide the necessary processing for the retail market. This led to integration of the production farms into the corporate structure of the processing and marketing companies. As competitive markets developed for further-processed meats, the turkey industry enlarged production units in response to increased demand. This expansion was usually financed by a feed company or processing plant anxious to get in on the rapid turnover of capital and the higher profit margin of further processed turkey. The industry has grown consistently since the mid-1940s. For the most part, it has grown in states that were originally concentrated production areas, but it also started up in new areas. The Southeastern states have been one of the most rapidly developing areas. United States turkey production has experienced a steady 172% increase since 1952, during which time output dropped only four times and was then followed by an abrupt rise. The three top pro-

FIGURE 1–4
Healthy and alert turkeys provide the answer to successful mass production of turkey meat. This has made possible the high protein, low fat, basic
meat now incorporated into many of the processed-meat products available to the consumer throughout the year. (Photograph by Marty Traynor.)

ducing states North Carolina, Minnesota, and California totaled 43% of
the United States production; 12 states produce 87%.

Supporting industries have followed the development of the poultry
industry very closely providing equipment and supplies, including feed
and medications, essential for large-scale production, processing, and
marketing. The poultry industry relies on quality equipment for hatching,
brooding, feeding, and processing its products. It requires transportation,
warehousing, refrigeration, energy, and people. The demand of the poultry industry for college-educated specialists as well as many technically
trained persons, provides many excellent employment opportunities.

POULTRY AS AN AMERICAN
AGRICULTURAL ENTERPRISE

Poultry is one segment of agriculture that has moved uniquely ahead in
its approach to the science, technology, and business of feeding people.

However, all phases of agriculture are interrelated in purpose, as well as in dependence upon each other for sources of supply and market outlets. For example, the poultry industry utilizes large amounts of grains, soybeans, and other feedstuffs.

The United States annually exports millions of metric tons of feed grains to other countries, primarily Japan, Western and Eastern Europe, the Soviet Union, the Peoples Republic of China, Southeast Asia, and South America. Fluctuations in grain supplies, demands, and prices have a very real effect on poultry production. Thus, world politics and trade can influence poultry production in any country, as all phases of agriculture can be effected. The agricultural production ability of any nation is a measure of its development and quality of life.

History books have not emphasized the fact that millions of tons of food are produced in the United States and exported throughout the world every year. Instead, we read in history books about the battles in Vietnam, Cambodia, Ireland, Iran, Argentina, and Africa. History books do not tell about the families who have helped build agriculture to provide for millions, but instead will tell about national political and military leaders. J. Henri Fabre said it quite well, "History . . . celebrates the battle fields whereon we meet our death, but scorns to speak of plowed fields whereby we thrive; it knows the names of the kings' bastards, but cannot tell us the origin of wheat. That is the way of human folly." This statement from the past continues to have particular significance in modern times.

> A sunburned man on a tractor plants the seed that eventually sustains life for us all. As the farmer turns his furrows he uses every imaginable form of know-how to obtain the best and most from his land. His contoured fields and automated feedlots attain a productivity unmatched by nonfarm industry, and unmatched in recorded time. He has harnessed sun and soil and science and left his mark on history.[1]

Although agriculture is the world's largest and most vital industry, since it affects the quality of life of virtually everyone, many consumers don't really know where food comes from . . . and don't really care. Many urban consumers think beef steak somehow "sprouts up" in the local food market, cellophane wrapped. They just don't picture the original source of a Burger King "Whopper" or a McDonald's "Big Mac" walking around on four legs! They don't associate food with live animals and plants (Figure 1–5). Many consumers take food for granted and strongly com-

---

[1] J. Hayes, ed., *The Yearbook of Agriculture*. United States Department of Agriculture, house document no. 349 (Washington, D.C.: The United States Government Printing Office, 1966), p. ix.

FIGURE 1–5
Retail poultry products bear little resemblance to the animal from
which they are derived.

plain when the price of food goes up, while voicing little objection to the
increased costs of other luxuries to which they have become accustomed.

In 1951, 23 cents of every dollar of take-home pay was spent to feed
the average family in the United States. Currently, out of every dollar of
take-home pay, only 16.6 cents goes for food. We are eating twice as
much poultry meat today as we did in the 1950s. Food is a much better
bargain today than it was 30 years ago, largely because food prices have
not risen nearly as fast as wages. Americans now enjoy more and better
foods for a smaller portion of their paycheck than ever before in the United
States and for less than citizens of most other countries in the world today.
In Japan and England, 26% of the consumers' take-home pay goes to feed
an average family; in Canada, Australia, and Sweden, 20%–30%; in
France, 31%; in Poland and Korea, 50%; in East India, 60%; and in Russia, 65% of the consumers' take-home pay goes to feed an average family.
In the United States only 16% of the consumers' take-home pay goes to
feed an average family. In Moscow, a person would have to work 99
minutes to earn enough money to buy a dozen eggs. A person in London
would have to work 20 minutes to earn enough money to buy a dozen
eggs. In Washington, D.C., a person would have to work only 10 minutes
to earn enough money to buy a dozen eggs. Nowhere else in the world
is food so good tasting and nutritious, so easy to prepare, and so plentiful
and inexpensive as it is in America.

The United States agriculture industry produces the largest, single, positive balance in international trade of any American industry. With only about 5% of the world's population, the United States supplies over 20% of the world's total food. United States farmers produce: 40% of the world's soybeans, 15% of the world's wheat, and 25% of the world's other grains. This accounts for 60% of our soybean crop, 46% of our wheat, and 27% of our feed grains that leave the United States. The export of these commodities provides an important part of the United States balance-of-trade in the world market.

The American farmer is the most efficient food producer in the world, and poultry leads livestock production efficiency. One American farmer can produce enough food and fiber for 78 other people, 26 of them residents of foreign countries. One Western European farmer produces enough food for only 19 other people. One Japanese farmer produces enough food for only 14 other people. One Russian farmer produces enough food for only 10 other people. In the United States today, 30% of all nonfarm workers in private industry depend upon the American farmer for a job. The 78 people each American farmer feeds can work in the city doing other things; they do not have to toil in the fields.

The farmer's cost of producing crops and livestock has increased drastically over the past few years and continues to escalate. During the same period of time, the prices the producer receives for the food have decreased, while wholesale food prices have increased more than 30% and retail food prices have increased more than 75%, and even more than 100% in some food categories. For the farmer, the demand for food is increasing, but the supplies are uncontrolled. The farmer is the only business person in America who buys equipment and supplies at retail, sells his produce at less than wholesale, and pays the transportation cost both ways. Eighty-seven percent of the rise in food prices since 1973 has occurred in the food after it left the farm. Most of the increase in food prices goes to the "middlemen," not the farmer. For example, if the average retail price of a small box of cornflakes was $1.15, less than ten cents is the on-farm production cost of the corn. In a box of cornflakes, the box costs more than the farm production cost of the corn; the "free" plastic toy in the box costs more than the corn; the advertising costs more than the corn; and also the farm-to-consumer transportation costs are greater than what the farmer receives for producing the corn. If the farmer made no profit in producing the corn, it would reduce the cost of the $1.15 box of cornflakes less than four cents. Farm prices and farm profits have very little impact on the price of food to the consumer today. So how have farmers made a living and how will they continue to make a living with these narrow profit margins? By becoming more and more efficient, through scientific agriculture and good management, and by avoiding overproduction.

Agriculture is the original solar-energy trapping system. Energy is collected from the sun and fixed in the form of plant and animal products including poultry and eggs, useful to humans. American agriculture produces 12 times as much energy in the plants it grows, as the energy it uses from fossil fuels. On a world-wide scale, there will be 200,000 additional people to feed by this same time tomorrow. World population by the year 2014 could total nine billion, two times what it is currently. With these additional people the world will have to produce an additional 30 million tons of food each year, at an annual increase of 2.5%, just to maintain present per-capita consumption levels—and people are starving today. In the next 30 years, enough food must be produced to equal all the food that has ever been produced in history up to now and the money must be available to purchase this food and pay the producer.

Poultry and egg production in developed countries is scientific, efficient, and big—and it will get bigger. It has to be done on a large scale if we are going to provide basic food for the masses of people on earth today and in the future, as inexpensively as it is being done today. The American poultry industry is a complex and vital industry in our society. Gone are most of the small barnyard flocks that we, our parents, and grandparents perhaps remember. We have long passed the point of producing food for a small number of people on a small acreage. Poultry production today is based on a highly advanced system of technology and science developed through research, requiring intelligent, well-educated men and women to make it work. When one agricultural producer in America stops producing food, 78 other people will have to produce their own food—or starve to death if they don't know how or don't have the facilities. William Jennings Bryan must have appreciated the importance of agriculture as early as 1896:

> . . . the great cities rest upon our broad plains and prairies. Burn down your cities and leave our farms, and your cities will spring up again as if by magic. But destroy our farms and the grass will grow in the streets of every city in the country.

Food is energy for us. Without food we could do nothing—we would not even be here. Today, food production is agriculture. Those who will be directly involved in modern agriculture are heading right into the most exciting and critical, the most dynamic and rapidly changing, and the most vital profession in the world today . . . "agriculture." They will be producing food, which fuels people and maintains their lives; without which nothing else in the world would be possible. There is no phase of agriculture more modern, more scientific, and more efficient than today's poultry industry. The poultry industry depends on advances in crop production, for the basic feed ingredients must be available at reasonable prices. The future broiler chicken will reach $3\frac{1}{2}$ pounds in four weeks instead of the now accepted seven weeks, and turkeys will show relatively similar gains. Egg production will increase and surpass 365 eggs per hen per year.

> "I can't believe that!" said Alice.
>
> "Can't you?" the Queen said in a pitying tone. "Try again: draw a long breath, and shut your eyes."
>
> Alice laughed. "There's no use trying," she said: "One can't believe impossible things."
>
> "I daresay you haven't had much practice," said the Queen. "When I was your age, I always did it for half-an-hour a day. Why, sometimes I've believed as many as six impossible things before breakfast . . . ."[2]

The poultry industry has believed and accomplished "impossible things." Step now "through the looking glass," and learn about the "beautiful" chicken: Truly, the most amazing and fascinating biological machine humans ever developed, from an animal God created, to serve their needs.

---

[2] Lewis, Carroll, *Alice's Adventures in Wonderland* and *Through the Looking-Glass*. (Cleveland: Collins World, 1974).

CHAPTER 2

CLASSIFICATION, NOMENCLATURE, AND SHOWING OF POULTRY

The origin and development of the modern-day fowl from a bird of many splendors is evident from the many breeds and varieties of poultry still maintained and utilized in shows, fairs, and for the sport of cock fighting. Domesticated chickens, turkeys, and waterfowl have been utilized in dietary patterns throughout the world for many years and have become an economically valuable commodity of commerce.

The principal purpose of poultry flock is to provide meat or eggs either as a home project or a commercial enterprise. The dual purpose "farm type" chicken may be a practical bird for specific use in small home flocks where economics of production is given less priority than other factors, such as the desire for fresh, "home-produced" eggs and meat. Commercial enterprises must place economics as a major factor, with due consideration of the costs of labor, capital investment, and mixed feed. It is essential for the commercial enterprise to plan the most efficient path to success. The breed and strain of poultry should be given due consideration. Most strains within breeds are developed by the breeder based upon optimal performance objectives of the specific production bird. A strain should be developed to meet specific production requirements of the commercial poultry enterprise. An understanding of classification and nomenclature of poultry provides a basis for selecting desired breed and strain characteristics in breeding and production stock.

DOMESTICATION AND DEVELOPMENT OF BREEDS

When birds first appeared on earth, they derived many basic characteristics from reptiles, such as scales on the shanks, a similar skeleton, and many other anatomical and physiological features. From Archaeopteryx (Figure 2–1), the earliest known bird that about 150 million years ago spent much of its time on the ground and climbed trees, to the modern highly specialized chicken, many changes have occurred.

Many years ago there lived in Southeast Asia, a bird that has been considered to be the first chicken, the ancestor of today's commercial chicken. As this bird was distinguishable from all other birds, it has been classified by taxonomists and assigned the Latin name *Gallus bankiva*, more commonly known today as the Red Jungle Fowl (Figure 2–2). Actually, four or more species of jungle fowl probably contributed to the present breeds of domestic fowl.

The earliest record of poultry dates back to about 3200 BC in India. In Egypt, chickens have been bred in captivity, their eggs artificially incubated, and the chicks grown for sale of meat and eggs since about

FIGURE 2–1
Archaeopteryx ("ancient winged creature") provides the evolutionary link between reptiles and birds.

FIGURE 2–2
The Red Jungle fowl is still prevalent in Southeast
Asia and is displayed in many zoos. (Courtesy of
Watt Publishing Company, Mount Morris, Illinois.)

1400 BC. Domestication of poultry in China also dates back to about 1400
BC. The Red Jungle Fowl was brought by explorers from the jungles of
Ceylon and India to Persia, Europe, and the British Isles. When the Romans invaded Gaul and England, domestic fowl were there. By the year
1 AD domesticated chickens were located in many parts of western Asia
and eastern Europe. From there they were taken by explorers to South
Africa, Australia, Japan, Russia, Siberia, and Scandinavia. In 1607 chickens were brought to the Americas by the English and became an important
part of the first permanent English settlement in North America.

Wild chickens of the *Gallus* genus still inhabit the jungles of Southeast Asia, and many colorful survivors of natural mating and selection
can be seen today roaming freely through the small villages as well as
large cities of the Phillipines, Indonesia, Malaysia, Vietnam, and Thai-
land.

The great variation in characteristics of chickens within the *Gallus* genus has allowed for development and maintenance of the standard breeds and varieties of fowl through both natural and artificial selection. The Red Jungle Fowl, which weighs about 2 pounds, only lays 10 or 12 eggs per year, enough to reproduce its species. The commercial laying hen may produce over 300 eggs per year; and the commercial broiler could, if allowed, grow to 12 pounds, yet neither produce any offspring. This discrepancy is entirely by human design and for human benefit, as will be learned from following chapters. Humans have selected from the wide variety of characteristics in fowl only those characteristics that are desired for specific purposes. These hereditary characteristics have been transmitted through specific breeding programs and improved through controlling the environment by confinement of the birds.

Humans have chosen to select a number of characteristics for maintenance and improvement in fowl. Cockfighting was once a major use of male fowl. From as early as the twelfth century, the popular sport flourished in England (Figure 2–3), until the nineteenth century when it was outlawed. However, cockfighting is still legal today in many parts of the world and even in some parts of the United States. Fighting cocks have beautiful plumage and are bred for strength, courage, and fighting spirit. The game pit attracts many spectators to observe the matches for a fight to the death, and bets are placed on which of the two birds will emerge victorious. Death often results from a punctured heart with an artificial spur (gaff) inflicted by the champion. Although cockfighting is considered inhumane and violent and is illegal in many countries for this reason, the wagering aspect of the sport has contributed to its demise in areas that prohibit organized gambling. However, as evidenced by the extent of gamecock breeding programs, one can usually find the location of a makeshift game pit in some obscure off-the-road barn on somebody's farm, where people will gather illegally to place wagers and watch brutal fights to the death of beautiful, bold, and courageous birds.

When cockfighting became illegal in England in the mid-1800s, the gamecock breeders started to breed chickens to exhibit. They were selected for uniform type, body form, and colored plumage patterns. These efforts were important in development of the standard breeds and varieties of chickens that are still used by fanciers today for exhibit and/or small home flocks. Even large-scale breeders of commercial egg and meat type chickens maintain many standard breeds as a gene pool from which their commercial strains are developed.

A similar interest in showing poultry developed almost simultaneously in America. A rivalry among breeders led to competition in poultry shows. This in turn stimulated an effort to maintain, perfect, and/or develop new breed characteristics. To judge these characteristics fairly re-

FIGURE 2–3
This print depicting a fifteenth century English game pit conveys some of the action of the ancient sport of cockfighting, currently considered inhumane and illegal in some areas of the world.

quired a standard. Therefore, in 1873, poultry breeders from the United States and Canada met in Buffalo, New York, to organize the American Poultry Association. The American Poultry Association, Inc., was the first livestock organization in North America. Its major goal has been to improve domestic poultry by maintaining purebred breeding stock. It functions to: (1) examine and license poultry judges, (2) establish official poultry show rules, (3) publish the *The American Standard of Perfection* which describes the recognized classes, breeds and varieties of poultry, and (4) recognize newly developed breeds and varieties.

Breeding of chickens for improved meat or egg production has been a relatively recent development. Using the same basic breeding techniques developed by the purebred industry for show characteristics, breeders were also able to select for and improve such characteristics as: (1) egg production, size, shape, color, and quality; (2) body weight and rate of growth; and (3) feed efficiency, high livability, and disease resistance. So, although commercial chickens today are primarily derived from basically four standard breeds, the prior development of over 200 varieties of chickens has played an essential part in the genetic development of the modern, food-producing chicken.

The wild turkey (Figure 2–4) is native to North and Central America. Native Indians hunted the turkey for food and used its feathers in clothes and headdresses. Aztec Indians of Mexico domesticated the wild turkey. The Spanish explorers then brought the turkey back to Spain. Domesticated turkeys adjusted well and were well-accepted by Europeans. By 1573 they were well-established in France, Italy, and England. Although these domesticated turkeys were brought back to America by the early settlers, the colonists had never before seen a wild turkey. Although the domesticated turkeys brought from Europe provided the basic genetic pool from which the commercial turkey of today developed, the more abundant wild turkey provided most of the turkey meat for the pioneers and became associated with the American holiday, Thanksgiving. The wild turkey can weigh over 50 pounds, run on the ground as fast as a horse, and fly through the air at over 50 miles per hour. Compared to many other wild birds including the bald eagle, it is much more intelligent, hardy, and courageous. It was for these reasons that Benjamin Franklin proposed that this noble native American bird be adopted by Congress as America's national emblem. Instead, the bald eagle with fewer and inferior credentials and of much less benefit to humans was selected.

Ducks were first domesticated in Asia, most modern breeds having mallard ancestry. Geese have been domesticated for hundreds of years,

FIGURE 2–4
The wild turkey, native to North and Central America, once domesticated, became established in many other countries of the world. The word *turkey* has thus been translated into many languages. (Courtesy of Austin Nichols Distilling Co., Lawrenceburg, Kentucky.)

most breeds being descended from the wild gray goose. Wild guinea fowl, from which the domesticated varieties descended, are found in Africa. Pheasants are native to China, and peafowl to India.

BREED IDENTIFICATION
AND CLASSIFICATION

In studying the many different types of poultry, desirable characteristics and features will be found, determining in each why one breed or variety was chosen over others for commercial use.

Purebred chickens may be identified according to their placement into a specific class, breed, variety, and/or strain. A class is a group of standard breeds that have developed in certain geographical regions of the world. Distinctive differences among breeds within a class are primarily those of body shape, size, and skin color. Distinctive differences among varieties within a breed are primarily those of feather color, pattern, and comb type. A strain is a chicken-breeding stock bearing a given name and produced by a breeder through at least five generations of closed-flock breeding. Distinctive differences are genetic and are selected by the breeder for specific purposes. The typical characteristics of each of the four major classes of chickens are summarized in Table 2–1.

Table 2–2 indicates some of the varieties of breeds within the classes of chickens, with their distinguishing characteristics. Two commercially important breeds, the Cornish (English class) and the Leghorn (Mediterranean class) are atypical in skin color. Their skin color is yellow. A description of some of the standard breeds of chickens is in Appendix 1.

Bantams are miniature chickens that originated in the Orient. There are many different types, colors, and plumage patterns. Most are exact miniatures of larger breeds and varieties, while some have unique colors

TABLE 2–1
Distinguishing Characteristics of the Four Major Classes of Chickens

Class	Skin Color	Ear-lobe Color	Egg-shell Color	Shank Feathering	Relative Size
American	Yellow	Red	Brown	No	Medium
Asiatic	Yellow	Red	Brown	Yes	Largest
English	White	Red	Brown	No	Medium
Mediterranean	(Yellow or white)	White	White	No	Smallest

TABLE 2–2
Distinguishing Characteristics of Some Varieties of Breeds Within Classes of Chickens

Class	Breed	Variety	Comb Type	Skin Color	Ear-lobe Color	Egg-shell Color	Shank Feathering	Mature Body Weight Male (kilograms/ pounds)	Female
American	Plymouth Rock	Barred	Single	Yellow	Red	Brown	No	4.3/ 9.5	3.4/ 7.5
		White							
		Buff							
		Silver Penciled							
		Partridge							
		Columbian							
		Blue							
	Wyandotte	Silver Laced	Rose	Yellow	Red	Brown	No	3.9/ 8.5	2.9/ 6.5
		Golden Laced							
		White							
		Black							
		Buff							
		Partridge							
		Silver Penciled							
		Columbian							
	Rhode Island Red	Single Comb	Single	Yellow	Red	Brown	No	3.9/ 8.5	2.9/ 6.5
		Rose Comb	Rose						
	Rhode Island White	Rose Comb	Rose	Yellow	Red	Brown	No	3.9/ 8.5	2.9/ 6.5
	Jersey Giants	Black	Single	Yellow	Red	Brown	No	5.9/13.0	4.5/10.0
		White							
	New Hampshire		Single	Yellow	Red	Brown	No	3.9/ 8.5	2.9/ 6.5
	Lamona		Single	Yellow	Red	White	No	3.6/ 8.0	2.9/ 6.5
	Dominique		Rose	Yellow	Red	Brown	No	3.2/ 7.0	2.3/ 5.0
	Java	Black	Single	Yellow	Red	Brown	No	4.3/ 9.5	3.4/ 7.5
		Mottled							

Class	Breed	Variety	Comb	Shank Color	Earlobe	Egg Color	Broody	Weights
	Buckeye		Pea	Yellow	Red	Brown	No	4.1/ 9.0 2.9/ 6.5
	Chantecler		Cushion	Yellow	Red	Brown	No	3.9/ 8.5 2.9/ 6.5
	Holland		Single	Yellow	Red	White	No	3.9/ 8.5 2.9/ 6.5
	Delaware		Single	Yellow	Red	Brown	No	3.9/ 8.5 2.9/ 6.5
Asiatic	Brahma	Light	Pea	Yellow	Red	Brown	Yes	5.4/12.0 4.3/ 9.5
		Dark						5.0/11.0 3.9/ 8.5
		Buff						5.0/11.0 3.9/ 8.5
	Cochin	Buff	Single	Yellow	Red	Brown	Yes	5.0/11.0 3.9/ 8.5
		Partridge						
		White						
		Black						
	Langshan	Black	Single	White	Red	Brown	Yes	4.3/ 9.5 3.4/ 7.5
		White						
English	Dorking	White	Single	White	Red	White	No	3.4/ 7.5 2.7/ 6.0
		Silver-Gray	Rose					4.1/ 9.0 3.2/ 7.0
		Colored	Single					4.1/ 9.0 3.2/ 7.0
	Redcap		Rose	White	Red	White	No	3.4/ 7.5 2.7/ 6.0
	Cornish	Dark	Pea	Yellow	Red	Brown	No	4.8/10.5 3.8/ 8.0
		White						
		White Laced Red						
		Buff						
	Orpingtons	Buff	Single	White	Red	Brown	No	4.5/10.0 3.8/ 8.0
		Black						
		White						
		Blue						
	Sussex	Speckled	Single	White	Red	Brown	No	4.1/ 9.0 3.2/ 7.0
		Red						
		Light						
	Australorp	Black	Single	White	Red	Tinted	No	3.9/ 8.5 2.9/ 6.5

TABLE 2-2 (Continued)

Class	Breed	Variety	Comb Type	Skin Color	Ear-lobe Color	Egg-shell Color	Shank Feathering	Mature Body Weight Male (kilograms/ pounds)	Female (kilograms/ pounds)
Mediterranean	Leghorn	Single-Comb Dark Brown	Single	Yellow	White	White	No	2.7/ 6.0	2.0/ 4.5
		Single-Comb Light Brown	Single						
		Rose-Comb Dark Brown	Rose						
		Rose-Comb Light Brown	Rose						
		Single-Comb White	Single						
		Rose-Comb White	Rose						
		Single-Comb Buff	Single						
		Single-Comb Black	Single						
		Single-Comb Silver	Single						
		Single-Comb Red	Single						
		Single-Comb Black-Tailed Red	Single						
		Single-Comb Columbian	Single						
	Minorca	Single-Comb Black	Single	White	White	White	No	4.1/ 9.0	3.4/ 7.5
		Rose-Comb Black	Rose					3.8/ 8.0	2.9/ 6.5
		Single-Comb White	Single						
		Rose-Comb White	Rose						
		Single-Comb Buff	Single						
	Spanish	White Faced Black	Single	White	White	White	No	3.8/ 8.0	2.9/ 6.5
	Blue Andalusian		Single	White	White	White	No	3.2/ 7.0	2.5/ 5.5
	Ancona	Single-Comb	Single	Yellow	White	White	No	2.7/ 6.0	2.0/ 4.5
		Rose-Comb	Rose						
	Buttercup		Buttercup	Yellow	White	White	No	2.9/ 6.5	2.3/ 5.0
	Catalana	Buff	Single	White	White	White	No	3.8/ 8.0	2.7/ 6.0

and characteristics not found in larger chickens. They are approximately one-quarter to one-fifth the weight of their larger counterparts. The American Bantam Association publishes a book of standards for bantams, and they are listed in *The American Standard of Perfection*. Bantams are raised primarily for exhibition or as pets. They are friendly, hardy, and efficiently convert feed into meat and small eggs.

The standard varieties of the single breed, Turkey, are Bronze, White Holland, Black, Slate, Narragansett, Bourbon Red, and Beltsville Small White. These varieties are described in *The American Standard of Perfection*.

The Broad Breasted Bronze variety (Figure 2–5) was developed by American breeders from the standard Bronze for the commercial turkey meat production industry. During the 1970s the turkey industry almost entirely changed to the Broad White variety (Figure 2–6), which was developed by commercial breeders from the Bronze and White Holland. The Broad White is essentially a Bronze turkey in all characteristics except white feathers. It is a fast growing, broad-breasted bird that efficiently converts feed to meat and has the white feathers that the proces-

FIGURE 2–5
The Broad Breasted Bronze Turkey provided the basic features required for commercial meat production until the broad white variety was developed for the convenience of the processor. (Colorado State University photograph.)

FIGURE 2–6
The Broad White Turkey predominates in the world's turkey industry and has surpassed the Broad Breasted Bronze in all features desired by the industry. (Photograph by Marty Traynor.)

sors prefer over the bronze feathers that leave objectionable dark pinfeathers and skin pigmentation.

There are one or more standard varieties of the following standard breeds of ducks: Pekin (White variety), Aylesbury (White), Rouen, Cayuga (Black), Call (Gray and White varieties), East India (Black), Muscovy (Colored, White and Blue), Crested (White), Swedish (Blue), Buff, Runner (Fawn and White, White and Penciled), and Khaki Campbell. These breeds are described in *The American Standard of Perfection*.

The White Pekin (Figure 2–7) is the most widely used duck for meat production, although the Muscovy is a popular farm duck, and the Khaki Campbell is a top egg producer popular in Europe. The Rouen is considered as a domesticated Mallard type. It matures slowly and has dark pinfeathers, making it less suitable than the Pekin for commercial meat production. The Runner has a small, long, and narrow body carried erect and is a good egg producer. The Khaki Campbell (Figure 2–8) was de-

FIGURE 2–7
The White Pekin duck is a popular commercial bird used worldwide for both meat and eggs. (Courtesy of Al Hollister.)

FIGURE 2–8
The Khaki Campbell duck is known for high egg-production.

veloped in England by crossing the Rouen with the White Runner. It is medium size with khaki colored plumage. It is an efficient egg producer, used commercially where duck eggs are marketable for food.

The standard varieties of geese described in *The American Standard of Perfection* are: Toulouse, Embden (Emden), African, Chinese (Brown and White varieties), Canada, Egyptian, Sebastopol, Pilgrim, and Buff. These have ultimately descended from the wild gray goose, having been domesticated worldwide for many centuries. Many crossbreed mixtures are found on small farms today.

Geese are raised primarily for meat production (Figure 2–9), usually near areas where a market exists. In some areas of the world, particularly in China, France, and Northern Europe, goose down is an important commercial commodity. Since older geese yield better quality down, breeders will often be plucked every six weeks when they are out of production (Figure 2–10). An adult goose will yield about one pound of feathers and down in a year.

Geese are relatively easy to raise in semiconfinement, since they will feed on weeds and pasture and are relatively resistant to disease. They can then be put on feed for desired weight gain just prior to market.

FIGURE 2–9
Geese, such as the White Embden, have many qualities that make them desirable as farm fowl and as commercial meat-production birds. (Courtesy of Al Hollister.)

FIGURE 2-10
Plucking geese for their down feathers at a commercial breeder farm in France to supply a worldwide market for goose down. (Courtesy of Al Hollister.)

The Toulouse and Embden breeds are of greatest economic importance, although the Chinese breed is also used commercially. Geese generally mate in pairs, but two to four females per male may be used. Also, artificial insemination can be used successfully in commercial production.

Many breeds of pigeons (Figure 2–11) are raised for exhibition, but only a few are raised for squab production. Pigeons typically mate in pairs and remain paired for life. A mated pair will produce from 1 to 12 pairs of squabs per year. Breeders are most productive between two and five years of age. Squabs are marketed at three or four weeks of age, at which time they have gained two-thirds of their adult body weight and are fully feathered under the wings.

Of the four major varieties of Guineas, the Pearl is more commonly used for meat production than the White African, Lavender, or Royal Purple. Guinea fowl (Figure 2–12) may be kept in small numbers on farms in the United States and used primarily as "watchdogs." If unconfined, they will roost on the roofs of buildings, mate in pairs, hide their nests, and will warn of approaching visitors with a loud, continuous cry. In France and other areas there is a commercial market for guinea meat. Male and female breeders are kept in cages (Figure 2–13); the semen is

FIGURE 2–11
The hobby of keeping pigeons can be easily adapted to large cities as well as to rural settings. The pigeon, however, holds in its many desirable features a potential for the production of poultry meat only partially developed.

collected, and the females are artificially inseminated weekly. Breeder females are kept through two or three egg-production cycles and can produce about 150 eggs per female per cycle. The fertile eggs are artificially incubated and hatched, and the keets are artificially brooded and grown for meat production.

There are several varieties of pheasant (Figure 2–14). The Ring-neck pheasant originating in China and a newly developed hybrid, the White pheasant, are most useful for food. However, other varieties such as the Golden pheasant, Lady Amherst, Silver, Imperial, and Reeves, are propagated for exhibition purposes. Although they are considered gamebirds, pheasants adapt well to confinement and can be propagated using many modifications of the methods developed for chickens. Meat-type pheasants are raised commercially primarily for stocking game shooting preserves or for release into the countryside.

Peafowl (Figure 2–15) are raised exclusively today for exhibition of their beautiful plumage. They will reproduce in semiconfinement; one peacock mating with four or five hens. Hens will lay five to ten eggs per year, starting the second year, which can be naturally or artificially incubated and hatched. The hatched birds may be naturally or artificially brooded.

FIGURE 2–12
Guinea fowl provide a durable barnyard bird with good potential for commercial meat and egg production. (Courtesy of Al Hollister.)

FIGURE 2–13
Male and female guinea fowl breeders in cages on a commercial farm in France provide the stock for specialized meat production. (Courtesy of Al Hollister.)

FIGURE 2–14
The Ring-neck pheasant, popular in the field as hunters' quarry, has also proven to have various domestic uses as a pen-reared bird. (Colorado State University photograph.)

FIGURE 2–15
The peafowl has very few features of commercial value, but is a beautiful ornament on some farms and large estates and is available in large city zoos for public enjoyment.

FIGURE 2–16
Swans are birds of beauty and grace. Although their meat is quite edible, swans are widely used to grace the appearance of private ponds and public parks. (Courtesy of Bonnie Bechtold.)

There are wild and domesticated swans (Figure 2–16). Domesticated varieties available are: White European Mute swans, Black swans of Australia, and Black Neck swans. They are used for exhibition purposes, being quite common in Europe. Swans are hardy and adapt well to all but the most severe cold weather. They can live on underwater vegetation or may be supplemented. Swans mate in pairs only and remain paired until death. They will lay six to eight eggs per year in ground nests made of sticks and twigs. The hatched young are called signets. Swans can live to be over 60 years old, the females breeding for up to 30 years.

TERMINOLOGY

To meaningfully study and recognize the distinguishing characteristics of the different species, breeds, and varieties of poultry, it will be necessary to know the proper nomenclature of the external anatomical features.

The male and female chicken (Figure 2–17) have some identical features. It is desirable to recognize and distinguish the features of the

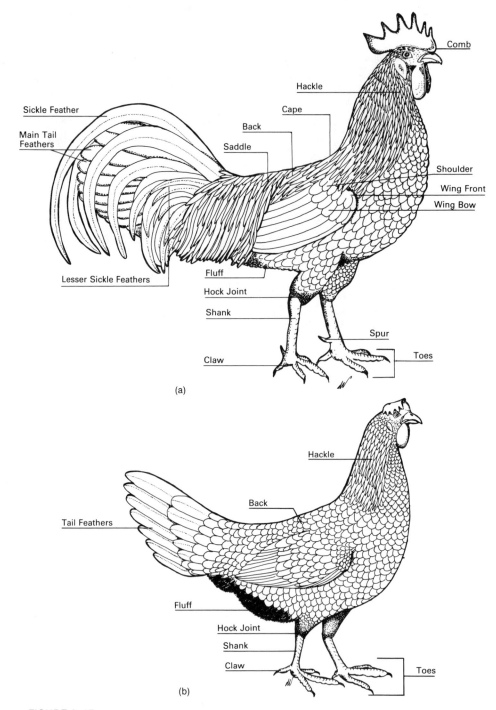

FIGURE 2–17
Although many features of the (a) male and (b) female chicken are similar, there are distinguishing characteristics. The term used to identify the characteristics is *sexual dimorphism*.

beak, comb, wattles, ears, earlobes, eyes, eye ring (eyelid), hackles, thigh, lower leg, hock joint (ankle), shank (foot), toes, and claw. The lower part of the beak is hinged at the jaw and is movable; the upper part is fused to the skull (Figure 2–18). The comb and wattles are red, soft, and warm. The ears are merely openings into the auditory canal protected by small feathers; the earlobes consist of tightly fitting specialized skin, devoid of feathers. The color of the earlobes, red or white, depends on the breed. The eyeball is covered by the eye ring which, when open, appears as a circle of skin defining the ocular opening. The hackles are the feathers of the neck. The thighs are not easily distinguished in the standing chicken as they are located along each side of the body and well-covered with feathers. The lower leg is feathered and articulates at the hock joint with the scaly shank. Since the chicken stands and walks on its toes, the shank is the foot and the hock joint is the ankle. Most chickens have three toes projecting forward and one claw projecting back.

There are different types of combs that are inherited characteristics of breeds and varieties. The single comb (Figure 2–18) is most familiar, having its base of attachment to the skull. Its posterior edge is the blade, and the spaces defined by its points are serrations. The pea comb (Figure 2–19) has three rows of bumps. The rose comb has many very small bumps and may or may not have a spike projecting back. The strawberry comb has a pitted texture, is relatively small, and sets well-forward on the head

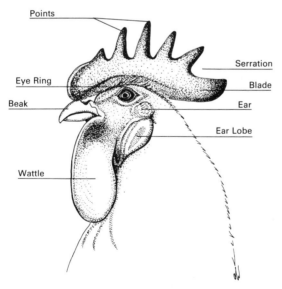

FIGURE 2–18
The head of the chicken has some unique features distinguishing it from other poultry.

FIGURE 2–19
Comb type is an interesting characteristic that distinguishes breeds and varieties of chickens:
(a) pea comb; (b) rose comb; (c) strawberry comb; (d) V-shaped comb; (e) buttercup comb; and
(f) cushion comb.

with its larger end forward. The V-shaped comb is associated with chickens that have a crest of feathers on the head, is very small, and sets well-forward on the head. These chickens may or may not also have muffs or a beard of feathers. The buttercup comb, starting at the base of the beak, forms a cup-shaped circle of points defining a deep cavity. It has a smooth, fine texture. The cushion comb is relatively small and smooth in texture, setting low and well-forward on the head.

The various wing feathers are not easily distinguishable in the standing bird. However, when the wing is spread out (Figure 2–20), the parts can be identified. The wing shoulder is that part nearest the wing's attachment to the body. The wing front is the front-most edge of unfolded wing extending to the tip. The wing bow is the upper surface portion of the wing just posterior to the wing front. The wing coverts are two rows of feathers extending out from under the wing bow feathers and covering the bases of the secondaries, providing a smooth and streamlining effect. The primary coverts are those toward the wing tip; the secondary coverts extend from the proximal portion of the wing. The primaries are the long flight feathers forming the posterior edge of the outer wing section; the secondaries of the proximal section. The axial feather is located between the primaries and secondaries.

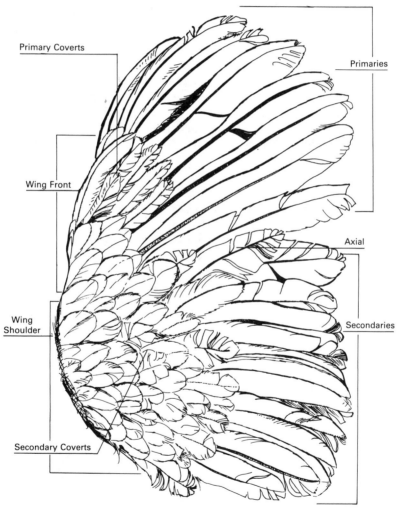

FIGURE 2–20
Distinguishing anatomical features of the wing.

The observable differences in secondary sex characteristics between the male and female chicken (Figure 2–17) are referred to as sexual dimorphism. The male has a larger body, comb, and wattles. In single-comb birds the male's comb will be turgid and stand erect, whereas the female's comb may flop over on one side. In multicolored varieties, the male will have more variety of coloring in his plumage than the female. The male has longer and more pointed hackle feathers than the female. The male and female both have main tail feathers. However, in the male only, the tail feathers are covered by sickle feathers. Also, only the male has saddle feathers. The male has a larger, more developed spur than does the female.

A young chicken from hatch to five weeks of age is called a chick. A male chicken less than one year of age is a cockerel; a female through her first laying year may be referred to as a pullet. A mature male chicken greater than one year of age is referred to as a cock or rooster; a mature female greater than one year old may be called a hen. A castrated male chicken is a capon.

The turkey has nomenclature similar to the chicken but with a few notable differences (Figure 2–21). It has no comb on its head, but does

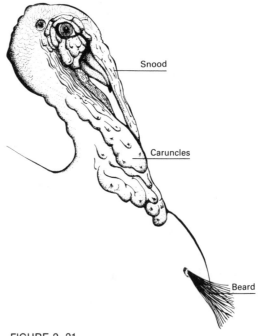

FIGURE 2–21
Distinguishing anatomical features of the turkey.

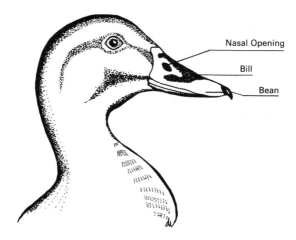

FIGURE 2–22
Distinguishing anatomical features of the duck.

have a fleshly growth from the base of the beak that is known as a snood, which is very long on males and hangs down over the beak. It has a wattle, but also bumpy, red, fleshy tissue covering the head and neck, called caruncles. Male turkeys have a tuft of long, bristly, black, coarse fibers attached to the breast, known as the beard.

A young turkey is called a poult. A male turkey of any age may be referred to as a tom; female turkey, a hen.

Ducks have nomenclature similar to that of the chicken, with the following notable differences (Figure 2–22). There is no comb or other head covering. The duck's bill is flatter than the chicken's beak and has

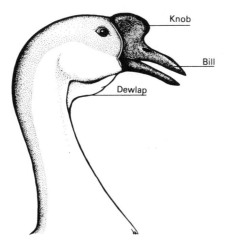

FIGURE 2–23
Distinguishing anatomical features of the goose.

a protrusion on the upper tip known as a bean. The duck has webbed toes used for swimming. Male ducks have curled feathers at the base of the tail distinguishing them from females. Male ducks emit only a hiss, whereas the female will also emit a squawk when handled.

A young duck is called a duckling. An adult male is a drake; and an adult female, a duck.

Geese have a few additional distinguishing features (Figure 2–23). Some breeds will have a horny knob at the base of the bill. Some geese also have a dewlap, which is a loosely suspended growth of skin extending from the base of the lower bill along the upper throat.

A young goose is called a gosling. An adult male is a gander; and an adult female, a goose.

SHOWING

The practice of showing birds has traditionally provided a very popular pastime as well as a professional endeavor for many people. As the poultry industry became commercialized, interest diminished to a point where those involved were only the most ardent exhibitors and 4-H Club members. However, the practice of showing poultry has been revived, and the opportunity to fit and show poultry provides an enjoyable challenge to the hobbyist. There are no poultry breed associations in the sense that exist among other livestock. Thus, there are no registries, and birds are usually not certified.

In preparation for the show it is important to know the various types of poultry (chickens, turkeys, waterfowl, and so forth) that may be accepted at a specific show. A working knowledge of breed and variety characteristics that relate to shape and color is necessary. *The American Standard of Perfection* provides this information and is the basic source of information for all judges. There are many sources of birds. A local hatchery, feed store, or mail order supplier may be able to provide purebred stock. Poultry and general farm magazines frequently contain advertisements for various breeds and varieties. The birds are obtained as chicks and reared to the desired size and weight. A good feeding and nutritional program, as well as disease control, vaccination, and other sound management practices are required.

Procedures for showing are basically the same for fitting and showing chickens, turkeys, ducks, geese, guineas, and many other fowl. The examples described refer to chickens in general. *The American Standard of Perfection* should be used as a reference for further details on individual breeds.

For showing, healthy, clean birds evidencing the basic breed and variety characteristics should be selected to fit and train at least three weeks prior to the show. There is nothing that disgusts a judge more than handling birds that are thin and emaciated and infested with lice and mites. Dusting birds properly with an appropriate insecticide available through feed stores or pet shops is recommended. You should wear a mask when dusting birds to avoid inhaling insecticide.

A coop for use in special training is handy to assist birds in becoming accustomed to close confinement. A coop approximately 24 in. high, 24 in. wide, and 30 in. long, consisting of a wooden frame and chicken wire or other wire netting for sides and top should be used. Wood shavings make a good bedding for the floor and should be clean and dry. Provide cups for feed and water and see that birds are well-fed and watered. Place the birds to be trained in the coop, one per pen, if possible; do not overcrowd. Birds should be handled carefully and quietly several times daily, taking them out and returning them to the coop. A judging stick or cane about three feet long may be used to train the birds to pose. Stroke and work the birds into position with the stick. Birds will soon learn to stand in certain positions and show off their points to the best advantage when being judged. Considerable patience is required to teach chickens to pose. Thus, when accomplished, posing may be considered a major accomplishment. Rewarding the birds with a few kernels of whole yellow corn may aid the learning process.

There are certain defects of plumage, color, and body shape so undesirable they have been designated as disqualifications. Go over each bird carefully to make sure it has none of these serious defects. A bird with a disqualification cannot win a prize. One disqualified bird in a trio entry will eliminate the entire trio. You can always find some defect in the color of plumage or the shape of the bird no matter how good the bird may be. The fewer defects a bird has, the nearer it comes to the standard in shape and color, and the better the chance of winning.

There are many color patterns represented in the different varieties of poultry. The more common color patterns are discussed below, and *The American Standard of Perfection* contains further details and photographs. The color pattern requirements and the defects in plumage color of the bread are important to know.

A white plumage should be chalk white. If soiled or dirty, the bird should be washed before exhibiting. Defects are creamy color or brassiness, and black or black specks in any part of the plumage.

Red plumage color is found in Rhode Island Reds and New Hampshires. The two colors, however, are quite different. The Rhode Island Red color should be a rich, brilliant red, uniform in shade throughout the body except where black is called for. The female is allowed a small amount of black ticking on the ends of the hackle or neck feathers, but the male's hackle should be free from any black. The tail feathers are black, and the primary and secondary feathers have edgings of black. New Hampshire plumage color is of a much lighter shade than found in Rhode Island Reds. It is a brilliant reddish bay to a medium chestnut red in some parts of the plumage. Defects of red plumage are: smut or black undercolor, parts of the plumage peppered with black, white in any part of plumage, uneven red color, light undercolor, and ticking or black on the hackle of the male bird.

Barred feathers are marked with narrow alternating black-and-white bars crossing the feather. Black bars are approximately twice the width of the white in the female. In the male, bars will vary in size on various parts of the body, but generally the bars are of equal width. Defects of barred plumage are: entire black feathers in plumage, white feathers, brown on surface, uneven barring, light undercolor, black bars wider or narrower than the white bars, and bars not going straight across the feather. Two or more entirely black wing or main tail feathers disqualifies a bird. Dark spots on the legs are defects but do not disqualify.

Buff feather color is described as being a rich, golden buff. The undercolor is lighter but should be an even buff throughout the body. Common defects of buff color are reddish buff, uneven buff coloring in different parts of the body, light colored and white feathers, and black or black peppering in feathers.

Body shape characterizes the breed; color or type of comb, the variety. Each breed has a particular type or shape of body. For example, the Leghorn's body is made up of long graceful curves. The Wyandotte is a bird of short curves. Its body will fit into a circle. The Rhode Island Red has a rectangular or brick-shaped body. The Plymouth Rock is bowl shaped.

For single entries, select the bird that has the best breed type and color, eliminating all that have serious defects. Health is very important, for a healthy bird will usually have good flesh and a bright plumage.

For trio entries, try to select two females that are as nearly alike in size, shape, and color as it is possible to get them. Sometimes birds that may not be quite as good as some other trio in type and color may win if they are uniform in these requirements. The male is one-third of the trio, pick the best one to go with the two females. One disqualified bird disqualifies the whole trio.

Exhibit birds in good condition. White-plumaged birds show soiled conditions very easily. When a white plumage is soiled and dirty, it does not look good in a show coop. Poultry raisers who raise white birds and show them usually wash their birds before taking them to the show. White-plumaged birds that have recently gone through a molt will usually not need to be washed unless the plumage has been stained. Birds with dark-colored plumages such as Barred Plymouth Rocks, Rhode Island Reds, and New Hampshires very seldom need to be washed unless their plumage becomes severely soiled.

Learning to wash birds is not a difficult task. With a little practice on birds not intended for exhibit, one can soon learn the proper procedures.

The room in which birds are to be washed should be 21°C–27°C (70°F–80°F) and free from drafts. Coops should be provided in which to place the birds after they are washed. Plenty of clean straw or shavings should be placed in the coop to keep the washed birds from becoming soiled.

Provide four tubs, setting them on boxes or benches (Figure 2–24). Fill the first two tubs with lukewarm water and the third and fourth with cold water. Place a few drops of bluing in the fourth tub to give the water a slight blue color, but take care not to get the water too blue for it will give the plumage a bluish tinge. The water in the first tub will be used for the actual cleaning, while the other tubs will be used for rinsing.

Soap the water in the first tub with a good grade of soap or detergent powder. Make a good suds before putting the bird into the water. Grasp the bird with both hands and lower it gently into the water, holding the wings so they cannot be flapped. When the bird's feet rest on the bottom of the tub, release one hand but hold the bird firmly with the other. With the free hand, gently move the feathers on all parts of the body so the soap and water will penetrate to the skin. Then with a small brush, sponge, or your hand, work the soapy water through the feathers. Rub the lather with the feathers from base to tip.

When the plumage has been thoroughly washed, transfer the birds to the second tub and thoroughly work out as much of the soap as possible. Then transfer to each of the third and fourth tub in turn, with the last

FIGURE 2–24
Procedure for washing show birds.

rinsing in the bluing water. It is important to remove all the soap, otherwise the webs of the feathers will stick and be streaked.

When the washed bird is removed from the final rinsing, the plumage should be dried as much as possible. Work as much water as possible out with the hands, then dry with a towel.

Shanks and toes may be examined at this time to make sure no dirt remains under the scales. If some is found, it should be removed with a toothpick. A small piece of cloth moistened with olive oil or vaseline should be rubbed over the comb, wattles, beak, and shanks of the birds. Do not apply too much as the plumage may become stained.

The birds should be placed in the drying coops in a warm room. Some shivering may occur. Do not place the birds too close to a heat source for they cannot stand too much heat. Also, the feathers will not be fluffy if they dry too fast. Care must be taken to see that the birds do not soil their plumage during the drying process; therefore, if two or more birds are involved, keep them separated. Wash birds only the day or night before they are to be exhibited or shipped to the show.

For shipping, a good, solid but light, shipping coop should be used. Never ship or bring birds to a show in a flimsy coop or box. Clean, dry straw or wood shavings should be placed in the coop, and a cup fastened in one corner for feed. Do not fill the cup with water for it will spill when the coop is moved and wet the straw, which will stain the plumage. In hot weather some provision should be made to provide water at intervals during shipping. Feed in the coop is not necessary if the birds are to be shipped only short distances or if they are not going to be in the coop for more than 24 hours. Water during this period is actually more important than feed for the bird.

Birds will be judged on their conformance to standards of the breeds and varieties for the following characteristics: weights, shape or type, color of plumage, color of shanks and skin, color of earlobes, color of eggs, and shape or type of comb. Some general disqualifications are:

Tail: Wry tail, split tail, squirrel tail, and entire absence of main tail feathers.

Wings: Split wing, slipped wing, clipped wing.

Back: Crooked or hunchback.

Beak: Deformed beak.

Twisted *feathers* in primaries, secondaries, main tail feathers, and sickles.

Weights: More than two pounds under standard weight, except Leghorns and Anconas, where it is more than $1\frac{1}{2}$ pounds underweight for males and more than 1 pound underweight for females.

Comb: Split single comb, sprigs on single comb. Absence of spike on rose comb and lopped comb, except on females of Mediterraneans, New Hampshires, and some rare breeds. A comb foreign to the breed.

Head and Adjuncts: Enamel white in the face of young Mediterraneans, and enamel white in the earlobes of common breeds of the American, Asiatic, and English classes.

Shanks and Toes: Decidedly bowlegs or knock-knees. Stubs or down on shanks or toes of all clean shank breeds. Entire absence of spurs on cocks. More or less than the required number of toes. Color of shanks, toes, or feet foreign to the breed.

Color: Red or yellow in any black variety. Black in quill of white varieties. Foreign color in any white variety.

General: unworthiness, disease, or deformity.

Some general defects are:

Undersized.

Too long or too short legs.

Too many or too few points on single combs.

Coarseness of comb and head.

Tail carried too high.

Exhibition birds may easily contract or transmit diseases at shows and fairs. Some basic rules and precautions related to disease prevention will provide protection to all concerned. A sick or ailing bird should never be brought to a public exhibition. In addition, it is a wise practice to keep healthy birds to themselves as much as possible during the exhibition. Equipment, feed, tools, or anything else that comes in contact with the birds should not be borrowed or loaned. Some birds may carry a specific pathogen without showing any major symptoms of the disease. Healthy birds, not previously exposed, can be extremely susceptible to unfamiliar pathogens. Sanitary procedures will prove to be a most profitable means of disease control. Minimize stress to birds from transportation, drafts, excitement, handling, and other unusual activities. Provide birds adequate feed and water. The use of antibiotics or other medications during these periods of stress can be effective if administered properly.

Fitting and showing poultry for fairs and shows is challenging, educational, and rewarding in many ways. Birds have the ability to learn and respond to specific training experiences. They are beautiful animals, and they reflect positively the exhibitor's care, knowledge, skill, and training, resulting in accomplishments not always possible for many individuals.

CHAPTER 3

AVIAN ANATOMY AND PHYSIOLOGY

A knowledge of the structure of the fowl is necessary to an understanding of functions related to its welfare for efficient production of poultry meat and eggs. Human regulation of the biological functions of this anatomy has resulted in the development of an "unnatural" animal better serving human needs, but also requiring care and protection through proper management.

As a flying machine, the bird has been endowed with structural features that provide some characteristics uniquely different from other animals. The very fact that the bird was designed to fly provided it the ability to maintain homeostasis over a relatively wide geographic area. Flight also provides a means of eluding enemies not available to other animals. Anatomical features such as hollow girder construction of the bones; fused vertebrae in the back, which are vital to providing a strong anchor for large flight muscles; and many other unique features provide the adaptation allowing birds to fly as well as walk. For example, the bird has developed unique respiratory and digestive systems adapted to sustained flight. The absence of teeth in the skull and the presence of feathers that form the outer covering of the body are more obvious examples of the unique adaptation of birds. A study of the structure of the fowl will provide a necessary basis for understanding its physiology in relation to its function as an agricultural food producer. Poultry management practices should be designed with the anatomical and physiological features of the bird in mind.

FEATHERS AND SKIN

The feather is a unique part of the bird. All birds have feathers, and no other animals do. Feathers replace many functions of the skin in other animals, such as providing protection from the elements and helping regulate body temperature. Feathers help streamline the body for flight. There are various types of feathers, each with a specific function and each with specific structural features enhancing its functional purpose. Quill feathers are found on the wings and tail, while contour feathers are the outer feathers covering the wings and body. Plumule feathers lie next to the body and are fluffy to provide the insulation needed to retain body heat in the winter and minimize absorption of environmental heat during the hot weather. A hair-like feather, the filoplume, appearing to be very rudimentary and biologically undeveloped, is located close to the body with no specific function identified. These hair-like feathers are singed from the carcass in processing for market.

Feather growth starts in a sheath of the feather follicle imbedded in the skin (Figure 3–1). At the base of this tubular pocket in the epidermal layer of the skin (Figure 3–2) there is a specialized group of cells from which many successive generations of feathers will be derived. These specialized cells consist of a core from the dermal layer of skin and a thin covering of cells from the outer epidermal layer. All parts of the feather are derived from the epidermal component, while the dermal cells provide the essential nourishment and pigments for the growing feathers. Following rapid growth to full size, the nutrient supply is stopped and the feather remains on the follicle as a nonliving structure. When the feather is lost, dormant cells on the follicle are stimulated to generate a replacement. Using its dermal muscles, the bird has the ability to move many of the feathers on the body, especially wing and tail feathers, with considerable precision and agility. This allows for maneuvering during flight and fluffing body feathers for insulation.

Although feathers may appear to have disadvantages and occasional interest has been shown in a specialized naked fowl, the absence of feathers would have an overall detrimental effect on the bird. A featherless bird, although developing a thickened skin, would be more subject to skin injury and would require considerably more heat to maintain body temperature. For commercial poultry, this would cost in terms of feed and controlled environment. Certainly there could be a possible saving too,

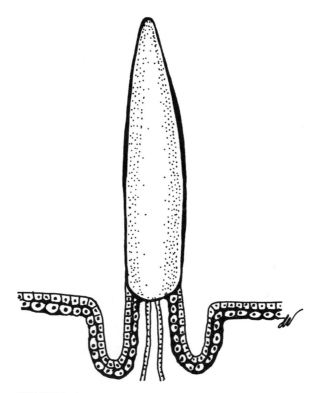

FIGURE 3–1
Specialized cells of the feather follicle consisting of a core
from the dermal layer of skin and a thin covering of cells
from the outer epidermal layer.

since feathers contain a high level of protein, and dietary requirements of this nutrient could possibly be modified. However, the advantages of a bird without feathers appear to be few, while feathers contribute much to domesticated as well as wild birds.

Feathers are the strongest natural structures of equivalent size and weight. The feather consists of a unique structure providing strength and durability for flight and protection. Figure 3–3 illustrates the typical structure of the gross anatomy as well as the detailed microscopic anatomy of a contour feather. The quill and contour feathers have a bilaterally symmetrical structure with a series of branching processes and an interlocking mechanism to provide a continuous airtight surface necessary for flight. Branching from opposite sides of the rachis or shaft are the barbs, which are visible without magnification. On microscopic inspection, it can be

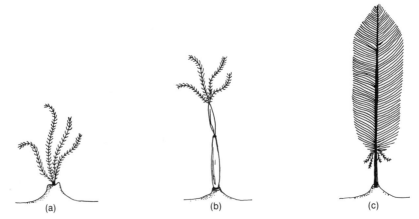

FIGURE 3–2
Development of the feather as growth from its base pushes the feather out of the follicle: (a) chick down in feather follicle; (b) sheath containing developing feather; and (c) fully developed feather in follicle, having shed sheath and down.

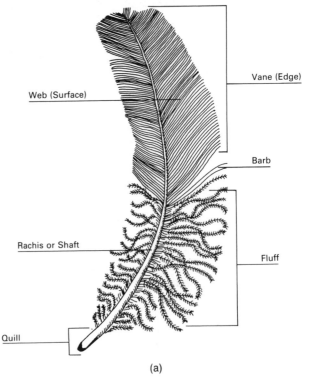

FIGURE 3–3
Anatomy of the feather: (a) gross; (b) microscopic.

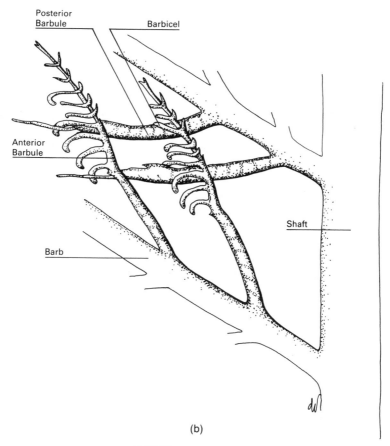

Posterior
Barbule

Barbicel

Anterior
Barbule

Shaft

Barb

(b)

FIGURE 3–3 (*Continued*)

noticed that branching from opposite sides of the barbs are barbules. Those barbules branching toward the tip of the feather are known as anterior barbules; those branching back toward the quill are called posterior barbules. It can be noticed that only the anterior barbules have branches known as barbicels, whereas the posterior barbules instead have a perpendicular ledge along their top edge. The barbicels have at their terminal end a small hook that is called the hamulus. These hamuli on the end of the barbicels of the anterior barbules hook over the ledge along the top edge of the posterior barbules projecting back from the adjacent barb. This interlocking mechanism provides the web or flight surface for pushing air when the bird flies. Plumule feathers are fluffy because they lack barbicels and hamuli. Even though a quill feather may become ruffled as the hamuli are unhooked or become disengaged they are easily hooked together again by the action of preening.

The skin of the bird is thin and pliable since the outer cover of feathers provides a protective cover. The skin possesses feather tracts that arrange feathers in a definite pattern. Feather tracts are easily identified on the plucked bird or even on the live feathered bird since they are raised above the general skin surface. These tracts contain sphincter muscles to hold the feather and usually are a point for accumulation of fat. Feather tracts are called pterylae, and the space between the tracts, apteria. A major anatomical feature of the skin of the fowl is that it does not contain any sweat glands or many sebaceous glands. There is only one major oil gland, the preen gland, located at the base of the tail. The oil is removed from this gland when it is squeezed by the bird's beak, and then the oil is spread over the body feathers by the bird's preening with its beak. Since the bird does not have the ability to perspire, the body is cooled by other means, mainly through respiration.

Specialized types of skin are found on various parts of the bird. The comb and wattles are unique skin types highly turgid in nature, while the scales of the shanks and toes provide a horny, hard type of covering. The beak is actually covered with a thin layer of skin. The earlobes are another rather special skin part.

In yellow skin chickens, a carotenoid pigment is deposited in the epidermal layer of skin. Although presence of this skin color is genetically determined, its intensity can be affected by the xanthophyll content of the bird's diet.

SKELETAL SYSTEM

The skeletal structure of the bird is designed for maneuverability and speed on the ground and for the unique ability to fly (Figure 3–4). In evolving from an ugly ground-dwelling reptile, the beautiful flying bird has necessarily undergone many adaptive modifications in its skeletal system. A reptile, or any other vertebrate, could not fly even if it had wings and feathers. A bird must support its weight, both by its legs and by its wings. Therefore, the skeleton of the bird is more highly differentiated than that of any other vertebrate. The avian skeleton must be both strong and lightweight. A basic engineering principle involved in meeting these requirements is similar to that applied to the building of any aircraft; a necessary economy of materials. Therefore, the most obvious adaptive changes differentiating the avian skeleton from that of other animals are:

1. fewer bones
2. many fused bones

3. higher mineral content of bones

4. pneumatic bones filled with air instead of marrow.

These adaptive changes in the skeletal system have increased its strength and reduced its weight, allowing the bird to fly as well as walk.

A study of the skeletal system reveals a small skull with fused bones and large ocular cavities but a small cranial cavity to hold the brain (Figure 3–5). The beak is devoid of teeth but has large nasal openings in the upper

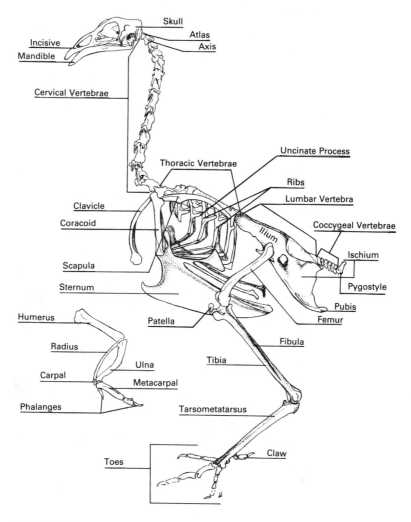

FIGURE 3–4
Skeleton of the chicken adapted for walking and flying.

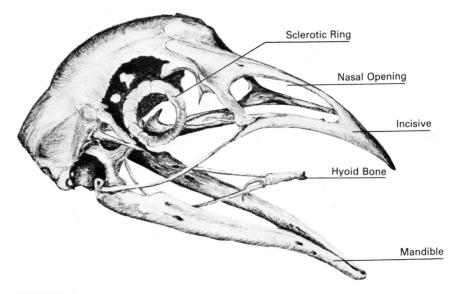

Sclerotic Ring

Nasal Opening

Incisive

Hyoid Bone

Mandible

FIGURE 3–5
Skull of the chicken showing the fused bones, absence of teeth, large ocular cavity, sclerotic ring, and hyoid bone.

mandible that is fused to the skull. The lower mandible is hinged at the jaw and is movable. Also hinged at the jaw is the hyoid bone, which extends into the tongue and aids in the passage of feed from the mouth into the digestive tract since the bird can't swallow. The skull is fused to the atlas, which is the first bone of the vertebral column. The cervical (neck) vertebrae are not fused, nor are the vertebrae in the tail. However, the thoracic and lumbar (back) vertebrae are fused for stress resistance and to provide a rigid attachment for the major flight muscles. The wing consists of the humerus, ulna, radius, metacarpals and digits, similar to other vertebrates.

The pectoral girdle (shoulder area) is particularly important because it relates to flight muscle function, and the bones in this area should be easily identified (Figure 3–6). The ends of the humerus, scapula (shoulder blade), coracoid, and clavicle (collar bone or "wish bone") all come together at the shoulder. The clavicle connects one shoulder to the other and provides an opening through which the digestive and respiratory tracts pass into the body cavity. The scapula lies along the back over the ribs, providing additional structural support. The thick coracoid connects the anterior part of the sternum to the shoulder joint and provides necessary structural support preventing the strong flight muscles from crushing the rib cage. The humerus provides necessary attachment for the flight muscles.

The sternum or breastbone provides a large, rigid anchor for the major flight muscles during movement of the wings and provides ventral support to the ribs (Figure 3–4). The sternum varies in size and shape depending on the species of bird. The rib cage provides protection to the viscera and, at the dorsal junction with a relatively fused region of the vertebrae, lends support for the flight muscles associated with moving the wing. There are seven pairs of ribs fused to the vertebrae and sternum, but hinged in the middle of each rib with flexible cartilage. Each rib has a fused process that overlaps the adjacent posterior rib providing additional structural support to the rib cage.

A series of fused flat bones in the posterior region is fused to the vertebrae in that area and provides a rigid base for the muscles associated with walking (Figure 3–4). The pygostyle, or tail bone, is the terminal point of the vertebral column. The tips of the pubic bones and the tip of the sternum project posterior on the skeleton and are utilized in predicting egg producing capacity in the culling process.

The leg consists of the femur (thigh bone), tibia (''drumstick''), fibula, and patella (knee cap), similar to other vertebrates (Figure 3–4). However, birds walk on their toes with their foot (metatarsus or shank, which is covered with scales) off the ground. The joint connecting the tibia to the metatarsus is the hock joint (ankle). The spur is connected to

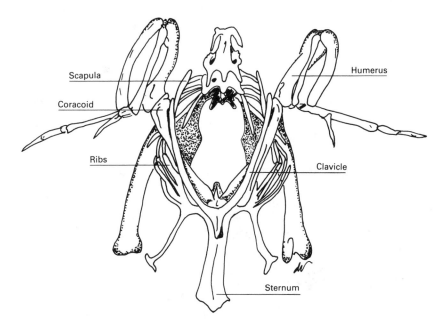

FIGURE 3–6
Pectoral girdle, anterior view.

the metatarsus but is not considered an integral part of the skeleton. The long bones of the leg allow the bird to maneuver on the ground and assist the bird to rest in a rather unique position known as roosting. Leg structure to the fowl has proven to be more important than flight. The rapid growth and development of commercial chickens and turkeys has resulted in leg weaknesses. Various forms of leg malfunction in poultry have been attributed to bone deformities closely associated with nutritional deficiencies and with muscle dysfunction, resulting in serious economic losses.

Preparation of a skeletal model provides an excellent opportunity to learn the structural aspects of the avian skeleton. (See Appendix 2.) The skeletal system of birds is an excellent example to study: (1) It is more easily obtained than many other animals; (2) The size of most birds, such as the chicken, duck and/or turkey, provides easily handled materials; (3) Nomenclature is basically the same as that of other animals; (4) There are fewer bones in the skeleton of a bird than there are in mammals; (5) Although there are differences between the skeleton of a bird and that of mammals the use, shape, names, and functions of the bones are very similar.

MUSCULAR SYSTEM

The muscular system is closely associated with the skeletal structure of the bird because muscles provide the source of power and locomotion and must attach to the structures they serve. All muscles work in pairs; as one contracts to cause movement of the skeleton, the other relaxes and vice versa.

Muscles in the breast area provide the major portion of meat on the bird. Although genetic selection has greatly enlarged these muscles, the bird's ability to fly has been hindered because the enlarged mass of muscle is not proportionally stronger. In fact, the large breast muscle has been thought to be the major reason modern, meat-type turkeys no longer have the capability to mate naturally and must be reproduced through the use of artificial insemination. Since the breast muscle comprises a major source of desirable white meat, its development has been favored in both chickens and turkeys. The leg and thigh have also increased in size as the breast muscle developed. However, leg muscle strength has not increased proportionally, which may be a contributing factor to leg problems. The thigh and leg muscles form the major sources of dark meat. In poultry, these dark muscles are used for walking and running (Figure 3–7). Since they do more work than the lighter-colored breast muscles, they have more blood capillaries, blood, pigment, and fat. In nonflying birds

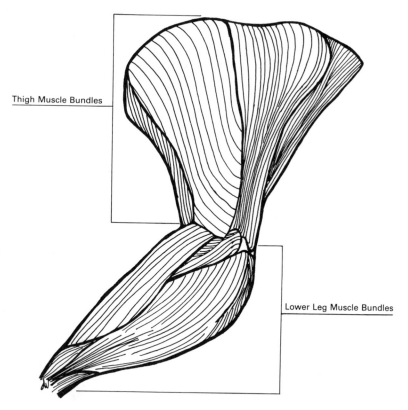

Thigh Muscle Bundles

Lower Leg Muscle Bundles

FIGURE 3–7
Major muscles of locomotion in the leg.

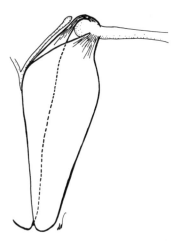

FIGURE 3–8
Major muscles of flight in the breast.

such as domestic poultry, the light-colored breast muscles are relatively weak, perform less work, and, therefore, have fewer blood vessels.

The flight muscles in birds are interesting to study since they are easily located and their function demonstrated on a dissected bird. The outer large breast muscle (Figure 3–8), the pectoralis major, is attached to the sternum and to the underside of the humerus. Obviously, when this muscle contracts it will pull the wing down during flight. The paired

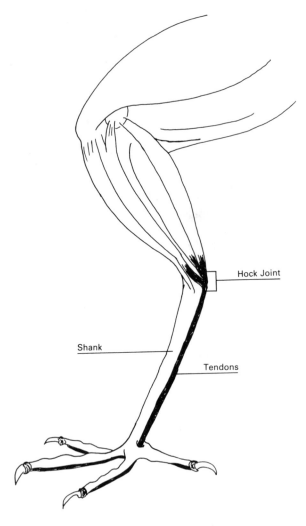

FIGURE 3–9
Tendons of lower leg muscles associated with action of toes.

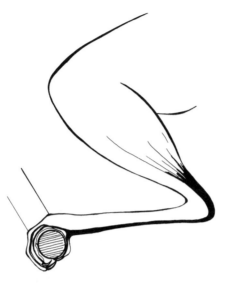

FIGURE 3–10
Stretched lower leg muscle tendons causing toes to grasp the perch. (After Peter-
son.)

muscle that will pull the wing back up would logically be located opposite
the muscle that pulls the wing down. However, to have that large a muscle
located on the back of the bird would not enhance the desirable stream-
lined contour of the "flying machine." Therefore, this muscle is also
attached to the sternum and is located deep to and separated by a membrane from the pectoralis major muscle. It extends along the coracoid
bone and is therefore called the supracoracoideus muscle. It is attached
to the top of the humerus bone by a tendon that passes behind the head
of the coracoid and over the notch of the scapula, much like a rope over
a pulley. Thus, contraction of the supracoracoideus muscle causes the
wing to move up. In flying birds, movement of the wing during flight
requires a great amount of energy; the breast muscles will therefore contain many blood capillaries causing them to be much darker than the breast
muscles of chickens and turkeys.

The muscle bundles on the lower leg are connected by tendons extending over the hock joint the length of the shank to the end of the toes
(Figure 3–9). When the bird stands or walks, the hock joint is relatively
unbent, allowing the tendons to slack and the toes to spread out. However,
when a bird perches on a rod or branch, or even falls asleep on the perch,
its lower leg muscles relax, its weight causes it to squat, bending its legs
at the hock joint (Figure 3–10). This involuntarily pulls the tendons tight

over the back of the hock joint causing the toes to curl and the claws to grasp the perch. The toes will remain locked in this position until the bird voluntarily uses its leg muscles to stand.

DIGESTIVE SYSTEM

The digestive system is a major component of the bird since it is the means by which food nutrients are converted for body use in the production of meat and eggs. The bird is basically a scavenger and thus has been provided with the ability to rip and tear flesh, scratch for seeds and insects, and consume its food in large pieces. The ability to eat its food and leave the scene in relative haste is one of bird's survival factors. The bird's high nutritive requirements and limitations on weight necessary for flight have necessitated unique adaptations in the anatomy and physiology of the digestive system. However, common to other animals, this system basically functions to accomplish the essential processes of food intake, storage, digestion, nutrient absorption, and waste elimination.

Any animal can be thought of as a biological "machine" that converts raw materials into a finished product: in the case of poultry, feed into meat and eggs; in the case of humans, food into happy, healthy, productive world citizens. The raw materials need to be processed (digested and metabolized) into desired end products (meat and eggs). The feed must somehow enter and become part of the body of the animal. This process intricately involves the digestive system and can be easily visualized if we consider the animal ("biological machine") as a three-dimensional, enclosed structure comprised of functional tissue with an opening in the front and an opening in the rear, with a tube through the structure connecting the two openings. This connecting tube with its various enlargements, linings, and attachments is the digestive system (Figure 3–11). The lumen of this entire tube can be thought of as being outside of the animal's enclosed structure (body), as it is exposed to the environment from which the raw materials, feedstuffs, are derived. The digestive process follows in a rather orderly manner as feedstuffs pass through this tube entering it at the front opening. The feed will pass in order through the following parts of the bird's digestive tract: mouth, esophagus, crop, lower esophagus, proventriculus (glandular stomach), gizzard (muscular stomach), small intestine, ceca, large intestine (rectum), and cloaca. Not all ingesta goes into ceca, which are mainly for further breakdown of dietary fiber.

A distinctive characteristic of birds is the absence of lips and teeth. Instead, the bird has a hard beak that can be used for grasping, tearing,

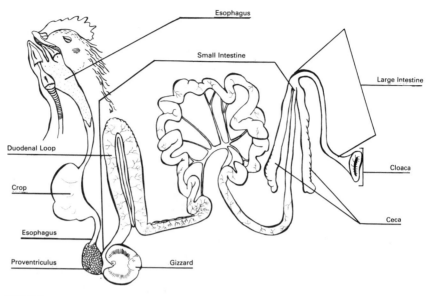

FIGURE 3–11
Digestive system of the chicken.

and scooping food. With the moistening and mastication of the food primarily taking place further along the digestive system, the absence of teeth may be advantageous. The digestive system works very efficiently in the handling of various types of food materials. The tongue contains the hyoid bone hinged at the jaw, and the tongue is pointed at the anterior tip with several barbed points projecting posteriorly on each side; this projects the appearance of a barbed arrowhead. Since the bird cannot swallow, the tongue moves back and forth forcing food down the esophagus. There are a few salivary glands in the mouth that contribute some moisture to the feed at this point.

The esophagus is the part of the tube that conveys feed from the mouth to the stomach. The crop is a storage pouch off of, but continuous with, the esophagus. The crop, located in the lower neck area, provides for storage of food materials hastily consumed by the bird. Here food is moistened and softened but to this point little, if any, digestion takes place. The food particles then move from the crop into the posterior segment of the esophagus and into the glandular stomach (proventriculus) where the first significant amounts of digestive juices are secreted. The proventriculus is located well within the body cavity. The digestive secretions contain the enzyme, pepsin, which starts protein digestion, and hydrochloric acid, which adjusts pH and helps dissolve minerals. The proventriculus is a relatively small and short enlargement of the esophagus. It provides no storage space, and within it there is little time for digestion of feed to occur. Thus, feed passes, with added digestive juices, rapidly into the muscular stomach (gizzard) where physical breakdown commences. The gizzard is a highly muscular organ used for the grinding and mixing of feed materials in preparation for digestion. As feed enters the gizzard, rhythmic movement of the muscles grind and crush the particles and mix them with the digestive juices, thus replacing the mastication function of teeth. The strength of the gizzard muscle and the tough leather-like lining allow utilization of grit as well as the feed particles producing much friction in the grinding process. The physical breakdown of large feed particles increases surface area, allowing more complete enzymatic digestion. When the gizzard is not heavily used because of the absence of grit and the presence of finely ground feed, the gizzard muscle may become flaccid and weak.

Leaving the gizzard, the food passes into the duodenal loop of the upper small intestine. The liver produces bile that is temporarily stored in the gall bladder, which is an enlargement of one of the two bile ducts connecting the liver to the posterior end of the duodenal loop (Figure 3–12). The presence of food entering the duodenal loop from the gizzard triggers the release of bile from the gall bladder. The bile mixes with the food slurry as it passes into the next portion of the small intestine. Bile is a green, alkaline fluid that emulsifies fat globules into smaller particles, greatly increasing the total surface area exposed to subsequent enzymatic digestion. Also, the alkaline bile neutralizes the hydrochloric acid secreted by the proventriculus, providing a more favorable condition for enzymatic digestive reactions to occur. Here in the duodenal loop digestion commences as the pancreas secretes digestive enzymes that aid in the breakdown of protein into amino acids, carbohydrates into simple sugar, and fat into glycerol and fatty acids. In the remaining area of the small intestine the digestive process is completed and absorption of nutrients takes place. Vitamin and mineral absorption takes place here too. The presence of many folds and villi greatly increases the surface area of the small intestine and the capacity to absorb nutrients. The small intestine in a mature chicken is 1.5 m (4.9 ft) in length and terminates at its juncture with the large intestine at the point of connection with the ceca. The large intestine is relatively short, only 10 cm (3.9 in.) in length, terminating at the cloaca. The ceca consist of two pouches that fill and empty from the same direction. Their main function is associated with the breakdown of fiber. Although the chicken and turkey cannot utilize large volumes of fiber in the diet, this mechanism makes possible the breakdown of small amounts commonly associated with some poultry diets. The major functions of the large intestine are storage of undigested waste material and

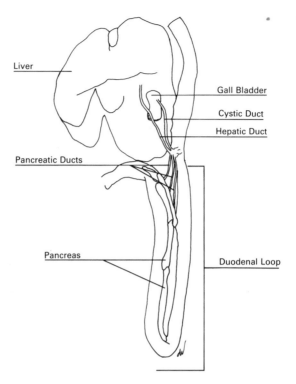

FIGURE 3–12
Liver showing bile duct connections to the duodenal
loop.

absorption of water from these intestinal contents. This process provides birds with a mechanism for recycling and for very efficient utilization of this important nutrient, water.

The cloaca is the common chamber into which the digestive, urinary, and reproductive tracts open. Its opening at the posterior end of the bird is known as the vent. When the bird eliminates fecal wastes from its digestive system, the cloaca actually folds back at the vent allowing the rectal opening of the large intestine to push out, as the opening to the reproductive tract is closed off. Thus, there is minimal chance of fecal wastes passing into the reproductive tract.

An understanding of the structure and function of the digestive system of the bird is important to understanding the need for highly specialized diets: low in fiber and containing all necessary nutrients in adequate amounts that are relatively easily digested. Basic knowledge of the nutrient requirements of poultry has developed into the very exact science of nutrition, which has aimed at maximum utilization of available feedstuffs for the efficient production of poultry meat and eggs.

URINARY SYSTEM

Closely associated with the digestive system in the process of excretion is the urinary system, or excretory system, which involves the elimination of the waste products of body metabolism. The kidneys are paired, each consisting of three lobes dorsally located along the vertebral column posterior to the lungs (Figure 3–13). The ureters are long tubes that connect the kidneys with the cloaca for the purpose of transporting the waste products out of the body. The bird has no urinary bladder and thus does not produce a watery urine as do mammals; it excretes the urates or products of metabolism as solids that are added to the feces as a white cap. The liver converts waste products of protein metabolism into uric acid, which is carried in the blood to the kidneys. This waste product, dissolved in water, passes through the blood capillary walls in the kidneys into collecting tubules. As this urine passes from the kidneys through the ureters, located next to the large intestine, much of the water is reab-

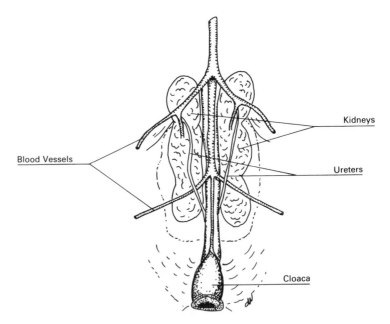

FIGURE 3–13
Urinary system of the chicken.

sorbed. As the urine enters the cloaca it combines with fecal wastes eliminated from the large intestine. The white pasty material in bird feces is uric acid that is insoluble and precipitates from the urine. Nitrogenous waste in the urine of mammals is largely urea that is soluble in the liquid urine.

CARDIORESPIRATORY SYSTEMS

Because of increased oxygen demand and greater capacity for heat regulation required by their relatively high body temperature, birds have evolved a respiratory system quite different from that of mammals. The system starts with the nasal chambers in the upper mandible of the beak, which open into the mouth. The trachea ("wind pipe") attaches to the throat at the larynx, which modifies the voice. The opening from the mouth to the larynx is the glottis, which is a slit that closes when feed is passing down the throat. The trachea is easily recognizable and distinguishable from the esophagus by its linear arrangement of cartilagenous rings that prevent its collapse from the negative pressure caused by inspiration of air. At the posterior end of the trachea is the syrinx (voice box), which then branches into two bronchial tubes. The syrinx is the point where the voice is produced by air pressure on a sound valve, and modified by muscle tension. This structure is fairly complicated in song birds compared to chickens, which only "cluck" or "crow." The physical anatomy of the syrinx allows hens, as well as roosters, to "crow." The reason hens don't crow is because they "don't feel like it" due to female hormone effects and the absence of sufficient levels of the male hormone.

The bronchi extend along each lung and are continuous with the air sacs, which are also continuous with the lungs. The lungs are relatively small and inexpansible, and firmly attached to the thoracic wall impressed against the ribs. The bird has no diaphragm that functions in respiration as mammals do. Respiration is accomplished by a unique association of the muscle, skeletal, circulatory, and respiratory systems, which rely on an interconnected system of nine air sacs (Figure 3–14). Located in the front of the body cavity near the clavicle and extending into the hollow core of each humerus bone is a single air sac called the interclavicular air sac. Portions of this and other air sacs will actually extend through small openings in some bones and fill their hollow centers. The other air sacs consist of four bilaterally symmetrical pairs, essentially consuming all available space in the body cavity with some portions extending into pneumatic bones. The two cervical air sacs are also located in the front of the bird but extend up into the cervical vertebrae of the neck. There

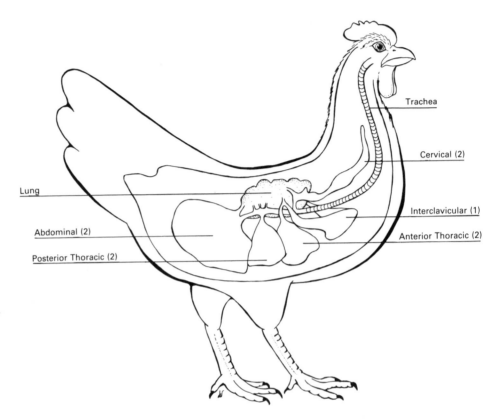

FIGURE 3–14
Respiratory system of the chicken.

is a pair of anterior thoracic air sacs plus a pair of posterior thoracic air sacs in the thoracic region of the body cavity. In the back of the body cavity and extending into the hollow core of each femur bone is the largest pair of air sacs known as the abdominal air sacs. The air sacs are continuous with the bronchi and lungs, which is essential to the proper flow of air during respiration. Also, an essential unique feature of the avian lung is that it has tubular parabronchi rather than the sac-like alveoli of mammalian lungs. Whereas alveoli are dead-end pouches receiving and expelling air intermittently as the lung expands and contracts, parabronchi in the avian lung are continuous tubes allowing air to pass through the lung in one direction. Both are laced with blood capillaries where gas exchange occurs.

Since there is no muscular diaphragm comparable to that in mammals, breathing is accomplished by muscular action of the entire thoracic and abdominal regions, with help from wing movements during flight. Since the ribs are somewhat flexible due to their cartillage "hinge," the sternum drops down when the bird's muscles relax, creating a negative pressure (vacuum) in the body cavity; it is similar to opening a bellows (Figure 3–15). Since the body cavity is filled with air sacs, in the vacuum they will expand; like a balloon in a vacuum jar. The air sacs, being continuous with the lungs and bronchi providing their only opening, will fill with air brought in through the trachea. However, the path of air flow is not as one might expect. An inhaled "breath" of air entering the trachea and bronchi mostly bypasses the lungs and directly enters the posterior air sacs from the bronchi. Then as the bird's muscles tighten, the sternum moves up, squeezing this breath of air, not out through the bronchi and trachea, but rather into the parabronchi of the lungs where gas exchange takes place. In the next respiratory cycle as the muscles relax and the sternum drops, the air sacs in the body cavity expand and the air in the lungs is drawn by vacuum on through the tubular parabronchi into the anterior air sacs. Simultaneously, a new breath of air enters the posterior air sacs as the previous breath did originally. Then as the bird's muscles tighten again and the sternum moves up, the first breath of air is forced out of the anterior air sacs through the bronchi and trachea and is exhaled

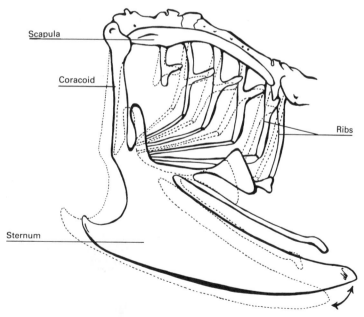

FIGURE 3–15
Flexible rib cage allowing movement of sternum, depicted.

through the mouth. Simultaneously, the second breath of air is forced into the parabronchi of the lungs. Thus, it requires two respiratory cycles of inhalation and exhalation for a single breath of air to enter and leave the respiratory system of birds.

This unique system of respiration may have evolved from a necessary efficiency of oxygen uptake by the blood of high flying birds and water-dwelling reptiles. These animals utilize low concentrations of oxygen where mammals could not breathe. Blood flows through blood capillaries lining the parabronchi of the avian lung in the opposite direction of the flow of air through the parabronchi. The blood takes up oxygen as it passes through the capillaries, but its affinity for oxygen uptake is greatest as it enters the lung at the distal end of a parabronchus where the oxygen concentration in the exiting air is lowest. Likewise, the blood's affinity for uptake of oxygen is least as it is about to leave the lung at the proximal end of a parabronchus where air is just entering from the posterior air sacs and is highest in oxygen concentration. Therefore, the blood can still absorb even more oxygen just before leaving the lung.

The respiratory system of birds functions not only to exchange oxygen and carbon dioxide in the blood, as it does in mammals, but, through its system of air sacs, it also provides cooling, moisture removal, and buoyancy to the body. Since birds lack sweat glands, they utilize the respiratory system for necessary cooling of internal organs and muscles. Panting in birds is not a sign of exhaustion, but rather an effort to speed up the dissipation of internal body heat by increased evaporation of moisture from the air sacs. The bird has a relatively high body temperature of 40°C–43°C (104°F–109°F). Also, large amounts of heat are generated during flight, at which time the air sacs function by greatly increasing the moist surface area over which evaporative cooling may occur. It has also been theorized that the air sacs function to cool the testes located in the body cavity of birds allowing spermatogenesis, which would probably not otherwise occur at the high body temperature of the bird. The air sacs also provide some buoyancy, which is probably advantageous to waterfowl.

The highly efficient avian heart is directly related to the high respiratory requirement imposed by flight (Figure 3–16). It is proportionally larger in size, beats faster, and pumps a greater quantity of blood per unit of time than the mammalian heart. Small birds have a basal heart rate of about 400–500 beats per minute and chickens about 300 beats per minute, compared with a rate of 60–70 beats per minute in humans. The rate in birds may even exceed 1,000 beats per minute under conditions of stress. Compared with other animals, birds have a relatively high blood pressure, relatively high metabolic rate, and a relatively high body temperature.

The blood circulatory system can be classified into five major cat-

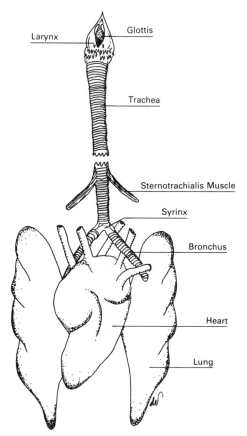

FIGURE 3–16
Cardiorespiratory systems.

egories: blood, heart, arteries, capillaries, and veins. The blood consists primarily of plasma, the liquid portion that carries digested nutrients in solution to the cells; waste products from the cells; tissue fluids; hormones; and the blood cells. Blood also plays a major role in the regulation of body temperature. The blood cells are the other component of blood, red cells (erythrocytes) and white cells (leucocytes). The red blood cell is small and oval in shape and contains a large nucleus, unlike mammalian red blood cells (Figure 3–17). The presence of nuclei provides a distinguishable feature in blood identification. The red cells in all animals, including birds, provide the means of carrying oxygen from the lungs to the body cells and carbon dioxide from the cells to the lungs for expulsion. Hemoglobin supplies the red color and is an iron-containing protein that provides the mechanism for this gaseous exchange. The leucocytes are larger in size and fewer in number than the red cells. Leucocyte numbers

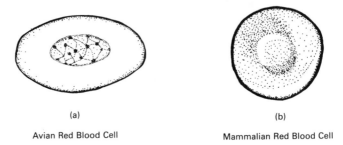

(a)   (b)

Avian Red Blood Cell   Mammalian Red Blood Cell

FIGURE 3–17
Red blood cells: (a) avian; (b) mammalian.

increase in body defense against disease. Approximately 5% of the live weight of the domestic fowl is blood. Seventy-five percent of whole blood is water and 25%, solids. Avian blood consists of 2–4 million red cells and 15,000–35,000 white cells per cubic milliliter. The blood of the fowl clots very rapidly. Fibrinogen in the plasma plays a major role.

REPRODUCTIVE SYSTEM AND THE EGG

One of the primary objectives of every living system is to perpetuate itself so that the species will be continued. There are numerous mechanisms of reproduction. Basically they are included in either asexual reproduction, where one individual can subdivide to produce two and subsequently more individuals, or in sexual reproduction where male and female cells are required to fuse to reproduce a new individual. The sexual reproductive systems of commercial fowl are of importance because of our interest in egg production in the female and production of high quality semen in the male.

Birds are unique among most animals as they reproduce through an egg, which contains all the necessary components for the commencement and maintenance of life processes during embryonic development. Also, the bird provides a protective package for these components in the form of a strong and durable egg shell. The hen actually does most of her reproductive work prior to the laying of an egg, since she provides all nutrient materials necessary to create and maintain early life. She can accomplish this just about every 24 hours. In order to accomplish this feat a profuse supply of blood must be available to the entire female reproductive system, which consists of the oviduct and the ovary. The ovary is involved in the production of the female reproductive cells or ova. The oviduct serves to transport the ovum from the ovary to the cloaca. All life in higher organisms is perpetuated through the ovum. The development of the mammalian embryo takes place within the body of the female, while embryonic development of birds takes place, for the most part, outside the body. It is for this reason that birds' eggs are extremely large in comparison with eggs of mammals. The yolk material, the albumen or white of the egg, and the shell provide nourishment and protection for the developing avian embryo.

The ovary is located on the dorsal wall of the body cavity posterior to the lungs and anterior to the kidneys. In the bird, only the left ovary is functional, while the right ovary is undeveloped. The ovary consists of many ova including yolks that are in various stages of development in the laying hen (Figure 3–18). Rapid development takes place in a period of five to ten days prior to ovulation. When the ovum is released, hor-

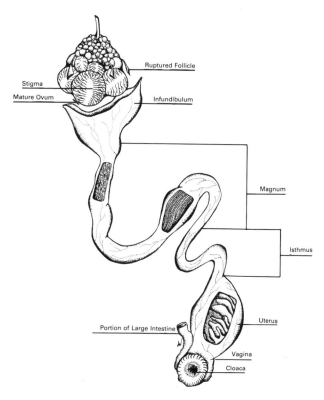

FIGURE 3–18
Reproductive system of the laying hen.

mones trigger the vascular sac (follicle), which holds the yolk to the ovary, to rupture along a line devoid of blood vessels, the stigma. Since this stigma is free of blood vessels, under normal conditions yolk release is free of hemorrhage. On occasion a small blood vessel may be ruptured causing blood to appear on the yolk as a "blood spot" or even as a "bloody egg."

Associated with the ovary, and corresponding to the vas deferens of the male, is the oviduct. In a laying bird, the oviduct appears as a large, highly vascular, folded tube occupying a large part of the abdominal cavity. The oviduct is divided into five regions: (1) the infundibulum, which receives the ovum; (2) the magnum, where the thick albumin is secreted; (3) the isthmus, which secretes the shell membranes; (4) the uterus or shell gland; and (5) the vagina, a passageway into the cloaca.

When the yolk comes to full size, it is released from the ovary by the rupture of the follicle along the stigma. The discharged yolk and its germinal disc are engulfed by the infundibulum, and within ten minutes the journey down the oviduct commences. It is in the infundibulum that fertilization will occur if the particular ovum is to become a fertile egg. Once the egg has passed through the infundibulum and the layers of albumen have started to be placed on the yolk, fertilization is impossible.

During the passage through the first part of the oviduct (the albumin-secreting magnum) the yolk acquires the mass of firm albumin that makes up about one-half of the total egg white. The yolk spends approximately three hours in the magnum. The remainder of the egg white is added after the shell membranes have been formed and the egg has entered the uterus.

The two shell membranes are formed in the isthmus during a period of 1.25 hours. The shell membranes influence the shape of the egg. However, the yolk and the thick albumen do not have the appearance of an egg until water secreted in the uterus, passes through the shell membranes, plumping the membranes, and giving the egg its characteristic shape. After the thin albumin has been formed inside the shell membranes and the egg assumes its normal size and shape, two spiral cords of thick albumen can be seen extending from the yolk toward the two poles of the egg. These spirals are known as chalazae. The twisted chalazae serve to anchor the yolk in the center of the albumen. The egg spends over 20 hours in the uterus, where calcium carbonate is deposited on the outer shell membrane. There is considerable shell material deposited on the shell membrane before the egg has acquired its full complement of thin albumen. The accumulation of the shell on the shell membranes is an interesting phenomenon, in that the shell is laid down as minute particles, deposited in tiny beads that build up several layers thick before hardening to form the shell. The rate of shell deposition is relatively slow during the first three hours, and then increases rapidly.

When shell structure is complete, the egg passes into the vagina where it may be retained for a few minutes while a very thin coat of albumen-like material is deposited over the shell. This material is referred to as the bloom or cuticle and functions to fill the pores in the shell.

The egg passes through the oviduct small end first, but just prior to laying the egg turns horizontally 180° so that the large end of the egg comes out first. This allows for more shell surface area on which uterine muscles may apply pressure prior to the egg-laying process. The egg-laying process, oviposition, consists of the cloaca folding back so that the vaginal opening deposits the egg directly outside of the body.

The male fowl possesses two testes that are located on the dorsal wall of the body cavity, posterior to the lungs and anterior to the kidneys (Figure 3–19). These never descend into an external scrotum, as is the case with most other animals. The testis consists of a large number of very slender, convoluted ducts. The sperm are produced in the linings of these ducts (Figure 3–20). The ducts are called seminiferous tubules; they appear in groups separated by delicate membranes that extend inward from a membrane surrounding the organ. These clusters of ducts produce the sperm, which then migrate through the ducts to central collecting points. Eventually, all of the ducts lead to the vas deferens, convoluted tubes that store and conduct the semen containing sperm to the outside of the body. Each of the vas deferens opens into a papillus, one located on each side of the dorsal wall of the cloaca. There is also a rudimentary copulatory organ, not connected with the vas deferens, located on the median ventral portion of one of the folds of the cloaca. It is this rudimentary organ, or male process, which is used in the classification of baby chicks according to sex on the basis of cloacal examination when newly hatched. Some birds, such as ducks and geese, possess a functional penis rather than papillae.

The process of spermatogenesis yields sperm cells, which subsequently become spermatozoa (Figure 3–21). Each spermatozoan has a highly specialized structure consisting of a pointed acrosome on the anterior tip of the slender head, which contains the nucleus, a middle piece posterior to the head, and a long tail or flagellum. The number of spermatozoa per unit volume of semen has been estimated at between a few hundred thousand to over 10 million per cubic millimeter of semen.

Although the mating process among most mammalian species is similar and generally understood by most observant people, the mating process of birds often remains a mystery even to many older adults. This probably stems from the fact that the reproductive organs of male birds are located internally, making their actual function in the mating process less obvious. Just prior to mating, a specific mating ritual takes place, finalizing with the male bird treading on the back of the female as she

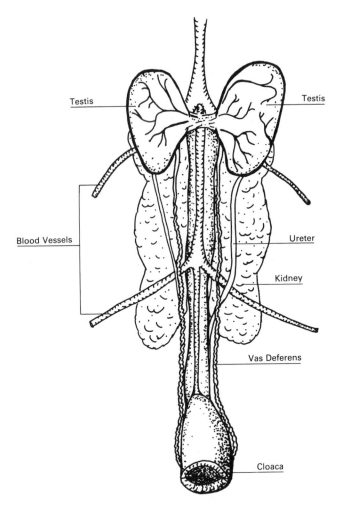

FIGURE 3–19
Reproductive system of the male chicken.

lays back her tail feathers. Male and female will then each evert their cloaca, closing off the rectal opening and allowing maximum protrusion of the vaginal opening of the female and the papillae of the male. The papillae, however, are only about 0.2 cm long. Copulation occurs merely by the male placing the two papillae at the vaginal opening of the female and releasing a small amount of semen. Then the vagina and papillae retract into the respective cloacal chambers as the male dismounts. The process is similar in natural mating with turkeys and similar in ducks and geese. However, male water fowl have a distinct and longer copulatory organs. The semen is ejaculated at the base and follows a corkscrew-like pathway around the outside of the organ rather than an internal route.

The bird's egg (Figure 3–22) is one of the most complex and highly differentiated reproductive cells. Its structural elements (Figure 3–23) are precisely arranged, as their total organization is essential to the specific function of each part. The avian egg is potentially able to maintain life: containing enough food material to sustain embryonic life, growth, and development prior to hatch. The "standard" chicken egg is described as follows:

Weight	58.0 g	Short circumference	13.5 cm
Volume	53.0 ml	Shape Index	74
Specific gravity	1.09	Surface area	68.0 sq. cm
Long circumference	15.7 cm		

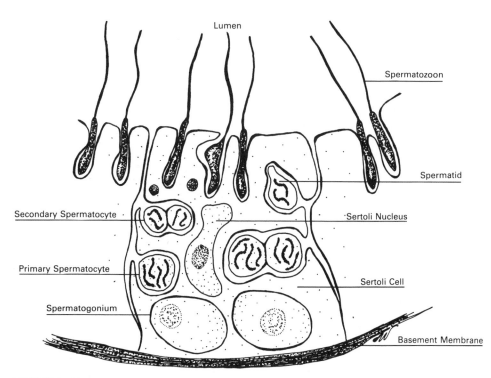

FIGURE 3–20
Cross section of seminiferous tubule of avian testis showing sperm-cell formation.

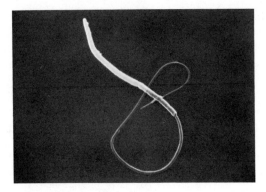

FIGURE 3-21
Spermatozoa of the turkey; magnification 2,000 X.
(Colorado State University photograph.)

When the egg enters the isthmus of the oviduct two thin membranes composed of fine fibers are secreted. They provide a surface on which the egg shell is deposited in the uterus. The shell structure is rather complex and has specific characteristics that directly support embryonic development. The egg shell is strong and rigid, to withstand the weight of the adult during natural incubation, thus the domed form and radial arrangement of crystals. It is porous to permit respiration of the embryo and moisture loss. The shell is a major source of the minerals required by the developing embryo.

The shell has an outer coating, the bloom or cuticle, that is glyco-

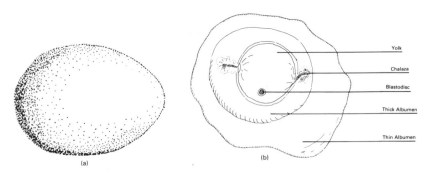

FIGURE 3-22
The chicken egg: (a) intact shell; (b) broken out of the shell.

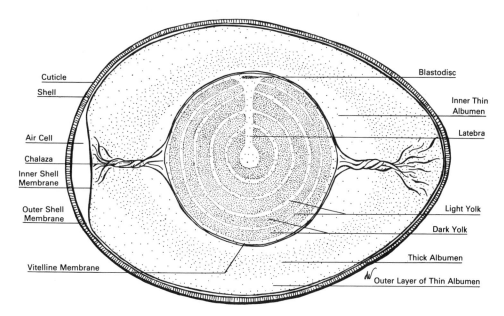

FIGURE 3–23
Structural features of the chicken egg.

protein (mucin) in nature. (Figure 3–24). The shell contains up to 8,000 pores per egg for the exchange of gasses and moisture. An outer crystalline layer is hard and compact and is made up of calcite crystals (calcium carbonate), the long axis of the crystal being perpendicular to the surface. The inner mammillary layer in which minerals are amorphous (noncrystalline) with no definite orientation contains more magnesium and phosphates, along with some knob-like crystals of calcite. There are two shell membranes located directly beneath the shell, the inner and outer (thicker), which separate as the egg cools and as moisture escapes, forming an air cell at the large end of the egg.

Shell strength is related to shell thickness. The breeder is interested in a quick, relatively accurate means of determining favorable shell thickness. Shell thickness may be estimated by specific gravity determination (Appendix 3). A simple test for the specific gravity of a very fresh hatching egg will give a determination of the thickness of its shell; higher specific gravity indicates greater shell thickness. The lower the specific gravity, the thinner the shell.

The yolk (vitellus) is spherical, yellow to orange in color, and located near the center of the egg (Figure 3–23). The "egg" or ovum contains the blastodisc, which is the germ spot or female reproductive cell. The yolk is enclosed in a vitelline membrane that maintains its shape. The

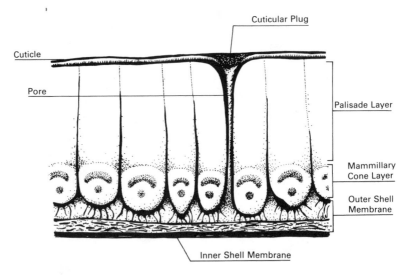

FIGURE 3–24
Cross-section of the chicken egg shell depicting microscopic structure.

latebra is a cylindrical core of white yolk connecting the center of the yolk with the blastodisc. Concentric layers of alternating light and dark yolk reflect recent yolk growth. The dark rings are caused by deposits of carotene (yellow) from the blood and are formed during the day when birds have been eating. The lighter rings are due to low levels of carotene in the blood and are formed during the night when birds are sleeping and not eating. This produces a series of rings in the yolk that provide a record of daily growth.

Albumin material is present in a number of forms of layers (Figure 3–23). The chalaziferous layer is a dense, matted, fibrous capsule of albumin around the vitelline membrane of the yolk. The matted fibrous capsule terminates on each end in the chalazae, which are twisted in opposite directions and keep the yolk centered. There are three other layers of albumin. The inner, thin (liquid) layer contains viscous albumin in which the yolk and chalaziferous layer float. The middle, dense layer surrounds the inner liquid layer. It is thicker and provides anchorage for the chalazae. The outer, thin layer is viscous and is located immediately below the surface of the inner shell membrane. The chalazae are twisted so that the blastodisc always orients itself toward the top. Specific gravity is a factor in this orientation.

From time to time, abnormal eggs or abnormal shell structure may appear as: double or multiple yolks, soft or thin-shelled eggs, an egg within an egg, watery white or flecked white, ridged egg shells, and odd-shaped eggs.

ENDOCRINE AND
NERVOUS SYSTEMS

The endocrine system (Figure 3–25) plays a very important role in regulating the functioning of the anatomical parts of the fowl. Behavior, appearance, growth, and reproduction can be regulated by humans in controlled environments for maximum performance. Hormones secretions of endocrine glands which enter directly into the blood system are carried rapidly to all parts of the body. Thus, the sites for hormone action or reception—other target glands or tissues—respond to endocrine secretions in relatively short periods of time. The pituitary is the master gland of the body located at the base of the brain behind the optic nerve. Through secretion of a number of different hormones, it controls action

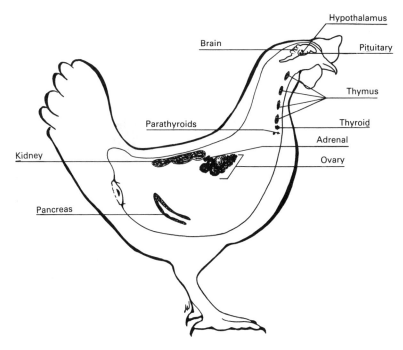

FIGURE 3–25
Endocrine system of the chicken.

of the entire endocrine system. The anterior and posterior lobes of the pituitary gland secrete hormones, which have a major role in regulating the action of other endocrine glands, thus affecting the bird's growth, development, metabolism, and sexual activity.

The thymus tissue is imbedded in fat along both sides of the neck. It is relatively prominent in chicks and immature birds but diminishes in relative size as birds mature and age. Its hormonal function is thought to regulate growth, specifically repressing development of the sex organs to delay their functioning until the bird reaches adequate physical size. With this function completed at sexual maturity, their relative size decreases as the bird ages.

The thyroid glands, located at the base of the neck, are oval-shaped, dark red or purple, and are imbedded in fat tissue. There are two of these glands, one on each side of the neck where it attaches to the body. The thyroids produce the hormone thyroxin, which increases the rate of body metabolism, body growth, and feather development and color. Birds with high metabolic rates utilize relatively more energy than birds with low metabolic rates. Attempts to regulate the metabolic rate of poultry as a means to affect growth and finish for favorable market characteristics have involved various methods of controlling thyroid function.

The parathyroid glands, of which there are two pairs, are closely associated with the thyroids. They consist of two very small glands near the surface of each thyroid. Their hormone secretions primarily function to regulate calcium and phosphorus metabolism, thus affecting egg shell formation.

The islets of Langerhans are located in the pancreas, which is attached to the duodenal loop. They secrete the hormone insulin, which regulates sugar metabolism thus controlling blood-sugar levels in the fowl.

The adrenal glands are located anterior to the kidneys on the vertebral column, are oval to triangular in shape, and yellowish in color. Being associated with the circulatory system of the body, blood vessels appear on their surface. They produce the hormone, adrenalin, which regulates carbohydrate metabolism, blood pressure, metabolic rate, and sex-gland activity. Adrenalin has been referred to as the "fear hormone" since it triggers the mobilization of carbohydrate to supply extra energy required by the animal under the stress of fear. Adrenal hormones also regulate the metabolism of sodium and potassium and thus control blood pressure.

The reproductive organs (gonads) have endocrine function, as they respond to direct stimulation of the pituitary gland hormones and produce and release hormones themselves. The testes of the male, located on the dorsal wall, anterior to the kidney, produce hormones known as androgens, including testosterone, which causes male secondary sex characteristics such as feather type, large combs, and crowing. Estrogens, the female sex hormones, are produced by the ovary and result in the female secondary sex characteristics as well as in the primary sex functions associated with reproduction, including egg production. Estrogens actually function to mask male sex characteristics, which the female bird would otherwise have due to her production of small amounts of androgens.

The nervous system of the fowl stimulates the function of the other anatomical systems as they react to the environment. This effect of the nervous system may be either direct or as a result of its effect on the endocrine system. There are very few endocrine effects that result from the simple and direct action of a single hormone. Instead, the physiological and psychological activities of the bird depend on very complex interrelations of neurohormonal effects.

A good example of neurohormonal interaction in the fowl is the control of ovulation and egg formation in the female (Figure 3–26). The light stimulus from the environment is absorbed by the retinal cells and is transmitted by the ocular nerve, which then stimulates the hypothalmus of the brain. This activates the anterior lobe of the pituitary gland to secrete follicle-stimulating hormone (FSH). The FSH stimulates growth of the ovarian follicles and regulates secretion of estrogens. When a follicle has reached ovulatory size, another hormone from the anterior lobe of the pituitary gland, luteinizing hormone (LH), is released and causes ovulation. The ruptured ovarian follicle then produces the hormone progesterone, which functions as a feedback control on the pituitary gland, synchronizing production and release of more LH. It thus contributes to the neural hormone mechanism that prevents another ovum from being ovulated prematurely before an egg is laid.

The oviduct is also under hormone control and is thus stimulated at precisely the right time to pick up and engulf the released ovum. Estrogen secretions from the intact ovarian follicles are responsible for enlargement of the oviduct to functioning size and its vascularization. Secreted estrogens also cause spread of the pubic bones and enlargement of the vent, necessary for oviposition. Estrogens trigger the mobilization of stored fat for yolk formation and of calcium stored in the bones for shell formation. Estrogens also are responsible for all female secondary sex characteristics such as plumage, voice, and behavior. The ovarian interstitial tissue secretes an androgen (male sex hormone) that controls egg white secretion and causes the good egg-producing female to also have certain male sex characteristics, such as a relatively large, red, waxy comb and wattles, comb turgidity, and aggressiveness associated with behavior.

Formation of the egg shell is at least partially under the control of hormones secreted by the parathyroid glands that regulate calcium and phosphorus metabolism. Here also, timing, both as to the beginning and

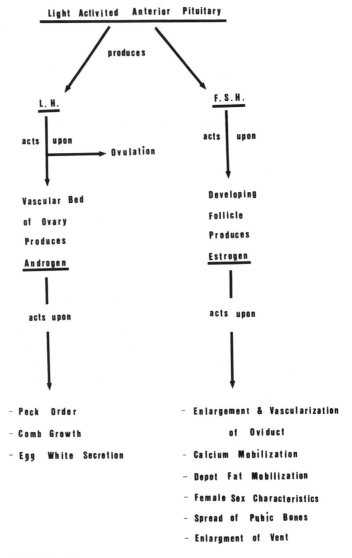

FIGURE 3–26
Neurohormonal control of ovulation and egg formation in the chicken.

end of shell formation, is remarkably and necessarily exact. Oxytocin is a hormone secreted by the hyopthalmus of the brain and stored in the posterior lobe of the pituitary gland. Experimentally it is known that a large dose of oxytocin administered intravenously will cause expulsion of a hard-shelled egg within three minutes. It, therefore, seems reasonable to postulate that in the normal chicken there is an accumulation or release of oxytocin sufficient to provide stimulation of the uterine muscles to cause oviposition. Oxytocin is believed to serve a similar function in other animals in initiating the contraction of uterine muscles during labor of pregnant females prior to giving birth.

The thyroid gland, in addition to influencing body growth, feather pigmentation, and molting, is partially responsible for regular seasonal changes in egg production, body weight, and egg weight. Prolactin, secreted by the anterior lobe of the pituitary gland, depresses the production of FSH and LH and initiates broodiness in fowl. Thus, they stop producing eggs and quickly become broody with a desire to set on eggs and care for hatched chicks. Prolactin is so named because it induces milk secretion in mammals. In pigeons, it causes the crop to produce "pigeon's milk," a milky fluid rich in calcium, which is in many ways similar to the milk of mammals. Pigeon milk contains fatty tissue cells shed from the epithelial lining of the crop.

Normal functioning of the entire process of egg production is completely dependent upon extremely precise synchronization of the production, storage, and release of endocrine secretions. If any gland begins to function on its own, without awaiting the proper "signal" for its hormone to be produced or fails to function when required, abnormalities such as yolkless eggs, soft-shelled eggs, and shell eggs within egg shells are likely to result.

Both egg laying and ovulation are also subject to the environmental influence of relative duration of light and darkness in a 24-hour day. Ovulation normally occurs about one-half hour after oviposition. Since it takes about 24.5 hours from ovulation to oviposition, a single egg production cycle will take about 25 hours. Therefore, if a hen lays an egg at 9 AM today, she will lay an egg tomorrow at 10 AM and the following day at 11 AM, and so forth. However, when laying takes place as late as 4 PM, release of the next ovum will not occur as light is decreasing in late afternoon and ovulation will be delayed until 10 or 12 hours later. Thus, no egg will be laid that day. It is for this reason that even the best hens do not produce 365 eggs per year. They must occasionally skip a day, thus defining a "clutch" of consecutive days on which eggs are laid. Thus also, any flock of hens will have less than 100% production on any day.

By controlling natural daylight through varying supplemental artificial light or regulating artificial light in a windowless laying house, commercial egg producers can affect the normal ovulatory cycle of the laying hen. They generally keep light duration constant at 14 or 16 hours of light per day to remove seasonal effects of decreasing day length and thus keep hens laying year-round. However, to provide 24 hours of light per day would not prevent hens from skipping an occasional day since other biological mechanisms override this effect of a light and dark cycle. Experimentally, chickens in light-tight houses have been induced to produce over 365 eggs per year by artificially shortening the light-dark cycle to fewer than 24 hours. This technique, if proven feasible in all respects, over a required laying period could significantly increase the yearly egg production per hen and find good commercial application.

The effects of human-controlled light on commercial pullet, turkey, and egg production will be discussed in subsequent chapters. It will be shown how humans have utilized environmental control to affect the neurohormonal interactions of poultry, to realize an increasing percentage of the genetic potential for food production provided by the poultry breeder.

The bursa of Fabricius is a gland found only in birds. It is a round or oval-shaped sac connected by a short stalk to the dorsal region of the large intestine at its junction with the cloaca. Removal of the bursa at an early age reduces or prevents antibody production.

Thus, any animal, but particularly the fowl, is an amazingly perfect "machine" with billions of functioning parts in the form of cells, tissues, and organs, comprising numerous systems and subsystems, all operating in synchrony. The normal functioning (physiology) of this complex, intricate structure (anatomy) depends on all parts operating at precisely the correct time, rather than independently. Very often metabolic products of one part or system will trigger the action, including the metabolic product production, of another part or system. The result of hundreds of these interrelated actions and reactions is a normal, healthy, productive, correctly functioning animal, reacting properly in an environment in which it was developed to live.

CHAPTER 4

GENETICS, BREEDING, AND CULLING AND SELECTION

From the show ring to the production unit the wondrous fowl has developed under the careful scrutiny of the master's eye. Attributes of feather patterns, color, and fighting spirit took precedence for the breeder until poultry meat and eggs became more important as food commodities. Now economic factors, such as feed conversion, egg production, and meat production, dictate desired traits in the eye of the breeder. Genes and chromosomes are "selected" to code for the characteristics required in a commercial food production bird. With further application of genetic engineering, there will probably be continued improvement in food production from poultry.

The commercial development of the domestic fowl may be looked upon as a successful attainment of genetic engineering, 40 years before the term became popular in the new world of genetics. The commercial chicken is an excellent example of genetic engineering: a mixture of genetic characteristics planned to produce an individual designed to perform with maximum efficiency under a variety of environmental conditions. The hybrid chicken that made its appearance in the late 1940s provided a "new model" that animal agriculture had not seen previously in the quest for increased productivity. The poultry breeder, through controlling genetics, not only achieved the goal of increased production, but just as importantly produced a remarkably uniform bird in production characteristics and in many other favorable attributes. The "engineering" process used to bring forth production gains in the "new chicken" was based on the selection of breeding stock or family rather than individual sire or dam characteristics. As a result, uniform breeding stock is available throughout the world from each of the relatively few commercial breeding companies. Although the poultry producer should not attempt to set up a breeding program, an understanding of avian genetics and poultry breeding techniques will provide a sound basis for evaluating flock performance and will provide the knowledge necessary to determine the best breeding stock for a particular application.

Poultry breeding has achieved a level of practical application that is not even approached in large-animal breeding. One has only to look at the relatively rapid advances made by the poultry industry since 1940 to appreciate the accomplishments attained through poultry breeding. This progress has been possible because of the biological advantages of fowl over mammals. Chickens reach sexual maturity at about 21 weeks of age. Also, the female chicken can potentially produce one fertile egg per day with relatively few nonproduction days per year. Embryonic development commences outside of and unattached to the dam's body, allowing continuing ovulation during the incubation period. The incubation period for the fertile chicken egg is only three weeks before hatching. Thus, many more offspring are available from which to select breeding stock than are possible with mammals. These unique biological advantages have been exploited by the poultry breeder, as exemplified by the chicken hen that can produce 150 progeny per year, about 100 times her body weight. The cow produces an average of only 0.7 progeny per year and thus reproduces two-thirds of her total body weight. The sow produces an average of 12 progeny per year, which is only eight times her body weight.

GENETIC INHERITANCE

The key to life itself and the code directing everything an animal is and does consists of four relatively simple nucleotides, each consisting of adenine, thymine, guanine, or cytosine, and their unique arrangement into a larger molecule known as deoxyribonucleic acid (DNA) (Figure 4–1). The DNA is present in every living cell in every animal and plant and is the active part of the chromosomes of living cells. "Genes" are segments of this DNA molecule that determine specific characteristics of the living organism. The manipulation of genes is the basis for all breeding programs, and DNA may be considered building blocks of the genetic foundation of an animal.

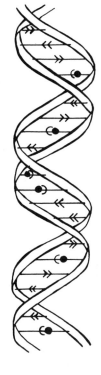

T A G C

FIGURE 4–1
The unique arrangement of nucleotides in DNA provides the basis for genetic traits. Nucleotides are the deoxy-acids of thymine (T), adenine (A), guanine (G), and cytosine (C).

The DNA has the unique ability among biochemical molecules to reproduce itself (Figure 4–2). As the DNA molecule reproduces itself, the chromosome of which it is the active part reproduces itself. Thus, the genetic code contained on the DNA molecule is duplicated exactly in the newly formed chromosome. Preserving this genetic code in every cell in the body is essential as the cells divide and multiply in number, as the animal grows. Chromosome and DNA replication prior to cell division assures that every cell in the body contains the same number and the same type of chromosomes. Also, each chromosome in each cell has an identical paired chromosome, both of which have the ability to reproduce themselves and their DNA code prior to cell division.

Cell division is the basis of growth and reproduction. Somatic cells form the body tissues and specialized reproductive cells are involved with the role of reproduction of the species. The nucleus of the cell contains the genetic information carried by the chromosomes, which divide during the process of cell division.

In all male chicken cells are 38 pairs of chromosomes plus one pair of complete sex chromosomes (ZZ), for a total of 39 pairs or 78 individual chromosomes. In all female chicken cells are 38 pairs of chromosomes

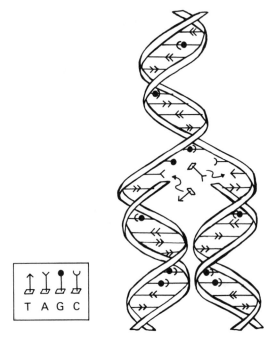

FIGURE 4–2
The DNA molecule has the unique ability to reproduce itself as nucleotides separate and bond to free
nucleotides. Nucleotides are the deoxy-acids of thymine (T), adenine (A), guanine (G), and cytosine (C).

plus one single complete sex chromosome (Z) plus one single incomplete
sex chromosome (W). Every tissue cell in a chicken has a chromosome
pair with a "gene" (DNA code) for feather color, not just feather cells.
Every tissue cell in a chicken has a chromosome pair with a "gene" (DNA
code) for comb type, not just comb cells. Every tissue cell in a chicken
has sex chromosomes, not just sperm and ova cells. Sperm and ova have
a sex chromosome plus 38 single chromosomes.

Birds differ from mammals in certain characteristics associated with
inheritance. One of the major differences is the genetic mechanism by
which sex of the offspring is determined. In mammals sex of offspring is
determined by the male gametes, but in birds it is determined by the female
gametes. Basically this procedure depends on the number of complete
sex chromosomes (Z) in each tissue cell. In birds there are two complete
sex chromosomes in the male but the female possesses only one.

The following diagram (Figure 4–3) illustrates sex determination in the fowl. Since all male cells contain a pair of complete sex chromosomes, after meiosis in the testes cells, only sperm cells with a single complete sex chromosome can be produced. Since all female cells contain only a single complete sex chromosome, after meiosis in the ovary cells, one-half of her ova will contain a complete sex chromosome and the other half will contain the incomplete sex chromosome. Ova from 50% of her ovulations containing the complete Z sex chromosome, if united with any male sperm cells, will produce male offspring containing both complete Z sex chromosomes, one from each parent. Ova from the other 50% of her ovulations not containing the complete sex chromosome, but containing the W chromosome, if united with any male sperm cells, will produce female offspring containing a single complete Z sex chromosome from the male parent and the incomplete W chromosome from the female parent. Thus, in birds, the female determines the sex of the offspring. The opposite is true in mammals, including humans.

Understanding inheritance of single gene characteristics in poultry necessitates reference to the following definitions related to basic genetics.

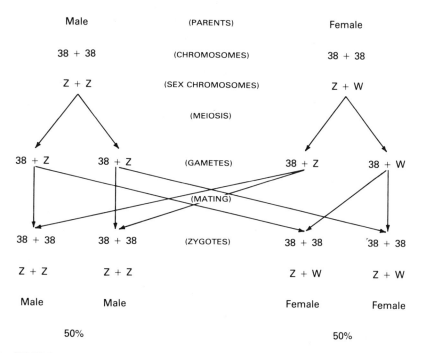

FIGURE 4–3
Sex determination in the fowl.

Homozygous   Paired genes (alleles) at the same locus on paired chromosomes code for the same characteristic (trait).

Heterozygous   Paired genes (alleles) at the same locus on paired chromosomes code for different characteristics (traits).

Dominant   The characteristic (trait) that masks the expression of its paired allele and is expressed in the phenotype.

Recessive   The characteristic (trait) that is masked by its paired allele and is not expressed in the phenotype.

Complete Dominance   The complete masking of the expression of one paired allele by the other allele.

Incomplete Dominance   Partial expression of both paired alleles resulting in a blending of the two traits in phenotype.

Genotype   Actual traits coded in paired genes (alleles) at the same locus on paired chromosomes.

Phenotype   The observable expression of traits coded in paired genes (alleles) at the same locus on paired chromosomes.

Simple inheritance can be illustrated in chickens by the transmission of comb type traits (Figure 4–4). Rose comb (R) is completely dominant to single comb (r). A homozygous rose comb parent can produce only gametes containing a chromosome with the "gene" coding for rose comb, since this characteristic is coded on both paired chromosomes. Likewise, the other homozygous single comb parent can produce only gametes containing a chromosome with the "gene" coding for single comb. When the gametes combine at fertilization all offspring will contain the heterozygous Rr genotype and have rose combs, since rose comb is completely dominant to single comb. When these heterozygous rose comb offspring are mated to each other in the second (F_2) generation, half of their gametes will carry the R genotype and half will carry the r genotype. Therefore, of their total offspring, 25% will be RR, 50% Rr and 25% rr, or 75% rose comb and 25% single comb.

Incomplete dominance can be illustrated by inheritance of the Blue Andalusian (see Appendix 1) feather color. In this case, black feather color is incompletely dominant to white and is also a single gene characteristic (Figure 4–5). The homozygous black parent can produce only gametes carrying the Bl (black) genotype. Likewise, the homozygous white parent can produce only gametes carrying the bl (white) genotype. When the gametes combine at fertilization, all offspring will contain the Blbl genotype, but will be blue (actually gray) since black is incompletely dominant to white and therefore does not mask it completely. When these heterozygous blue offspring are mated to each other in the second (F_2) generation, half of their gametes will carry the Bl genotype and half will

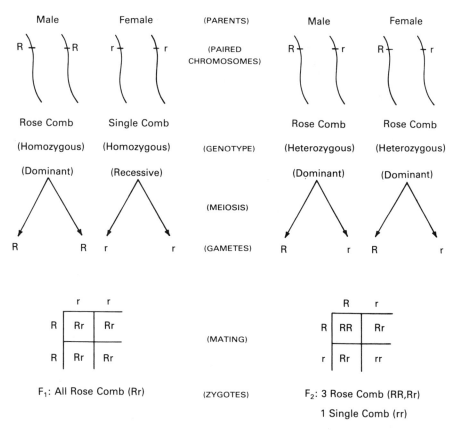

FIGURE 4–4
Single inheritance illustrated by transmission of comb type in chickens, rose comb (R) and single comb (r).

carry the bl genotype. Therefore, of their total offspring, 25% will be black (BlBl), 50% will be blue (Blbl), and 25% will be white (blbl).

Sex linkage can be illustrated by inheritance of the barred feather color pattern, since this characteristic is coded on the sex chromosomes (Figure 4–6). Since barred (B) is completely dominant to nonbarred (b), a nonbarred male, New Hampshire for example, must be homozygous recessive bb. In order for a female to be barred she must carry the dominant "gene" for barring on her single complete sex chromosome (Z). The homozygous nonbarred male (bb) can produce only sperm carrying the b (nonbarred) genotype on the sex chromosome. The barred female will produce half of her ova carrying the B (barred) genotype on the sex chromosome (Z) and the other half of her ova not even containing a com-

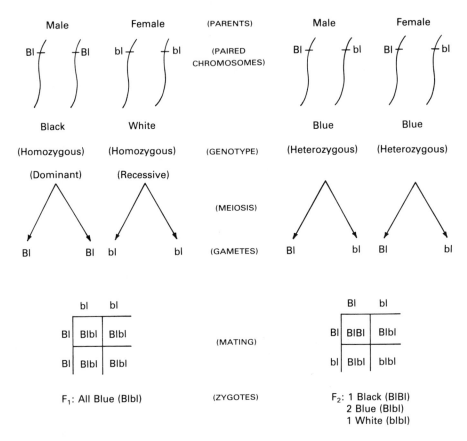

FIGURE 4–5
Incomplete dominance illustrated by inheritance of feather color pattern in the Blue Andalusian, blue (Blbl), black (BlBl), and white (blbl).

plete sex chromosome and therefore devoid of the B (barred) genotype. When the ova containing the sex chromosome carrying the B genotype combine at fertilization with any sperm cells carrying the b genotype on the sex chromosome, the offspring will be barred (Bb), since barred is completely dominant to nonbarred. These offspring will all be males, since they will contain two paired sex chromosomes (ZZ), one from each parent. However, half of the barred female's ovulations will produce ova devoid of a complete sex chromosome. When these ova, containing only the shorter W sex chromosome, combine at fertilization with any sperm cells carrying the b genotype on the sex chromosome, the offspring will be nonbarred (b−) since the barred female fails to contribute any "gene" locus for barring. These offspring will all be females, since they will contain only a single complete sex chromosome (Z) from the male parent. Thus, a female chicken can transmit a sex-linked characteristic to her sons, but not her daughters. If the male is homozygous barred (BB), he will produce only sperm carrying the B (barred) genotype on the sex chromosome. A nonbarred female must carry the nonbarred genotype in the half of her ova containing a complete sex chromosome (Z); and the other half of her ova will be devoid of the barring gene locus since it will contain only the incomplete sex chromosome (W). Therefore, at fertilization the combination of any sperm cells (B) with any ova (b or −) will produce barred male (Bb) and barred female (B−) offspring. Thus, a male chicken can transmit a sex-linked characteristic to his sons and daughters.

Female birds contribute their only complete sex chromosome to their male offspring and the male contributes one also. The female, having only one complete sex chromosome, cannot contribute one to her daughters. Therefore, any characteristic carried on the sex chromosome by the

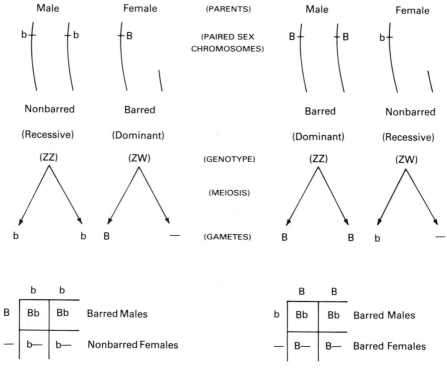

FIGURE 4–6
Sex linkage illustrated by inheritance of the barred feather color pattern, barred (B) and nonbarred (b).

female cannot be transmitted to her female offspring. The very fact that only one complete sex chromosome from the male parent is transmitted makes these particular progeny female. Knowledge of these facts has been very important in poultry breeding for the transmission of desired characteristics and, specifically, has been utilized for sex determination through feather characteristics at the time of hatching. In some instances feather color has been utilized as a means of "labeling" where this phenotypic (physical) characteristic may be closely associated with a particular genotype. In a breeding program where specific characteristics that are located on the sex chromosome are required in the female they must be obtained through the male parent. Should it be a physiological characteristic that cannot be easily determined by gross observation of the male, egg production for example, then progeny tests are required and extensive evaluation of the male line for the specific characteristic in his female progeny is necessary.

Heredity and environment interact to produce the actual characteristics of any individual bird. Those inherited characteristics, which may be the result of single gene pairs or a combination of many genes, are bred into an individual bird and may express themselves in two ways: (1) physiological—those we cannot readily see, such as egg production, rate of growth, early maturity, and broodiness; and (2) physical—those we can readily observe, such as body size and shape, comb type, and plumage color. Physiological characteristics generally result from the DNA code of multiple genes at multiple loci on more than one pair of chromosomes. They are affected by environmental factors. Many physical characteristics are each generally due to single gene pairs on single paired chromosomes and are not affected by environment. Characteristics may be either dominant or recessive, and they may depend on the existence of other characteristics for their full expression. Thus, poultry breeding requires more than just guesswork where birds would be crossed at random. It requires a controlled environment to optimize the expression of genetic potential.

There are a number of complications affecting theoretical phenotypic selection in breeding. Complete dominance always masks the recessive gene, making it difficult to determine whether or not the bird is "pure" (homozygous) for its expressed characteristic. For example, a slow feathering bird may be genetically KK (homozygous) or Kk (heterozygous), whereas for a bird to be rapid feathering it must be kk (homozygous). Rapid feathering is highly desirable and closely associated with rapid growth. Its recessiveness makes selection for this trait much more difficult than if it were a dominant characteristic as it cannot be identified in the heterozygous state. Some genes may display incomplete dominance. Thus, when white-shelled egg and brown-shelled egg breeds are crossed, a "tinted"-shelled egg bird is obtained, representing a blending of characteristics rather than one characteristic dominating over the other completely.

There are many other variations from simple, single gene action that further complicate theoretical phenotypic selection. Modifying action of a pair of genes on the expression of a specific character may alter expected ratios among the offspring and make prediction of progeny performance more complicated than one would expect. Inheritance of feather color in the fowl and factors affecting the expression of feather color patterns are influenced by combinations of genes as well as by specific individual genes, their modifiers, and physiological functions. In some breeds, feather color is based upon a relatively simple combination of genes. However, more elaborate feather color patterns may involve physiological factors that prevent the direct transmission of the genetic code. It can be visually demonstrated through inheritance of feather color and pattern that the genetic code is not always directly transmitted from parent to all offspring. Feather color inheritance may be physiologically influenced by different feather patterns between the male and female of the same breed, since sexual dimorphism is associated with the sex hormones produced. Hen feathering in the female and the existence in the male of sickle feathers over the tail feathers, pointed hackle feathers on the neck, and saddle feathers on the back are examples of physiologically determined differences in feathers between the sexes. Difference in the width of bars between the sexes of Barred Plymouth Rocks and even more distinct sexual dimorphism differences in some other breeds demonstrate the physiological effect on expression of the genetic code.

There are many variations in feather-color inheritance. White is an interesting example. There are two types, dominant white and recessive white. Many strains of White Plymouth Rocks are dominant white. However, the original White Plymouth Rock is recessive white, but all White Leghorns are dominant white. The expression of either of these two types of white depends upon the presence of a set of genes associated with the expression of feather color in the fowl. It must be present in a specific combination. White is a color where pigment is involved and should not be confused with lack of pigment. Dominant white is a very desired characteristic among meat type birds and, in its dominant form, almost completely masks most of the other color patterns when the birds are crossed. White feathering in meat-type birds is desirable since it eliminates dark feather pigment deposits in the skin and the appearance of undesirable color in pinfeathers that may remain after processing. There are no direct relationships between feather color and egg shell color. For example, White Leghorns lay white-shelled eggs, as do Brown Leghorns and Black Minorcas; but White Plymouth Rocks and Rhode Island Whites, as well as other heavy breed whites, all lay brown-shelled eggs.

Inheritance of feather characteristics in the chicken has been studied extensively and many interesting applications have been found. Feather growth rate, which is independent of feather color, has been found to be closely associated with the individual's growth rate and is also very useful for feather-sexing. Feather-sexing of white commercial chickens has provided a significant economic advantage to the poultry industry. Feather color is also the basis for certain auto-sexing breds, which allows chicks to be distinguished as to sex at hatching, based upon down color.

Inheritance of feather color in turkeys provides an outstanding example of genetic diversification and the variation experienced in the expression of specific characteristics. The breed, turkeys, are divided into varieties on the basis of plumage color. There are seven standard varieties: Bronze, White Holland, Black, Bourbon Red, Narragansett, Slate, and Beltsville Small White. The genetics of these traits (Table 4–1) demonstrate some simple as well as some more complex modes of inheritance. For example, there are two types of Slate (sl sl) = light-colored slate, and Slate (DD) = pure. When variations occur such as Dd (heterozygous), the bird appears as a black-winged bronze, which is determined by b', another gene that is part of a triple allele series with B = black, b = bronze and b' = black-winged bronze. The following genotypes and phenotypes are of interest: BB = black, bb = bronze, b'b' = black-winged bronze, and Bb = black bronze. Modifiers may change this color pattern as follows: Bb = black bronze; however, Bb' = a completely

TABLE 4–1
Color Patterns and Genotype of Turkeys

	Males					Females				
Bronze	WW	dd	NN	bb	RR	WW	dd	NY	bb	RR
Bourbon Red	WW	dd	NN	bb	rr	WW	dd	NY	bb	rr
Narragansett	WW	dd	nn	bb	RR	WW	dd	NY	bb	RR
Black	WW	dd	NN	BB	RR	WW	dd	NY	BB	RR
Slate*	WW	DD	NN	bb	RR	WW	DD	NY	bb	RR
Blue*	WW	DD	NN	BB	RR	WW	DD	NY	BB	RR
Buff	WW	dd	NN	BB	rr	WW	dd	NY	BB	rr
White	ww (with any combination of the others)					ww (with any combination of the others				

* Either of these colors is acceptable as "Slate."

The Palm Turkey has the same genotype as the Bronze, except that it is recessive for the palm pattern (pp), whereas the Bronze is dominant (PP). Black-winged birds that are bronze have the same genotype as Bronze except they have b'b', where Bronze have bb in their genotype. Y is used to represent the nonfunctioning sex chromosome of the female.

TABLE 4–2
Results of Mating Rusty Black

		Male Gametes (Four Kinds, Derived from Rusty Black, BbRr)			
		BR	*Br*	*bR*	*br*
Female gametes (four kinds derived from rusty black, BbRr)	BR	BBRR pure black	BBRr black red	BbRR black with a few bronze feathers	BbRr rusty black
	Br	BBRr black red	BBrr homozygous buff	BbRr rusty black	Bbrr heterozygous buff
	bR	BbRR black with a few bronze feathers	BbRr rusty black	bbRR pure bronze	bbRr bronze red
	br	BbRr rusty black	Bbrr heterozygous buff	bbRr bronze red	bbrr pure Bourbon Red

black individual, since b′ to show its effect must appear in the homozygous state. When a gene prevents the expression of other genes it is referred to as being epistatic.

The triple allele series may further demonstrate gene action. For example, N = non-Narragansett (Bronze), n = Narragansett, and n^a = albino (white with faint bronze pattern). When the genotype, n^a, appears in females, 75% die as embryos, and those that do hatch are completely blind. This is an example of gene action that demonstrated how a relatively simple combination may influence function. Bourbon Red (rr) is brownish red and is derived from the Bronze. The double recessive bbrr = Bourbon Red. However, bbRR = Bronze, BBRR = Black, and b′b′RR = black-winged bronze feather patterns. Specific matings reveal some interesting variations. Bourbon Red X Bronze = reddish bronze (bbRr); Bourbon Red X Black = rusty black (BbRr); and Bourbon Red X black-winged bronze = bronze red (bb′Rr), similar to the bronze-red cross. Offspring resulting from the mating of rusty black turkeys are illustrated in Table 4–2. This demonstrates the reason for inaccuracies when selecting strictly upon phenotype. In another example, white in the turkey is absence of color due to gene c or w., completely recessive to C or W. that permits color to be expressed. The appearance of a bird at hatching that is white with buff down indicates a genotype bbcc or bb'cc and clear yellow down indicates BB or Bb or Bb' or b'b'.

Some interesting variations in feather patterns in the turkey are seen in the mosaic hybrid (Figure 4–7), which exhibits certain alternative traits (alleles) of both parents in juxtaposition and are unblended. This pattern is considered by some to be due to somatic gene mutations although other explanations such as "nuclear shifting" also have been offered. In another example referred to as "hairy type," the poult has down that appears as wiry, coarse hairs laying close to the skin. In the adult the features have a coarse ragged appearance (hair-like) and the plumage has a damp-like appearance and texture.

Breeding for complex physiological characteristics, such as egg production and growth rate, involves precise genetic manipulation requiring much time-consuming work with large numbers of birds. Progress toward improving these two commercially important traits has been very rapid since 1940, due partially to the positive influence of controlled environment on genetic progress. Although the poultry used in today's industry

FIGURE 4–7
Mosaic hybrid turkey. (Colorado State University photograph.)

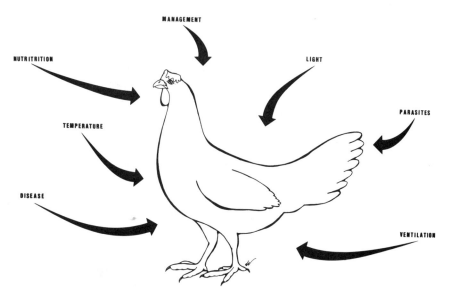

FIGURE 4–8
Genetic potential of the chicken is influenced by many external factors.

have many genetically superior characteristics, they must be provided an environment within which they can express their genetic potential (Figure 4–8). The impact of this genetic-environment interaction must be appreciated by the commercial poultry producer. Although many growth-promoting or egg-production-stimulating feed additives have been made available, they may merely compensate for deficient environmental conditions and should not replace good management or proper environmental control conducive to top performance. Conversely, environment-induced performance is limited by the genetic make-up of an individual bird. No amount of environmental control can cause a bird without the genetic potential to produce efficiently to equal production levels of birds with that genetic potential. High efficiency production can only be accomplished through the combination of both favorable genetic make-up of an individual or flock and the favorable environment through which this potential may be fully expressed. The modern poultry industry has utilized this combination to advantage. Future growth and progress of the industry will depend upon the continued maximization of this genetic-environment interaction incorporating favorable combinations of genes with optimal nutrients, light, temperature, and many other factors comprising the total environment of the bird.

Genetic resistance to disease is quite unspecific for a particular pathogen, but has been successfully accomplished through the attainment of characteristics associated with general health and vigor. Reports suggesting successful selection for increased resistance to specific diseases have provided some promise; however, there are presently many more practical and economically efficient methods of disease control. Selection for general health and vigor incorporate many natural body defense functions that provide protection from the many pathogens.

BREEDING PRACTICES

In order to understand this rather complicated and unique form of animal breeding, certain terms must be defined.

Inbred   An individual resulting from several generations of the mating of relatives so that the inbreeding will exceed the equivalent of two generations of brother-sister mating. (An individual exceeding 33.3% coefficient of inbreeding.)

Inbred Line   A group of inbreds in which the relationship is sufficiently close so that the offspring of any pair within the group will be inbred to exceed the equivalent of two brother-sister matings (exceeding 33.3% coefficient of inbreeding).

Hybrid   The first generation resulting from the cross between unrelated inbreds.

Hybrid Vigor   Performance characteristics of the offspring that exceed performance characteristics of either parent.

Heritability   The degree (or percent) of the influence of heredity on the expression of a given character.

Traits of 40% of greater heritability are said to be highly heritable, which means they are relatively easily transmitted to progeny. Fifty percent heritable means about half of the gain that can be accomplished from a particular trait may be made through breeding, while environment will determine the other half. In turkeys, for example, body weight at 26 weeks of age has been determined to be 52% heritable in Broad Breasted toms, whereas in Beltsville males it is reported to be only 20% heritable. With the same degree of selection, therefore, one could make much more rapid progress toward a given "size" with the Broad Breasted turkey. Simple characteristics, those influenced by a single pair of genes (feather color), have high heritability; but more complex characteristics, which involve multiple gene action (growth or egg production), are of relatively low heritability.

The following concepts are basic to understanding poultry breeding practices. The male parent transmits genetically coded characteristics for egg production to his female offspring and male offspring in the same proportion as the female parent transmits genetically coded characteristics for egg production to her female and male offspring. A chicken breeder hen can lay a fertile egg on many consecutive days, potentially producing over 250 offspring per year. This is over 200 times more progeny per year than many other agricultural animals. A chicken's generation time is less than one-half year, allowing progeny to be bred much sooner than other agricultural animals.

Breeding practices of commercial poultry vary to a certain extent among poultry breeders, with the basic concept applied to variations of the technique of reciprocal recurrent selection. The major emphasis, however, is to select breeding stock based upon its family performance rather than individual performance. This selection not only relates to a particular desired trait, but the breeder is also very concerned with ability of a selected genetic line (family) to transmit the desired characteristic to progeny. The ability of one line to genetically combine with another line to produce progeny with superior performance is referred to as combinability. Careful evaluation of a line or family is necessary to produce the desired performance in offspring when they are crossed with other families. Selection of superior parents based on their phenotypic characteristics is seldom given a high degree of merit unless these characteristics are prevalent in a high proportion of the progeny in cross-family matings.

Specific knowledge of avian genetics provides the basis on which evaluation of the genetic worth of an individual or family is made. Outstanding individuals may be mixtures of many genetic traits (heterozygous), a result of many genetic combinations, and should not be used for breeding. Selection of outstanding individuals as parents for the next generation does not guarantee that the sons and daughters produced will all resemble their parents in performance traits. The poultry breeder may discard these outstanding heterozygous individuals from the breeding stock, utilizing them for food production, rather than using them for breeding future generations. Crossbreeding of superior, commerical, food production birds is no longer utilized as a basic breeding practice to produce additional progeny for commercial use because of the lack of uniformity of progeny and almost equal numbers of unfavorable and favorable offspring produced. The ultimate goal of the poultry breeder should be to obtain many, uniformly high-performing, commercial birds. The great grandparent, grandparent, and parent lines are maintained for the sole purpose of breeding improvement and for producing the commercial bird.

Systematic intercrossing is a procedure by which the small poultry breeder may successfully avoid accumulating a high degree of inbreeding while still maintaining a closed flock and a relative amount of flexibility in selection. A given number of birds are maintained in four separate flocks; A, B, C, and D. At each breeding season the males are mated to the females of the next flock, thus "A" males are bred to "B" females and so on. In the next generation, then, instead of flocks A, B, C, and D, there are now second generation flocks AB, BC, CD, and DA. In the subsequent breeding season the same breeding pattern is followed with AB males mated to BC females and BC males to CD females, and so forth. This rotation of males assures a diverse genetic background and minimizes the detrimental effects of inbreeding while maintaining a distinct family line. This procedure is not used in large commercial poultry breeding systems.

Inbreeding in poultry is defined as the mating of closely related individuals. Brother-sister matings, for example, will produce an inbred line with a coefficient of inbreeding of 33.3%. The coefficient of inbreeding is a measure of the degree of the relationship between the sire and dam, adjusted for the inbreeding of a common ancestor. Coefficient of inbreeding is calculated according to the formula of Sewell Wright as follows:

$$F_x = \sum [(1/2)^{n+n'+1} (1 + F_A)]$$

when x = the inbred individual; A = ancestor common to x's sire and dam; F_x = coefficient of inbreeding of x; n = number of generations from sire of x back to the common ancestor; n' = the number of generations from the dam of x back to the common ancestor; and F_A = the coefficient of inbreeding for the common ancestor of A. If A is not inbred, this portion of the formula is not used.

As the calculated percentage coefficient of inbreeding increases, the actual or true degree of inbreeding may be less than that which has been calculated. The inbreeding coefficient actually is calculated to express the degree of homozygosity, in other words, the so-called pureness of a trait within a line. Highly inbred lines are desired by some breeders because their characteristics are theorized to be firmly established. However, inbreeding concentrates both favorable and unfavorable characteristics. This has advantages, since it may reveal weaknesses in a line, which then may be eliminated while selecting for only those desired traits to be ultimately incorporated in the commercial production bird. This bird is usually produced by crossing more than two inbred lines to produce many heterozygous individuals uniformly incorporating all the desired characteristics of the basic lines in the final cross. These heterozygous birds should be considered a terminal product to be used only for commercial food-production purposes. They should not be mated among themselves regardless of their superiority, since they will produce offspring with great genetic diversity, resulting in variable performance.

The commercial food egg producer requires birds that have uniformly good characteristics so the flock average is high. It is relatively unimportant to have a few 300 egg-per-year birds in the flock, but more important to have many 265 egg-per-year layers. In order to obtain this desired uniformity, it is necessary to mate genetically similar females with a group of genetically similar, but unrelated males. This is accomplished by close inbreeding in the grandparent lines in order to concentrate the genes and develop parent birds highly homozygous in their genetic traits. Through the technique of inbreeding and hybridization (crossing inbred lines), the commercial "hybrid" chicken is produced. This commercial production bird exhibits "hybrid vigor" with expression of favorable performance characteristics exceeding those of either parent line. It has good vitality, is well adapted to the environment, and has commercially important characteristics, such as high egg production and/or rapid growth and feathering (particularly in broiler production stock).

The basic concept of "crossing inbred lines" may be diagramed showing a relatively simple theoretical example utilizing four great grandparent (GGP) pure pedigree lines, each selected primarily for a single desired characteristic (Figure 4–9). Each grandparent line is inbred for several generations and selected for desired characteristics prior to crossing offspring (parents) with another similarly inbred and selected line. These inbred grandparent lines are referred to as expansion flocks because large numbers of progeny are being propagated, grown, and inbred over several generations, resulting in many individuals with identical, homozygous desirable traits to be used as parents (P) in the final hybrid cross. In order to identify which of many possible lines will successfully transmit desired selected characteristics to offspring, test crossing of the various lines, reciprocally alternating males and females, is employed with a relatively small sample of birds before lines are expanded. When two lines are identified by test crossing to produce uniformly outstanding offspring, these lines are then each reproduced by inbreeding as great grandparent or grandparent stock for eventual cross mating of selected lines for production of commercial strain cross chicks. This final mating of parent stock is done at local hatcheries throughout the world. Parent stock is obtained as chicks from primary poultry breeders and grown to sexual maturity at local hatcheries prior to mating.

The male line is that inbred family from which the male parent stock is selected for the final cross. The female line is that inbred family from which the female parent stock is selected for the final cross. Male family lines necessarily contain females of the same genetic strain for use in

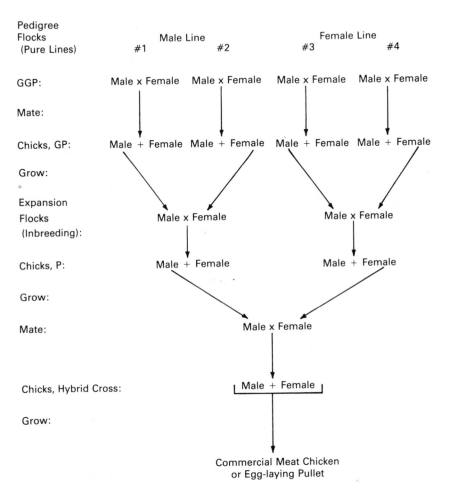

FIGURE 4–9
Basic concept of "crossing inbred lines" used in commercial poultry breeding.

inbreeding, but only the males are selected and utilized for the final hybrid cross. Likewise, female family lines necessarily contain males of the same genetic strain for use in inbreeding, but only the females are selected and utilized for the final hybrid cross. Thus, in broiler breeding the White Cornish female is mated with the White Cornish male in the grandparent expansion flocks; and the White Plymouth Rock male is mated with the White Plymouth Rock female in the grandparent expansion flocks.

A successful method of determining sex of chicks at time of hatching has been accomplished by observing specific, sex-linked characteristics associated with feather color and feather growth. Slow feathering (K) is dominant to rapid feathering (k) and is sex linked. Here is an example of an undesirable dominant characteristic, slow feathering, that will predominate in offspring if not properly handled in breeding, but it has been used to advantage by the breeder as a tool in sexing chicks at hatching time. In the rapid feathering chick, the primary and secondary wing feathers are longer than the coverts; although in the slow feathering chick, the primaries and coverts are about the same length (Figure 4–10). Rapid feathering and rapid growth are closely associated. Therefore, the broiler producer prefers rapid feathering birds, but rapid feathering also has other attributes. Less feather picking and cannibalism is found when birds are rapidly feathered.

This sex-linked characteristic of slow feathering has been developed by some commercial breeders in their production layer stock to more easily sex chicks at hatching time, since male Leghorns are not kept. The genetic scheme for utilizing this sex-linked characteristic to sex chicks at commercial hatcheries is illustrated in Figure 4–11.

The rapid feathering female chicks are easily distinguished from the slow feathering male chicks on day of hatch by simple observation of wing feather growth (Figure 4–10).

There are three mating systems commonly used in commercial poultry breeding: pen mating, flock mating, and artificial insemination. Pen mating is used by the chicken breeder for test-crossing great grandparent pedigree lines. Flock mating is used for inbreeding to multiply selected

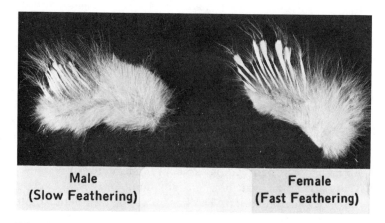

Male
(Slow Feathering)

Female
(Fast Feathering)

FIGURE 4–10
Early wing feather growth in some commercial strains of chicks distinguishes rapid and slow feathering birds and illustrates a practical application of sex-linkage in sexing chicks. (Colorado State University photograph.)

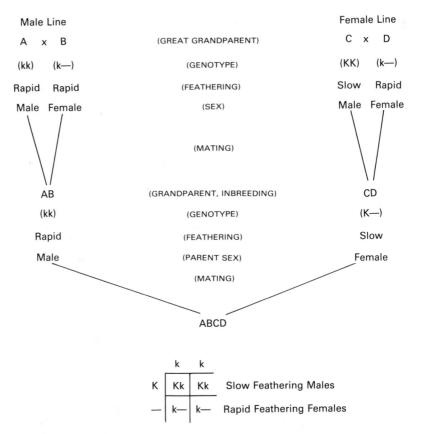

FIGURE 4–11
The genetic breeding scheme used for the establishment of rapid feathering in a commercial line for the purpose of "feather sexing" chicks.

grandparent family lines and in crossing inbred parent lines. Artificial insemination is used commercially for turkey breeding and propagation of meat production turkeys, for commercial turkeys do not produce high enough fertility when mated naturally.

In pen mating, a small flock of 10–20 females are naturally mated to a single male in a pen containing trap nests. Each female is wing banded for identification. The hen is trapped in the nest after laying an egg and must be removed by a caretaker who records her wingband number on the fertile egg. This allows each offspring to be identified as to its parents, which is necessary when its performance is later evaluated. Grandparent lines will be selected for inbreeding based, in part, on performance of offspring from these test crosses. One problem with pen mating is that flock fertility may be low due to preferential mating by the single male.

In flock mating, a number of males are present in a large flock of females at a ratio of one male to 10–20 females, depending on the size and age of the hens. Here trap nesting is unnecessary, since the breeders have already been selected for propagation of an inbred line and mating is random. Flock mating usually provides better flock fertility than pen mating because of more males and some male competition, which results in most females being mated. Flock fertility of 90% can be expected with the flock mating system, which requires about ten days for 20 hens to be mated by a single male.

Artificial insemination may be used instead of these methods of natural mating. The males are kept separate from the females and at weekly or biweekly intervals mated by artificial insemination. Artificial insemination offers many advantages to the poultry breeder to assure specific matings in a given period of time. The techniques and procedures are discussed in detail in Chapter 5.

CULLING AND SELECTION

Culling involves identifying and removing nonlaying and low producing hens from a flock. It is not related to breeding for it deals with removing the least productive fraction of the flock. It is aimed at the prevention of retrogression in an egg production flock, rather than aimed at progress in a breeding flock.

Culling is an indirect method of applying breeding knowledge to the production poultry flock. It has been shown that through identification and elimination of the weak, the poultry producer can be assured of economically sound production stock and at the same time be quite sure of retaining birds with superior genetic background.

Culling the small poultry flock is one of the most important jobs that can be carried out in efficient management. Yet, this is a procedure that is frequently neglected. If culling is practiced, it is much too lax because producers don't have time or do not take time. They believe a poor hen may lay a few eggs; supposedly that is better than none. The individual chicken is an important economic unit in the poultry flock, and even though the cost per bird is relatively low, any breakdown of one or more of these units results in a loss of income and is a potential threat to the economic and physical structure of the flock. Poorly producing hens eat more than they can earn and should be eliminated from the poultry operation. A bird in poor health is not only a poor producer, but is a potential source of disease, since disease invariably attacks the weak to gain a foothold. From the unthrifty bird, disease spreads to the strong, healthy individuals, and then more birds die and the flock's egg production decreases.

Extensive culling of large, commercial laying flocks is often not practiced because it may not be practical or economical. Modern, commercially bred, ready-to-lay pullets will be uniformly good egg producers. Many large egg production flocks are only retained for 12–15 months of production and are then replaced. Therefore, except for removing a few obviously poor producers, it may not be practical to cull large laying flocks. However, commercial egg producers who plan to keep their flock for a second production year should employ a more extensive culling program.

In general, there are four reasons for culling: (1) Salvage the poor producer before the bird becomes too emaciated for market or before she dies. (2) Increase the efficiency of production, which is reflected as a higher percent production of the flock. This also reduces the number of pounds of feed required to produce a dozen eggs, thus giving the producer a more favorable egg-feed ratio. (3) Increase the amount of floor and feeder space available for the good producers, with a resulting increase in efficiency of space and labor required. (4) Control spread of disease.

In order for a chicken to be a good producer and an economic asset to the operation, she must have the potential characteristics for extended egg production. The bird that should be given space in the laying house exhibits high vitality, is alert, friendly, active, and has a good appetite. Her body has the capacity to produce many eggs as shown by well-sprung ribs, a wide back that carries straight to the base of the tail, and a shape that is long and moderately deep so as to form a parallelogram. The legs of a good egg producer are strong and parallel, and her keel bone is long and straight. She carries her body in a stylish manner and, when satisfied, she cackles contentedly. The feathers of a good producer are clean, but may be broken and ragged since she puts her energy into egg production and does not regenerate feathers that become damaged.

The bird that should not be allowed to take up valuable space in the laying house is the one that does not lay at all or lays very few eggs. She can easily be picked out of the flock if the general standard of the flock is high, for she will stand out as obviously inferior. If the poor producers are numerous, the job of culling becomes more of a task and is discouraging to the flock owner. In general, the poor egg producer will be dull, listless, and quiet, and will not spend much time eating. She generally will be wild and difficult to handle. Her head and face will be coarse and possibly shallow, long and narrow, and contain a lot of pigment. Her back will be narrow. She will have a turned-up keel, indicating limited body capacity for egg production. Her feathers often will be close, tight, and in good condition, as more of her energy is used for their replacement instead of egg production.

When a hen is examined to determine whether to "cull" her or "keep" her in the laying flock, there are five things you want to know about the individual:

1. Ability to lay. Body capacity, stamina, general health, and alert appearance. This may be determined before production begins or anytime during the first production year.

2. Present production. This may be determined at any season of the year to distinguish between those birds that are laying and those that are resting at the time of handling.

3. Indications of past production. These characteristics are usually not apparent in the pullet that has just started to lay, since it depends upon the length of time a bird has been in production. However, these can and should be used for measuring the worth of a bird any time after she starts laying.

4. Rate of production. The number of eggs laid in a given length of time is important; the higher the rate of production, the more valuable the hen.

5. Health and vitality. The ability of the bird to withstand the strain of egg production may be determined anytime before or after the egg-laying period.

The comparative characteristics of a good producing hen and a poor producing hen are summarized in Table 4–3.

When culling a laying flock, look over the entire flock before handling any of the birds to get an overall picture. Note the health and vitality of the bird before you pick it up. Also, note body conformity and size and look for any abnormalities or defects. Pick the bird up and examine these characteristics closer. Also, note the temperament and feather condition. Examine the comb, wattles, face, and eyes. Examine the vent for size and moistness. Determine the pubic bone spread and pubic-to-sternum bone spread. Note the pliability of the abdominal skin. Fat deposits make the skin feel hard.

If the hen has the ability to lay and if the hen is presently in production, examine the vent, eye ring, and the beak for yellow pigment and examine the shanks for yellow pigment and roundness. Determine the body conformity and size, check for abnormalities and any indications of disease, and examine for wing molt. Taking all points into consideration, the future potential of the hen as an egg producer may be evaluated. One can determine approximately how long a hen having yellow skin has been in or out of production by checking for the presence and absence

TABLE 4–3
Comparison of the Characteristics of a Layer and Nonlayer

Character	Good Producer	Poor Producer
Head	Clear-cut, rugged, alert, fine quality	Coarse, phlegmatic masculine, "beefy"
Face	Bright red, clean cut, rather thin	Yellowish tint, puffiness
Eye	Full, round, prominent	Dull, defects
Comb and wattles	Large, full, smooth, hard, waxy, bright red, glossy	Limp, dried, shrunken, cold, dull, shriveled, scaly
Skin	Soft, loose, velvety	Thick, underlaid with fat
Abdomen	Full, soft, pliable, flexible, enlarged	Contracted, hard, fleshy
Pubic bones	Thin, pliable, spread apart, elastic	Blunt, rigid, close together, thick, stiff (two fingers apart)
Keel	Spread apart from pubic bones	Close to pubic bones (three fingers from pubic bones)
Vent	Large, smooth, moist, dilated, pliable, bleached	Shrunken, puckered, dry, hard, yellow or flesh colored
Eye ring	Bleached, white	Yellow
Ear lobe	White	Yellowish
Beak	Bleached	Yellow
Shanks	Bleached, flattened	Yellow, round
Feathers	Worn, soiled, trim, frayed	Smooth, clean, not worn, sleek, glossy
Molting	Late, rapid	Early, slow
Temperament	Active, alert, easy to handle, good appetite	Less active and alert, more difficult to handle, eats less
Health	Good	Disease
Body capacity	Large, increased	Small, decreased
Legs	Strong, straight	Weak, crooked, crippled

(bleached) of yellow skin pigment in the vent, eye ring, beak, and shanks (Table 4–4). When coming into egg production a hen will lose yellow pigment first from the vent, followed in order by the eye ring, beak from base to tip, and then shanks. When going out of egg production, the yellow pigment will return to these areas of skin in the same order as it left and twice as fast.

The presence or absence of yellow pigment in the subcutaneous fat and shanks of yellow-skin chickens is directly correlated with the presence or absence in the feed of a yellow carotenoid pigment. For this reason, a hen fed on a ration devoid of such feed ingredients as yellow corn and green forage, which have considerable amounts of carotenoid, might have the appearance of laying so far as pigment is concerned, though she may have never produced an egg. The character of the feed the hen has been receiving should, therefore, always be considered in relation to her condition with reference to pigment. Obviously, skin pigment could not be used to cull white-skinned chickens from a laying flock since these breeds do not have the genetic trait for depositing carotenoid pigment in the skin.

You should use proper technique for removing the bird from the cage and handling it. Approach the cage slowly and make some noise so as not to startle the bird. Open the cage and stand close to the opening so the bird can't fly out. If the bird flies to the top of the cage, let it settle down before trying to get hold of it. Turn the bird so that it is facing you and place your middle finger between its legs with the first and third fingers tight against the outside of each leg, and the thumb and little finger each holding down a wing. Firmly grasp the legs, not the breast or wings, and immediately lift the bird off the floor of the cage. The bird will quit struggling as soon as its legs are immobilized and off the floor. Do not remove the bird from the cage until it is under control. Remove the bird from the cage head first. Let the bird's body lay on your arm with the head tucked under your arm for examination of the pubic bones, sternum, and vent. To examine the head, hold the bird up on your hand, but retain control of its legs. Set the bird back in the cage head first. Use the same procedure for roosters as described above for hens, except grasp both legs with all fingers quickly and at the same time to avoid getting scratched by the spurs. Then maneuver the bird so that it can be removed head first.

TABLE 4–4

Sequence and Rate of Pigment Loss in Laying Hens

Yellow Pigment	Egg Production	
	IN (bleached)	OUT (yellow)
Vent	1–2 weeks	1/2–1 week
Eye ring	2–4 weeks	1–2 weeks
Beak	6–8 weeks	3–4 weeks
Shanks	2 months	1 month

Molt, or loss of feathers, may be used to indicate a bird's laying ability. Commercial egg producers and some breeders use molting as a production indicator. Both time and duration of feather molt should be considered. The bird loses old feathers and grows new ones in the following order: head, neck, body, wings, and tail. Wing primaries drop before secondaries. When the molt extends to the body and wings, the hen usually stops laying and the molt becomes complete.

The wing consists of ten primary feathers on the outer portion, one axial or short feather in the center and approximately 10–12 secondary feathers on the innermost area next to the body (Figure 2–20). A primary wing feather is replaced in approximately six weeks. An early molter loses one primary every two weeks, whereas a late molter loses two or three feathers at a time every week. New feathers appear glossy, bright, full, soft, and have large quills. Old feathers are worn, soiled, dry and frayed, and quills are small, hard, and transparent.

It is possible to estimate when the wing molt began by determining the number, size, and condition of primary wing feathers. Early and slow molters are poor egg producers and generally drop only one or two primary feathers at a time. Late and fast molters are good egg producers and shed three or more primary feathers at a time. Since it takes six weeks to grow a new wing feather (two-thirds of growth during the first three weeks), one can estimate time and rate of wing molt by observing the number and length of new primary wing feathers (Figure 4–12).

Chickens generally molt annually in the late summer or fall at the close of each laying year. An early molter is a poor layer. It takes six weeks for a new feather to grow out in a high or low producer. The high producer molts later and grows more feathers at a time, completing the molt much more rapidly (two to three months) than a low producer, which may be out of production for four to six months. A high producer will lay eggs until the wings molt. Wing molt will indicate when a hen stopped laying and also the rate at which she laid. The hen with the most, new, primary wing feathers probably has been out of production the longest.

Poultry managers must decide whether or not they should incorporate forced molting into their replacement programs. Many who do have their molt age "locked in" rather rigidly with very little consideration given to the advisability of molting a particular flock a few weeks earlier or later. This policy would be justified if egg prices were constant throughout the year, but is not justified when egg prices fluctuate by plus or minus 20% within a year. Manipulation of molting dates can actually increase the income from a flock. Changing the molting date by as little as five weeks may improve income as much as ten cents or more per hen. A projection of future flock performance and profitability for various alternative molting dates can easily and rapidly be accomplished by using available computer programs.

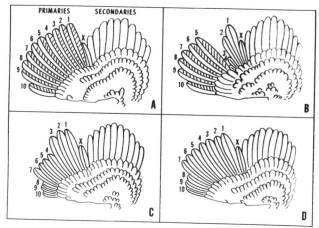

A. Normal wing showing primary feathers (1 to 10), axial feather
(x), and secondary feathers (right).

B. Wing of a slow molter at 6 weeks. Primary feather 1 is fully
grown. Feather 2 is 4 weeks old, 3 is 2 weeks old, and 4 has
just appeared. Other primaries have not been dropped.

C. Wing of a fast molter at 6 weeks. All primaries have been
dropped. Feathers 1 to 3 are fully grown; 4 to 7 (which were
dropped in a group) are 4 weeks old; 8 to 10 are 2 weeks old.

D. Wing of a fast molter at 8 weeks. Feathers 1 to 7 are fully grown;
8 to 10 are two-thirds grown. Hen completed molt at 10 weeks.

FIGURE 4–12
Wing molt and feather growth. (*Culling Hens.* U.S. Department
of Agriculture Farmers' Bulletin No. 2216, 1966.)

Selection involves identifying and selecting superior birds for breeding stock. It deals with the most productive fraction of the flock (top 10%, 15%, or 25%), and is aimed at progressively improving the breeding flock. The selection of individual males and females for breeding may be based on:

1. Past performance. The pedigree of the individual is examined for several preceding generations.

2. Present performance. The appearance and performance of the individual and its sibs (sisters and brothers) are studied. Body capacity, stamina, health, and vitality are important factors since the hen must have the ability to withstand the strain of egg production. The higher the rate of egg production (number of eggs laid in a given length of time), the more valuable the family is for breeding.

3. Future performance. The appearance and performance of the progeny (sons and daughters) of an individual are measured.

In selecting hens for breeding, first look at the gross structure of the individual, her posture, body shape, and general appearance. Then handle the individual and choose her according to the qualities outlined in Table 4–3. Hen selection is based on several traits. The more important are the handling qualities, head, pigmentation, molt, and the breed characteristics.

The selection of males for the poultry breeding flock is equally as important as the selection of the females, since the male contributes to the offspring in the same proportion as the female. In selecting the male for breeding, follow the same points of consideration that are followed in selecting the female, the only difference being that you cannot use such characteristics of production as pigmentation and pubic-bone spread. Note the appearance and evaluate the male's vigor and health. Select a bird that is large and has good body capacity and posture. His legs should be strong and straight and they should be relatively rich in pigment. The bird should be alert and active, have a strong head, and a broad yellow beak. His feathers should be tight and well-groomed. He should have a wide straight back, hold his tail well above the horizontal plane of the back, and have a straight breast bone that carries well back to the abdomen. This type of phenotypic selection generally reflects the physical well-being of an individual bird and may be applied to males that have been genetically selected for the desired egg production characteristics, based on family performance records.

CHAPTER 5

REPRODUCTION, EMBRYONIC DEVELOPMENT, AND INCUBATION

The jungle fowl, which needed only to produce enough eggs to reproduce its species, has been taken by humans out of the jungle, domesticated, and scientifically altered to produce an ancestor very much modified to meet the food production needs of a modern well-nourished society. In helping the fowl become more prolific in its reproductive cycle, humans have improved artificially on what came naturally to the rooster and hen. Today, the chicken hen leads the animal kingdom in reproductive capacity. Artificial control of the mating, egg laying, incubation, and hatching environments has increased egg production, fertility, and hatchability and improved overall efficiency of reproduction to more efficiently provide food for humans.

REPRODUCTION

The Basis of Fertility

The term fertility refers only to the percentage of eggs that have been fertilized. Since most hatcheries include early dead embryos among the eggs reported as infertile, fertility figures require careful interpretation. For example, research reports of 90% fertility may be equivalent to 75%–80%, as reported by commercial hatcheries. All steps in the reproductive process are vital in a commercial poultry production program, though some may be more important to breeders and others more important to hatchery operators.

One of the basic definitions of fertility commonly used in mammalian reproduction is, "the ability to produce offspring." However, in reference to poultry, it is useful to focus attention on many separate components of the fertility complex that are more easily observed in birds. Fertility may be defined as the ability to produce fertile eggs, implying equal contributions of male and female parents. A highly fertile flock is one that produces a relatively large number of fertile eggs. Fertility is the percentage of the eggs laid that are fertile. Egg production and egg fertilization are separate functions. Although infertility may be misinterpreted as a malfunction of the male, the hen should not be ignored since apart from her role as an egg producer, her reproductive tract either rejects the sperm or is a recipient of the sperm.

Very few species of birds are as machine-like in egg production as the domestic chicken or turkey. Females of most species must engage in more or less elaborate courtship rituals before eggs are produced. These include choosing or accepting a mate, defending territory, building a nest, and actually displaying courtship behavior. These procedures are important in at least one domestic avian species—the pigeon—which rarely lays eggs unless paired. However, actual mating isn't necessary—even if the pair is separated by a wire partition the male can stimulate the female pigeon to lay—and females can be fooled by a mirror in the cage or even by being stroked by the caretaker. In turkey hens there are problems of receptivity to be considered. Also, various conditions may affect the hen's ability to retain functionally normal sperm after mating.

The testes start producing sperm at about 100–250 days of age. In the process of maturing, these sperm cells pass through several stages requiring approximately 30 days to complete. The mature sperm leaves the testes and travel down the vas deferentia. There is apparently only very little storage of sperm in the vas deferentia of the fowl. The bulbous ducts extending through the wall of the cloaca serve as short-time storage organs. These terminate in narrow papillae that release semen onto the surface of the copulatory organ. This organ contains erectile tissue, but differs from the mammalian reproductive organ in that it is relatively small and it becomes erect instantly and loses erection very quickly. During copulation the bulbous ducts are squeezed by contraction of the muscular sphincter and the semen pours out onto the surface of the small copulatory organ in the everted cloacal wall.

During copulation the female extends the vaginal opening beyond the lips of the everted cloaca. The male then mounts onto the back of the female, makes everted cloacal contact, and semen is deposited at the vaginal opening. The female immediately withdraws the vaginal opening into the cloaca, retaining the semen in the vagina. Sperm move out of the seminal fluid and into secretions coating the oviduct wall. Using their motile flagella, aided by vaginal motion, they migrate ("swim") the length of the oviduct. Only the strongest complete the trip. Once in the anterior end of the oviduct they "lie in wait" for a freshly ovulated yolk and many then attach to the ovum in the infundibulum. This is the only time an egg can be fertilized. As soon as the yolk is coated with albumen, the sperm can no longer penetrate to the ovum and as the vitelline membrane starts to thicken, the sperm cells are unable to penetrate it. Thus, eggs laid the same day as the first mating or first insemination are never fertile, and eggs laid the next day are rarely fertile unless the insemination is carried out in early morning. Sperm can survive in the oviduct of a hen for several weeks and remain viable. Fertile eggs have been reported to have been laid as long as ten weeks after a single insemination but these are very rare; fertility drops quite abruptly after about two to three weeks.

There are some interesting differences between mammalian and avian sperm as indicated in Table 5–1. Thus, avian semen must be used in artificial insemination of hens within a few minutes of its collection, but a hen need only be inseminated as often as once per week. Varying durations of fertile egg production in different birds may depend on inherent differences in the hen. Low fertility immediately after artificial insemination may be due to an exceptionally large proportion of embryos

TABLE 5–1
Distinguishing Characteristics of Mammalian and Avian Sperm

	Mammals	Birds
Development of sperm:	below body temperature; scrotum is regulator	at body temperature, except air sacs may regulate otherwise high testes' temperature. High environmental temperature may terminate semen production
Viability of collected sperm:	several days; best if chilled to 0°C(32°F)	hours, or even minutes for *high* fertility; killed below 4.4°C(40°F)
Viability of sperm in female:	hours	days or weeks

that die before the eggs are laid or may result from a poor insemination technique, resulting in inadequate sperm numbers. Inadequate numbers of sperm shorten the duration of fertile egg production following an initial high fertility level. For chickens, an amount of semen containing at least 100 million sperm is necessary for maximum fertility. Although this number may be adequate for turkeys also, larger numbers are frequently used for artificial insemination. Turkey semen contains about 11 billion sperm per milliliter, but the concentration may vary up to about 20 billion sperm per milliliter. Chicken semen is less concentrated than turkey semen.

Infertility in healthy flocks may be due largely to inadequate mating frequency under natural mating conditions. This can result from a combination of infrequent periods of receptiveness on the part of the hen and of low mating efficiency of the male. A successful mating is the end result of a chain of actions and responses as follows:

1. The hen initiates action by approaching the male
2. The male struts
3. The hen squats and spreads her tail feathers
4. The male mounts, orients to the hen's head, and grips her wings
5. The hen elevates her tail and everts her cloaca
6. The male treads, everts his cloaca, and they copulate

The mating will not succeed if there is failure at any step. However, if it proceeds to step five, and the hen everts, she then becomes nonresponsive for a variable period of time. Some hens become responsive again within a day or two, but most require longer periods, and some birds have been observed to remain nonresponsive for as long as 30 days. Male mating efficiency also varies widely. As a result, the average interval between successful matings may be nearly twice as long as the interval between periods of responsiveness. With increasing age of sperm in the oviduct, the embryos produced from fertilization become progressively less capable of survival; embryo age at death is inversely correlated with sperm age. Thus, when mating frequency is inadequate, the chick or poult yield will suffer not only from true infertility, but also from a high percentage of dead embryos.

Low fertility in a poultry breeding flock may also be attributable to other factors. Males not in semen production are worse than useless in a breeding flock: They can't mate, and their aggressive behavior frequently prevents more functional males from mating. Seasonal variation in semen production is well-known since the male responds to environmental conditions. Fertility may be high at the start of the breeding season or it may be low if inadequate mating has occurred immediately before the start of egg production. Fertility ordinarily declines after mid-season, in part due to a natural decline in semen production and a decrease in the number of males producing semen. Fertility has been observed to decline in artificially inseminated flocks given a constant dosage of semen. The loss in fertility may be the result of high summer temperatures that limit the life of the sperm in the oviduct. Advancing age in the hens also may be associated with failure of the sperm transport mechanism. In some experiments, chickens and turkeys that failed to produce any fertile eggs after insemination produced fertile eggs when sperm were introduced directly into the upper oviduct by surgical methods. Much remains to be learned about the physiology of sperm in the oviduct.

Breeding

Sound decisions regarding breeder flock management must be made on the basis of the known characteristics of a specific strain. No two strains are exactly alike, and, hence, no two will respond equally to the same changes in the environment at any given age and season. The males of some strains mature earlier, produce larger volumes of semen with higher concentrations of sperm, and are continuously fertile over longer periods of time than are males of other strains. These traits may be inherited and, therefore, modified by selection. Heritability (the percentage of the total variation that is caused by inheritance as distinct from environment) of these traits is medium to high, so selection of the best individuals is an effective method of improving breeding flocks. With chickens it is advisable to permit most strains to reach a minimum age of 21–23 weeks before they are brought into production. More dependable results are obtained from slightly older birds. Since rapid growth of the yolks starts about two weeks before egg production commences, it is obviously necessary to provide an adequate breeder ration at least two weeks prior to bringing the birds into production.

Light is an important factor in controlling reproduction (Figure 3-26). Light can be used to bring hens into egg production when days are short or when light is drastically reduced. This can be achieved in one of two ways; (1) by lengthening the day to 14 hours, or (2) by breaking the night with about one hour of light such as from 9PM–10PM. A light intensity of about two foot candles on the birds should be provided. Continuous 24-hour light is not recommended because more thin-shelled eggs are laid and egg production tends to decrease more drastically after the first two months on this regimen. Physiological response of males to light is in much the same way as hens. Males may respond more slowly than hens, which in turkeys justifies lighting the males two or three weeks prior to lighting the hens. Males also molt and decrease semen production as a result of excessive lighting. The response of birds to light is dependent on a preconditioning dark period prior to light exposure. Increased darkness (reduced length of day) speeds recovery when both males and females go out of production. The important factor here is the length of the continuously dark period. After three or four weeks of increased darkness, the birds will respond to light stimulation with increased reproduction. Extreme weather changes or any change in the environment that makes the birds uncomfortable may reduce fertility.

When selecting breeders on the basis of body weight or conformation, attention should be given to reproductive capacity. Otherwise a low fertility strain may be developed. There is very little relationship between body weight of the male and semen production measured by volume. Strains that differ in egg production may also show differences in male semen production. About two-thirds of natural chicken matings may be successful. There is little relationship between the size or appearance of the male and mating activity or success. Nevertheless, males should be carefully selected to the standards set for the strain. The hen has an important influence on fertility. Variation in the duration of fertility is attributable to differences in survival of sperm in the oviduct. Standard good practice would be to start mating the birds about a month prior to the time hatching eggs are needed. Males should be placed with the hens at least one week prior to the time the hens are to be brought into egg production. Hens should not be overstimulated to bring them into production too fast. It is best to utilize a proven lighting program and stay with it. Hasty action and change in management after the birds start to lay can result in considerable loss in fertility and egg production. Comfortable housing as well as ample feeder and waterer space are essential to achieving high reproductive performance.

Artificial Propagation

Artificial insemination of chicken breeder hens is usually considered impractical under floor management conditions. However, some breeding companies find that, in carrying out pedigree work, maintenance of breeder hens in cages, and utilization of artificial insemination provide for efficient recording of egg production, identification of eggs, and assurance of individual matings. Artificial insemination of turkeys is necessary, due to their large body size and frequent inability to carry through conception in natural matings. All commercial turkey breeder flocks are artificially inseminated on one-to-two week intervals.

The basic procedures for collection of semen from turkeys and chickens are similar. Generally, two people are needed, although there is a one-person technique whereby the male may be held between the knees of a single operator, or the operator may use a "milking bench" to secure the tom turkey (Figure 5–1). For the two-person technique, one operator holds the male, while the other stimulates it to ejaculate and collects the semen. In order to obtain semen, it is very important the bird be held in a resting, relaxed position. This can be accomplished in chickens and small turkeys by one person holding the bird under his arm with each hand grasping a thigh, so that as much weight as possible is supported without any particular strain on the legs of the bird (Figure 5–2). For large tom turkeys, the operator should rest the bird on a platform about four feet high and grasp the shanks, as shown in Figure 5–3. Stimulating the male to protrude its papillae and "milking" the semen from these bulbous ducts is the most exacting part of the technique. The protrusion of the papillae is brought about by massaging the soft parts of the abdomen with

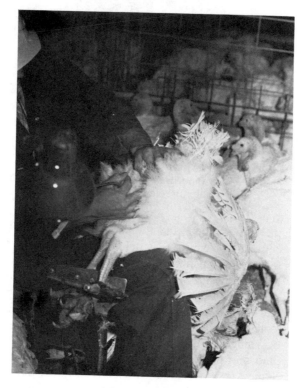

FIGURE 5–1
Obtaining turkey semen for use in artificial insemination by utilizing a "milking bench" in a one person technique. (Photograph by Marty Traynor.)

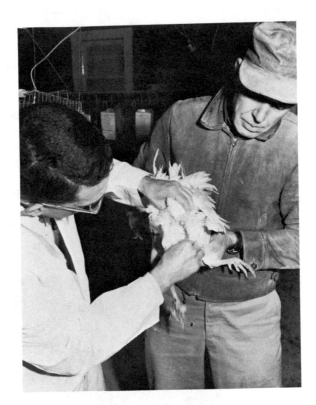

FIGURE 5–2
Obtaining semen from a rooster for use in artificial insem-
ination, by holding the bird gently by the thighs. (Colorado
State University photograph.)

the three fingers and thumb of one hand. At the same time a small receptacle or aspirator is held in the other hand to collect the semen. The
tail is then pushed forward toward the male's back. The bird is further
stimulated, and the thumb and forefinger are in a position to "milk" the
semen from the ducts of the papillae the instant they are protruded, and
ejaculation takes place (Figure 5–4). During the first few attempts to collect semen from a particular male none may be obtained and feces may
be voided. After a few attempts, the male is trained to protrude the papillae and can easily be stimulated to ejaculate without voiding feces.
Semen contaminated with feces, urates, dust, or blood should be dis-
carded. The male should be handled carefully in order to avoid excessive
excitement, fright, and physical harm.

Semen of good quality should be creamy white, thick, and sticky in
nature. About 0.2–0.5 ml semen can be collected from a tom turkey and

0.75–1.0 ml from each male chicken at each ejaculation. Best results are obtained by collecting from the same male only once every other day. Semen should be used for inseminations within 10 to 15 minutes after collecting. Holding semen longer than 30 minutes after collecting should be avoided, since sperm do not live long outside the body. Sperm survive better at temperatures of 7.2°C–12.8°C (45°F–55°F) than when kept too warm or too cold. The fertilizing capacity of avian semen is destroyed rather rapidly at 4.4°C (40°F) or below. Therefore, care should be taken to avoid excessive chilling of semen during the time that elapses between collection and insemination. Avian semen has not been successfully frozen and stored to date, as has mammalian semen. However, research is progressively moving toward solving the problem.

Inseminate hens in the afternoon, preferably between 2PM and 4PM to reduce the chances of a hard-shelled egg being in the uterus; at this

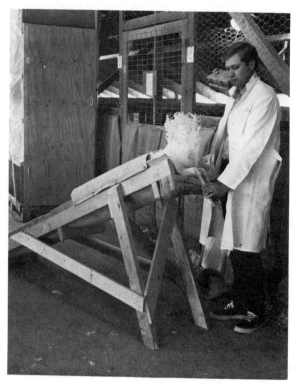

FIGURE 5–3
A platform provides support for large turkeys while semen is obtained for use in artificial insemination. (Colorado State University photograph.)

FIGURE 5–4
Semen is ejaculated from papillae and collected by an aspirator. (Colorado State University photograph.)

time insemination will be easier and result in higher fertility. The amount of semen usually used is 0.05 ml per bird per insemination. This dose may vary with different operations.

There are two basic techniques for inseminating caged chicken hens. The first technique requires that the bird be removed from the cage; this is the common procedure that is followed in inseminating hens caught from floor pen flocks or removed from a cage. It is the slower technique when utilized on caged birds. With the bird resting in a horizontal position and firmly against the operator's side, the operator's thumb is placed against the bird's tail pushing it toward the bird's head, and the index and middle fingers are placed just below the vent. The female's abdomen is tightened by upward pressure of the fingers and downward pressure of the thumb, which forces the oviduct to evert. A second operator inserts a tuberculin syringe or dispensing straw containing the desired quantity of semen into the everted oviduct. Then after all pressure has been released from the hen's abdomen allowing the oviduct to return to the normal position, the semen is ejected into the oviduct.

The in-cage technique may be used for chickens. A female to be caught for insemination by this technique should be facing the rear of the cage. Both legs are grasped by the hand at about the level of the hock joints and the shanks are pulled through the cage door and over the feed trough (Figure 5–5). Generally, this leaves the bird with her head near the floor of the cage and the posterior end of her sternum resting against the cage side of the feed trough. While holding the hen's legs firmly together to apply some pressure on the abdomen, one person places the thumb below and the fingers above the vent and applies pressure in a downward direction, causing eversion of the oviduct. A second person approaches the cage from either side and inserts a syringe or dispensing straw into the everted oviduct and ejects semen after all pressure has been released from the abdomen.

A technique similar to that described for chickens is utilized for turkeys. Turkey hens should not be inseminated when there is a hard-shelled egg in the uterus. The best part of the day for inseminating turkeys appears to be early morning or late afternoon. One person, kneeling or

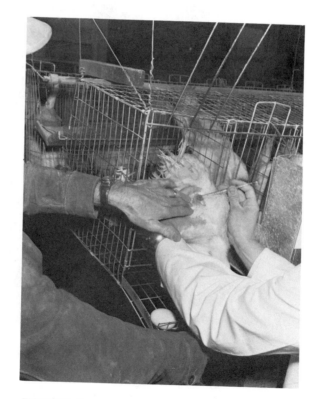

FIGURE 5–5
Removing the hen partially from the cage provides the opportunity for rapid insemination of caged birds. (Colorado State University photograph.)

in a sitting position, holds the hen between his knees by the shank with her head down and back out (Figure 5–6). Pressure is then exerted on the abdomen of the hen with the fingers of one hand to expose the opening and force the oviduct to evert, while the tail is pushed back (Figure 5–7). The oviduct can be everted with little difficulty if the hen is in full-laying condition, but even if she is not in full-lay, it can be forced out with considerably more pressure. The term commonly used for everting the oviduct is ''breaking the hen.'' A second person fills the syringe or dispensing straw with the proper quantity of semen and inserts it at least one inch into the everted oviduct (Figure 5–8). Pressure on the abdomen is then released and 0.025 ml–0.033 ml ($\frac{1}{40}$ ml–$\frac{1}{30}$ ml) of semen is dispensed. The tail is pressed back into normal position, and the hen gently released to keep her from discharging the semen.

FIGURE 5–6
Artificial insemination of the turkey hen. (Photograph by Marty Traynor.)

FIGURE 5–7
Everting the cloaca of the hen turkey to expose the opening to the oviduct in preparation for artificial insemination. (Courtesy University of California—Davis, F. X. Ogasawara.)

The anatomical structure of the reproductive organs of geese differs markedly from that of chickens and turkeys. Instead of a rudimentary sex organ, the gander has a penis that becomes quite enlarged during the breeding season and that is extruded prior to mating or when the bird is handled to obtain semen artificially. It is not possible to evert female geese to show the opening of the oviduct, as is the procedure in chickens and turkeys. The following is an outline of the artificial insemination procedure that has been found to be effective with geese.

A person seated on a stool, places the gander on his lap with its head to the left. Using one hand to stroke the back from about the middle toward the tail, the other hand is used simultaneously in a similar way, stroking the abdomen toward the vent. After this procedure is followed several times, the thumb and forefinger of the hand are brought in contact with the pubic bones in a very light massaging motion. This usually causes the gander to extrude the penis (Figure 5–9) and will also result in ejaculation if the bird is producing semen. A simultaneous, firm hold of the tail with the other hand is helpful. A second person is necessary to collect the semen with a suitable receptacle. The semen is released at the base of the penis, but it may run along a canal that extends the length of the penis and may be collected at the end or anywhere along its length. The proper type of receptacle is, therefore, important; a centrifuge tube will meet the requirements quite well. Ganders produce 0.05–0.6 ml of semen per ejaculate. It is advisable to remove feed from the ganders about six hours before they are handled to prevent fecal contamination of the semen. It is important to handle the males carefully since excessive pressure in the region of the reproductive organ will cause bleeding. Ganders can be trained to respond to such handling and will not struggle or make any attempt to escape after having semen collected two or three times.

One person holds the goose by both legs in the horizontal position with its head under the arm. The second person does the inseminating,

FIGURE 5–8
Artificial insemination into everted oviduct of turkey hen. (Courtesy University of California—Davis, F. X. Ogasawara.)

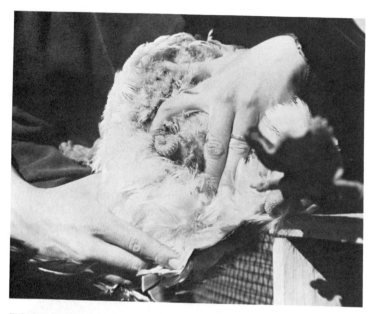

FIGURE 5–9
Protruding penis of gander in preparation for semen collection. (Courtesy
of Al Hollister.)

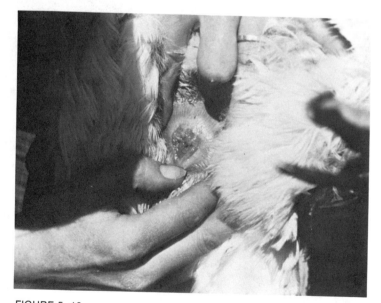

FIGURE 5–10
Everting the cloaca of the female goose to make the opening to the oviduct
more accessible in preparation for artificial insemination. (Courtesy of Al
Hollister.)

using a one-milliliter tuberculin syringe containing a dose of semen. The forefinger of the hand is inserted into the cloaca and, by palpation, the opening of the oviduct is located slightly downward along the left side (Figure 5–10). The glass tube attached to the syringe is then guided along the finger through the cloaca and into the oviduct, whereupon the plunger is pressed and the dose of semen released. The dosage of semen generally recommended to inseminate geese is 0.05 ml.

The equipment used for artificial insemination varies considerably for various conditions under which the inseminations take place, particularly related to the season of the year. The receptacles used for collecting semen vary widely. Particularly in turkeys, to prevent chilling of the semen, it is advisable to use a vacuum bottle aspirator to collect and hold the semen (Figure 5–11). A one-milliliter tuberculin syringe has been utilized frequently and with good success for insemination of hens. Disposable glass "straws" are utilized in turkey insemination in order to reduce

FIGURE 5–11
Vacuum bottle aspiratory is frequently used to prevent chilling of collected semen. (Colorado State University photograph.)

the spread of disease from hen to hen, with a new straw used for insemination of each hen.

Spermatogenesis and Avian Semen

The primordial sex cells (Figure 3–20) in the male are located in the testes. During the first nine weeks of life, these primordial cells organize in the seminiferous tubules. The cells of the basal layer of the seminiferous tubules begin to multiply, gradually increasing the diameter of the tubules. When sexual maturity is reached, the cells that line the tubules are called spermatogonia. The spermatogonia multiply by mitosis to form replacements for themselves as well as primary spermatocytes. The primary spermatocytes then undergo meiotic (reduction) division, which results in the secondary spermatocytes. During the weeks that follow, spermatids are formed by growth and maturation of the secondary spermatocytes. This process is aided by Sertoli (nurse) cells in the tubule lining. The spermatids gradually migrate from the seminiferous tubules into the efferent ducts and out into the epididymis where a final process produces mature sperm. Prior to this waiting period in the epididymis, the sperm are not capable of reliable fertilization or viability. The entire process by which mature sperm are produced in a mature bird takes approximately one month.

The mature sperm in semen pass out of the epididymis into the vasa deferentia, two long convoluted tubes or ducts leading to the cloaca. Some semen storage takes place here. The posterior end of the vas deferens is thick and expanded to form a bulbous duct that terminates in the narrow papillus. The bulbous ducts also provide for some semen storage. When the area of the papillae and the phallus surface becomes engorged with lymph, it protrudes slightly and the ejaculated semen flows out.

The semen is composed of various cellular fluids and mature sperm. Avian semen is normally thick and creamy white. When spermatozoa are viewed under a microscope, a swirling movement is observed indicating high sperm motility. Any variation from this normal state will indicate decreased fertility, increased embryonic mortality, or some other defect. Observed variations from normal may be:

1. Brown or watery semen found to have only about 60% of the live, normal sperm of good semen.
2. Old or "stale" sperm (shown to decrease fertility and increase embryonic mortality). This condition can develop in storage or in the hen's oviduct.
3. Contaminated semen (blood, feces, or foreign material contamination that can lead to decreased fertilizing capacity and sperm death).
4. High percentage of abnormal sperm.

5. Nonmotile sperm (High motility is necessary for high fertility and embryonic viability).

Mammalian semen is less concentrated than avian semen and can be successfully diluted and stored for long periods of time outside the body. Inside the female it survives only a short time (up to 72 hours). Avian semen, however, is very concentrated (turkey: 11 billion sperm per milliliter; chicken: 3,200,000 sperm per milliliter). Utilizing semen extenders, semen diluted up to 1:1 can be utilized successfully with commercial flocks. Although semen should be used within 30 minutes after collection, extenders appear to enhance survival time beyond this limit. Inside the female, however, avian sperm normally survive much longer than mammalian sperm. (4 weeks in turkeys, and 10–14 days in chickens).

Various techniques and procedures have been developed to evaluate avian semen. Fertilizing capacity of sperm appears to depend upon a variety of factors, and no one factor alone may be totally indicative of this function. However, actual insemination of a group of hens provides the most accurate evaluation of the fertilizing capacity of males.

Individual sperm volume can be measured through collection of semen from each male utilizing single aspirator vials (Figure 5–11). Each collection vial should be calibrated or a one milliliter tuberculon syringe may be used to withdraw semen from the tube for measurement. Volumes should be measured to the nearest 0.1 ml. Separate collecting vials prevent mixing of semen among males in pedigree mating. Some loss may be expected when transferring semen from the collecting recepticle to the calibrated vial or syringe. It is important to standardize collecting and measuring equipment and technique so results are comparable among males.

Sperm-cell numbers may be counted by means of a hemocytometer (used for counting blood cells) to determine concentration. From each ejaculate collected, a sample of 0.01 ml is removed, using a serological pipette, and diluted in a test tube containing 10 ml of 0.9% (physiological) saline solution. All semen should be thoroughly flushed out of the pipette by drawing some of the diluent up into the tube and then flushing it out into the test tube. The resulting dilution of 1:1,000 should be thoroughly mixed by inserting a stopper in each test tube and inverting 20 times. This mixture is satisfactory for both haemocytometer and photometer readings. A 40% formaldehyde solution and a Napthol Blue Black protein stain should be added in minute amounts to each semen sample following dilution. This immobilizes and outlines the spermatozoa to assist with counting. A Hausser and Levy-Hausser "Hy-Lite Corpuscle Counting Chamber" should be observed at 430X magnification for all counts. Application is made of the red-blood-cell-counting technique for counting the spermatozoa. Duplicate counts for each diluted sample should be made utilizing a hand counter.

A Bausch and Lomb Spectronic "20" has been found to be adaptable to estimate sperm numbers photoelectrically. This instrument should be set at 650 mμ, a wave length that has been demonstrated to provide optimal light absorption for avian semen. Manufacturer's instructions for the operation of the instrument should be followed. Immediately following the dilution and mixing procedure each diluted semen sample is poured into a spectrophotometer test tube, which is placed into the machine and the percent light transmittance recorded. A calibration curve can be determined for specific conditions.

TABLE 5–2
Variation in Quality of Turkey Semen Ranked on a Percent Fertilizing Capacity Basis*

Male No.	Semen Volume (ml.)	Percentage Progressive Motility	Sperm Conc. (millions/ c.m.m.)	No. Motile Sperm per Ejaculate** (billions)	Percentage Fertility
1	0.80	55	8.2	3.6	93
11	0.40	65	7.6	2.0	92
10	0.34	60	5.8	1.2	92
14	0.49	60	6.9	2.1	91
6	0.66	40	6.5	1.7	89
16	0.65	65	8.9	3.8	89
9	0.46	68	10.3	3.2	89
17	0.76	30	9.1	2.1	88
7	0.40	60	7.0	1.7	83
15	0.60	45	6.6	1.8	83
19	0.49	68	8.8	2.9	81
20	0.55	50	8.3	2.3	80
2	0.44	73	6.9	2.2	80
4	0.56	50	7.3	2.0	76
3	0.45	62	7.9	2.2	72
18	0.42	63	8.9	2.4	72
8	0.66	20	11.1	1.5	67
12	0.50	53	6.8	1.8	61
5	0.46	68	5.1	1.6	49
13	0.27	68	2.6	0.4	45
Ave.	0.52	56	7.5	2.1	80

* Total mean values for insemination and evaluation periods 8, 10, 12, 14.
** (semen volume) × (semen conc.) × (percent motility) = Number motile sperm per ejaculate.

To determine percent sperm motility, a water bath maintained at 27°C should be utilized to maintain all collecting aspirator tubes at a constant favorable temperature. Immediately following collection of an individual semen sample, an aliquot is removed with a disposable pipette and diluted in an equal amount of physiological saline solution. The dilution is made on a microscope slide maintained at 32°C on an electrically heated stage. A cover slip is then placed over the diluted semen, which is observed at 430X magnification for percent motile cells. Number of motile sperm cells per ejaculate (an index) can be calculated by multiplying semen volume by semen concentration by percent motility.

The best technique to evaluate semen is to obtain evidence of its capacity to fertilize an egg. Table 5–2 provides percent fertilizing capacity for male turkeys correlated to semen volume, percentage progressive motility, sperm concentration, and number of motile sperm per ejaculation. A sharp decline in fertility, below 88% occurs when a combination of these factors provides a total, negative influence.

EMBRYOLOGY

Embryology is the science dealing with the formation, early growth, and development of living organisms. It encompasses the biological processes occurring between fertilization and birth or hatch; the development of a single microscopic cell, the zygote (or fertilized egg), into a complete, functioning living animal (a chick, poult, kitten, puppy, foal, calf, piglet, lamb, . . . or a human baby). It is the study of the beginning of life. People of all ages are interested and inquisitive about this particular phase of the reproduction of life. A child only a few years old will invariably ask the inevitable question, "Where did I come from?" And a person never becomes too old, too sophisticated, or too wise to humbly look in wonder at the natural phenomena involved in the creation of new life.

Mating is an observable, experiencible process in animals, as is birth. Most men, as well as women, will eventually observe and/or experience both processes in humans, or at least in some animal. But many people never will observe the many fascinating events that naturally occur during that period of time between mating and birth when functional life is "created." The avian species, with its unique variation of sexual reproduction whereby the fetus develops unattached to the mother, provides an excellent system for studying the fascinating science of embryology. The study of avian embryology will include a study of each of the processes of fertilization, cell division, differentiation, growth, and finally hatching (Figure 5–12). Much of the total developmental process

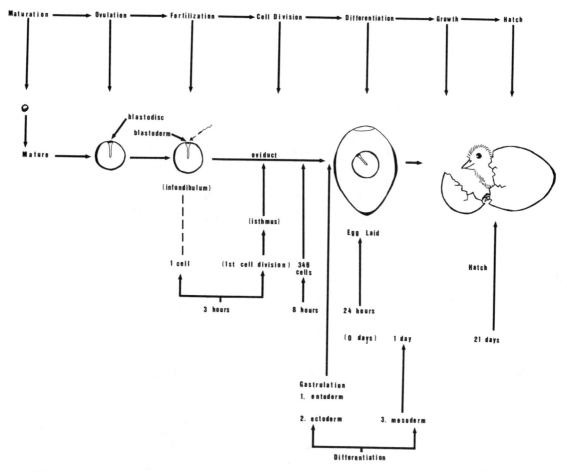

FIGURE 5–12
Processes involved in reproduction in the female fowl.

observed in the avian embryo can be directly related to a similar developmental process in many other animals, but cannot be as easily studied as in the embryonated avian egg.

Fertilization involves the penetration of the sperm (male gamete) into the ovum (female gamete) and the subsequent fusion of their pronuclei into a single nucleus with paired chromosomes in a single cell. Of hundreds of sperm cells that may attach to a single ovum, only one will penetrate, and its pronucleus fuse with that of the ovum. This fertilization takes place in the infundibulum of the female bird's oviduct soon after the yolk is ovulated. The fertilized ovum may be referred to as the zygote.

Early changes in the zygote take place in the oviduct, before the egg is completely formed (Figure 5–12). First cell division begins about three hours after fertilization as the yolk enters the isthmus of the oviduct.

In the human, this corresponds to 24 hours after fertilization. Continued, more rapid cell division forms a thin, undifferentiated layer of cells on the yolk, the blastoderm (Figure 5–13). Eight hours after fertilization there will be 346 undifferentiated cells.

First differentiation of the layer of cells occurs in the uterus very shortly before the egg is laid. This process is called gastrulation and involves a thickening of the disk of cells along one part of the periphery with an ingrowth of a second layer of cells from this thickening. This inner layer of cells is the entoderm; the original outer layer of cells is called the ectoderm (Figure 5–14). The cells of the blastoderm at this stage are attached to the yolk surface only at the periphery, forming a space into which the entoderm grows. This center portion of the transparent blastoderm will appear darker than the periphery attached to the yolk. The transparent portion is called the *area pellucida* and the peripheral attached portion appears opaque and is called the *area opaca*. At this point, about 24 hours after fertilization, the chicken zygote corresponds in development to the human zygote 12 days after fertilization.

After the fertile egg is laid, cell division and differentiation will con-

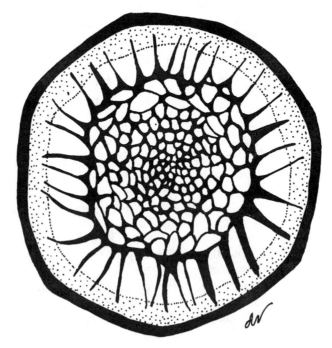

FIGURE 5–13
Thin undifferentiated layer of cells on the yolk comprising the blastoderm.

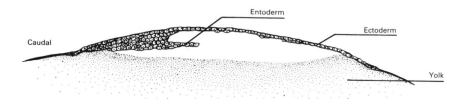

FIGURE 5-14
Formation of the three basic layers of the chick embryo shortly before oviposition (longitudinal section).

tinue at temperatures over 27°C (81°F), but are optimal when eggs are properly incubated at 37.5°C (99.5°F). During the first day of incubation, a thickening of the layer will occur due to an uneven rate of cell division across the diameter of the ectoderm (Figure 5–15). This structure is the primitive streak and will define the longitudinal axis of the embryo. From the primitive streak a third layer of cells will immediately differentiate and grow out on both sides between the ectoderm and entoderm. This newly differentiated layer of cells is the mesoderm. Further growth of these three layers of cells with an uneven rate of cell multiplication within each layer will cause portions of the layers to fold, forming further differentiated tissue comprising the various parts of the embryo. The ectoderm, or outer layer, will eventually differentiate into the skin, feathers, beak, claws, nervous system, lens and retina of the eye, and the lining of the mouth and vent: primarily the outer parts of the bird. The entoderm, or inner layer, will later differentiate into the digestive, respiratory, and endocrine systems: the innermost parts of the bird. The mesoderm, middle layer, will differentiate into the muscles, bone, blood, reproductive system, and excretory system: the middle tissues of the bird.

During the first day of incubation, the primitive groove develops along the longitudinal thickening of ectoderm. This will become the neural

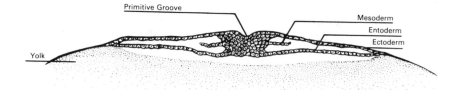

FIGURE 5-15
Formation of the three basic layers of the chick embryo during first day of incubation (cross-section).

groove, which will later develop into the spinal cord of the central nervous system. By 22 hours of incubation, the head fold will be noticeable. The foregut tissue will have differentiated by 24 hours of incubation, as will the primordial sex cells. As the embryo starts to take form due to the rapid multiplication of dividing cells, the resultant folds of embryonic tissue develop up and away from the blastoderm that is enlarging more uniformly down over the surface of the yolk. Continued development in both directions will remain connected by a constricted stalk. As the *area opaca* of the original blastoderm continues to enlarge on the surface of the yolk during the first day of incubation, small red blotches begin to appear in this tissue. This is actually blood being formed even before containment in a developing vascular system. These small spots of blood are called blood islands. This stage of chick embryo development at 24 hours of incubation corresponds in the human embryo to 2.5 weeks of development.

During the second day of incubation as the chick embryo continues to grow up and away from the yolk it begins to roll over onto its left side, still remaining connected to the enlarging blastoderm by what will become known as the yolk stalk. The blastoderm enlarging over the surface of the yolk will now be referred to as the yolk sac, which by the tenth day of incubation completely engulfs the yolk. Also, during this second day of incubation the primary cell divisions of the brain differentiate, the eyes and earpit are differentiated, and the tail fold and vascular system is formed. This stage of development corresponds in the human to about three of four weeks of embryonic development. At this time, perhaps the single most vital development event occurs: the heart is formed and starts to beat. The vascular system develops around the blood islands simultaneously with development of the heart.

Starting early in the second day of incubation, two transparent tubes, projecting from the head fold down either side of the embryo forming an arch, start to fuse together at the anterior apex of the arch. Fusion continues posteriorly forming a larger tube, and the wall thickens as cell division progresses rapidly to form heart muscle tissue (Figure 5–16). As fusion and tissue growth continue in limited longitudinal space, the thickening, elongating tube starts to buckle, pushing out a section at the anterior end. This first bulge in the anterior part of the fused tube will actually become the ventricles of the heart. Further growth and fusion increase the size and weight of this anterior protruding portion, causing it to drop, assuming a position below the also enlarged and bulged posterior portion of the tube. This posterior portion of the tube will become the atria of the heart as it assumes a position above the dropped ventricle portion. During this final transposition of the heart, the ventricle begins to twitch, progressing to a slow but rhythmic beat. Then the atrium picks

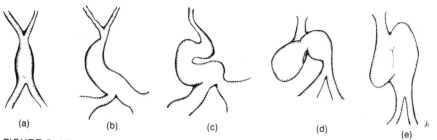

FIGURE 5–16

Formation of the heart: (a) fusion of two tubular vessels; (b) continued fusion and thickening of walls, (c) buckling of elongating tube; (d) enlarged anterior portion of tube positioning below enlarged posterior portion; (e) transposed tube with ventricle bulge below atria.

up the beat at a more rapid rate, followed by the ventricle increasing its rate to catch up, and then the entire heart starts to beat faster. These initial contractions of heart muscle start the blood moving in the vascular system. At first there is a back surge of blood when the heart muscles relax since valves are not yet formed in the arteries. During the third day, the ventricle becomes positioned even further behind the atrium. The ventricle and atrium each become divided into two chambers during the fourth day, and by the fifth day of incubation, heart development is complete.

The developing yolk sac is one of four extraembryonic membranes (Figure 5–17) that has some unique characteristics related to its function. It is a vascular membrane comprised of a layer of mesoderm over a layer of entoderm, which directly contacts the vitelline membrane of the yolk. The blood islands develop from the mesoderm layer. The entoderm layer differentiates into glandular epithelial cells, which secrete digestive enzymes to digest yolk nutrients, and other cells, which absorb these digested nutrients into the blood system. The vascular system of the yolk sac is continuous with that formed in the embryo and thus transports necessary nutrients from the yolk to nourish the growing embryo.

A second extraembryonic membrane, the amnion (Figure 5–17) starts to form on the second day of incubation. It is a nonvascular, transparent membrane comprised of a layer of mesoderm under a layer of ectoderm. It grows up and over the embryo completely engulfing it, as it becomes completely enclosed at 3.5 days of incubation. The amnion becomes filled with a clear, colorless fluid in which the embryo is immersed. This fluid allows the embryo to move naturally while it buffers it from excessive external forces. Thus, it is analogous in function to the amnionic fluid in humans. Growth of the amnion constricts the tube connecting the yolk sac to the embryo forming the yolk stalk.

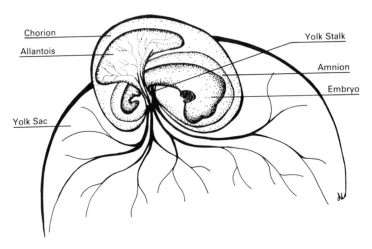

FIGURE 5–17
Development of the four extraembryonic membranes of a chick embryo
at about five days incubation.

During the third day of incubation the limb buds are formed. The esophagus starts to develop during the third day, and the yolk sac becomes larger and more vascular.

The fourth day of incubation of the embryonated chick egg, which corresponds to about two months of human pregnancy, is particularly significant in that by the end of this day differentiation of all parts of the embryo is complete; only growth and development continue during further incubation. Analogously in the human, by the end of the tenth week of pregnancy, before the woman even knows for sure she is pregnant, the fertilized ovum has developed into a complete, very complex, living human being, slightly less than three centimeters long, weighing a little less than six grams.

By the fifth day of incubation in the chick, the already differentiated lungs, trachea, esophagus, liver, proventriculus, gizzard, pancreas, and sex organs can be identified by observation. Through this day, the chick embryo has a striking resemblance to the embryos of many other animals at a corresponding stage of development. (Figure 5–18).

During the sixth day of incubation, the chick embryo becomes visibly distinguishable from that of other animals. Main structural divisions of the wings and legs can be observed. The duodenal loop forms in the small intestine. The first voluntary movement of the embryo commences during this day to be followed by more rapid growth and development of the body.

On the seventh day of incubation, the mouth (beak) is distinctly bird-like, digits are noticeable on the legs and wings, and the ceca start to enlarge. The abdomen has become more prominent, because of the growth of the visceral organs.

During the eighth day, feather tracts appear in the skin and the crop becomes completely formed. The head is proportionally large in relation to the body, and the eyes are very prominant. By the ninth day, the contour of the body is distinctly that of a bird. By the tenth day, the forelimbs look like wings and the digits of the feet have completely separated.

By the tenth day of incubation, the other two of the four extraembryonic membranes have enlarged and started to function. Back on the second day of incubation, the chorion originated with the amnion from a fold near the head consisting of a layer of ectoderm and a layer of mesoderm. However, rather than growing closely around the embryo, as did the amnion, it formed a larger balloon-like sac that enclosed the embryo and amnion (Figure 5–17). The chorion, with an outer layer of ectoderm and an inner layer of mesoderm, continues to expand until it eventually fuses to the inner shell membrane of the egg. Late in the third day of

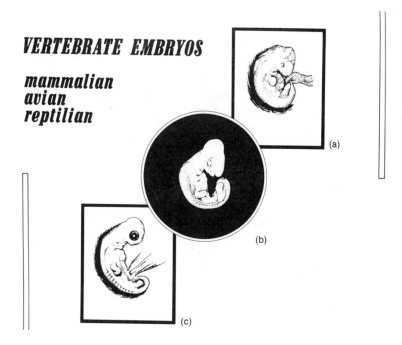

FIGURE 5–18

Vertebrate Embryos: (a) mammalian, human (1.5 months); (b) avian, chicken (5 days); (c) reptilian, turtle. (Illustration by Gary Raham.)

incubation a fold of entoderm under a layer of mesoderm pushes out from the abdominal area of the embryo and balloons out as it grows out away from the embryo into the space between the chorion and amnion. This is the allantois, which develops a highly vascular blood system continuous with that of the embryo. It continues to expand within the expanding chorion and, by the seventh day of incubation fuses its outer mesoderm layer to the inner mesoderm layer of the chorion, forming a single fused membrane called the chorioallantois. As early as the fifth day of incubation, the chorion has contacted and started to fuse to the inner shell membrane. By the ninth day, the fused chorioallantois has fused to about half of the inner surface of the inner shell membrane, becoming completely fused by 12 days of incubation (Figure 5–19). The chorioallantoic membrane, while expanding, contacting, and fusing to the inner shell membrane, also wraps around the yolk and albumin. Thus, it is in surface contact with the shell, as well as with the egg albumin. This is particularly significant to the digestive function of the vascular allantois. The allantoic membrane secretes enzymes that digest albumin. The digested nutrients from the albumin as well as calcium from the shell are absorbed by the blood capillary system of the allantois and transported to the developing embryo. The allantois serves two additional, equally important functions. It receives metabolic waste products from the embryo's kidneys, depositing them from the blood into the egg cavity. The allantois also provides for embryonic respiration prior to functional lung development, receiving oxygen from the shell pores. The blood capillary system of the allantois, tightly fused to the shell membrane through the chorion, will absorb oxygen and release carbon dioxide, which will pass out of the pores in the shell. Thus, it functions as the temporary embryonic lung since the entire egg actually "breathes" through its shell pores. The only function of the chorion, which is nonvascular and indistinguishable from the allantois once fused to it, is to attach the vascular surface of the allantois to the inner shell membrane.

After ten days of incubation, growth and development continue more rapidly. On the twelfth day, down starts to grow out of the feather follicles and is quite noticeable by the thirteenth day. Now scales start to appear on the shanks and nails on the toes. Up until the fourteenth day, the embryo was perpendicular to the longitudinal axis of the egg, but now it has become too long to fit and must turn parallel. On the fifteenth day, the abdomen starts to enclose the small intestines. On the sixteenth day, the scales and nails become hard, the albumin is nearly gone, and the yolk from now on will supply most of the nutrient. Dark residues of undigested yolk material have already appeared in the yolk sac. During the seventeenth day, the embryo begins final preparation for hatching. The amnionic fluid is nearly depleted, although the amnion still adheres to the

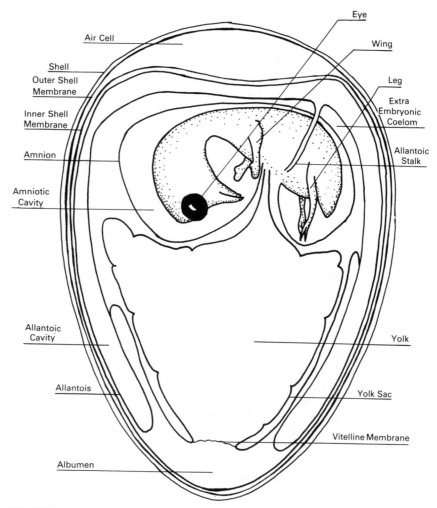

FIGURE 5–19
The chick embryo at ten days of incubation.

wet, down-covered embryo; the embryo now fills most of the egg-shell space. On the eighteenth day the remaining yolk material starts to enter the abdomen of the embryo by retraction of the yolk sac through the umbilical opening. This retraction will continue through the nineteenth day (Figure 5–20) and the umbilical opening will not be completely sealed until shortly before hatching. During the nineteenth day the beak, which has developed a hard pointed cap called an "egg tooth," will pierce the air cell in the large end of the egg and pulmonary respiration will com-

FIGURE 5–20
The chick embryo
at 19 days of incu-
bation.

mence as allantoic respiration continues. However, as the lungs gradually assume greater responsibility for respiration, the chorioallantoic membrane begins to dry up, and allantoic respiration and circulation rapidly decrease during the first few hours of the twentieth day and finally cease. It is essential that this vascular membrane dry up at this time to prevent hemorrhaging during hatching. Pulmonary respiration will be completely functional by the end of the twentieth day.

The incubation period of birds' eggs varies depending on the genus and species (Table 5–3). Normal hatching of the chicken "embryo" (chick) will occur on the twenty-first day of incubation. The chick at this time completely fills the egg shell, with its head in the large end of the egg tucked under its right wing and its legs drawn up toward its head. The hatching process, starting with pipping, when an initial hole is broken in the shell, may take three or four hours. It is started by an involuntary muscle spasm that forces the head of the chick forward causing the egg tooth on its upper mandible to break the small hole in the shell. It may be a few minutes before the chick again is thrust forward to enlarge this opening. Periodically the chick will reposition itself slightly in the shell so that the pipping eventually forms a ring of cracks around the shell, finally allowing the end of the shell to be pushed away as the bird emerges. The chick will be breathing well and perhaps even chirping inside of the egg during the pipping process.

The newly hatched chick has just completed a few hours of hard physical "labor" in breaking out of the shell and is understandably exhausted. Like most other newly born animals, including humans, the chick is wet, sleepy, and ugly. However, in the warm dry environment of the hen's feathers or the artificial hatcher, it soon dries and fluffs its down, starts to chirp loudly, and begins to explore its newly discovered "world" (Figure 5–21).

From this amazing chicken egg, that only twenty-one days ago contained less than 60 g of all the nutrients and materials necessary for converting what originally started as a single invisible cell into a complex and functioning living organism, what is left? Almost nothing! Only a brittle shell depleted of a great amount of its calcium, some dried-up

TABLE 5–3
Artificial Incubation Requirements for Birds' Eggs

Forced-air Incubator Requirements[1]	Chicken	Turkey	Duck	Muscovy Duck	Goose	Guinea	Pheasant	Peafowl	Coturnix Quail
Incubation period (days)	21	28	28	35–37	28–34	28	23–28	28–30	17
Temperature[1] (degrees C/F., dry bulb)	37.6 99.75	37.4 99.25	37.5 99.5	37.5 99.5	37.4 99.25	37.6 99.75	37.6 99.75	37.4 99.25	37.4 99.25
Humidity (degrees C/F., wet bulb)	29.4–30.6 85–87	28.3–29.4 83–85	28.9–30.0 84–86	28.9–30.0 84–86	30.0–31.1 86–88	28.3–29.4 83–85	30.0–31.1 86–88	28.3–29.4 83–85	28.9–30.0 84–86
Do not turn eggs after	19th day	25th day	25th day	31st day	25th day	25th day	21st day	25th day	15th day
Temperature during last 3 days of incubation (degrees C/F., dry bulb)	37.2 99.0	36.9 98.5	37.1 98.75	37.1 98.75	36.9 98.5	37.2 99.0	37.2 99.0	36.9 98.5	37.2 99.0
Humidity during last 3 days of incubation (degrees C/F., wet bulb)	32.2–34.4 90–94	32.2–34.4 90–94	32.2–34.4 90–94	32.2–34.4 90–94	32.2–34.4 90–94	32.2–34.4 90–94	33.3–35.0 92–95	32.2–34.4 90–94	32.2–34.4 90–94

[1] For still-air incubators add 1–2°C. (2–3°F.) to the recommended operating temperatures.

FIGURE 5–21
The newly hatched chick, ready to face the world.

membranes and some crystalline waste deposits. Essentially all of the yolk and albumin and a high percentage of the shell have been converted from fewer than ten cents worth of inanimate "chemicals," into functioning life with unlimited potential worth. With recent advancements in genetic engineering and cloning of living cells and organisms, it is still rather humbling to realize that no human has ever created from nonliving elements, a "machine" as complex and perfect as a chick (or any animal or plant). Humans have played with, regulated, and changed the biology of plants and animals, and particularly that of the chicken, to better serve their needs. However, humans must humbly sit back in awe as they contemplate the total complexity of any living "machine," and appreciate the phenomenal "engineering" achievement of its construction, which can occur naturally without any input of human knowledge and technology.

INCUBATION

Incubation Principles and Practices

The artificial incubation of the bird's egg is an art studied and practiced since 2000 BC. The ancient Chinese and Egyptians operated large hatcheries that were quite successful; they utilized the latent heat produced by developing embryos held in baskets. The history and development of artificial incubation from the wild birds that bury their eggs in decomposing organic matter or the cuckoo who lays her eggs in another bird's nest, to the development of the modern machines that hold thousands of eggs provides an interesting pattern of development with some reluctance to attempt to "improve" on nature. For example, in the early 1920s, Dr. S. B. Smith received a patent on the "forced draft" incubator, which provided the basis for circulation of air, a giant step forward in artificial incubation. However, at that time the hatching industry was not ready to accept the patent and pay the royalty. A long court battle resulted and, over a period of approximately five years, a number of lawsuits developed. Finally, the patent was invalidated because the procedure had been in use by others prior to the filing of the patent.

Incubation of birds' eggs has been carefully studied (Figure 5–22) throughout the many years that this "magic" process has caught the attention of humans. The apparent wonder concerning conversion of the contents of an egg into a baby chick or poult (Figure 5–23) has stimulated a more far-reaching and basic wonder of the beginning of life itself. After working with artificial incubation, one may wonder how the "dumb

FIGURE 5-22
A study of embryonic development by direct observation of living embryos. (Photograph by Marty Traynor.)

FIGURE 5-23
Newly hatched turkey poults. (Photograph by Marty Traynor.)

chicken" accomplishes results in her hatch comparable to that of machines. The incubation process may be considered relatively simple, and it is, providing some very basic rules are closely followed.

Only eggs obtained from healthy, vigorous birds from a well-managed flock in high production will hatch well. These eggs must have sound, clean shells and should be normal in all respects. Chicken eggs should weigh approximately two ounces or 57 g each. Some eggs should be eliminated as undesirable for hatching. Certain characteristics of individual eggs are known to interfere with hatchability: size (too large or too small), interior quality (blood spots, abnormal air cell), shell quality (rough, thin, or cracked, misshapen eggs), age (too old), dirty shell. Selection of eggs without these detrimental characteristics will effectively increase the hatching percentage. Some of these physical characteristics are inherited and may be bred into poultry by continued selection. Shell quality is under the influence of heredity as well as environment. Therefore, it can effect loss of moisture during incubation and, thus, hatchability, and can also influence the shell quality of market eggs later produced by the offspring.

When the egg is set in the incubator (Figure 5–24) the large end should be up so the embryo will not develop with its head in the small,

FIGURE 5–24
Turkey hatching eggs set in incubator, small end down. (Photograph by Marty Traynor.)

more pointed end without the air cell. Eggs may also be incubated on their side in small hand turned incubators. The yolk will turn so that the embryo will be toward the top of the egg, that is, up rather than down, regardless of the position of the egg. As a result, embryos may suffocate when pulmonary respiration commences on the 20th day of incubation if there is no air cell in the end where the chick's head is located. Also, pipping is unsuccessful in the small end of the egg as there isn't sufficient room for the embryo to reposition after pipping and only one hole is made. Eggs incubated large end down develop tremulous air cells more frequently than eggs set with pointed (small) end down. Eggs containing loose air cells have a low percent hatchability.

Procedures are recommended to provide clean and sanitary eggs to set in the incubator. Although washing removes the bloom (cuticle) so that too much moisture may be lost during incubation and also results in the entrance of bacteria and other contaminants, it is preferred to setting dirty eggs. If possible, washed eggs should not be stored longer than one day prior to setting. Clean, unwashed eggs are the best to set, and every effort should be made to obtain nest clean eggs. Avoid setting eggs laid on the floor. Good breeder-house management is the key to obtaining clean eggs for hatching. Adequate nest space (one nest for every ten hen's eggs), with plenty of clean nesting materials, as well as clean, dry building floors and frequent egg gathering (at least three times per day) will aid in obtaining good setting eggs.

Fertile hatching eggs may be properly stored up to one or two weeks with very slight decrease in hatchability. This allows accumulation of enough eggs to completely fill incubators and allows some flexibility in scheduling setting and hatching dates. Fertile eggs may be stored on egg flats in corrugated cardboard cartons as received from the breeder farm (Figure 5–25). A plastic wrap or sack directly enclosing the eggs in the cartons will slow detrimental moisture evaporation through pores in the egg shells. Moisture evaporation from eggs is also controlled by regulating the humidity of the storage room at 75%–80% relative humidity. Humidity of the storage room can be increased by mist-fog-generation equipment available commercially. Optimal storage temperature for fertile eggs is 10°C–13°C (50°F–55°F), which necessitates controlled refrigeration of the storage room. To obtain maximum hatchability it is recommended that entire cases of fertile eggs be carefully turned on either side periodically during each day to prevent blastoderm from contacting the inner shell membrane.

There are four basic environmental factors, which the bird would provide for naturally, that must be provided for in artificial incubation of birds' eggs.

FIGURE 5–25
Cases of turkey hatching eggs in storage where temperature and humidity are monitored and controlled. (Photograph by Marty Traynor.)

1. Temperature control. Forced draft incubators, or those with fans to circulate the air, require a temperature of 37.5°C ± 0.5° (99.5°F ± 0.5°). In "still air" machines—those with no fan and dependent upon convection currents to move air—a temperature between 38.3°C (101°F) and 39.4°C (103°F) is required; depending on the size of the machine and the recommendations of the manufacturer. Fluctuations in temperature will seriously alter the progress of embryonic growth and development. Although the embryo is relatively resistant to short periods of low temperature exposure, it is very sensitive to high temperatures. Large commercial machines contain a cooling unit that activates to prevent temperature increase which occurs during the latter stages of development.

2. Humidity. The amount of moisture in the air within the incubator is very important to the normal development and subsequent hatching of the egg. Maintaining a relative humidity of approximately 65% prevents, under normal conditions, excessive moisture loss from the egg. In small incubators, where hand turning of individual eggs is accomplished by opening the machine, rapid decrease in humidity occurs each time the incubator is opened. Although water is present in the machine, recovery of adequate humidity draws heavily from the eggs, causing excessive evaporation. As a result, hatching chicks may stick in the eggs and not emerge. A dry climate, of course, increases the risk of excessive dehydration. Small machines contain water pans that must be kept filled with warm soft water and may require light sprinkling of the eggs with water every time the machine is opened. Large commercial incubators contain relatively elaborate control mechanisms for automatic humidifying systems.

3. Turning. To prevent adherence of the developing embryo to the shell membranes, turning eggs at least five times per day is very important. Eggs that are incubated on their sides should be marked with an "X" and rolled over one-half turn so the marked side goes directly opposite its previous position. Most large incubators position eggs large end up at a 45° angle, and turn eggs through a 90° angle. Some incubators turn the individual eggs within the trays, others turn the whole tray, while another type turns the complete incubator. Turning is best practiced throughout the incubation period up until three days prior to hatching.

4. Ventilation. The incubator must be provided a continuous change of air to remove the carbon dioxide produced by respiration of the embryo and to supply oxygen to the embryo. The rate of ventilation must be precisely regulated to accomplish the exchange of air without excessive loss of heat or humidity from the machine. It is also important to ventilate the incubator room in order for the machine to have an available supply of fresh air (Figure 5–26). Sanitation is extremely important in hatchery management as dirty eggs and incubators may negate all other efforts of good incubation practices. Incubators and hatchers should be thoroughly cleaned of down and debris and disinfected and fumigated on a specified schedule. Soiled eggs should never be set in an incubator. If eggs are

FIGURE 5–26
Positive pressure duct in incubator room provides for distribution of air. (Photograph by Nancy Nydegger.)

washed, they should be carefully scraped of adhering dirt first in order to minimize contamination. The eggshell has many small pores through which contaminants may enter the egg after it has been washed and the bloom or cuticle removed. Cracked shells and mishapened, or otherwise abnormal eggs should never be set.

Incubated eggs are transferred from incubators (setters) to hatchers three days prior to hatch (Figure 5–27). The hatcher can be a similar machine, but since no turning is necessary, eggs are placed on their side in hatching trays in which chicks will hatch. The hatcher should be adjusted to provide a slightly lower temperature [37°C (98.5°F)], higher relative humidity (70%), and increased ventilation. Chicks and poults are removed from the hatcher at the termination of the incubation period (Figure 5–28) and taken to the hatchery service room (Figure 5–29).

Fumigation of eggs prior to incubation and sometimes at setting is practiced in large hatcheries to disinfect the shells. The embryo is extremely sensitive to formalin during the period 24–96 hours. Fumigants may damage the early embryo, so care is practiced not to fumigate during the first week after incubation has commenced. Some hatcheries, how-

FIGURE 5–27
Incubated turkey eggs being transferred to hatching trays. (Photograph by Marty Traynor.)

FIGURE 5–28
Pulling hatched turkey poults from hatcher. (Photograph
by Marty Traynor.)

ever, fumigate eggs immediately after they are set in the incubator. Many
incubator manufacturers provide detailed directions for fumigating their
incubators. There are two basic techniques:

1. The "cheesecloth method" utilizes a measuring cylinder or glass,
clean cheesecloth, formalin, and wire hooks or a small glass rod on which
to hang the cheesecloth. Calculate the number of cubic feet of space in
the incubator (length × width × height). Measure 15 ml (0.5 ounce or
14.3 g) of formalin for every 2.8 cu m (100 cu ft) of space. Dip enough
cheesecloth in the formalin to soak up all of it. Several cloths may be
used in large machines rather than one large cloth. Hang the cloth near
the fans in the incubator about three hours. If a still air incubator is used,
hang near the door. During the hatching process, fumigation should first
be carried out when one-tenth to one-fifth of the chicks are out of the
eggs, and then again about 12–15 hours later. The process is not generally

FIGURE 5–29
Transferring hatched poults to plastic boxes for servicing. (Photograph by Marty Traynor.)

recommended unless a high level of pullorum or typhoid is suspected. A relatively high humidity, 68%, is conducive to efficient penetration of the gas.

2. The "potassium permanganate method" utilizes potassium permanganate crystals, formalin, a measuring cylinder, and a deep enamel pan. Relative humidity in the incubator or hatcher should be about 68%. A single fumigation is used in the incubator for disinfecting the shells of incubating eggs. Do not overfumigate in the incubator. Calculate the number of cubic feet of airspace in the incubator as described for the cheese-cloth method. For each 2.8 cu m, (100 cu ft) use 30 ml (1 ounce or 28.7 g) of formalin and 17.5 g of potassium permanganate crystals. Place the potassium permanganate crystals in an enamel pan large enough to hold about ten times as much fluid as will be used. If necessary, use more than one pan. Do not use a glass or earthenware pan(s) as the reaction produces heat. The pan(s) should be set near the fan. Pour formalin over the crystals, and formaldehyde gas will be released immediately. Do not inhale the gas, and do not add potassium permanganate crystals to formalin. Fumigate the closed incubator for three hours. In large commercial hatcheries and egg holding facilities, electrically heated formalin containers with automatic controls are used.

Fumigation of the incubator should be carried out before eggs are set (double strength) and immediately after eggs are set (single strength). Fumigation of the hatcher should be done before eggs are transferred (double strength). The incubator and hatcher are fumigated to kill pathogenic bacteria, thus preventing the spread of disease from one hatch to another. A contaminated hatcher or incubator is an excellent place for cross-contamination of eggs. Pathogenic bacteria from diseased chicks, egg shells, chick down, and debris are frequent sources of contamination.

Additionally, fertile eggs may be dipped in an aqueous, antibiotic solution cooler than the temperature of the eggs, allowing the antibiotic to penetrate the shell pores. This provides internal and shell-surface residual antibacterial protection during the subsequent incubation and hatching periods. A large commercial egg dipping tank is shown in Figure 5–30. The immersion time is about three minutes. The dipping solution may contain approved combinations of more than one antibiotic plus perhaps a disinfectant.

An incubation record should be kept for each setting using a hatching record sheet (Table 5–4).

FIGURE 5–30
Antibiotic immersion tank for hatching eggs. (Photograph by Marty Traynor.)

TABLE 5–4
Hatching Record Sheet

Incubation record of _____ Machine _____

Date set _____ Number eggs set _____

Test for infertiles, date _____ Number _____ Percentage _____

Test for dead germs, date _____ Number _____ Percentage _____

Hatched _____ chicks; this is _____ percent of fertile eggs

Record of temperature

Date	Day	AM	N	PM	Remarks
	1				Preliminary run for regulating
	2				temperature. *Note* the temperatures.
	3				Apply to a still-air incubator 39°C
					(102°F). Forced draft incubators 37.5°C
					(99.5°F).
	1				Put eggs in incubator.
	2				
	3				Start turning eggs.
	4				
	5				Begin cooling.
	6				
	7				Test for fertility.
	8				
	9				
	10				
	11				
	12				
	13				
	14				Test for dead germs.

TABLE 5–4 (*Continued*)

15	
16	
17	
18	Stop turning.
	Still-air incubators:
19*	Increase temperature to 39.7°C (103.5°F)
20*	Increase temperature to 40°C (104°F)
21*	Increase temperature to 40.5C (105°F)
	* Forced draft incubators should drop to 37°C (98.5°F) from 19 through 21 days.

High Altitude Incubation

High altitude should be considered a suboptimal environment for the incubation of chicken and turkey eggs, for it accentuates some of the problems related to artificial incubation. Therefore, special attention to factors relating to ventilation and humidity control is required. Chronic hypoxia (oxygen deficiency) is produced in sea-level-dwelling animals when moving them to high altitude. Physiological mechanisms within the animal's body attempt to bring it into equilibrium with the new environment. However, the degree of adjustment as well as the effects of the stress will depend upon the altitude differential, the functional efficiency of adaptive mechanisms, and duration of exposure to higher altitude.

Detrimental effects of altitudes above 914 m (3,000 ft) on hatchability of fertile eggs have been observed under commercial production conditions during the artificial incubation of both chicken and turkey eggs. At an altitude of 1,524 m (5,000 ft) the depression in hatchability of commercial chicken eggs does not economically warrant the procedures necessary for increasing oxygen concentration in the incubator. Turkey hatcheries, however, do find an economic benefit to the addition of oxygen during the incubation period.

Wild birds living in high mountain areas have adaptive mechanisms that allow them to reproduce under conditions adverse to hatchability. For example, bird eggs differ in the number of pores in the shell. This may be an adaptive evolutionary change probably to control moisture loss from eggs in relatively dry climates. Many investigations have attempted to explain the mechanisms involved in the reaction of birds' reproductive systems to altitude adjustment. Genetic selection for factors influencing adaptation to high altitude conditions appears to provide a logical approach. Birds under natural environmental conditions have adapted. At an altitude of 2,073 m (6,800 ft) and up to 3,048 m (10,000 ft) poultry have been reported to reproduce well under natural conditions with broody hens. A decrease in hatchability of chicken eggs of 10% from sea level to 305 m (1,000 ft) and a 20% decrease to 610 m (2,000 ft) has been found under artificial incubation conditions. As elevation increases, hatchability decreases, generally due to the accompanying reduction in partial pressure of oxygen. A hatchability decrease of 17% at 1,183 m (3,881 ft) and 32% at 2,180 m (7,151 ft) above sea level has been reported from controlled research studies. When eggs from White Leghorn lines selected for slow and fast hatching were incubated at three locations differing in altitude 183 m (600 ft), 1,585 m (5,200 ft), and 2,134 m (7,000 ft), significant differences in hatchability were observed between lines and among locations.

The addition of oxygen to the incubator is practiced in some commercial turkey hatcheries as a means of adjusting for the loss in available oxygen due to lowered partial pressure in high altitude environments (Figure 5–31). Oxygen is usually metered into the incubator and/or hatcher, and the level of oxygen in the machine is monitored to maintain a concentration of 23%–23.5%, not to exceed 26%. When this procedure is followed, ventilation must be restricted to conserve oxygen. This could be detrimental to the embryo since CO_2 buildup occurs and toxic levels may be reached. Therefore, CO_2 concentration should be monitored and maintained at 0.5%; lower levels have been reported to prolong the hatch; and higher levels can be toxic. Instrumentation is required to obtain accurate measurements of both gasses, which must be monitored at regular intervals (Figure 5–32). Care should be exercised in handling oxygen, and recommended safety measures followed. The addition of oxygen has been reported to add from 5% to 10% to live poult production costs. The technology of incubating eggs in high altitude environments has potential for development considerably beyond that exhibited by the modern incubator.

The stress of low humidity at high altitudes is compounded by an increased evaporation rate of water through the shell pores. Evaporation rate increases as atmospheric pressure decreases. The adaptation of chick embryos to a high altitude environment of 3,658 m (12,000 ft) is characterized by a decreased total pore area of the egg shell, which allows the egg to reduce moisture loss. Attempts to explain differences in birds' reproductive response to altitude change as well as mechanisms for adaptation have been based upon gas exchange, oxygen consumption, water

FIGURE 5–31
Liquid oxygen storage tank at Mile High Turkey Hatchery, Inc., Longmont, Colorado. (Photograph by Marty Traynor.)

loss during incubation, water vapor conductance of the shell, and pore number as they all relate to egg mass. Exposure of avian eggs to high altitude incubation requires a delicate balance be maintained between water loss and metabolic adaptation capacity.

Effects of exposure to high altitude—hypoxic stress—and the functional adaptation of avian embryos may be explained in part by the decreased partial pressure of oxygen in the atmosphere as the altitude increases. The relative concentration of oxygen in the atmosphere (20.98%) remains constant with respect to other elements as altitude increases. However, the actual number of molecules of oxygen in a unit volume of space is less at high altitudes than at sea level. This is because there is less pressure at higher altitudes and therefore fewer oxygen molecules available in any unit volume of space. If the partial pressure of oxygen (pO_2) is reduced significantly from that at sea level, there will be a re-

FIGURE 5–32
Portable carbon dioxide and oxygen analyzer. (Photograph by Marty Traynor.)

sultant reduction in the oxygen saturation of the blood that reduces the oxygen available to body tissue. Adaptation may occur on a short-term adjustment basis in order to meet the immediate body requirements. However, long-term effects sometimes manifest themselves as chronic disorders. Genetic and physiological adaptation also combine for long term adaptation to the suboptimal environment. Problems associated with poultry production in the Rocky Mountain areas of the United States are limited to the incubation process, since relatively few turkeys and almost no chickens are reared above 1,524 m (5,000 ft). However, in Central and South America high mountain valleys with relatively cool climates provide a rather large high-altitude population of broilers and laying hens.

At altitudes above 914 m, (3,000 ft), design and engineering of incubators and hatcheries should focus on the problems associated with the total environment, since many unique conditions have been identified with specific geographical locations. The potential economic advantages of controlling total environment to enhance hatchability at high altitudes has been demonstrated. Even at sea level, environment may be adjusted to significant advantage in some situations. It is quite feasible that imaginative design of incubators, rooms, and buildings may easily and economically provide some of the basic requirements for improvement of incubation. The potential of genetic adaptation should not be overlooked, and breeder flocks might best be located in close proximity to the altitude in which the eggs will be hatched. However, eggs produced in high altitude locations, when incubated at lower altitudes, have been reported to exhibit excellent hatchability. Pressurization of incubators under conditions of a sea-level environment may also provide enhanced embryo development and improved hatchability, especially for turkey eggs, which hatch at a rate considerably below that normally expected for chickens.

CHAPTER 6

BROODING, REARING, HOUSING AND EQUIPMENT, AND PRODUCTION OF POULTRY

The hen is still a good mother for from 10 to 12 chicks, but for the vast number of offspring produced commercially, mechanical surrogate "mothers" have been designed to incubate, hatch, brood, and rear the young ones. Properly managed housing and equipment provide fresh air, a dry, warm climate, well-balanced diets, and the basic elements of tender loving care. The business of brooding, rearing, and housing poultry involves science and technology and still a certain amount of "art," all of which require uniquely qualified managers to realize maximum potential from today's very specialized poultry. Housing and equipment should serve the bird to provide a comfortable environment with minimum stress for optimal production of eggs and meat.

Exactly when birds were domesticated by humans may be disputed. It may be hypothesized that when early humans were tired of climbing trees and looking among rocks, in crevices, and under brush for elusive birds and their eggs, they then first thought of domesticating the birds. Penning a few birds made them more readily accessible when needed. With protection, feed, and water provided, as well as security and comfort in which to raise their young free of predators, some "captive" birds increased egg production. The protection and services humans offered provided the key elements for successful domestication. An environment favorable for reproduction of the species was essential for wild birds naturally adapted to a much more primitive environment. Through adaptation and pressures of artificial selection, the domesticated fowl has become the most protected and productive food animal known to humans. With humans providing protection from weather, predators, and disease and also easily accessible and highly nutritious food, the bird no longer needs to devote a large portion of its life's efforts toward survival. Therefore, it may devote its energy to growing and reproducing more effectively.

Design of a poultry house should be based on the production objective and focused on standards for maximum reproduction or growth. Protection from the weather and extremes of heat and cold, adequate insulation and ventilation, and efficient labor utilization are some major objectives of housing poultry. Comfort of the birds is of prime importance. Carbon dioxide as well as high levels of ammonia, methane, or other gases in the air that irritate the respiratory system, eyes, or skin, resulting in bird discomfort, will have an adverse effect on growth, egg production, and disease resistance. Although birds may appear to be more tolerant to these irritants than humans, an environment that provides severe discomfort to the caretakers will no doubt have some adverse effect on the birds. The fact that the poultry house must also accommodate people necessitates modifying the house design to meet requirements of both poultry and people. For example, the bird requires considerably less height than is required by humans who provide the necessary services. By increasing the height of the ceiling the volume is greatly increased. Thus, the body heat of the bird is dissipated more rapidly than may be desirable in cold weather. In order to overcome this problem additional birds are added to a specific floor area, reducing air volume per bird substantially. Conserving the body heat of all birds in the house filled to capacity, with a specially designed house having a low ceiling and adequate insulation, generally eliminates the need for a supplemental heat source in most poultry houses. In cold weather, burning feed-energy through the bird's body should be minimized and, if necessary, supplemental heat provided to avoid extreme low temperatures.

Ventilation in poultry houses may depend upon natural air movement or may be provided by electric fans. Ventilation must be regulated to control heat loss by varying fan speed or intermittent use of multiple fans and adjusting air intake openings. Thermostats and electric timers may be used to regulate mechanical ventilation systems. The ventilation system must adequately remove carbon dioxide, ammonia, methane, and other gases produced in the house, as well as water vapor, to provide uniform distribution of fresh, dry air with a minimal draft.

In hot climates maximum ventilation is required to remove heat, moisture, and waste gases. However, in cold climates when maximum air exchange is attempted to remove odors, house heat is severely reduced, lowering not only temperature, but also the moisture-holding capacity of the air. Condensation then results on equipment and litter; manure retains too much moisture; and walls, ceilings, and insulation may accumulate moisture. Increasing ventilation rate to compensate for the lowered moisture-carrying capacity of the air lowers the temperature further and negates the objectives of a ventilation system. Well-located thermostats and variable speed ventilation fans may provide the necessary control, but in extremely cold climates or through extended periods of cold weather even the most elaborate fan systems are inadequate to prevent severe cold stress in birds. In such extremes, supplemental heat from natural or manufactured fuel may be the only alternative.

BROODING AND REARING

The "brooding process" is the nursery period for the baby chick and poult. This is a very critical time in the life of a growing bird. Not only its survival but its present and future production performance depend on various factors affecting optimal growth during this period.

Brooding may be carried out in cages or on the floor. The objectives are to provide warmth, protection, and easily accessible feed and clean water. Modern commercial strains of chickens and turkeys have many inherent advantages of health and vigor to start them without a mother hen. However, they must be provided with the basic requirements for optimal growth and welfare: heat, fresh air, moisture control, and adequate space. A single brooder setup requires a heater, feeders, waterers, litter, a confinement ring, and a light.

Natural or propane gas flame brooders are commonly used to provide heat (Figure 6–1). The heat from the flame is reflected by a large metal hover. The entire unit can be raised or lowered on pulleys to regulate the temperature at the floor. Alternatively, an electric heat lamp may be used, but it may be more expensive to operate. It may have either a white or infrared bulb and a smaller reflector and may also be raised or lowered to regulate temperature. Oil flame, electric element, hot water, and hot air brooders have been used, but not normally as suitable as gas flame or electric lamp brooders. Cage brooders have electrical heating elements and are used commercially for specific brooding requirements. Battery cage brooders are best used for research projects where relatively small numbers of birds must be kept separated.

There are a variety of feeders and automatic feeding systems available commercially. Individual feeders may be trough-type (Figure 6–2), which stand on the floor, or tube-type (Figure 6–3), which hang from the

FIGURE 6–1
Gas flame brooders providing heat for growing turkey poults. (Photograph by Marty Traynor.)

ceiling. Automatic feeders utilize either a chain-drag or auger (Figure 6–4) to convey feed along a trough or pipe from a bulk storage container. Feeders for growing birds should be maintained at about the bird's shoulder height, with the height adjusted as the bird grows.

Water containers and automatic water systems are available commercially. Individual waterers are either glass, plastic, or metal, closed-vacuum reservoirs that flow into a pan to a level determined by a single opening at the bottom of the reservoir (Figure 6–5). Automatic trough waterers (Figure 6–6) are connected to a water tap and may be regulated by a float valve. Automatic cup waterers (Figure 6–4) are connected by plastic pipe to a water reservoir or pressure-regulated tap. They are activated by the bird's beak pressing on a trigger on the cup, which when moved allows water to partially fill the cup. Hanging bell waterers (Figure 6–7) are connected to a fresh-water source and are self-filling to maintain an adjustable water level as the birds drink. Waterers also should be raised as the birds grow to about the bird's shoulder height. Drinking water, if not provided continuously, should be changed at least once per day. Water

FIGURE 6–2
Trough-type feeders being used during early brooding. (Photograph by Marty Traynor.)

FIGURE 6–3
Tube-type hanging feeders.

FIGURE 6–4
Auger-type automatic pan feeders and automatic cup waterers.

FIGURE 6–5
Pan-type waterer with vacuum reservoir.

FIGURE 6–6
Automatic trough waterer connected by hose to water
supply.

FIGURE 6–7
Hanging bell waterer.

spillage should be minimized, since wet litter around the waterer can favor the proliferation and transmission of disease microorganisms.

Litter material must be absorbant and nontoxic. Sawdust and wood shavings are commonly used commercially when available (Figure 6–2). However, locally available materials may be used. Straw and rice hulls are often used successfully for smaller flocks. Start chicks or poults on a five-centimeter (two-inch) depth of litter and increase depth as necessary to maintain adequate dryness.

A confinement ring to keep the birds from straying too far from the brooder heat can be made of corrugated cardboard, metal, wallboard, or wire hardware cloth (Figure 6–8). Solid materials serve as a draft guard if necessary. Wire hardware cloth may prevent suffocation if birds pile up against it and allow for adequate air flow, preventing buildup of CO_2. The confinement ring should be about 50cm–60cm (20 in.–24 in.) high and 0.6 m.–1 m (2 ft–3 ft) from the edge of the reflector. The confinement ring can usually be removed after one or two weeks.

Light over the brooding area will attract birds to the heat, feed, and water since they will associate light with these items. Also, light may help prevent piling by providing security to the birds. A 40-watt incandescent lamp is adequate if no other light is available.

FIGURE 6–8
Confinement rings made of wire hardware cloth in place around brooders. (Photograph by Marty Traynor.)

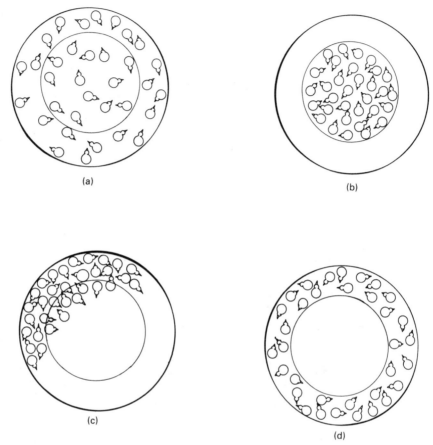

FIGURE 6–9
The distribution of the chicks within the confinement ring indicates their comfort: (a), satisfactory; (b), too cold; (c), draft; and (d), too warm.

Brooding temperature should be started at 32°C–37°C (90°F–100°C), measured at the edge of the heat reflector (hover) 2.5 cm–5 cm (1 in.–2 in.) above the litter. The temperature should then be reduced 3°C (5°F) per week and then maintained at 21°C–24°C (70°F–75°F). The temperature can be regulated by raising or lowering the brooder over the chicks. The position of the chicks within the confinement ring provides a good indication of their comfort (Figure 6–9). If most of them are piled together under the heat reflector, they are probably too cold and the brooder should be lowered. If most of them are piled around the confinement ring, they are probably too hot and the brooder should be raised. If most of them are piled at one side of the confinement ring, there is probably a draft

under the brooder. If they are comfortable, they will be uniformly distributed within the confinement ring, moving about freely. Since newly
hatched chicks and poults have not fully developed their body-temper-
ature-regulating mechanisms, a brooder must supply enough supplemental heat to maintain optimal body temperature. For efficient control of
brooder heat, the room temperature should be about 5°C (10°F) lower
than the brooder temperature.

Ventilation in the brooder house must be adequate to remove moisture, allowing the litter to dry, and to remove carbon dioxide expired by
the birds, ammonia from the feces, and carbon monoxide from gas flame
brooders. Ventilation must not cause drafts. Ventilation must be limited
in cold weather since it also removes heat; whereas in warm weather heat
removal may be desirable.

The optimal relative humidity in the brooder house is 50%–60%.
Extremely high or extremely low humidity should be avoided. Moisture
is reduced in a brooder house by ventilation.

Adequate floor space must be provided for the maximum size of the
birds until they are moved from the brooder house. Floor space, feeder
space, and waterer space are directly related to the growth of the birds.
Specifications vary depending on the type of bird being brooded and
reared.

Proper arrangement of brooding equipment and materials should be
done at least a day before the chicks or poults arrive. Temperature should
be adjusted and all equipment functioning properly. In a proper brooder
setup (Figure 6–10) small trough feeders should be positioned parallel to
the radii of the confinement ring from the center under the heater out
perpendicular to the arc of the ring, as spokes on a wheel. Thus, the birds

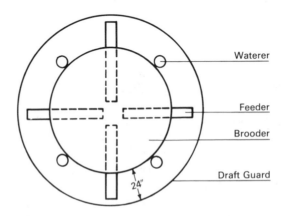

FIGURE 6–10
Typical brooder equipment setup.

can feed where they are comfortable along the feeder and are not prevented by the feeder from moving toward the heat if they become chilled (Figure 6–8). If trough feeders are placed perpendicular to the radii of the confinement ring, the birds on the outer side of the feeder away from the heat may pile together when they become cold and will be blocked by the feeder from moving toward the heat at the center of the ring. The waterers should be placed one between each feeder at the edge of the heat reflector. As birds become older and the brooder is raised, the feeders and waterers can be moved out farther from the center. The birds throughout their growth period should never be required to move more than three meters (ten feet) to eat or drink; and it should be much less than this during the first few weeks of growth.

Chicks should be carefully placed on the litter at the edge of the heat reflector after dipping their beaks first in water and then in the feed so they get their first taste of feed and an incentive to continue to drink and eat. It is recommended for the first three days to place some feed on paper towels or shallow cardboard box lids allowing the birds to walk through the feed, thus locating it and starting to eat sooner. Turkey poults particularly may require special help to locate the feed. Since young birds do have a natural instinct to peck at noticeable objects on the ground, a contrasting red color on the feeders or even in the feed can help them first locate and taste the feed. Feeders during the first three days should be filled to the top. Thereafter, feed troughs should be approximately two-thirds full to control wastage caused by birds scattering the feed into the litter (Figure 6–11). "Starve outs" can be easily identified during the first three days as those birds that stand around and show no interest in drinking or eating. They usually begin to exhibit signs of dehydration: thin spindly legs, hunched-up appearance, and general listlessness. Time should be spent to pick up these birds and dip their beaks in the water. Once the birds begin to drink they will eat, but they will not eat until they have learned to drink. A technique of forced feeding about one milliliter of tap water alone or with sugar and vitamins added has been used successfully. A five-centimeter (two-inch) piece of tubing is attached to a syringe and inserted through the mouth to the crop area where the solution is deposited.

"Warm-room brooding" is a system in which the whole room is heated, usually by a central heating system. In this procedure similar recommendations are followed. However, usually temperatures approximately 3°C (5°F) lower are used. In fact, some investigations have indicated that lowered temperatures to conserve energy in the brooder house result in favorable response by the birds. Lower, but not cold, temperatures will stimulate feather growth, appetite, and body growth. Rapid feathering and rapid growth are closely correlated and are desirable

FIGURE 6–11
Pan feeder filled to the top to encourage turkey poults to find the feed during first three days, and a trough feeder approximately ⅔ full to control feed wastage. (Photograph by Marty Traynor.)

in growing birds to reduce feather picking and cannibalism. However, it is less expensive to heat the environment than to produce additional body heat through increasing feed consumption.

Knowledgeable regular surveillance of the brooder house conditions should be practiced throughout the brooding period. Birds should be observed for signs of discomfort or disease, feather picking, and cannibalism. Mechanical and automatic equipment should be inspected at least daily, and basic troubleshooting techniques employed when necessary. Expect the unexpected and try to prevent problems before they occur. Last, but not least, provide tender loving care through the use of good animal management, and the birds will respond optimally to their properly controlled environment.

HOUSING AND EQUIPMENT

Poultry housing should provide minimal stress and reasonable comfort for the birds, along with necessary production efficiency and convenience for the manager. A poultry house should be clean, well-ventilated, and reasonably dry and comfortable. The house must be designed for effective control of temperature, humidity, and ventilation.

After the brooding period, a bird's body temperature is 40°C–43°C (104°F–106°F). Since this is higher than air temperature, the bird is constantly losing heat. This heat must be replaced so the bird's body temperature will not decrease. When the rate of heat loss from the bird is increased, heat production by the bird must be increased proportionally. Also, when heat production in the bird is increased, there must be a corresponding increase in heat loss. The nonbrooding bird can adjust to a limited but relatively wide range of environmental conditions by its ability to regulate its close body environment within its covering of feathers. However, a minimum of energy should be used by the bird to keep itself either warm or cool so its energy is available for production of meat (growth) or eggs. At temperatures less than −9.5°C (15°F), poultry must use excessive amounts of stored nutrients, originally obtained from feed, for heat energy necessary to maintain normal body temperature. Thus, feed will then be diverted to body storage of these depleted nutrients rather than to growth or egg production and this desired production will then be greatly decreased. This, of course, will decrease the efficiency of the entire poultry production unit.

Ideally, poultry housing should provide a temperature zone or range of thermoneutrality within which the bird feels neither hot nor cold (Figure 6–12). Since birds have more body surface area per unit of body weight than most larger animals, any sudden decrease or increase in air temperature will affect birds to a greater extent than it will larger agricultural animals. However, some temperature fluctuation within the range of thermoneutrality is desirable as it has been shown to stimulate egg production from laying hens. However, this temperature fluctuation out of the optimal range of egg production and feed efficiency between 20°C and 30°C (68°F–86°F) should not be for more than a few hours and should not extend below 0°C (32°F) or above 35°C (95°F). Air temperatures in the laying house of 38°C (100°F) or above for only a few hours can cause extensive mortality in a flock and may be a problem during extended periods of hot weather in warm climate areas. Air temperatures in the laying house of less than −12°C (10°F) for only a few hours may result in frozen combs and wattles and may stop egg production.

Although these extremes are seldom reached inside a properly designed poultry house, extended periods of relatively high or low temperature inside the house can drastically affect production efficiency. High temperature in a laying house, consistently above 27°C–30°C (80°F–85°F), can cause a decrease in egg production, production of thin shelled eggs, poor internal quality of eggs, reduced size of eggs, and reduced fertility and hatchability of breeder flock eggs. It can also result in increased

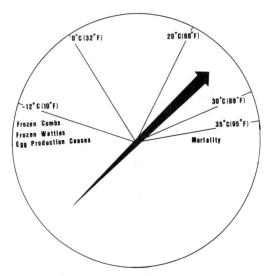

FIGURE 6–12
Critical environmental temperatures affecting performance of laying chickens: optimal range, 20°C–30°C (68°F–86°F); short-term tolerance range, 0°C–35°C (32°F–95°F).

mortality and cause the birds to decrease their activity, drink more water, and consume less feed. Breeds of chickens differ in their ability to tolerate extended periods of hot weather; Leghorns are less affected by heat stress than heavier breeds. Low temperature in a laying house, consistently below 7°C (45°F), can cause a decrease in egg production and feed efficiency and reduced fertility and hatchability of breeder flock eggs. Extended periods of high temperatures are much more detrimental to poultry than extended periods of low temperatures.

The design of a poultry house should provide for features that will avoid temperature extremes and prove to be economical over a period of time. However, maintaining constant temperature within a narrow range probably would not result in sufficient improvement in production and egg quality to justify additional costs of required air-conditioning and heating equipment.

The primary sources of moisture in a poultry house are the exhaled air from the birds, manure, and spillage from waterers. Moisture and heat are expired from the respiratory system of birds as their primary method of cooling the body. The air warmed in the air sacs from internal muscle and organ heat can hold a considerable quantity of moisture. In hot weather, birds will start to pant, which causes a marked increase in their respiration rate, facilitating the vaporization of water through their air sacs and allowing them to lose heat and maintain body temperature. Poultry manure is 70%–80% water, which adds considerable moisture to the air if not periodically removed. One hundred laying hens consume 19 l–23 l (5 gal.–6 gal.) of water and 9 kg–11 kg (20 pounds to 25 pounds) of feed per day and produce 11 kg (25 pounds) of manure per day. The contribution of waterers to the humidity of air in a poultry house depends on total surface area of water, air temperature, spillage, and ventilation rate.

Floor space and feeder space required for laying hens reared on the floor will differ considerably depending on the type of housing. Space in cages depends on the cage design. During the laying as well as the rearing period overcrowding should be avoided. Provide approximately 0.3 sq m (3 sq ft) per bird of floor space for light breed layers and about 0.4 sq m (4 sq ft) per bird for heavy breed layers when birds are in a continuous confinement situation. In small home flocks where birds are allowed to leave the building approximately half the floor space is required.

In a complete confinement laying house suitable litter material should be placed on the floor before the birds are housed (Figure 6–13). Occasionally a new layer of litter material should be added and the litter should be stirred frequently during cold months. When the building is closed, this may result in a buildup of 15 cm–20 cm (6 in.–8 in.) of litter material over a period of approximately six months after housing pullets. This method has been called the deep litter technique and when properly managed allows for some bacterial heat production in the litter, which enhances drying.

Feeder space should be provided floor birds at a minimum of 10.7 m (35 ft) of linear space or six 18 kg–22 kg (40 pounds to 50 pound) capacity hanging feeders per hundred layers. Provide at least 24 box type nests for 100 hens. Nests should have a 18 cm × 20 cm (7 in. × 8 in.) opening for the light-breed layers and an opening of 25 cm × 30 cm (10 in.–12 in.) for heavy-breed birds. A minimum of one round automatic waterer or its equivalent is recommended for 100 birds. With trough type automatic waterers, provide a minimum of 2.4 linear meters (8 linear feet) per 100 layers.

In some housing methods, laying hens on the floor are provided with roosts, particularly in small flock situations. Roosts, although not necessary, do have advantages in the small floor flock since they tend to discourage birds from sleeping in the nests at night, thus resulting in cleaner eggs. Manure will accumulate underneath the roosts and must be periodically removed. When roosts are used, 18 cm–20 cm (7 in.–8 in.) per bird should be provided depending on the size of the bird.

Cages were introduced into the poultry business in the mid-1920s.

FIGURE 6–13
Complete confinement floor-type laying house. (Colorado State University photograph.)

Cages for growing birds and for layers have certain advantages. One of the major advantages to caged birds is that the need for litter materials is eliminated. Manure from the bird accumulates underneath the cages (Figure 6–14). Various ideas and management techniques for ease of manure removal have been developed over the years. All have had certain disadvantages as well as advantages. The industry has not completely solved all problems involved in manure handling. One system involves deep pits under cage units where manure may accumulate for the entire time the laying flock is housed. These deep pits are relatively dry and have a minimal amount of odor and fly problems in a negative pressure fan ventilation house. However, when a water line overflows and wets a large portion of the manure, this advantage may be lost. Manure pits and other areas of accumulation have a tendency to attract mice and sometimes rats because of the spilled feed as well as the high nutrient value of the manure. This problem is particularly noticeable in cold climates during the winter because the warmth of the decomposing manure also attracts the rodents.

The major objective of housing birds under any conditions should be the well-being of the individual bird and the flock as a whole. This state of well-being is economically desirable since it not only enhances production characteristics, but it assures a minimal loss through mortality and morbidity. Over 90% of all commercial laying hens in the United States are housed in cages. These cages are quite satisfactory as measured by the fact that the birds will produce large numbers of eggs under these conditions of complete confinement. Reproduction is one of the first physiological functions that is adversely affected when an animal is uncomfortable or in poor health. Birds housed in cages are protected from many diseases and stress conditions that they would face in a floor-type confinement unit. Cannibalism is a much more serious problem when young pullets are beginning to lay in laying flocks on the floor than it is in cages of fewer than 10–15 hens. Caged hens also are not faced with the stress and trauma of obtaining feed and water in competition with large numbers of birds, and adequate feeder and waterer space is more likely to be available under cage conditions than it is under floor conditions. Today's commercial layer has been designed to function very well in a cage, and diets are designed to meet the requirements of cage conditions. This bird would be at a physical disadvantage under floor or barnyard conditions.

For the poultry manager, cage egg production provides many advantages not obtained in floor units. Perhaps the most noticeable advantage is that fewer dirty eggs are obtained in cages than on the floor. Floor

FIGURE 6–14
Manure accumulation underneath laying hens in cages. (Photograph by Marty Traynor.)

birds contaminate eggs with feces and litter materials from their feet whereas cage eggs roll out of the cage into a special area that prevents contact with the birds. There is some concern as to whether or not egg breakage in cages is reduced or increased. This depends upon management. Basically, there may be fewer cracks and checks in cages if the pitch of the floor allows the egg to roll out slowly. An egg-eating habit can spread very rapidly through a floor unit and is very difficult to eliminate. Birds in cages occasionally will try to reach out and break an egg, but this is a relatively rare problem.

When birds are housed in laying cages, various cage dimensions may be considered. In situations where there are fewer than five birds per cage, cage floor space should range between 348 sq cm–465 sq cm (54 sq in.–72 sq in.). This would require a standard cage 3.05 cm (12 in.) wide, 457 cm (18 in.) deep and 35.5 cm (14 in.) high (Figure 6–15). Five to nine birds per cage require a cage 40.6 cm × 45.7 cm × 35.5 cm (16 in. × 18 in. × 14 in.); 10–19 birds per cage, 60.9 cm × 60.9 cm × 35.5 cm (24 in. × 24 in. × 14 in.); 20 or more birds per cage, sometimes referred to as colony cages, 12.2 cm × 60.9 cm × 35.5 cm (48 in. × 24 in. × 14 in.). The recommended slope for the bottom of cages is 2.5 cm (1 in.) per 30.5 cm (12 in.) of cage depth. The cage bottom must slope to permit eggs to roll out of the cage to prevent cracking and to facilitate gathering.

There are numerous commercially available cage systems utilizing multiple decks and a variety of automatic feeding, watering, manure removal, and egg collection systems. A relatively recent innovation is the reverse or shallow cage system (Figure 6–15). It has the same floor space as the standard cage, but is 45.7 cm (18 in.) wide and only 30.5 cm (12 in.) deep. This provides the birds more feeder and waterer space and allows four birds to feed and drink simultaneously.

Variations in flock performance can be brought about by inadequate equipment. Poorly designed equipment not only costs through lowered production, but also may consume a great deal of the caretaker's time. Whenever tedious, routine jobs can be minimized, this should be done by proper use of equipment. Also, a minimal amount of time should be consumed in repairing equipment. Old and faulty equipment may cost more to operate than to replace. Failure of feeders and waterers can be very detrimental to efficient weight gains, and waterers that overflow cause damp conditions suitable for spreading disease.

The use of hanging feeders and automatic feeders and waterers provides benefits that hand-filled feeders do not. Hand-filled trough feeders require excessive labor and should not be used if hanging feeders or automatic feeders are available. Automatic feeders with a moving chain, cable, or auger (Figure 6–16) are considered the most efficient way of feeding large commercial flocks and have the advantage of providing fresh

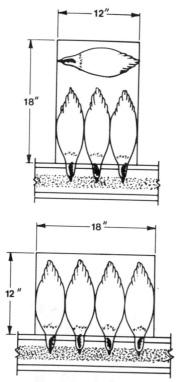

FIGURE 6–15
Standard cage, 12 in. (305 cm) wide, 18 in. (457 cm) deep; reverse cage, 18 in. (457 cm) wide, 12 in. (305 cm) deep. Reverse cage provides more feeder space than standard cage and allows four birds to feed simultaneously. (Courtesy of A. R. Wood Manufacturing Company, Luverne, Minnesota.)

FIGURE 6–16
Auger-type automatic pan feeders supplying fresh feed to a commercial flock of turkeys. (Photograph by Marty Traynor.)

feed at all times. To reduce feed wastage, avoid overfilling feeders. Birds, whether in cages or on the floor, should have to stretch in order to reach the feed. Floor-type units should have feeders at birds' shoulder height. In cage units, feeders should be located outside the cage so birds must stretch to reach the feed (Figure 6–17). Automatic cage feeders may involve a cable or chain-drag system (Figure 6–18) or an auger system (Figure 6–19) to move feed in a trough along the row of cages from a bulk storage container. Water should be supplied to both floor and cage birds in a continuous flow system via a shallow trough (Figure 6–20) or a dew drop or cup waterer activated by the bird's beak (Figure 6–21). Allow one dew drop or cup for each three to five birds. Water temperature should be maintained between 13°C and 18°C (55°F and 65°F) if possible.

Proper adjustment of feeders and watering devices is a factor that should receive constant attention. Feed troughs, for example, should be maintained at a level that allows the birds free access to the feed, but at

FIGURE 6–17
Automatic feeding of caged layers. (Photograph by Marty Traynor.)

FIGURE 6–18
Chain-drag automatic feeder system for caged layers.

FIGURE 6–19
Auger automatic feeder system for caged layers.

the same time does not provide an area for the bird to "play" and shove feed out of the trough onto the floor. Constantly adjust feeder height as the bird grows to the shoulder height of the bird. Other methods for preventing feed wastage are various guards and lips on equipment. The purchase of feeding equipment should be based upon the ability to easily adjust these factors.

Location of feed and watering devices is very important in a floor operation. In cages there is less chance that birds will be far removed from either. However, consideration must be given to location of feeders and waterers in relation to the work pattern and general management conditions either on the floor or in cages. In cage egg operations the trends have been toward a shallow cage unit that allows all birds access to feed simultaneously. In many cage units there is sufficient feed space for only approximately half the birds to eat at one time. There is some controversy as to whether or not this is a significant point since there is ample time available for all caged birds to eat and drink during a 24-hour period. However, in floor operations the competition for feeder space and waterer space results in more timid birds being less likely to obtain sufficient time at the feeders and waterers. Birds do tend to cycle and eat at certain times of the day; for example, following egg laying, early in the morning, and

FIGURE 6–20
Continuous-flow shallow trough water system for caged layers.

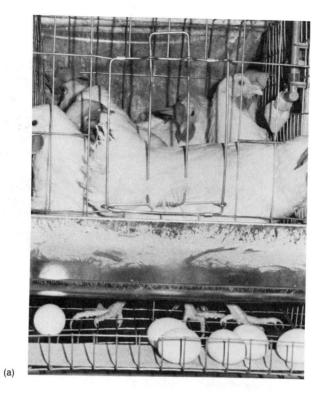

(a)

(b)

FIGURE 6–21
Automatic cup watering systems for caged layers activated by bird's beak.
(Photograph (b), courtesy of Swish Watering Systems.)

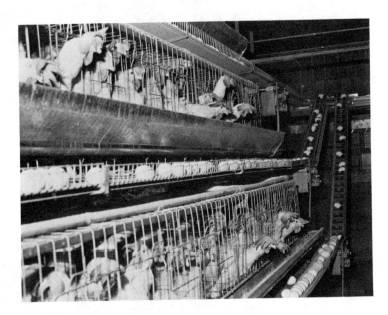

FIGURE 6–22
Automatic conveyer-belt egg-collecting system for caged layers. (Photograph by Nancy Nydegger.)

before the lights go out in the evening. Therefore, birds will compete for feeder space, and the less aggressive individuals may not have opportunities to obtain their full complement of feed when needed.

Eggs should be collected at least three times a day on flats. Wire baskets are not recommended for collecting eggs because the weight of the eggs upon one another causes some cracked shells. A variety of automatic egg-collection systems are available for large commercial caged flocks (Figure 6–22). Eggs should be washed as soon as possible after collection and then cooled immediately. Eggs should be washed in clean, warm water to prevent bacterial migration through the shell pores. Eggs should be stored at approximately 7°C–13°C (45°F–55°F) and at a relative humidity of 70%–80% until they are marketed.

Lighting in floor and cage laying houses should provide about one foot-candle of light per bird at bird's heated level and be evenly distributed. This can usually be accomplished through the use of a 25 watt to 40 watt incandescent bulb approximately every 37 sq m (400 sq ft of floor space). It is important that bulbs be kept clean since dust, which accumulates rapidly in laying houses, will greatly reduce the amount of illumination received by the birds.

VENTILATION SYSTEMS
AND ENVIRONMENT

Housed poultry must be provided fresh, relatively dry air along with the removal of moisture, heat, and gases. If ventilation is adequate to maintain a dry environment, it will probably be providing enough fresh air. In order for ventilation to cool house air and remove moisture, the temperature and relative humidity of the outside air must be lower than that of the inside air.

Ventilation systems fall into two major categories, gravity convection and forced air. Forced air systems utilize fans and provide either positive pressure or negative pressure ventilation. A pressure system allows a mixture of air and provides more efficient air exchange. Where air is merely exhaused without building up pressure, there is a tendency for certain streams and passages of least resistance to develop, which may cause drafts in a marginally designed system.

In a gravity convection system (Figure 6–23), warm, moist air produced by the birds rises through an opening in the top of the building. This causes a partial vacuum at the floor, which allows for fresh air to enter along the sides of the building. This ventilation can be controlled by adjusting the openings along both sides of the house. These openings are usually covered by adjustable curtains. Often fans will be placed within gravity convection houses to circulate air but they are not used to move air into or out of the house.

Positive pressure ventilation systems (Figure 6–24) typically employ a fan mounted at the end of the house that pushes air into a duct along

FIGURE 6–23
Gravity convection ventilation system.

FIGURE 6-24
Positive pressure ventilation system with intake fan on near end of building; exhaust tower on far end.

the ceiling spanning the inside length of the house (Figure 6-25). The only air exits in the duct are small holes along the length of the duct on either side, totally equalling the area of the air intake. This provides a draft-free supply of fresh air that mixes with house air as it is forced from the many duct holes. As air pressure builds up in the house, the stale warm air is forced out through an opening near the floor at the end of the house and up through an exhaust tower on the outer wall.

Negative pressure ventilation systems (Figure 6-26) typically employ exhaust fans mounted along one side of the building that pull air out of the house. The fresh air enters through openings under each eave, controlled by an adjustable baffle. In negative pressure systems where fans pull out the old air and allow the new air to enter through specific openings, drafts can be a problem. The exhaust fan should move from 0.06 cu m–0.23 cu m (2 cu ft–8 cu ft) of air per minute per bird. This rate of air movement may be increased in warmer climates and may be decreased to as low as 0.02 cu m (0.5 cu ft) per minute per bird in cooler locations. Specific recommendations will depend on the type of housing, the climate, and the number of birds in the confinement. In humid climates a minimum of 0.01 cu m (0.3 cu ft) per minute per bird is required to control humidity.

In cold climates it is difficult to control ventilation when the outside air being drawn into the building may be considerably below freezing, but some air movement is always recommended. Cold weather ventilation can be accomplished by using multiple speed fans. In some areas supplemental heat in laying houses is recommended for periods of low environmental temperature in order that some degree of air exchange may be accomplished. In low temperature areas, loss of heat may be compensated for by increasing the concentration of birds. This may be satisfactory, but has a limitation since in extended periods of cold weather it may be more expensive to produce heat through the bodies of additional birds than through a supplemental heating system requiring some form

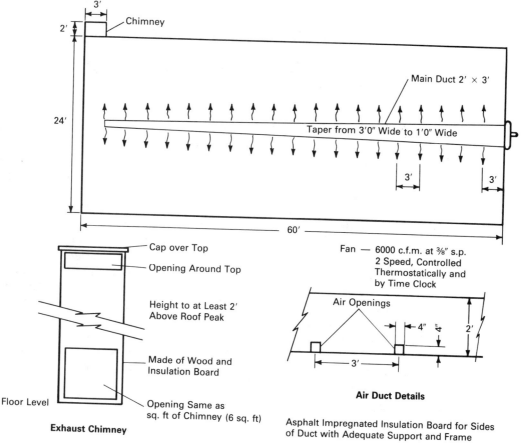

FIGURE 6–25
Positive pressure ventilation system providing balanced distribution of air throughout the poultry building.

FIGURE 6–26
Negative pressure ventilation system with exhaust fan on one
side of building.

of fuel other than feed. Supplementation with a solar heating unit may be
in order where ample sunshine is available during the day.

Housing design is very important in controlling the direct environment of poultry. Insulation in the ceilings and walls is essential; it helps
to keep the house relatively warm in cold weather by conserving heat and
relatively cool in hot weather by preventing heat from entering. Insulation
should be thick and soft, providing a minimum R value of 12–15 ceilings
and 8–10 in the walls. A polyethylene vapor barrier should be installed
on the inner side of the wall and ceiling insulation. The moisture-proof
vapor barrier must line the inside of the building, the source of heat during
cold weather. This required location of the moisture barrier prevents migration of warmed, moist air into the walls and the ceiling area so that
the condensation does not take place at the studs and ceiling joists causing
deterioration of the structure and does not saturate the insulation causing
it to become a conductor of heat. Ideally, it keeps the moisture in the air
allowing it to be removed from the building by the ventilation system.

WASTE DISPOSAL
AND UTILIZATION

Accumulation of manure offers a physical and economic challenge that
must be met for all confined domesticated animals. Concentration of birds
in economic units has resulted in large accumulations of manure (Figure

6–27). A flock of 100,000 laying hens can produce 11,340 kg (25,000 pounds) of manure per day. Manure removal systems utilizing mechanical scrapers as well as water wash-down techniques or raised slatted floors all provide labor saving advantages, but they also bring with them some disadvantages. For example, removal utilizing a water wash-down results in the need to remove and dispose of about four times the weight and volume of the original manure. Water solutions of manure may be deposited into a pond and, through bacterial action under favorable conditions, digestion allowed to proceed, yielding methane gas and a stable by-product, sludge. However, in cold climates the winter months result in a very slow action by the bacteria and as a result rapid accumulation of solids may result. Liquid manure spraying onto crop fields requires considerable energy and many acres of crop land. Poultry manure is high in nitrogen and may burn crops unless properly diluted or spread thinner than other manures. However, corn will grow well in soil fertilized with poultry manure. Uric acid in poultry manure is utilized by plants.

Poultry manure is too valuable biologically to become an economic burden and should be utilized as an asset rather than disposed of as a liability. Digestion, drying, and/or single-cell protein production are potentially feasible uses of manure. Poultry manure can be dried and utilized

FIGURE 6–27
Accumulations of manure and used litter from poultry houses being loaded into manure-spreading truck for use as fertilizer. (Photograph by Marty Traynor.)

as a feed ingredient in the diet of larger animals, particularly ruminants, either as a pure product or mixed with organic litter materials commonly utilized in poultry houses. Pure poultry manure is a good source of crude protein, calcium, and phosphorus. Lambs fed dehydrated poultry manure have shown superior performance to those fed alfalfa. Dried poultry manure is a satisfactory dietary supplement mixed with corn or other energy sources in diets of beef cattle. These examples of biological utilization of poultry waste as an animal feedstuff indicate a potential for poultry and livestock waste recycling combinations. Accumulation of certain heavy metals, drug residues, and medications and the potential for interactions are problems that must be prevented. The future for recycling or otherwise utilizing poultry manure may hold much promise.

POULTRY PRODUCTION

Broiler Production

Broilers should be brooded and reared under complete confinement during the growing period in one building. Floor space should be calculated based on the chickens' size at seven weeks which would be as much as 2 kg (4.5 pounds). However, partial house brooding may be used successfully to save on fuel during the first three weeks of the brooding period. A removable plastic or plywood partition confines young brooding chicks to half or one-third of the house, thus concentrating brooder heat. If the unused portion of the house remains empty and unheated for these first three weeks, a fuel savings of 25%–40% can be realized with possibly greater savings during cold winter months. However, excessive humidity and ammonia can cause problems that need to be adequately compensated for. A variation of partial house brooding involves multiple age growout. Chicks are brooded on one-third of the house until three weeks of age. They are then moved to the other two-thirds of the house where they are grown to market age, while new chicks are placed on the one-third section and brooded simultaneously. This may realize a fuel savings of as high as 70% or more and allow 10 or 12 rather than 5 or 6 flocks in the house per year. However, ventilation and prevention of disease in young chicks requires more precise management.

Brooders can be removed from use at four to five weeks of age, depending on ambient temperature of the house. Usually a grower ration will be substituted for the chick starter for the last two or three weeks prior to market.

Floor area for broiler chicks under individual brooder units should be 45 sq cm (7 sq in.) per chick, with about 500 chicks per brooder. House temperature should be at least 18°C (65°F) for the first two weeks and at least 15°C (60°F) thereafter. Allow 0.04 sq m–0.10 sq m (0.5 sq ft–1.0 sq ft) of total floor area per bird to seven weeks of age. A confinement ring or draft guard should be placed around the brooder about 0.5 m–1.0 m (2 ft–3 ft) from the edge of the reflector. Provide at least 5 cm (2 in.) of a suitable litter material on the floor. This material may be wood shavings, crushed corncobs, chopped straw, peanut or rice hulls, wood chips, or other available absorbant materials. A good litter material is absorbant and free of toxic substances and should not become excessively dusty.

Built-up (deep) litter has certain advantages over starting with new litter for each flock. Chicks actually can perform better on old litter from previous flocks than when placed on new litter in a sanitized building. This is due to the old litter's providing a gradual acquiring of resistance to pathogens due to exposure before their natural resistance is lost, similar to the effects of vaccination. Also, built-up litter is a good source of nutrients, including animal growth factors such as vitamin B_{12}. Management of built-up litter systems is critical as its advantages depend on maintaining proper depth, stirring, moisture and heat, and providing adequate housing.

Broiler growing in cages has met with limited success. Although cages are used quite extensively for pullet rearing in certain areas, broilers, which grow more rapidly, are not well adapted to cages. Foot problems and breast blisters developed, resulting in carcass blemishes that are unsatisfactory for market purposes. Recent attempts at growing broilers in cages indicate that some of these problems may be overcome in the future. If the cage method is acceptable, it will eliminate many of the problems now faced by broiler growers, particularly some diseases. Catching of the birds at the time they go to market may be more labor efficient in cages than in floor rearing operations.

Broilers usually are loaded onto trucks to go to the slaughter plant at night in order to minimize the amount of excitement caused in the house and to meet time schedules of the processing plant. This also allows the labor crews to work during the cooler part of the day. It is a problem to acquire labor when needed for this type of job at the pay scale to meet competitive markets. However, loading broiler chickens requires concern for the birds' welfare, so the broiler producer must minimize handling costs as well as losses from mortality, bruises, broken wings, and skin tears.

Roaster Production

Broiler stock may be used for roaster production. However, advantages can be gained by developing breeding stock specifically for yielding roaster production birds with characteristics commercial broilers would not exhibit after seven weeks of age. Since roasters may be grown out to 12 through 15 weeks of age, leg problems and breast blisters may become excessive in commercial broiler stock. Since feed efficiency will drop off during this later growth period, optimal nutrition becomes a critical management decision. Genetic selection in the primary breeding program for optimizing roaster production parameters from 7 to 20 weeks of age may prove more profitable than merely growing out commercial broiler stock.

Roasters should be brooded and reared in complete confinement, but transferred at seven or eight weeks to another building. They should receive at least three different feed rations during their growth: a chick starter, followed by a grower, and then finisher ration. Slaughter age will depend on market weight demand.

Capon Production

The purpose of caponizing chickens is to provide higher quality meat for a specialized market. Caponized males grow more slowly than normal males and accumulate more body fat. The caponized males exhibit some female characteristics since they do not produce testosterone, and when cooked are more tender, tastier, and juicier than noncaponized males. Removal of the testes and thus elimination of the male sex hormones they produce reduces the male sex instinct and changes their behavior. They will become more docile and less active. Energy that is normally expended in fighting, courting behavior, and territorial protection is greatly reduced, allowing more efficient conversion of feed into growth, fat deposition, and improved meat quality.

Surgical caponizing involves total removal of the testes at about two to three weeks of age. At this age heavy breeds should weigh about one pound. The operation may be performed on older birds, but the younger birds suffer less adverse effects and survival rate is higher.

Feed and water should be withheld from the cockerel for 12–18 hours prior to surgery to assure the intestines are empty. The partially empty intestines settle away from the testes, thus providing improved visibility within the body cavity. The bird must be penned on wire or a clean floor or it may ingest litter material.

Adequate light, proper instruments, and adequate restraint of the bird are necessary. Clean and sanitary facilities free of dust are desirable, although sterile equipment is not necessary because the bird is highly resistant to infection. The bird is fastened on a surface on its left side with the wings held together above the body. The legs are also fastened together and the bird stretched out to its full length in order to expose the lateral rib cage area. Feathers in this rib area must be removed and the skin disinfected with 70% ethanol or another skin disinfectant. Merely swabbing the skin with clean water may be adequate if a disinfectant is not available.

Using a sharp scalpel or knife, the capon producer should make a one-inch incision through the skin and other tissues between the two posterior ribs. The incision should be deep enough to expose the abdominal air sac covering the intestines and other abdominal organs. Care must be used to avoid cutting a large vein in the skin that runs diagonally between the thigh and wing. A rib spreader is then inserted with handle toward the back of the bird. The abdominal air sac is punctured with a sharp hook or probe to expose the internal organs. The testes are located on the dorsal wall at the anterior end of the kidneys, posterior to the lungs. The testes of a three-week-old cockerel are about the size of a large wheat kernel and may be yellowish, white, gray, or black in color.

Both testes should be removed from the single incision, the lower or left testis removed first. The testis is grasped with special forceps and then twisted free from its connective tissue while slowly pulled from its attachments. Care must be taken not to rupture large blood vessels located between the two testes. The upper, right testis is then similarly removed. Removal of both complete testes is necessary since any fragments that remain will grow and produce enough male hormone to create a "slip," which will not be a normally functioning cockerel, but will also not yield the desirable meat qualities of a good capon. Electrically heated cautery equipment is available for incising skin and removing testes. It prevents excessive bleeding and may reduce the incidence of slips. The rib spreader may now be removed and tension on the bird released, allowing the skin and thigh muscle to slip back into place. Once the bird is released, the incision should close without need for sutures or bandage.

Following surgery the birds should be provided feed and water in a clean pen where they are not crowded. Crowding may cause cannibalism, prolonging healing of the incision. "Windpuffs" may develop within a few days due to a buildup of air under the skin that escapes from air sacs cut during the surgery. Carefully puncturing the skin with a sharp instrument will effectively release entrapped air and may be repeated if necessary.

Chemical caponizing is accomplished by implanting a natural plant estradiol hormone in the bird's neck at the base of the skull. This produces female characteristics that may last for four to five weeks. Birds are slaughtered at about six weeks after implant. These birds are sometimes referred to as "caponettes" and yield meat that can be sold at the same premium price as surgically produced capons.

Turkey Production

Turkeys are preferably brooded under complete confinement and then transferred to another building or semiconfinement drylot shelter at 8–12 weeks of age for rearing. This semiconfinement is still commonly practiced in major turkey production centers in the United States. Some producers, who have also used complete confinement, find better overall production characteristics in semiconfinement, drylot-reared turkeys. However, complete confinement, particularly in climates where weather can be unpredictably severe, may prove to be an economically wise management decision and become the rearing system of the future.

A number of different feed formulations may be used in growing a turkey from poult to market age. Feed should be formulated on a least-cost basis, determined, not only by cost of ingredients, but by optimal utilization related to age, sex, and various management parameters. At least a starter, grower, and finisher ration should be used consecutively to produce market turkeys.

A minimum of 65 sq cm (10 sq in.) of floor space per poult under the hover is recommended during the first five weeks of the brooding period (Figure 6–8). A maximum of 600 poults per gas brooder and 100–300 poults per electric lamb brooder are recommended. At least 0.1 sq m (1 sq ft) of brooder house floor space per bird is recommended through eight weeks of age. If outdoor pens are provided adjacent to the brooder house, a slight reduction in floor space may be made. Feed and water must be available to poults as soon as they are placed under the brooder. Turkey poults may be slow in learning to eat. Since adequate feed and water must be consumed during the first two or three days of the brooding period, it is recommended to dip their beaks in the water and the feed as they are placed under the brooder. Allow at least two linear meters (six linear feet) of feeder space per 100 poults during the first two weeks of the brooding period (Figure 6–11). From three to eight weeks this space should be doubled. Linear waterer space per 100 poults during the first two weeks should be at least 0.6 m (2 ft) or two 3.8 l (1 gal.) water founts. From three to eight weeks, 1.2 linear meters (4 linear feet) or two 19 l (5 gal.) founts are recommended. Additional watering space should be provided during hot weather.

The confinement ring of hardware cloth should be approximately 457 mm (18 in.) high and placed 1 m (3 ft) from the edge of the hover when starting day-old poults (Figure 6–8). It may be enlarged in diameter of confined floor space after about seven days depending on the type of building. At two weeks of age the confinement ring may be removed although in small buildings it may be moved to round the corners of the building walls. Turkeys will crowd into corners, pile, and suffocate. If drafts are a problem, a draft guard of corrugated cardboard may be used instead of hardware cloth.

Continuous light, one 40-watt bulb per 46 sq m (500 sq ft), should be provided for at least the first three days of brooding. Light duration may then be reduced to 14 hours per day for seven to ten days and further reduced gradually to nine hours per day.

Climate and weather permitting, turkey poults may be moved to an outside range or pasture at eight weeks of age. About half the flock should be moved to range the first day, the remainder the following day. They must be provided feed and water, regardless of the growing vegetation available. Range vegetation will depend on geographical location. Green grass and alfalfa provide the best range cover. The maximum number of birds per acre of range is 250, with a limit of about 5,000 birds per flock. Waterers, feeders, and small shelters should be moved each week to maintain clean, dry range. Ranges should be rotated out of use at least yearly. Open ranges are not usually used among commercial turkey growers because they require excessive labor for care and feeding the birds.

After transfer of turkeys to the rearing facility, additional requirements must be considered. Portable range shelters should supply about 0.5 sq m (1.8 sq ft) of space per turkey. Feeder space should be about 18 linear meters (60 linear feet) or five, round, range-type feeders per 1,000 birds (Figure 6–28). Three automatic waterers or 10 linear meters (35 linear feet) of water trough space per 1,000 birds is recommended. Additional watering space is required in hot weather. Where complete confinement is used (Figure 6–29), a minimum of 1.5 sq m (5 sq ft) of floor space per bird is recommended. Ventilation should provide at least 0.03 cu m (1 cu ft) per minute. Either litter or slatted floors can be used for confined turkeys. Slats should be placed 25 cm (1 in.) apart and be strong enough to support the birds with a surface width of approximately 5 cm (2 in.) per slat. It is best to introduce turkeys to slat floors at about eight to ten weeks of age before they gain too much body weight and their feet can become accustomed to the slats. Otherwise, sore feet can be a problem as the birds gain body size at market age.

Waterfowl Production

Brooding and rearing requirements for waterfowl (ducks and geese) are similar to requirements for broiler chickens. Brooder temperatures may be maintained a few degrees lower for waterfowl; initial brooding temperatures of 28.9°C–35.6°C (85°F–95°F), reduced approximately 2.2°C (5°F) per week are recommended. Waterfowl do not require swimming water, only water for drinking, and preferably they should be kept away from puddles, ponds, and streams. Waterfowl will pollute water if allowed

FIGURE 6–28
Round range-type feeder for turkeys reared in semiconfinement. (Photograph by Marty Traynor.)

FIGURE 6–29
Complete confinement rearing of turkeys. (Photograph by Marty Traynor.)

to swim in a confined area. This pollution will result in an unsanitary environment for disease dissemination and cause many offensive odors. Waterfowl have been used for pond weed control and geese have been used specifically to control weeds in certain crops such as raspberries and cotton. However, commercial rearing of ducks and geese for meat production is done under complete or semiconfinement with environmental control employing management methods similar to those recommended for growing broilers or turkeys.

Pullet Production

Commercial pullets are brooded and reared in complete confinement to facilitate necessary control of light. They are normally brooded and reared in the same building. They are brooded on litter-covered floors along both sides of the house until five or six weeks of age. When the brooder heat is removed, they are allowed to move into the center of the house onto either a solid, litter-covered floor or wire or wood-slatted floor. Battery cages can be used to brood and rear pullets until they are transferred to the laying house. Pullets are reared to about 20 weeks of age when they become sexually mature and are then transferred to a laying house. Feed formulation may be changed frequently during the growing period as recommended by the primary breeder. At least a chick starter and pullet developer ration should be provided, it should be changed to the pullet developer at eight weeks of age.

Floor space requirements for growing pullets may be calculated as for broilers. Although broilers may grow more rapidly and take up more space, they only require this space until they reach seven weeks of age. Pullets will grow more slowly and should have a little more space so that they mature and develop without crowding. Therefore, the floor space requirements of pullet chicks to ten weeks is the same as for broilers to seven weeks. Under ten weeks of age, pullets should have access to a watering system that will provide the equivalent of approximately 30 l (8 gal.) of water per 100 birds per day. Waterers are placed no farther than 4.6 m (15 ft) from the feeders. Approximately 3.8 cm (1.5 in.) of feeder space should be provided per chick. For example, a 1.5 m (5 ft) feeder open to the birds from both sides provides adequate feeding space for 80 chicks. In confinement rearing, from ten weeks until transfer to the laying house at 18–20 weeks of age, space required for pullets is generally 0.3 sq m–4.5 sq m (1 sq ft–1.5 sq ft) per bird for light breeds and up to 0.6 sq m (2 sq ft) per bird for the heavy breeds.

Control of artificial light is essential for year-round pullet and egg production. Also, it will synchronize a flock of growing pullets so they will all respond uniformly to the stimulus of increasing light when placed in the laying house. Duration of light, or day length, has a profound effect on development of sexual maturity in pullets. Increasing day length during the growing period results in early maturity, with pullets starting to lay small eggs prior to 18 weeks of age, before their body size is adequate. Decreasing day length will delay sexual maturity until adequate body size is achieved and pullets are placed in laying cages. Light intensity of about one foot-candle at bird level is adequate, and variations above this will not affect sexual maturity.

There are many variations on recommended lighting programs for growing pullets either exposed to daylight or in light-tight houses. In open houses, artificial lights are regulated to provide constant or decreasing day length by a timer that is adjusted according to when the sun rises and sets. In windowless houses, timer adjustment need not take into account varying natural day length. Pullets may be provided eight hours of continuous light per day until they are transferred to the laying house at 20 weeks of age. At this time, light would be increased gradually 0.5 hour per week until 14–16 hours per day are achieved, after which light duration is maintained constant. Pullets will start into production within four weeks of starting the stepped up lighting program. A variation on this lighting program starts pullets at 15 hours of light per day, gradually decreasing light duration 20 minutes per week until 8 hours per day is reached just prior to placement in laying house at 20 weeks. Then light may either be stepped up directly to 14–16 hours per day or to 12 hours per day followed by a gradual increase of 0.5 hour per week until maintained at 14–16 hours per day throughout the subsequent laying period. Pullet chicks should be started with 24 hours of continuous light for the first two days to facilitate their early feeding and drinking. The light from a gas flame brooder is not enough to affect a controlled lighting program. Even if electric lamp brooders are used, the controlled lighting program can be started after the brooder lamps are removed.

Light duration during the laying period must never decrease, as this would cause egg production to stop. If layers receive more than 18 hours of light per day, some strains will become hyperactive. Also, it is an unnecessary expense. This control of artifical light is essential for year-round pullet production and egg production, which otherwise would be seasonal due to annual variation in day length in countries not located near the equator.

There are many advantages to growing chicken pullets for replacement purposes in cages. Pullets reared in cages can be more easily watched than floor-reared birds, have less stress prior to being housed, and will be acclimatized to a cage. When pullets are reared on the floor, some trauma is experienced by the birds when placed in a cage. This frequently causes the birds to be nervous and flighty. In order to adjust the birds at a slower pace, some cage-laying managers have adapted a program whereby the birds are put in cages at an early age, two or three weeks prior to egg laying. The important point in providing pullets for egg production is to obtain maximum egg-laying ability with a minimum amount of stress and trauma to the birds. This will provide the necessary economic returns and minimize problems associated with egg production and mortality in cages.

Breeder Flocks

Managing the breeder flock in any type of poultry operation requires a great deal of refinement beyond the basic needs of the production flock. For example, in turkey reproduction, management of the toms as well as the hens requires careful consideration of environmental factors that are involved in the reproductive cycle. Egg production is stimulated by lighting programs accompanied by a proper level of nutrition, comfortable quarters, and proper care of the breeders. In turkey flocks where artificial insemination is practiced on a weekly or biweekly basis, frequent handling of the birds is required and care must be taken to minimize the trauma involved. Collection of semen from the males is a rigorous task since turkey males may weigh between 30 and 50 pounds. Emphasis on careful handling is essential, and any employee who does not exhibit a reasonable amount of patience and concern for the animal's welfare should be eliminated from the team. In turkey flocks, adequate numbers of nests equipped with gates that will allow only one bird at a time to enter a nest are required to assure sound, clean hatching eggs. In chicken-breeding operations the problem of multiple occupancy of nests frequently results in broken and soiled eggs. The details involved in obtaining semen and managing breeder flocks has been discussed in another section of this book. General management and care of the breeder birds either for artificial insemination or natural mating will be reflected through fertility and hatchability of the eggs produced.

CHAPTER 7

NUTRITION
AND
FEEDING

The major objective of poultry production is to efficiently and economically convert relatively unpalatable and unattractive feedstuffs into nutritious, palatable, and attractive food for humans. A trip through the digestive system allows visualization of the accomplishment of this objective. Optimally balanced diets using least-cost, available ingredients are specifically formulated for a variety of types and ages of poultry.

The basic reason and justification for the existence of animal agriculture today is that relatively affluent humans in developed countries of the world prefer and can afford to eat meat, eggs, and milk, rather than legumes, grains, and roots and leaves of plants. People in developed countries will eat these more expensive forms of protein and other nutrients not only because they more conveniently provide a balanced diet of the essential (high quality) nutrients, but more because they taste good and people have acquired a desire for them. These relatively affluent people are willing and able to pay animal producers to take feed, comprised primarily of plant nutrients, and pass it into an animal, which will convert it into animal nutrients in the form of meat, eggs, and milk. At best this conversion of food is not efficient, although poultry is much more efficient at it than larger agricultural animals (cattle, sheep, and swine). It is expensive to feed plants (that humans can eat) to animals for the purpose of converting these plants to animal products. However, this may be justified on an economic basis because grain and roughage can be produced in excess of human food requirements.

Comparing the nutritional health and well-being of most people in developing areas of the world with those people in developed areas, it is apparent that a balanced diet containing meat, eggs, and milk is preferable to a nonbalanced diet from only plant nutrient sources. Although it is possible to obtain a balanced, totally vegetarian diet resulting in good nutritional health, this balanced diet is not easily obtained without precisely combining optimal amounts of a wide variety of plant foodstuffs to obtain all essential nutrients. The expertise and patience required to provide this necessary delicate balance is not found in most developing areas of the world. Even in developed countries this expertise is not readily available to, or even desired by, the general food consumer. It is much more convenient and less expensive for the consumer to obtain a properly balanced diet comprised partially of meat, eggs, and milk. This is evidenced by comparing the price per unit weight of balanced vegetable foodstuffs ("health foods") with the much lower price per unit weight of meat, milk, and eggs. This great price advantage of animal food products becomes even a greater advantage when price is compared on a per-unit-of-usable-nutrient basis.

Poultry converts feedstuffs into human food (meat and eggs) much more efficiently than any other common agricultural animal. Broiler chickens convert feed to live tissue at a ratio of two kilograms of feed per kilogram of live weight gain; turkeys have a feed conversion ratio of three kilograms of feed per kilogram of weight gain. Commercial laying hens convert feed into eggs at a ratio of 2.6 to 1. Therefore, the potential use of poultry in improving nutrition in developing countries is reasonable to consider. Also, as long as feedstuffs can be produced in abundance in developed areas of the world, poultry will be the most feasible animal to convert the feedstuffs into desired human food in order to maintain nutritional health standards at a relatively low cost.

POULTRY NUTRITION

Required Nutrients, Feed Ingredients, and Additives

The commercial chicken that has been bred for maximum growth or egg production requires a diet that will permit the full expression of genetic potential under the existing environment. Unlike its predecessor, today's chicken is not adapted to scavenging the jungle or barnyard to obtain required nutrients from insects, green plants, and miscellaneous seeds. Poultry nutritionists have identified the nutritive requirements for maximum performance, and today's poultry rations are the most complete of any diet fed to animals, including humans. Inadequately fed birds will very rapidly reflect deficiencies through a decline in rate of growth, egg production, and general performance. The young growing bird will soon exhibit signs of classical nutritional deficiency diseases. Symptoms of marginal deficiencies will first appear in the most rapidly growing or high egg-laying birds, which have nutritive requirements exceeding those of the average flock. Diets may be relatively simple or very complex, and the form in which they are fed will vary with the type of feeding system. Only a few carefully selected feed ingredients may be used to formulate a poultry ration that is economical and also adequate to meet the nutrient requirements of high egg production or rapid growth.

The nutrients that comprise a poultry diet, as any animal diet, are water, protein, carbohydrate, fat, minerals, and vitamins. Although all are essential, adequate water may be considered the single most important nutrient. Water should be provided continuously and be easily accessible to all birds throughout the poultry house. Water is necessary for many body functions, particularly absorption and assimilation of nutrients from the digestive tract and metabolic reactions. Without ample amounts of water, production performance will suffer. All feed ingredients contain some water, but this is not adequate to meet the needs of the bird. Although water is one of the least expensive ingredients available, it frequently is inadequately supplied. The waterer should be free of excess minerals and salts, free of high bacterial contamination, low in nitrates, and of a quality suitable for human consumption. Waterers must be constructed so that minimal contamination can occur from bird's feces, litter, and other foreign materials. Founts, troughs, and drinking cups with automatic regulation are preferred to devices that must be hand filled. Birds require at least twice as much in weight of water as they require in weight of dry feed. They may require more water if there are excess salts in the diet.

Protein provides the amino acid "building blocks" for tissue growth and egg production. It is the most expensive nutrient and one that must be provided from a high quality source. Protein quality is generally based on two major factors, amino acid composition of the feedstuff and availability of these amino acids from the feedstuff through digestion in the gut of the bird. Amino acids are considered as the building blocks of proteins (Table 7–1). Of 19 total amino acids required by poultry, 13 are considered as essential amino acids, because they cannot be produced in the bird's body and must be supplied in the diet, and 6 are considered as nonessential, because they are synthesized by the body and need not be

TABLE 7–1
Amino Acid Requirements of Poultry

Essential Amino Acids[1]	*Nonessential Amino Acids*[2]
Arginine	Alanine
Cystine	Aspartic acid
Glycine	Glutamic acid
Histidine	Hydroxyproline
Isoleucine	Proline
Leucine	Serine
Lysine	
Methionine	
Phenylalanine	
Threonine	
Tryptophan	
Tyrosine	
Valine	

[1] Amino acids that must be supplied by protein in the diet because they cannot be synthesized in required amounts in the bird's body.

[2] Amino acids that can be synthesized in required amounts in the bird's body if not supplied by protein in the diet.

supplied in the diet. Feedstuffs differ qualitatively and quantitatively in their amino acid composition. Therefore, in order to supply all necessary amino acids in the feed, high protein feed ingredients should be obtained from various plant and animal sources. Poultry diets consist mainly of plant materials. However, a portion of the protein may be provided from animal products to assure adequate levels of some amino acids that are not adequately supplied by present plant materials. Some synthetic amino acids are economically feasible for use in poultry diets. Methionine and lysine are generally low in plant products, but adequate in animal products. Addition of these two synthetic amino acids to an otherwise adequate all-plant diet can provide a complete diet for both growing birds and laying hens. High lysine corn provides an improved source of this amino acid. Also, other small grains are being developed with improved lysine levels.

Soybean oil meal, a by-product of the soybean oil industry, has become the major source of plant protein for poultry diets in most areas of the United States and throughout the world in general. Other oil meals are utilized in varying amounts according to geographic and economic availability. Cottonseed meal, for example, is available in areas of high cotton production and may, through special processing, be made usable in starting and growing diets. However, in laying-hen diets high levels of cottonseed cause undesirable mottled yolks in table eggs. Gossypol, the responsible agent in the cottonseed, can be partially removed or deactivated, allowing some cottonseed oil meal to be used in layer rations. Other high protein sources are listed in Table 7–2 and can be used in poultry diets with careful consideration given to amino acid content and economic availability.

Animal by-products (tankage) provide a source of some of the essential amino acids, but are usually used at a relatively low level in most poultry diets, primarily to provide methionine and lysine. Animal protein products are usually more expensive than plant protein ingredients and, therefore, have limited use in many parts of the world. Major sources of animal protein are: meat scrap, a by-product of the slaughter house; rendered offal and animal wastes; and fish meal, which may be a by-product or specifically made of certain fish, such as menhaden or anchovy. Anchovy meal is manufactured in large quantities in Peru.

Feedstuffs high in carbohydrate constitute the major volume of poultry diets. Carbohydrates are the primary source of energy for the bird. Major carbohydrate sources are grains, primarily corn and milo. Barley, oats, wheat, and other grains usually do not compete favorably with corn

TABLE 7–2
Sources of Nutrients Required by Poultry

Nutrient	Sources
Protein	Meat scraps (lysine), fish meal (lysine, methionine), poultry by-product meal (tryptophan, lysine), blood meal, liver and glandular meal, feather meal (hydrolyzed), animal tankage, milk products, cottonseed meal, peanut meal, soybean meal (lysine), corn gluten meal (methionine), saffflower meal, sesame meal, sunflower seed meal.
Carbohydrate	Corn, sorghum grains (milo), barley, rye, oats, wheat, wheat middlings, various grain by-products.
Fat	Animal tallow (beef), lard, corn oil, other vegetable oils.
Minerals	Meat scraps, fish meal, milk products, ground limestone (calcium), ground oyster shells (calcium), dicalcium phosphate (calcium, phosphorus), defluorinated rock phosphate (phosphorus, calcium), steamed bone meal (phosphorus, calcium), salt (sodium, chlorine, iodine), manganese sulfate (manganese), manganese oxide (manganese), zinc carbonate (zinc), zinc oxide (zinc).
Vitamins	Yeasts, fish solubles, distillers' solubles, liver meal, alfalfa meal, milk by-products.

and milo as the prime ingredient when compared on a least-cost basis. Since wheat is used widely as a food for humans, it usually brings a price higher than can be justified for use in poultry diets. Oats are too high in fiber. Barley is intermediate in these factors. Carbohydrate sources are listed in Table 7–2. No source of feed should be overlooked because geographic location, availability, nutrient value, and cost should be considered for each individual situation.

Fats and oils are placed in a single category of nutrients since they are utilized for a specific purpose. They have high energy values, but can only be used at relatively low levels in poultry diets for at about 5% added fat, the feed will begin to lose optimal flow characteristics. Animal tallow is a major fat source, although vegetable oils are also commonly used (Table 7–2). Fats and oils added to the diet reduce dust (fines) in the feed and improve palatability.

Minerals are present in many of the ingredients in the diet. Good supplemental sources of minerals are listed in Table 7–2. The major minerals required are calcium and phosphorus. They are used in the formation of egg shells and bone. Limestone and oyster shells are two major ingredients incorporated in poultry diets to provide calcium. Bone meal and defluorinated rock phosphate are major sources of phosphorus. Copper, zinc, manganese, iron, and other minerals in trace amounts are required for many metabolic functions. Interaction of minerals with other nutrients is an important function in the efficient digestion and utilization of feed. Marginal mineral deficiencies may interfere substantially with optimal feed conversion, growth, egg-shell structure, and general health of the bird. Although the salt requirement of birds is relatively low, adequate levels are essential and excessive amounts are highly toxic. Birds require a sensitive balance between necessary and toxic levels of salt.

Vitamins may be categorized as fat soluble, (A, D, E, and K) or water soluble (the B-complex vitamins). Many vitamins are quite stable, but some deteriorate rapidly on exposure to heat, sunlight, or air. Major sources of vitamins for a poultry diet are listed in Table 7–2.

Vitamin A is found in many naturally occurring plant products and is associated with carotene, which is found in many plant pigments. High levels are found in yellow corn, but not in white corn or sorghum. Bright green alfalfa dried by kiln is higher in vitamin A than sundried alfalfa. Green grass, other leafy food materials, and carrots are high in vitamin A as long as they retain their bright color. Vitamin A is necessary for the health and maintenance of epithelial tissues, such as the lining of the bird's respiratory system. Common symptoms of deficiency occur around the eyes, with crustation appearing and night blindness, which as in humans effectively reduces the bird's ability to see in the dark. Because it increases exposure to air, grinding of whole or other course feed materials will hasten the deterioration of this vitamin during storage, particularly if storage areas are warm or hot. As a result, the poultry industry does not depend upon the bird's receiving their vitamin A from ingredients in the diet. Dry or stabilized vitamin A is added to diets to meet the requirements of the bird. This form of the vitamin is not easily oxidized by adverse storage conditions since vitamin A particles are given a protective coat that prevents oxygen from entering and oxidizing that particle.

Vitamin D is associated with sunlight, for sunlight provides irradiation that stimulates the manufacture of vitamin D in the skin of the bird. Fish oils are high in content of vitamin D. However, the poultry producer normally adds vitamin D to the poultry diet in required amounts to meet productive objectives rather than relying on synthesis or feed ingredients. The vitamin D_2 that is adequate for most mammals is not of value to birds; thus, it is important to have vitamin D_3.

Vitamin K is necessary to control hemorrhage and maintain tissue health and function. It occurs naturally in green plants such as alfalfa, but may be destroyed by heat and light. Kiln-dried alfalfa-leaf meal added to the diet is an excellent source of vitamin K. However, poultry diets are usually supplemented with a manufactured form of vitamin K to assure the required level.

Vitamin E (tocopherol) has been identified as playing an important role in antibody production and in increasing resistance to disease. Although vitamin E occurs naturally at relatively high levels in whole grains and alfalfa meal, it is easily oxidized, particularly in the presence of minerals and unsaturated fatty acids. Therefore, it should be added to the poultry diet in order to assure adequate levels, and an antioxidant should be added to reduce loss.

The B-complex vitamins are identified with energy metabolism and the general health and well-being of the nervous tissue and body muscle development. A deficiency may appear as muscle paralysis of varying degrees, depending upon the specific B vitamin or vitamins deficient. Often the birds will appear sleepy and lethargic and prefer to sit rather than stand and be active. Slipped tendon, for example, is due to the lack of tension in the muscle, which results in slippage of the tendon from its position over the long bones of the legs. Slipped tendon is mostly caused by defective long bone growth; the condyles are improperly formed, allowing the tendon to easily slip over the side of the bone. The bird in early stages of the deficiency may appear normal except that one or both legs cannot be held under the body and will extend out to the respective side. These symptoms may be more prevalent during early growth of birds and may more frequently appear in the rapid growing strains or in individuals throughout the flock that are growing most rapidly. Thus, the largest, most vigorous birds with higher vitamin requirements than the slower growing may be the first to exhibit deficiency symptoms. The symptoms may be confused with infectious diseases affecting the nervous system, such as Marek's disease, leucosis, or Newcastle disease, which makes laboratory diagnosis necessary. Many of the B vitamins were first specifically labeled as unidentified growth factors associated with normal growth, any specific deficiency causing a specific set of symptoms.

High environmental temperatures have been shown to have a negative effect on some vitamins in feed ingredients. Hot weather has also been shown to cause a substantial increase in vitamin A, C, and K requirements. These were the vitamins studied most, therefore there is more information available for them on this subject. Storage conditions of the ingredients, as well as manufacturing conditions such as pelleting, have a profound influence on the stability of many nutrients, but vitamins appear to be the most sensitive to high temperature. Vitamins incorporated into premix ingredients are subjected to variations in temperature, humidity, time in shipping, and storage, as well as the effects of any added mineral salts. Vitamin E and other antioxidants aid in the prevention of degradation of vitamin A and probably several other vitamins. In addition, there are a number of other specific factors to consider: (1) Feed consumption regulates vitamin intake; it is closely associated with environmental temperature, because high temperatures suppress feed intake. (2) Management factors closely interact through their influence on growth rate, egg production, and bird activity. (3) Energy-protein ratio interacts with genetic makeup of the bird to influence feed utilization; these directly affect nutrient requirement.

Fiber occurs in just about all sources of animal and plant products except fats and oils. It generally is not added to poultry diets. Fiber is required to provide a certain amount of bulk in the diet and is necessary for efficient digestion and physical consistency and movement of food materials through the digestive tract. Unlike the ruminant, the digestive system of the bird is not designed to handle large amounts of fiber. Food moves quite rapidly through the digestive tract of birds, whereas the movement in the cow, for example, is much slower to allow digestion of fiber by bacteria. Sources of fiber sometimes added to the diet are oat hulls, wood shavings, corncobs, and other products high in cellulose. Dietary fiber may be effective in controlling cannibalism and feather picking under the confinement conditions of commercial poultry housing.

Unidentified growth factors, antibiotics, hormones, and other growth stimulants are continually being investigated relative to their specific roles in enhancing the growth and well-being of poultry. Many interactions occur, and frequently it is found that a specific nutrient limits or enhances the availability and/or assimilation of other nutrients. For example, specific amino acids have been found to limit the assimilation of other amino acids, and the minerals, calcium and phosphorus, must be in the ratio of approximately 2:1 for maximum utilization. Many growth factors still may remain unidentified. For example, advantages gained in feeding poultry certain industrial by-products, such as brewers' dried grains, suggest the existence of growth factors resulting from the production process. Also, the effect of antibiotics at low levels in the diet suggests they function to enhance growth, unrelated to disease control. This beneficial effect has been demonstrated to be greater when birds are reared in old, unclean buildings under relatively poor management rather than in new buildings or ones in which a vigorous cleaning and disinfection program has been practiced. This suggests a relationship of bacterial flora of the environment and their competitive role in the gut for nutrients required by the bird. Although certain antibiotics and medications have been demonstrated to provide a beneficial influence on growth and egg production, the exact mechanism of action is not completely understood. Furthermore, certain anticoccidials enhance production even without evidence of coccidia infection. Growth hormones as feed additives are not used in commercial poultry production at the present time. Feed additives that enhance growth and egg production have been proposed over many years. Only those that have stood the test of careful investigation in research laboratories and proven themselves safe and effective in the field have been established for use in the poultry industry. Frequently, new products obtained from the earth or as a by-product from some industrial process have been proposed for use in feeding other animals or poultry or as a fertilizer, since recycling and waste utilization appear to be wise practices. However, these must pass many safety and efficacy tests before being incorporated into poultry diets. Such new uses of waste products should be approached with great caution in spite of promising claims for nutritional and economic advantages.

Digestion, Absorption, and Metabolism of Nutrients

To convert chicken feed into meat and eggs, the feed must be passed into the anterior opening of the chicken. In the chicken it is converted into eggs that come out the posterior opening or it is converted into meat that is harvested in a somewhat different manner (Figure 7–1). The analogy one might draw is that the chicken is a food production "factory."

Like any factory producing a marketable product, the chicken must be appropriate for efficiently producing its intended product. Just as it would not be efficient to manufacture watches in an automobile factory,

FIGURE 7-1
Conversion of feed to human
food by poultry.

likewise it would not be efficient to produce eggs from a meat production chicken, or vice versa. Thus, we use a different type of chicken for each purpose.

Also, like a factory, the chicken must have adequate high quality machinery to efficiently produce a high quality product. Just as it would not be efficient or even possible to mass produce quality automobiles in a backyard garage with inadequate equipment, it would also not be efficient to mass produce meat from just any chicken. Thus, the type and quality of the chicken producing the meat (or eggs) is determined by the breeding of the bird.

In order to get the full potential out of a properly equipped factory, the working conditions must be optimized. To get full potential in production out of a genetically optimal, correct type of chicken, the bird must remain healthy in an optimally, controlled environment. Thus, in either case, time and energy do not have to be expended on unnecessary stresses and thus be diverted from production of product.

Essential to the manufacture of any quality product are appropriate, high quality, raw materials. To produce automobiles, the company requires iron ore of designated quality, not wooden logs or sand. The chicken, as a manufacturing unit for eggs or meat, also must be provided appropriate, high quality raw materials. Feed ingredients must meet or exceed designated quality standards and must be appropriate for the desired end product. Just as an automobile factory could not directly use logs or sand to produce major parts of a marketable automobile, a chicken could not efficiently use cellulose, sand, or iron ore to produce eggs or meat.

Continuing the logic of this analogy of the chicken as a food producing "factory," it will be instructive and very interesting to tour this factory and learn exactly how the raw feed ingredients are converted into meat and eggs. Much of the machinery in this factory and its function should already be familiar to you (Chapter 3), so that will not be reviewed here in any great detail.

In producing meat or eggs, the raw materials in the feed will be given first consideration. The total of feed ingredients must contain optimal amounts of the six basic nutrients, protein, carbohydrate, fat, vitamins, minerals, and water. Protein is made up of many amino acids chemically bonded end-to-end in long chains. Carbohydrate is made up of many simple sugars (monosaccharides), chemically bonded. Fat (triglyceride) consists of glycerol bonded chemically to three long-chain fatty acids. Vitamins are smaller organic chemicals than the first three nutrients discussed; and minerals are very small inorganic nutrients. Although feed contains a certain amount of water, it must also be provided separately from the mixed feed. In changing these nutrients from poultry feed into animal products (meat and eggs), the nutrients must be digested, absorbed, and then metabolized.

The process of digestion has been described in Chapter 3 as it related to the physiology of the organs of the digestive system. In touring this food production factory, the chicken, it may be necessary to review the anatomy of the digestive system and its functions. In preparation for this tour, we are required to become completely enclosed in a controlled-environment suit and helmet, similar to that which astronauts wear in space, so we are indestructible and can live fairly comfortably in the chicken. We also must now undergo a drastic reduction in size. As we are becoming smaller, as if this weren't frightening enough, we now find ourselves being devoured along with the chicken feed by a hungry chicken (Figure 7–2). As we enter the "factory," being picked up by the beak, we are tossed along with large "boulders" of various feed ingredients to the back of the mouth and are then literally shoved by the back of the tongue, over the closed "trap door" entrance to the larynx, down the esophagus, to fall into the gaping pouch of the crop. Here we come to rest for a moment, catch our breath, and look around.

We notice large boulders, many times our size of what appear to be crushed soybeans and corn covered with a layer of an oily lubricant, and some large, jagged, hard "rocks" that appear to be mineral. Some of them appear to be large, transparent, "ice-like glaciers." From our knowledge of the expected components of poultry feed, we rapidly identify these materials as vegetable oil and various minerals including salt. We notice some sheets of green organic material and rapidly identify them as alfalfa.

We are small enough to see with our unaided eye the chemical structure of these feed ingredients. We realize that these ingredients, being

FIGURE 7–2
To better visualize the conversion of feed into meat and eggs, the poultry producer may perhaps dream of being devoured along with the chicken feed by one of the hungry chickens he feeds, and thus start a tour of this food production "factory" (Sketch by Susan Gruhlke).

the raw materials of the factory and being temporarily stored here in the crop, must contain optimal amounts of the six basic nutrients including water. Just as we are thinking about this separately supplied nutrient, water, we notice the surroundings becoming slightly more fluid as water molecules start to flow over some of the boulders and rocks of feed ingredients. In closely examining the surface of the various sized forms, we notice the soy boulders are made up of long folded and intertwined chains of amino acids. The corn boulders are made up largely of long chains of monosaccharides. The oily coating over these structures is made up of many glycerol molecules, each with three long chains of fatty acids attached.

We find ourselves hanging on tightly to a single protein chain on the surface of a large soy boulder as suddenly it is moved forcibly along with all the surrounding forms back into the tube of the esophagus. After a short passage it enters a widening in the tube that must be the proventriculus. The wall of this stomach is slimy and secreting fluids from its cells. The fluids literally bathe the boulders and smaller forms with a flexible protein coat that we suspect is the soluble enzyme, pepsin. We also notice a nonprotein fluid, probably hydrochloric acid, that appears to have little immediate effect on most of the larger forms, but seems to dissolve the mineral rocks as their surface starts to erode away.

After a very little time in the proventriculus, the boulders and rocks, bathed now in a considerable amount of fluid, pass into the gizzard lined with a thick leathery pouch. This pouch contains powerful muscular walls that immediately start to squeeze in on the entering forms, crushing them against each other, and breaking them into smaller pieces. As the organic and inorganic forms rub against each other with tremendous force and break into smaller pieces, the sound of rumbling and scraping is deafening, not unlike that of a "landslide" or waves pounding on a beach. Moisture in the form of digestive juices mix with the crushed boulders as they break apart as additional water now enters the gizzard and is mixed with the increasing number of smaller particles of soy and corn. The rocks of minerals are completely dissolving in the highly acid fluids, and everything is in a thick "muddy" slurry as it passes into the anterior end of the duodenal loop. We are still clinging to a relatively long protein chain that was originally part of a longer protein molecule and is part of only a small piece of what originally was a gigantic boulder.

We are completely immersed in fluid as we start to pass along the duodenal loop. We soon notice more fluids being "piped" into the loop; they contain protein enzymes in solution from the islets of Langerhans of the pancreas. Then the slurry meets head on and mixes with a green wave of bile. Now large spheres of oil and globs of fat, which have been formed in the increasingly aqueous environment, start to break up into smaller pieces as the green bile surrounds them. This emulsification process continues until the smaller pieces are reduced to free triglycerides, which then can be chewed apart by lipases (enzymes) that come along with the pancreatic fluids.

The liquid slurry is then squeezed further into the next portion of the small intestine, which appears from the inside as a long, folded tunnel with folds in its lining. The entire surface is lined with finger-like villi projecting perpendicularly into the lumen. Protected from digestion by our enclosed, controlled-environment suit, we find we have some control over where we can "swim" in the fluids of the intestine. We now let go of the protein chain that we have been clutching since it was part of a large boulder of soybean tissue and "swim" over close to the villae lining the intestinal wall. The wall of the tubular villus is transparent, being made up of a monolayer of absorptive epithelial cells and relatively few secretory goblet cells (Figure 7–3). Behind this transparent wall of the tubular villus is a blood capillary. Upon even closer examination it is noticed that each intestinal epithelial cell has many microvilli projecting into the lumen of the intestine (Figure 7–4). Only when one considers the total microscopic structure of the intestinal lining is it possible to begin to estimate the vast total absorptive surface area of the lumen of the small intestine. It now starts to become more evident that further breakdown

FIGURE 7–3
Two villi of the intestinal wall of a chicken. (Photograph
by Dian Webster.)

of the protein, carbohydrate, and fat will be required if these raw materials must pass into the blood capillaries of the villae for transport to the growing egg or muscle tissues where they are required. Up to this point, although much physical breakdown of the raw materials has occurred, relatively little chemical digestion of protein, carbohydrate, or fat has yet occurred. In fact, a number of additional digestive enzymes are now being secreted by cells lining the small intestine.

So, digestion of protein, carbohydrate, and fat will be completed in this portion of the small intestine since these long-chain nutrients are simply too large to pass through the cells lining the villae and enter the blood capillaries. Digestion can be defined as the breakdown of feed nutrients in the intestinal tract into its smaller and simpler parts for subsequent absorption into the blood system. Perhaps a good vantage point from which to view this digestive process would be from inside one of the cells lining a villus. We will then reduce ourselves in size even further and grab onto a free amino acid that is about to be transported through the cell wall lining a villus. Once inside the cell we then turn and look out through the microvillae into the lumen and watch what happens.

Out in the lumen we see many long chains of amino acids (protein), many long chains of glucose and other monosaccharides (carbohydrate), and many triglyceride (fat) molecules. We are now small enough to see individual atoms bonded together to form molecules. Just as we learned in chemistry class, protein is zig-zagged in shape (Figure 7–5). Sugars do have carbon rings, each with one oxygen and with perpendicularly bonded hydrogen atoms and with a methanol group attached to one of those carbons in the ring (Figure 7–6). Triglycerides do have a three-carbon backbone with three fatty acids, one branching out of either carbon of glycerol. It is shaped like an "E" (Figure 7–7).

We will watch now as these large molecules react with water (H-OH) and specific enzymes to break some of their bonds (hydrolysis), releasing free amino acids from protein, free monosaccharides from carbohydrate, and free glycerol and fatty acids from triglycerides (Figures 7–5, 7–6, 7–7). This hydrolysis occurs rapidly but not instantaneously with the gradual breaking of more and more carbon-nitrogen bonds on proteins and carbon-oxygen bonds on carbohydrates and triglycerides to produce shorter and shorter chains of molecules and eventually many free

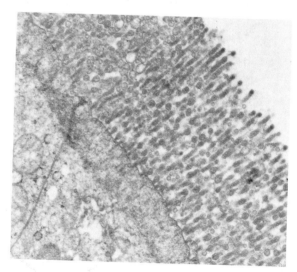

FIGURE 7–4
Microvilli of two epithelial cells of a villus projecting into the lumen of the intestine of a chicken. (Photograph by Dian Webster.)

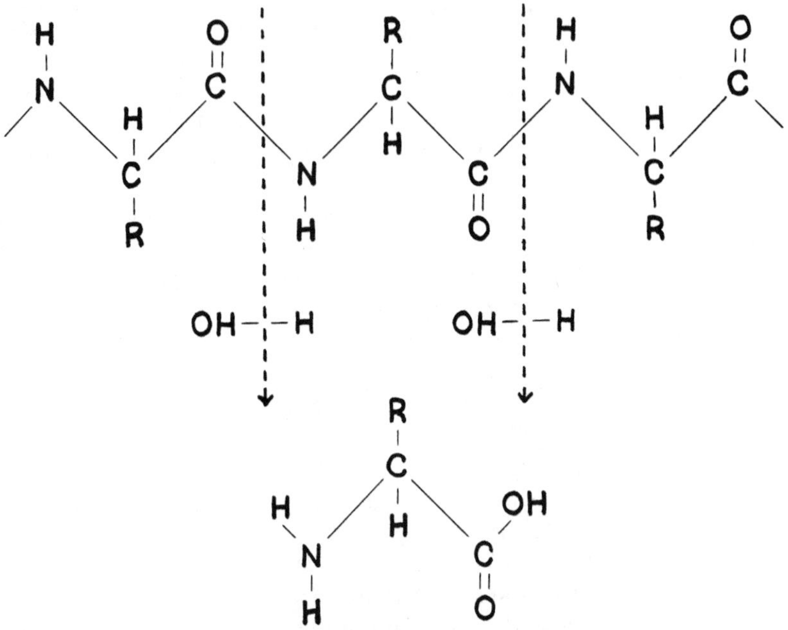

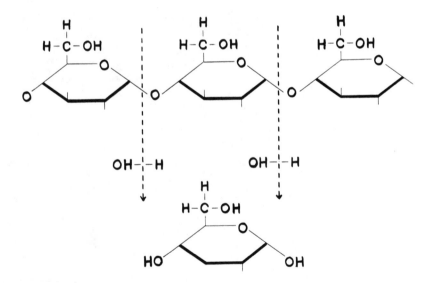

FIGURE 7-5
Digestion of protein by hydrolysis of carbon-nitrogen bonds releasing free amino acids.

FIGURE 7-6
Digestion of carbohydrate by hydrolysis of carbon-oxygen bonds releasing free monosaccharides.

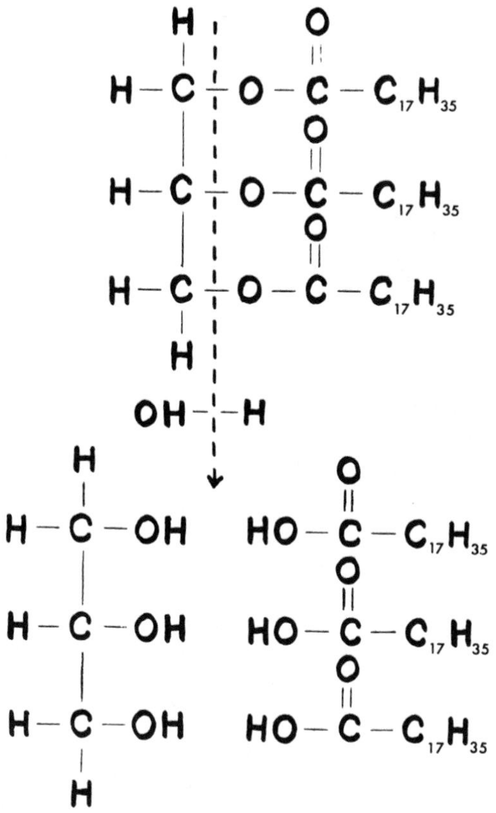

$$
\begin{array}{c}
H - \overset{\displaystyle H}{\underset{\displaystyle |}{\overset{\displaystyle |}{C}}} - O - \overset{\displaystyle O}{\overset{\displaystyle \|}{C}} - C_{17}H_{35} \\
H - \overset{\displaystyle |}{\underset{\displaystyle |}{C}} - O - \overset{\displaystyle O}{\overset{\displaystyle \|}{C}} - C_{17}H_{35} \\
H - \overset{\displaystyle |}{\underset{\displaystyle |}{C}} - O - \overset{\displaystyle O}{\overset{\displaystyle \|}{C}} - C_{17}H_{35} \\
\overset{\displaystyle H}{} \\
OH - H
\end{array}
$$

$$
\begin{array}{cc}
\overset{\displaystyle H}{\underset{\displaystyle |}{\overset{\displaystyle |}{}}} & \overset{\displaystyle O}{\overset{\displaystyle \|}{}} \\
H - \overset{\displaystyle |}{\underset{\displaystyle |}{C}} - OH & HO - C - C_{17}H_{35} \\
H - C - OH & HO - \overset{\displaystyle O}{\overset{\displaystyle \|}{C}} - C_{17}H_{35} \\
H - C - OH & HO - \overset{\displaystyle O}{\overset{\displaystyle \|}{C}} - C_{17}H_{35} \\
\overset{\displaystyle |}{H}
\end{array}
$$

FIGURE 7–7

Digestion of a triglyceride by hydrolysis of carbon-oxygen bonds releasing free glycerol and free fatty acids.

amino acids, monosaccharides, and glycerol and fatty acids. These products of digestion come in contact with the membrane of the microvilli and are transported across it into the cytoplasm of the absorptive epithelial cell by active transport systems. If any very short polypeptide chains are transported into the cytoplasm of the absorptive cell, they are digested to free amino acids before passing out of the cell into the blood capillary. Hydrolysis of fat is not always complete, but it is broken down sufficiently to allow its absorption through the intestinal epithelial cell into the blood system and into the lymphatic system.

So the digested nutrients have now attached to, and been actively moved across, the membrane of the microvilli and are released into the cytoplasm of this absorptive intestinal epithelial cell, as the process of absorption is now occurring. These free digested nutrients now pass through the cytoplasm of the cell and then pass out through the cell wall and enter the blood capillary of the villus. The portal vein then carries these materials to the liver where certain products are put into general circulation while others are screened out. Absorption of digested nutrients from the lumen of the small intestine into the blood circulatory system has now occurred. Dissolved minerals and vitamins are absorbed into the blood system without being digested.

Once in the blood system, nutrients are transported to those organs and tissues of the body where they are needed for any of various life processes. This is where the nutrients undergo metabolic reactions. Thus, metabolism is a distinctly different chemical process from digestion and can be defined as all processes that digested nutrients undergo from the moment they enter the circulatory system of the body until the end products of reactions are eventually excreted or stored in the body.

All monosaccharides are metabolized to glucose, which is transported by the blood system to those cells of the body requiring energy. Thus, the primary use of glucose is oxidation in cells, which produces heat and energy with carbon dioxide and water as by-products (Figure 7–8). If there is more glucose in the blood than is required by the bird for heat and energy, a very limited amount of excess glucose may be converted back into polysaccharides and stored as the carbohydrate component of the cells. Any additional surplus glucose in the blood at this point goes to the liver and is bonded back together in long chains to form glycogen (animal starch), which can be stored in a limited amount in body muscles and primarily in the liver. When more glucose is required for energy, liver glycogen is converted to glucose, enters the blood, and is taken to that part of the body where it is needed. Synthesis and hydrolysis of glycogen, and glucose metabolism are under hormonal control, allowing a constant concentration of glucose in the blood. Any remaining excess glucose in the blood is metabolized into body fat for which there is nearly unlimited storage.

Digested fat absorbed into the blood is first transported to those cells of the body requiring its oxidation for heat and energy (Figure 7–8). Any excess fatty acids may be transported to become a necessary component of body cells and tissues. Any additional excess blood fat components can be used to synthesize skin oils and, finally, fat for storage in the body. There is essentially no limit to the amount of excess fat that can be synthesized and stored in the body.

The primary use of amino acids in the blood is in the synthesis of new protein for cell and tissue structure (meat and eggs) and enzymes (Figure 7–8). Once this need is met, surplus amino acids are transported in the blood to the liver, where they are deaminated by enzymatic hy-

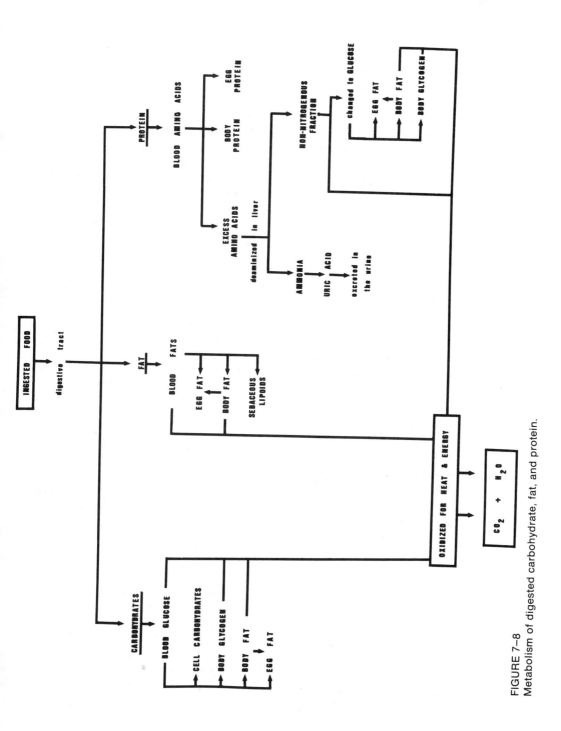

FIGURE 7-8
Metabolism of digested carbohydrate, fat, and protein.

drolysis of the carbon-nitrogen bond, which frees ammonia gas. The ammonia may be metabolized to uric acid and small amounts of urea for excretion with the urine or, if necessary, may be used as a nitrogen source in the synthesis of required nonessential amino acids. The nonnitrogen part of deaminated excess amino acids may be oxidized in any cells to heat, energy, carbon dioxide, and water. When this energy requirement is met, the acid may be metabolized to glucose, which can be stored as body glycogen or converted to fat if not also oxidized for heat and energy.

Minerals are directly necessary for many metabolic reactions and some are used in tissue structure such as bones and egg shells. Vitamins are not provided in the diet for use as a source of energy, although excess quantities may be oxidized or metabolized into waste products for excretion. Vitamins are primarily used to form coenzymes necessary for metabolic reactions. Excess vitamins may be stored to a limited extent in the egg and liver, which are relatively high in vitamin content.

If we are to continue our journey through this food manufacturing factory, the chicken, we must also pass with the digested nutrients out of the absorptive epithelial cell from which we have watched the digestion and absorption processes. We will now enter the blood capillary of the villus with a free amino acid to which we have attached. We will travel with this amino acid to a growing muscle cell. Since muscle cells contain considerable protein, the growing cells must be able to synthesize protein from the raw materials supplied by the blood from the liver. The liver acts like a switchyard, providing the redirection and make-up of new packages of nutrients to be sent out into the bloodstream. As we enter a series of blood vessels and capillaries and finally arrive at a muscle cell, the amino acid on which we are riding and many other identical and different amino acids pass out of the thin capillary wall and are actively transported through the muscle cell membrane.

Thus, we enter the cell and proceed to identify some familiar organelles we studied in cell biology and try to determine the fate of many free amino acids that now have entered the cell and are floating suspended in the cell's cytoplasm (Figure 7–9). We rapidly locate the largest single structure in the cell, the nucleus. We may consider the cell as a single production unit of the "factory," and the nucleus is the "control room" of this production unit. We notice, as expected, that the cell not only is filled with cytoplasm, but is infiltrated with a lacy curtain-like transparent membrane, continuous with both the nuclear membrane and cellular membrane. This extensive membrane, continuous but filled with holes, is the endoplasmic reticulum. Attached to this membrane surface are thousands of small, roughly spherical structures known as ribosomes, which we soon discover are the protein synthesizing "machines" in the factory production unit. It is obvious that long chains of protein are being "extruded"

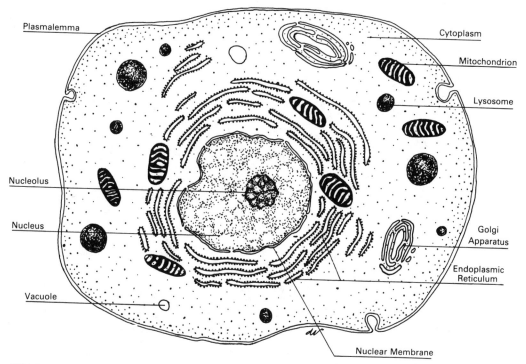

Plasmalemma

Cytoplasm

Mitochondrion

Lysosome

Nucleolus

Nucleus

Golgi Apparatus

Endoplasmic Reticulum

Vacuole

Nuclear Membrane

FIGURE 7–9
A typical animal cell.

from most of these machines. However, even from this interior view, it is not obvious exactly how the ribosomes are synthesizing protein. It will probably be most understandable to check first in the control room (nucleus) to learn the manufacturing process from the beginning.

Entering the nucleus we immediately observed the familiar chromosomes, some with segments of their deoxyribonucleic acid (DNA) uncoiled and with broken cross-bonds allowing a segment of the double helix to separate or "unzip" (Figure 7–10). As the cross-paired nucleotides unbond, free nucleotides take their place as a strand of messenger ribonucleic acid (m-RNA) is synthesized, replicating the coded linear arrangement of nucleotides from the separated DNA helix. When a segment of the code has been transcribed onto the newly synthesized m-RNA, it detaches from the DNA and leaves the nucleus. In the cytoplasm it attaches at one end to a ribosome and starts to feed through (Figure 7–11).

What has happened is that the pattern determining exactly what type of protein will be synthesized on that specific ribosome at that time was

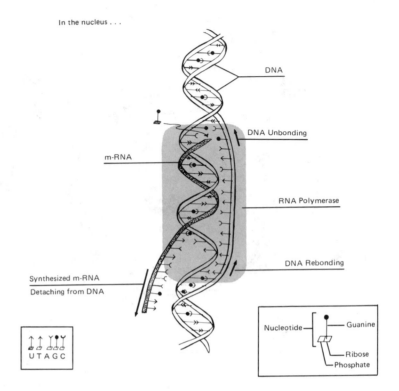

In the nucleus . . .

DNA

DNA Unbonding

m-RNA

RNA Polymerase

DNA Rebonding

Synthesized m-RNA
Detaching from DNA

U T A G C

Nucleotide — Guanine
Ribose
Phosphate

FIGURE 7–10
Transcription of the genetic code from an uncoiled segment of deoxyribonucleic acid (DNA) onto synthesized messenger ribonucleic acid (m-
RNA), catalyzed by the enzyme, RNA polymerase. Nucleotides are the
deoxy-acids of uracil (U), thymine (T), adenine (A), guanine (G), and cytosine (C).

coded in the DNA of one of the chromosomes that contain the "master
pattern" for all products the cell produces. Since DNA is part of the
chromosomes it cannot leave the nucleus. Therefore, it must transcribe
its coded pattern onto m-RNA, which exactly duplicates the pattern. The
m-RNA can and does detach from the DNA and leaves the nucleus carrying the specific pattern for synthesis of a specific protein to a protein
synthesizing machine (ribosome).

The m-RNA then feeds through the ribosome, stopping momentarily
whenever each consecutive set of three nucleotides are at the center of
the "machine" (ribosome). Every three, consecutive, adjacent nucleotides comprise a codon, which specifies a specific amino acid to be fed
into the machine for attachment end-to-end to other, similarly specified

amino acids as the m-RNA pattern has moved and continues to move through the machine.

Since free amino acids (raw materials) in the cytoplasm cannot recognize the m-RNA codons in the ribosome, transfer ribonucleic acid (t-RNA, analogous to a "factory worker,") picks up a free, specific, amino acid and feeds it into the ribosome just when and where it is required by the m-RNA pattern. The t-RNA is a relatively short RNA molecule that is folded back and bonded to itself in four places, making a three-looped molecule with a fourth nonlooped tail that bonds to an amino acid (Figure 7–12). The end of the loop opposite this tail carrying an amino acid has a linear arrangement of three adjacent nucleotides that are not cross-bonded but project out. The specific linear arrangement of these three nucleotides constitute a codon that matches and bonds only to its three complementary nucleotides in a consecutive linear arrangement on the m-RNA when that specific pattern is stopped in the center of the ribosome. This coded pattern on the t-RNA not only allows it to bring into the center of the ribosome an amino acid bonded to its opposite end, but this amino acid is specifically identified with the three-nucleotide codon. Thus, any t-RNA can recognize and pick up only the specific amino acid that corresponds to its specific mucloetide codon. Therefore, as the m-RNA passes through the ribosome, only specific amino acids determined by the respective nucleotide patterns of both m-RNA and t-RNA can be brought into the ribosome. Once t-RNA bonds to its complementary seg-

In the cytoplasm . . .

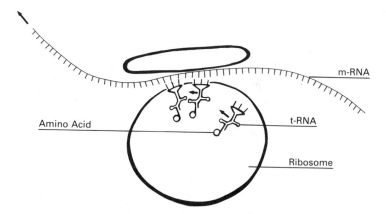

FIGURE 7–11
Messenger ribonucleic acid (m-RNA) providing the transcribed genetic code to the ribosome, the site of protein synthesis.

On the ribosome . . .

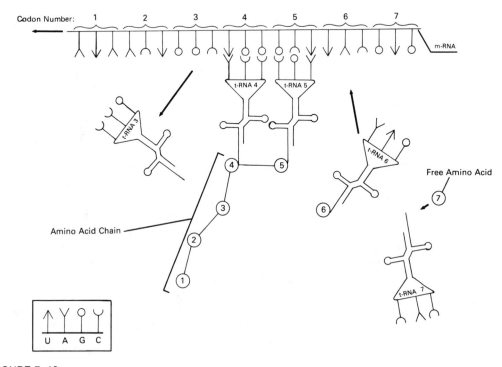

FIGURE 7–12
Transfer ribonucleic acid (t-RNA) moving a specific amino acid to the site of protein synthesis on the ribosome, determined by t-RNA's specific bonding to coded triplet nucleotides (codons) on m-RNA. Nucleotides are the deoxy-acids of uracil (U), adenine (A), guanine (G), and cytosine (C).

ment of m-RNA momentarily in the center of the ribosome, the t-RNA releases the amino acid, which immediately forms a carbon-nitrogen bond to the amino acid on the end of a growing protein chain. As the m-RNA moves through, positioning the next three consecutive nucleotides in the center of the ribosome, the t-RNA that just released its amino acid detaches from the m-RNA and moves out into the cytoplasm to find another identical amino acid.

By repeating this process as the m-RNA feeds through the ribosome—with each triplet codon of nucleotides on m-RNA in the center of the ribosome "calling for" a specific coded t-RNA which carries a specific amino acid for release at the ribosome—a specific protein molecule, originally determined by the genetic code in DNA, is synthesized on the ribosome. There are many identically coded t-RNAs in the cytoplasm for each specific amino acid. Also, as m-RNA feeds through one ribosome, it will start feeding into another ribosome, thus obtaining multiple use of its pattern. When one considers there are hundreds of ribosomes per cell and billions of cells comprising the tissues of the bird, the magnitude of this synthesis is difficult to relate to events occurring on a single ribosome. It must be realized that through this intricate process, only the type of protein determined by the genetic code in the DNA in the nucleus of a cell can be synthesized at any one time on any one ribosome in that cell.

The sum total of billions of such syntheses of many end products and their organization and assembly into growing and multiplying cells results in tissue growth and production of food products by animals. Also, it should be realized that many of the amino acids that are part of meat protein were the same identical amino acids that were in plant protein in the chicken feed. They have been unbonded by digestion, absorbed, and bonded back together in a different but specific sequence to form meat protein.

What if an essential amino acid, such as lysine, is coded for in the m-RNA feeding through the ribosomes in a protein-synthesizing cell, but there is no lysine available in the cytoplasm of the cell because there was a lysine deficiency in the chicken's diet? If the m-RNA calls for a specific amino acid and the t-RNA does not bring it to the ribosome because none is available, protein synthesis on that ribosome will stop at that point, rather than produce an imperfect protein omitting that amino acid. When this stop in protein production is projected to all ribosomes in billions of tissue cells due to a protein (amino acid) deficiency in the feed, the bird stops growing or producing eggs.

Some amino acids, if not present in protein in the diet, can be synthesized in the chicken's body from simpler compounds as long as excess nitrogen is present. These are known as "nonessential amino acids," and for poultry are: alanine, aspartic acid, glutamic acid, hydroxyproline, proline, and serine. To call these "nonessential amino acids" implies they do not need to be present in the diet since they can be synthesized. This word, *nonessential*, may be misleading and should not be interpreted in the broader sense that these amino acids are "not necessary." As explained previously, they are indeed absolutely necessary for protein synthesis to occur on the ribosomes in the body cells. Those amino acids that cannot be synthesized in the body from simpler compounds are called "essential amino acids," meaning they must be present in the diet. The essential amino acids for poultry are: arginine, cystine, glycine, histidine, isoleucine, leucine, lysine, methionine, phenylalanine, threonine, tryptophan, tyrosine, and valine. All of these are also necessary for protein synthesis to occur on the ribosomes in the cells. A protein or amino-acid deficiency in the diet will result in slow growth, poor feathering, poor egg production, and disproportionally high fat content, because protein synthesis on many of the ribosomes will stop. A deficiency of nonessential amino acids will increase the requirement for essential amino acids.

FEEDING POULTRY

In feeding poultry we are, in effect, concentrating protein (Figure 7–13). On a dry-weight basis, a poultry feed may be 29% protein, 69% carbohydrate, and 1% fat. Also on a dry-weight basis, a broiler carcass may be 77% protein, 20% fat, and negligible carbohydrate. Thus, protein has been concentrated from 29% to 77% just by passing feed into a chicken. However, this is not without cost. We haven't really manufactured any more protein than was originally in the feed and probably somewhat less, but the relative concentration of protein in the broiler is increased because the carbohydrate concentration is negligible. Where did the carbohydrate go? The carbohydrate was used to provide heat and mechanical and chemical energy for the growing broiler.

Energy is the largest, single, dietary requirement of poultry. Larger birds require more total energy than smaller ones. Thus, a relatively small

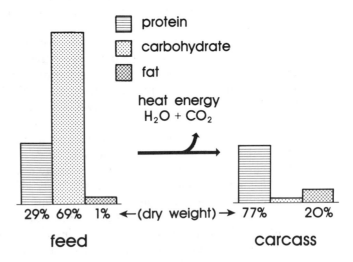

FIGURE 7–13
Concentration of protein in the conversion of poultry feed to poultry carcass.

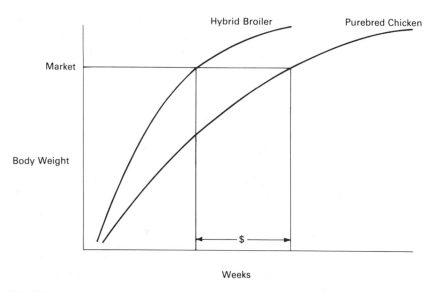

FIGURE 7-14
Growth curve of a rapidly growing hybrid broiler chicken compared with a growth curve of a slower growing heavy-type pure breed chicken.

chicken, the Single Comb White Leghorn, has been favored for commercial egg production over larger breeds. Because she requires less energy for body maintenance, she more efficiently converts feed into eggs. Unlike pure heavy breeds, the commercial broiler chicken has a rapid early growth rate, reaching market weight much sooner on less total energy (Figure 7-14). The slower growing, heavy chicken is older by the time it reaches the same market weight as the broiler and has required perhaps twice as many weeks to feed a large, slow growing body, requiring much more feed and total energy. Thus, a more efficient feed conversion is achieved by the bird with early rapid growth, which can be marketed much earlier in its life than the slow-growing bird. Feed efficiency is measured in terms of kilograms of feed required to produce a kilogram of growth or eggs produced. Since feed is the single most costly factor in producing poultry meat or eggs, feed efficiency very significantly affects the economics of poultry production.

Poultry will regulate the volume of feed they consume in order to obtain a given required quantity of energy. Therefore, the amount of feed consumed by a flock will be largely determined by the energy content of the ration. Birds will maintain growth rate and egg production within a wide range of energy levels, since the bird will adjust the amount of feed consumed to maintain a constant energy intake. However, overall efficiency of production is reduced when energy content of a feed varies outside of a relatively narrow range. Feeds too high in energy will not be consumed in large sufficient quantities to supply adequate amounts of other required nutrients. Feeds too low in energy will be consumed in larger amounts, perhaps supplying more than the optimal amounts of other nutrients. For example, protein in the feed in excess of what is required for optimal growth rate or egg production is oxidized for energy, particularly in a low energy ration. Since protein is the most expensive ingredient in the feed, much more expensive than carbohydrate, excess protein should not be supplied for energy. It is important to feed high quality protein from a variety of sources, but to feed no more protein than is needed. Excess protein is broken down in the liver to provide energy. Protein energy is about two to three times more expensive than carbohydrate energy.

Thus, poultry-feed formulation is extremely precise and must be related to the specific requirements of the bird, based on its purpose and total management. Poultry diets vary widely, as explained, but generally more protein is required in the diet of a growing bird than in an adult bird's and a relatively large amount of protein is required for laying hens at maximum rate of production. Also, laying hens will require more calcium in the feed than growing birds. They need it for egg-shell production. Environmental factors, particularly temperature, will affect the optimal amount of energy required in a feed: more energy being required at low temperature. Also, calcium may need to be increased in a diet for laying birds kept at a high temperature for prolonged periods. Many other factors also dictate what exact feed formulation should be used for maximum efficiency. In no way is it acceptable to just supply plenty of everything and hope for the best. One simply cannot afford a haphazard approach to feeding poultry. Good, sound technical and scientific advice is required today to feed poultry for efficient food production.

Nutrients are supplied by the ingredients of the poultry ration. Ingredients vary in their nutrient content as well as in the availability of the nutrients to the bird. Feed ingredients may be evaluated to determine their potential usefulness in a poultry feed. Any ingredient may be analyzed to determine its content (percent) of crude protein, crude fiber, nitrogen-free extract, crude fat, ash, and moisture. A nutrient composition table (Appendix 4) lists the average quantity of the nutrients in each of a number of feed ingredients. If you have the ingredients and their percentage concentrations in a feed, it is possible to calculate the nutrient composition of the feed using values obtained from a nutrient composition table. Thus, a feed can be characterized and evaluated on chemical composition basis. However, chemical analysis of poultry feed ingredients will not accurately predict the usefulness of the nutrients to the bird.

Therefore, feeding experiments may be conducted to determine the digestibility and usefulness of an ingredient for the purpose of supplying the nutrients determined by chemical analysis.

Metabolizable energy is a feed ingredient characteristic that provides a more meaningful measure of the feeding value of the ingredient for poultry than a measurement of its digestible nutrients. Any organic feed ingredient has a characteristic total or gross energy level that can be measured in kilocalories (Figure 7–15). This is the ''combustible (gross) energy'' or that energy released and measured when the ingredient is burned in a calorimeter. For any given level of feed intake by a bird, the total gross energy can be determined (Figure 7–15). Not all of this energy, however, is available to the bird for production. A considerable amount of energy is lost in the feces, and when this is subtracted from the gross energy of a given intake of feed, what is left is called ''digestible energy.'' Part of this digestible energy is also unavailable for the bird's use and is lost in the urinary wastes. This leaves what is known as ''metabolizable energy,'' which is an estimate of the feed ingredient's useful energy. Generally a feed ingredient with a high metabolizable energy value will be a highly digestible material. However, not all metabolizable energy of a complete feed is available for production of meat or eggs. A considerable amount of metabolizable energy may be lost or used in the form of heat. This energy loss, which depends on the environment and management, leaves the bird a ''net energy'' that is available for work and body main-

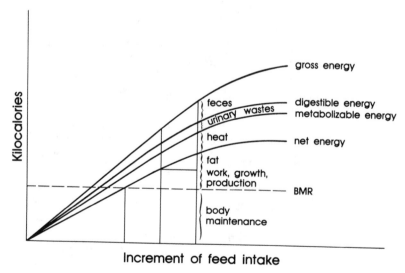

FIGURE 7–15
Energy utilization in poultry based on increment of feed intake.

tenance. From this net energy value, the "basal metabolic rate (BMR) energy" is subtracted, leaving the amount of energy that is truly available for production of body tissue such as meat and eggs. The BMR is constant for any individual bird at a given age and does not vary with feed intake. It is the energy required for the bird to just maintain life without doing any work or production. The amount of energy truly available for production of meat and eggs will be further decreased if the bird is required to do other forms of work, such as walk, run, fly, or fight. Therefore, commercial poultry should be provided comfortable confinement and easily accessible feed and water, and should not be allowed excessive stress or exercise. When these conditions are provided, most of the available energy from the feed can go into efficient production of meat or eggs. If the feed increment is increased beyond the bird's capability for production or other work, the extra available energy will be converted into fat and stored in the body, thus decreasing the efficiency of feed conversion to human food.

Since feed constitutes a major cost of poultry production, correct formulating and mixing of poultry diets has great economic significance. For example, the requirements of the growing bird will change as it grows, and its requirements differ significantly from those of the mature laying hen. Eggs utilized for reproduction have different nutrient requirements than those produced for human food. Various types of poultry require different levels of nutrients. The growing turkey, for example, requires a higher level of protein than does the growing chicken during specific periods of growth.

Least cost formulation of poultry diets is extremely important in order to meet the competitive market for poultry products. Least cost diets are formulated to provide all necessary nutrients from ingredients available at the lowest possible price. These diets may be computer formulated, with alternative ingredient sources considered as their prices fluctuate and substitutions made within the nutrient limitations set. Performance must be related to cost, and frequently cost is tempered by other factors and various limitations which determine the amount of an ingredient used in a specific diet. Diets may be formulated to meet the requirements of the average bird or perhaps the top one-third or three-quarters of the flock in order to obtain efficient conversion of feed to the desired product (meat, eggs, and reproduction). Maximum efficiency in conversion of feed to product is the major objective to effectively compete in marketing poultry. Maintaining disease resistance and absence of nutritional deficiency symptoms are also important objectives; they usually will be achieved if the major objective is accomplished.

In formulating and mixing a diet for a small home poultry flock, the same basic considerations of nutrition and economics must be carefully evaluated as in the large commercial flock. Factors such as production objectives, age of birds, climate, and season of the year must be considered. The nutritional value of ingredients and their relative costs are important in determining dietary goals. In addition, one of the most important factors to consider in formulating a diet is the ingredient availability. Location of production, required transportation, and year-round accessibility are necessary to consider since poultry diets should undergo minimal change throughout a cycle of growth or egg production. Dietary changes, when made, should be gradual to minimize adverse adjustment effects.

Mixing of feed for the small home poultry flock is generally not feasible because of the rather complex nature of the poultry diet. To properly prepare a finished poultry feed, an understanding of feed mixing procedures is required and an appreciation of the need for accuracy is necessary. However, the home farm may have grains available that can be utilized in feeding poultry for either eggs or meat. These grains may be mixed with a concentrate purchased from a local feed dealer. Even in these situations, the economics may not justify mixing your own finished feed or even having a small poultry flock. However, the convenience and satisfaction of having a home poultry flock may make the added expenditure of time and money justifiable. Diets may be formulated from grains to supply carbohydrate; a plant protein supplement, such as soybean oil meal, cottonseed meal, or linseed meal; some form of animal protein, such as skim milk, meat scrap, or fish meal; and a pre-prepared mixture to supply necessary minerals and vitamins.

Large commercial poultry operations frequently mix their own feed to control consistency, uniformity, and composition of the diet and to assure quality and least cost. Smaller commercial poultry farms, however, may purchase ready-mixed feeds providing other desired advantages. For example, the financing and technical advising service of a large feed company can be a valuable asset. Some large feed mills will underwrite poultry production units as a means of assuring mill operation at capacity and as a means of distributing the economic pressures of costs and profits.

Feed formulation requires ingredient quality and consistency. Large feed mills will test ingredients to determine their quality before using them in the diet. For example, moisture is of great importance because of its effect on ingredient weight and the proportion of other nutrients contained in a particular feedstuff. A certain amount of water is contained in most ingredients. However, since water is one of the least expensive nutrients it should not be derived from a relatively high priced ingredient. Furthermore, excess water may shorten storage life of the ingredient and enhance spoilage and mold growth. Protein content of soybean-oil meal may only vary a fraction of a percent. However, when soybean-oil meal is purchased on a carload basis, this fraction of a percent may result in a significant economic advantage or disadvantage to the purchaser. Ingredient purchase, therefore, should be based upon a guaranteed analysis and priced accordingly.

Examples of specific poultry diets are shown in Appendix 5. They illustrate the variability in formulation of the various uses of feeds.

CHAPTER 8

MANAGEMENT FOR DISEASE CONTROL

Many diseases can occur among the various types of poultry. Brief descriptions are presented for some of the major problems most commonly encountered throughout the world. Within the total management of the birds, sanitation and disease prevention are fundamental. A healthy flock is attained through a total disease control program. It is important to recognize disease problems early and immediately respond with knowledgeable timing and treatment, which may necessitate seeking immediate professional advice.

Disease may be defined as a deviation from the norm. Some diseases may be highly infectious and spread from bird to bird, and other problems classified as disease may not be transmitted at all. Nutritional disorders are sometimes referred to as diseases; deviations from the normal condition to be sure, but many birds may display deficiency symptoms, and these symptoms are not transmitted from bird to bird. As birds have been housed and subjected to high density management, many respiratory diseases have become serious problems. Inadequate ventilation and close bird to bird contact have enhanced transmission of respiratory diseases.

Microorganisms may enter a bird's body through a number of common pathways. The skin, eyes, mouth, and nasal passages leading to the respiratory and digestive systems are major pathways by which disease organisms enter the body. Pathogenic microorganisms are bacteria, viruses, protozoa, parasites (both internal and external), and fungi. Many of these microorganisms are generally resistant to the environment and multiply rapidly on a warm, moist substrate, particularly living tissue. Microorganisms are not only transmitted from bird to bird but on equipment, shoes, and clothing of humans and on vehicles, feed, water, air, and in the litter. Air is a very common transmitter when it contains dust particles on which bacteria and viruses are carried. Buildings are especially well-suited for harboring lice and mites as well as many other disease microorganisms. The floor and the floor materials are excellent places for multiplication of pathogenic microorganisms. Most broiler and turkey buildings have dirt floors, and egg-laying houses may have a solid floor of concrete or asphalt.

Initial design of poultry houses should consider construction features that will allow thorough cleaning and adequate maintenance of sanitation. Installation of the watering system should provide a medication dispenser that will provide accurate and prompt treatment of birds through the water when properly used. When birds are ill, they will frequently drink water when they will not eat.

Disease control is a challenge in high density poultry housing, and prevention must be continuously practiced to minimize potential for infection. Preventive measures are best accomplished through a well-planned and well-managed sanitation program. A vaccination program should be designed to provide protection from specific diseases known to be prevalent. A vaccination schedule should be employed along with a continuing sanitation program, and applied specifically to the requirements of the management program; in no way should vaccination be considered a substitute for a well planned management program.

DISEASES

Many terms are used in conjunction with the description of disease and associated problems. For example, disease may be defined as any deviation from the normal state of well-being whether it be a slight ailment or one endangering life, and therefore is not necessarily something that can be transmitted from bird to bird. Chronic diseases are of long duration, but acute disease outbreaks are of short duration. The commonly used term, *infection*, refers to the invasion of the tissue by microorganisms; these microorganisms grow and produce toxins or otherwise injure the body tissues and organs. These microorganisms are called pathogenic microorganisms, which means they have the ability to cause infection and disease. When the term *immunity* is used, the reference is to the power of the animal to resist and overcome infection. Immunity may be initiated by a vaccine—a suspension of disease-producing microorganisms produced in the laboratory and administered to the bird before the disease is picked up from other uncontrolled sources.

Agents of Disease

1. Viruses are a common cause of poultry diseases. They are easily transmitted through the air or by contaminated feed, equipment, and clothing. The microorganisms are extremely small in comparison to other pathogens and can replicate only inside living cells. They are highly resistant to sanitizing and cleaning agents and thus difficult to eliminate.

2. Bacteria are microscopic one-celled microorganisms. They cause many poultry diseases but may be readily controlled by the proper use of antibiotics. There are specific antibiotics that are effective against specific types of bacteria. Broad-spectrum antibiotics may be effective against a number of types of microorganisms. Careful use of antibiotics is emphasized since bacteria will develop immunity to the antibiotic, diminishing its effectiveness over a period of time. (Bacteria are easily spread in many ways; very careful sanitary procedures must always be followed.)

3. Protozoa are microscopic single-celled animals that are generally highly resistant to disinfectants and that may live for long periods of time in the ground. They multiply rapidly in the gut, producing tissue damage and toxins detrimental to the well-being of the host.

4. Parasites live off of the host and are either external or internal. They are multicellular, and they frequently cause the host's death because they take products essential to the welfare of the body. They may exist for long periods of time away from the host and may be spread easily from bird to bird or from equipment, soil, litter, buildings, and human clothing. They grow rapidly in warm, moist conditions, but are highly resistant to dry, cold environments too.

5. Fungi are low forms of multicellular plants, which are prevalent in warm, moist conditions. They are prevalent in feeds. Grains and other products that are not heated during processing are frequently a major source of fungi.

Most diseases are easily transmitted through direct contact with other birds or by contact with contaminated quarters and equipment. They are spread through litter and soil, feed and water, by wild birds, and attendants and visitors. Disease microorganisms usually gain entrance into the body through the nose, mouth, eyes, skin, cloaca, or through the egg.

Viral Diseases

Marek's disease may affect chickens at ages of about 6–16 weeks of age. In general, pathologists accept this disorder to be caused by one or more herpes viruses. Chickens appear to be most susceptible to contact infection during the early life, hatching and brooding periods; however, death may not occur until late in the growing period or at laying age. Many birds will die within a few weeks after becoming infected, and mortality will continue through the lifetime of the flock. There is no known treatment, but in recent years an effective vaccine has been developed. It must be administered immediately after hatchings before the birds leave the hatchery. Lameness or weakness of one or both legs is the major symptom, and diseased birds may lie paralyzed with one leg stretched backward and the other leg forward.

Lymphoid leukosis, sometimes known as big liver disease or visceral lymphomatosis, is a virus-caused disease of semimature or mature chickens. The disease is characterized by a gradual onset of persistant low mortality among the flock. Tumors may be present, and the birds are emaciated or unthrifty with pale combs and wattles. Thickening of the long bones of the legs and especially the shanks may be observed. There is no treatment; the best control at present is to obtain stock that has been genetically bred to have resistance to the viruses.

Gumboro disease or infectious bursal disease (IBD) is an acute, contagious, viral disease of chickens that causes severe kidney damage. It is highly infectious and spreads by many of the common routes. Ruffled feathers, droopiness, trembling, and a drop in feed consumption, accompanied by a white or greenish diarrhea, are major symptoms. Kidneys are pale, swollen, and are filled with urates (a paste-like material). There is no treatment, but a vaccine to prevent the disease is available. Most outbreaks occur at an early age, three to six, thus vaccination at hatching time is generally recommended. The most effective treatment is good husbandry to reduce the severity of the disease.

Chronic respiratory disease (CRD) is caused by *Mycoplasma gallisepticum*, a bacterium lacking a rigid cell wall. There are two species of *Mycoplasma, M. gallisepticum* and *M. synoviae*, that affect all ages of chickens and turkeys. In turkeys, they cause infectious sinusitis and synovitis, respectively. If the breeder hen carries the microorganism, it may be transmitted to the chick through the egg, but it can also be transmitted by direct contact with other birds that are infected and by contaminated equipment or through dust. Frequently, the symptoms are similar to other respiratory diseases—the primary signs being swollen face and head, labored breathing, and weakness. Accumulation of a yellow, cheesy exudate in the air sacs, lungs, or heart sac may be observed. No single drug has been found effective in all cases. Antibiotics and sulfonamides may prevent some serious secondary infections and will help maintain the appetite, which assists the bird in fighting off the infection. There is no satisfactory vaccine, and good preventive management is the best means of control. Some foundation breeder companies maintain *Mycoplasma*-free breeder stock enabling hatcheries to sell *Mycoplasma*-free chicks.

Epidemic tremor (avian encephalomyelitis) in chickens is characterized by nervous symptoms caused by a virus infection. Mortality may occur in chicks less than three to four weeks of age, but not in laying hens. Droopy, dull, and sleepy signs in young birds, accompanied by partial-to-complete leg weakness and paralysis may be seen. A severe drop in egg production is the most obvious sign in outbreaks among laying hens; there are no obvious postmortem lesions. No specific treatment exists at this time. Vaccination of pullet chicks to be used as breeders is recommended at the ages of 8 and 16 weeks.

Fowl pox is a viral disease commonly seen among chickens and turkeys. Lesions appear on the unfeathered skin areas as well as the upper respiratory tract and digestive tract. A large DNA poxvirus is the causative agent. Pox is spread by biting insects such as mosquitoes and by contact with infected birds; poxvirus is resistant to environmental conditions and may persist for many months. Pox can be prevented by vaccination during the early growth period; it is best to vaccinate pullets well before egg production commences. The vaccine used is a pigeon pox preparation for chickens, and turkeys are usually vaccinated with fowlpox vaccine. Chickens are usually vaccinated using the wing web method, and turkeys are vaccinated through the use of a thigh-stick method at two to three months of age.

Enteritis of chickens and turkeys is a viral disease characterized by a sudden onset of bloody droppings, depression, and frequently high mortality. The virus is transmitted by many types of wild birds and from ingestion of feces of infected individuals. Sudden death is usually the first sign, and a concurrent drop in feed and water consumption may be noted. The birds that die may be well-fleshed with small hemorrhages appearing at various sites such as the breast, thigh muscles, on the heart and liver, and on the gizzard. There is no treatment, therefore good care and careful management are most important to minimize losses.

Infectious bronchitis (IB) among chickens is an acute, highly contagious, virus-caused respiratory disease. The disease occurs widely in all countries where chickens are raised. The disease may occur among growing birds, broilers most frequently, and less often among laying hens. Among baby chicks, coughing, sneezing, and other signs of respiratory distress may be observed. There may be weakness, depression, and huddling near the heat source. Mortality is quite low. Among laying chickens similar symptoms are observed, accompanied by a drop in egg production (20%–50%). Modified virus vaccines are used in young chickens for prevention; in the event of an outbreak there is no treatment other than careful management, although sometimes antibiotics are administered to control secondary infections from other bacteria.

Infectious laryngotracheitis (LT) is an acute viral infection of chickens characterized by marked respiratory problems, coughing, sneezing, and gasping. Birds may be immunized prior to acquiring the disease, but it should be done only if the disease has been previously observed in the area. Birds should be at least four weeks old when vaccinated. A number of vaccination techniques are acceptable, such as the eye-drop method and the wing-web technique.

Avian influenza is a viral disease that affects the respiratory and nervous systems. Sometimes referred to as "fowl plague," it occurs throughout the world and is a major problem of the world's poultry industry. In most outbreaks the signs are predominantly those of a respiratory disease—coughing, sneezing, and labored breathing; however, there may also be diarrhea, edema of the head and face, or/and nervous disorders. Mortality may be highly variable, and outbreaks in laying birds will be accompanied by reduced egg production. Frequently those birds that are still laying or have recovered produce abnormal egg shells. There is no effective treatment, but good husbandry, proper nutrition, and broad-spectrum antibiotics may assist to reduce the detrimental effects of secondary invaders.

Newcastle disease infects chickens, turkeys, and many other wild and domesticated birds. It is caused by a virus. The birds may exhibit respiratory distress, diarrhea, and paralysis prior to death. Among laying birds an abrupt drop in egg production may occur with little or no mortality. The disease may be controlled through the use of a carefully planned vaccination program. Exotic Newcastle is similar in its effect on the birds; however, mortality is very high. This disease is usually introduced by exotic birds—parrots, lovebirds, and many illegally introduced birds. Treatment of the disease is of no value, and to date the best method of control has been complete depopulation of the birds in an infected area.

Bacterial Diseases

Pullorum disease or bacillary white diarrhea (*Salmonella pullorum*) was at one time one of the most serious diseases of young chickens in the United States. It is still a very serious problem in many countries throughout the world. It provides an excellent example of a disease that at one time seriously threatened the industry, but that is now very well-controlled although not eliminated completely, a fact that must be remembered. The causative agent, *Salmonella pullorum*, may be carried by rodents, lizards, and many other cold-blooded animals, as well as by all types of wild birds and poultry. It is transmitted by the hen to her chicks (Figure 8–1) through the egg, as well as by bird contact, and, in the hatchery, by infected down from chicks carrying the organism. High mortality among chicks results, and the birds that recover may become carriers and a source of further infection. Best control has been through blood testing of the breeder flock and disposal of the "reactors." The National Poultry Improvement Plan provides an effective means of control through the application of systematic testing and breeder flock and hatchery inspection. Mortality in young birds can be controlled by application of furazolidone, sulfa drugs, or broad-spectrum antibiotics. In addition, good husbandry practices can be highly effective.

Fowl typhoid is caused by a bacterium, *Salmonella gallinarum*, which is spread by equipment, feed, people, and rats and can be transmitted from hen to chick through the egg. This disease is similar in many ways to pullorum disease, and the blood-test technique is effective when utilizing an antigen to test for both pullorum and typhoid. Common symptoms of listlessness and sudden death are observed, and acute outbreaks occur in young birds as well as in mature birds. Control is similar to that

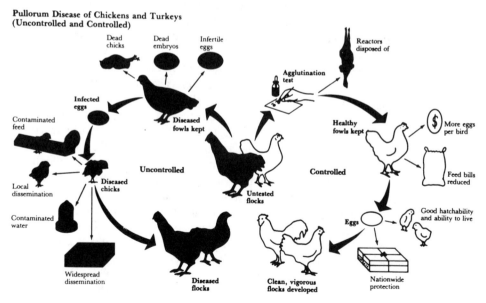

Pullorum Disease of Chickens and Turkeys
(Uncontrolled and Controlled)

FIGURE 8–1

Cycle of transmission of *Salmonella pullorum* in poultry (pullorum disease). (Courtesy of National Poultry Improvement Place.)

used for pullorum disease and is accomplished under National Poultry Improvement Plan procedures.

Fowl cholera is a highly infectious, bacterial disease of chickens, turkeys, waterfowl, and other birds, with most outbreaks occurring in growing and adult birds. Acute and chronic forms of the disease can be identified, with death of apparently healthy birds occurring suddenly. In the chronic form, symptoms are swollen combs and wattles that may also exhibit a dark bluish color. Infected birds are listless, sleepy, and feverish, sitting with their heads drawn to the body or turned and resting on their wings. Birds will respond to medication, but with limited success, and those that recover may become carriers. Prevention may be accomplished in part through the administration of a bacterin under the skin of the neck between 12 and 16 weeks of age or through administrations of a live "vaccine" strain of *Pasteurella multocide* in the drinking water.

Infections caused by *Escherichia coli* are becoming more and more prevalent among all poultry. This microorganism is widely spread in nature and is a normal, permanent inhabitant of the lower intestines of all animals, including man. However, when sufficiently large numbers are present, infections occur that result in 2%–10% mortality among young birds, frequently at an age of seven to nine weeks. Conditions favorable to the rapid multiplication of this microorganism must be avoided. An outbreak of *E. coli* infection indicates poor sanitary conditions exist, so a great deal of care should be exercised to maintain a high level of sanitation. Stressful conditions frequently result in an outbreak where marginal levels of the microorganism may be present. Adequate ventilation without excessive dry, dusty conditions, avoidance of overcrowding, and clean and regularly disinfected waterers are important factors in maintaining a favorable environment for the bird to maintain good health.

Botulism is caused by the ingestion of toxins produced by *Clostridium botulinum*. It occurs frequently in the warmer months in chickens, waterfowl, turkeys, and domesticated pheasants. Birds show drowsiness, weakness, and loss of control of the legs, wings, and neck, which results in death. Good management is necessary to prevent ingestion of spoiled feed materials, decaying carcasses, decaying vegetation, and certain beetles in the litter. An antitoxin is available for certain forms, and the use of selenium and antibiotics has been found effective. It is important that the birds have access to fresh, clean, nonalkaline water. Careful disposal of dead birds must be done to avoid access to all other animals.

Erysipelas is an acute disease primarily of turkeys. It is one of the very few diseases that may be contracted by humans through direct transmission of body fluids, including blood, into an open wound. Outbreaks may be characterized with sudden mortality among a few birds and a swollen snood or irregular, dark red skin lesions on the caruncle, face, or head of turkeys. Infected flocks may be treated with penicillin and simultaneously inoculated with erysipelas bacterin. Tetracyclines can be added to the feed for long-term treatment while immunization is developed in the flock. Workers in processing plants may contract the disease from infected birds and first observe infection, swelling, and soreness of fingers, hands, and arms as the disease progresses. Immediate medical attention is necessary as death can occur.

Infectious coryza (roup) is characterized in chickens by swelling of the face, sneezing, and discharge from the nasal passages and eyes. All ages are susceptible, although birds that are half grown or older are most frequently infected. Management practices for control may require depopulation to eliminate all carrier birds followed by thorough cleaning and disinfecting of the house. A bacterin can be used to immunize birds in areas with a history of high infection. Sulfonamides and antibiotics may be effectively used to treat outbreaks.

Paratyphoid infection is an acute or chronic disease of poultry and may be caused by one of the many species of *Salmonella*. Signs of the disease are usually seen in young birds up to about seven weeks of age. Profuse diarrhea followed by dehydration, build up of feces (pasting) around the vent, drooping wings, shivering around the heat source, and death are the major symptoms observed. To control the disease young birds should be obtained from breeder stock known to be free of the infection. Strict sanitation management measures must be followed for all birds through thorough cleaning and disinfecting of premises and equipment. Treatment of infected birds with antibiotics and other drugs is reasonably effective.

Ulcerative enteritis, sometimes referred to as quail disease, may affect all poultry and is spread primarily through the droppings. The disease is highly contagious. The symptoms of the disease are similar to coccidiosis and include listlessness, humped-up appearance, retracted neck, drooping wings, partially closed eyes, ruffled feathers, diarrhea, anemia, and bloody feces. Mortality may occur. Intestinal ulcerations and distinctive colorful lesions of the liver characterize the disease. Sound management and selection of disease-free stock are of prime importance. Old birds should be kept separate from young stock, a good practice in control of all diseases. Most of the antibiotics are effective at low levels for control and at high levels for treatment.

Protozoan Diseases

One of the oldest known and most destructive diseases of poultry is a protozoan infection known as coccidiosis. There are at least nine species of the genus *Eimeria* that infect chickens and seven others that infect turkeys. The same species of coccidia found in chickens are not found in turkeys or other animals; coccidia are host specific. Coccidiosis commonly occurs in two forms: cecal where it may be in the acute form or intestinal where it is frequently a chronic infection. Young birds appear to be affected most severely, and those that recover infrequently suffer severe damage to the lining of the intestine, with a resulting loss in the ability to absorb nutrients. Thus they become culls in the laying house. Bloody droppings as well as paleness of the head, loss of appetite and weight, and occasional diarrhea, and a general unthrifty appearance are common symptoms of the infection. Although older birds may not display the symptoms to the extent that younger birds do, egg production among layers is substantially reduced. Vaccinations are effective to control the disease although the economics of this procedure is questionable and excellent management is essential to its success. Drugs for treatment or control are effective, and most broilers are produced with a level of medication which is successful for the prevention of an outbreak under good management conditions. Damp litter and dampness around feeders and waterers are conducive to the multiplication and spread of the organism.

Histomoniasis, or blackhead, severely affects turkeys and has also been reported in chickens, pheasants, partridges, and other birds. The etiological agent is the protozoan, *Histomonas meleagridis,* carried by chickens infested with cecal worms. It is characterized by listlessness, drooping wings, and yellow (sulfur colored) feces. Head parts may be black. The bird may be emaciated, and there may be high mortality. Medication to prevent outbreaks in turkeys has proven to be quite effective. In addition, several drugs are available for treatment, and good management of turkey premises is of the utmost importance in controlling the spread of this microorganism even in the absence of carrier chickens in close proximity to turkeys.

Parasitic Diseases

Parasites include internal as well as external parasites. The external fall into two major categories, lice and mites. Lice are most prevalent. They are flat, wingless, brownish-yellow insects that move very rapidly. There are a number of different types. The chicken body louse, the shaft louse, the chicken head louse, and the wing louse all are adapted to specific conditions in the area of their existence. They act as a nuisance to the bird, causing constant irritation and reducing the normal performance of the bird. Northern fowl mites suck blood and resemble the red mite in appearance. Eggs are clustered at the base of feathers. Mites are vicious blood suckers that cause scabs to form on the skin, thus impairing the appearance of the dressed carcass. Sprays and dusts are effective against the parasites, but must be applied so as not to contaminate feed and water. Frequent examination of chickens will aid in preventing serious trouble; also, good nutrition and careful management to avoid undue stress will help prevent infection.

Worms are internal parasites. Worms are prevalent in warm climates where extended periods of cold, dry weather are not common. Worms, which exist in a number of forms, compete with the bird for the digested nutrients in the gut. Large numbers in the intestine cause irritation and inflamed and thickened walls. Good sanitation and management practices are necessary for the control of both external and internal parasites, although the parasites differ somewhat in their mode of infection. Specific drugs are required for each specific type of worm, and frequently additional nutrients may be recommended in order to compensate for the loss of nutrients to the worms.

Fungal Diseases

Mold and fungal diseases generally invade the respiratory system and the upper digestive tract. Aspergillosis, a disease of chicks and poults caused by a fungus, is characterized by respiratory symptoms and lesions in the lungs and air sacs. The use of moldy litter and feed should be avoided, and the birds should be kept in good condition through proper diet and dry, clean, uncrowded housing. Feed can be a major source of these organisms, and careful monitoring of ingredients (grain) is highly recommended.

MISCELLANEOUS DISEASE PROBLEMS

Dissecting aneurysm, or aortic rupture, is a fatal disease of turkeys but is less frequently observed in chickens. It is most frequently observed in large toms at puberty and appears to be associated with genetic susceptibility. Large masses of blood are observed in the dead birds' abdominal cavity due to rupture of a major blood vessel. Frequently this problem is observed in birds at times when they are handled for marketing or artificial insemination. Overfeeding protein and fats at these times should be avoided. There is no treatment although Reserpine has been used to lower blood pressure in older birds and lessen the occurrence of this stress-related problem.

Perosis, or slipped tendon, is a deformity frequently involving young chickens, turkeys, and gamebirds. It is a most frequent problem when birds are reared on wire or slat floors and is associated with overcrowding.

The hock is flattened, widened, and enlarged. Prevention by feeding an adequate diet is most effective; however, frequently the problem is observed among the faster growing, larger individuals of a flock. Prompt supplementation of the diet with manganese, choline, and the B-complex vitamins may minimize the outbreak.

Rickets is caused by a nutritional deficiency: the lack of the proper balance of calcium, phosphorus, and vitamin D_3. Most frequently, the use of vitamin D_2 rather than D_3 is the cause of the problem; however, high levels of calcium may cause an imbalance of phosphorus and vitamin D_3. Young growing birds exhibit a lame, stiff-legged gait and retarded growth. Birds often rest in a squatting position and may exhibit enlarged hocks. Laying birds drop in egg production and lay thin-shelled and soft-shelled eggs, and may also get down on their hocks and become paralyzed. Soft rubbery bones and beading of the ribs are frequently observed, and the beak becomes soft and rubbery. A balanced ration eliminating possible deficiencies is the best control or treatment.

Vitamin A deficiency usually occurs in young birds up to seven weeks of age through cessation of growth; birds exhibit drowsiness, combs and wattles may be pale, eyelids become inflamed and swell, and a cheesy exudate may accumulate under the lids of survivors. Decreased egg production among layers, inflammation of the eyes with cheesy exudate and symptoms of conditions associated with "a cold" are frequently reported. Prevention and treatment are accomplished by feeding diets with adequate levels of vitamin A supplied through feedstuffs high in vitamin A or by adding a synthetic form of the vitamin.

Vitamin E deficiency is exhibited as three possible disorders: (1) encephalomoslacia (crazy chick disease), (2) exudative diathesis, and (3) muscular dystrophy. Vitamin E deficiency is most frequently observed in young poultry and may be seen in diets of flocks fed high levels of fat. Loss of balance, sudden prostration, and problems of locomotion may be observed in the various forms. The use of stabilized fats in the feed is an important means of control as well as adequate levels of vitamin E (10,000 units per ton of feed). Treatment with oral administration of 300 IU of vitamin E per bird may be effective depending upon the form of the deficiency.

Bluecomb disease, pullet disease, and summer disease are a few terms applied to a condition in chickens that primarily occurs in pullets as they commence egg production. This problem appears to be associated with stressful conditions and is characterized by loss of appetite, depression, watery diarrhea, bluish appearance of comb and wattles, decreased egg production, dehydration, and some mortality. Proper sanitation and good husbandry practices should reduce the potential for this problem to develop and treatment varies from use of antibiotics to providing adequate supplies of clean, fresh feed and water.

OTHER ABNORMAL CONDITIONS

Breast blisters are generally caused by an irritant that produces a large, blister-like lesion on the keel bone area of the breast. This problem appears most frequently on birds reared in cages or on slat floors and is undesirable because it causes the carcass to be downgraded at the time of slaughter. As a result, very few broilers have been successfully reared in cages. It is generally not treatable; the best procedure for dealing with it is to control management and eliminate the cause.

Bumblefoot is a food pad infection caused by bruising from irritants in the litter; hard or sharp surfaces on the floor area will also induce the condition. The treatment should include lancing the infected area and thoroughly cleaning it with warm salt water and iodine. The foot must be kept clean and alowed to drain.

Cage layer fatigue is the name given to a condition in layers in which bones become very brittle. It may also be associated with fatty livers. There is evidence that a calcium-phosphorus imbalance may be associated with the condition (there also may be a need for specific vitamin supplementation.) When the bird is removed from the cage the condition frequently corrects.

Pendulous crop is an enlargement of the crop in both chickens and turkeys. It commonly appears under conditions of poor management where birds are not fed or watered regularly, especially during hot weather. Evidence of a genetic tendency toward weak crop muscles and physical obstructions in the upper digestive system will also increase the occurrence of the problem. The best cure is to eliminate the cause through improved management practices. The treatment involves cleaning the crop thoroughly and removing it through a surgical procedure, since once the muscles in the crop wall are stretched there is very little chance that they will retain their ability to function properly and the condition will persist.

Omphalitis is a condition usually observed in young poultry during the first week following hatching. This is an infection of the naval area and abdomen caused by poor sanitary conditions during hatching. Antibiotics may be effective in minimizing the growth of the infection in the chicks, but high mortality may be expected.

Cannibalism usually starts among young chicks with toe or tail picking and feather pulling. Vent picking in older birds is an added form and is usually prevalent among birds commencing to lay eggs when prolapse may occur and the bright red tissue attracts other birds to pick at the area. Prolapse, or blow out, is characterized by eversion of the oviduct through the vent, a normal process during laying. Prolapse occurs when the tissue does not retract to its normal position. If vent picking becomes a habit, birds will literally eat one another alive. High mortality and a loss of growth or egg production may occur. There are many treatments recommended, including the use of blinders, but the most effective is debeaking. Cannibalism is frequently brought about by poor management, excess light, overcrowding, overheating, or other stressful conditions. There are many theories covering a host of causes that should not be ignored, and that are paralleled by treatments of equal number.

Internal laying is caused by ova being deposited in the body cavity instead of passing through the oviduct to produce hard-shelled eggs. Since the body cavity does not have the capacity to absorb these ova as rapidly as they may occur, the body cavity soon fills with unabsorbed yolk material, the bird's abdomen descends very close to the ground, and the bird acquires a duck-like stance. Affected birds should be euthanized.

DISEASE PREVENTION AND CONTROL

One major step in the control of disease is proper personnel management. Visitors should be prohibited or limited to an isolated area of the premises. It is a natural desire to wish to show visitors a successful poultry operation. Owners and managers are usually proud of their units and like to show off the results of their efforts, new innovations, designs, and management techniques. Visits to units in other towns or other states provide a means of learning and exchanging information and good fellowship. However, that may also lead to transmission of microorganisms. Microorganisms present under a particular set of environmental conditions may not produce an active disease outbreak because of the biological balance that exists, but in a different and new environment there may exist conditions favorable to the rapid multiplication of these same microorganisms. Microorganisms may be transmitted on boots, shoes, clothing, and hair of visitors, and by the same route, visitors can easily pick up disease microorganisms to take home to their flocks. Likewise, your employees can transmit disease to your flock from contact with their own birds or a neighbor's small flock. Because your employees work on a poultry farm, they may be considered by some as experts and may be called upon for advice and asked to observe diseased flocks. Once exposed to other flocks, they will endanger your flocks as they are potential carriers of disease. It is best to discourage all employees from keeping any kind of poultry, particularly pet house birds. Offering an employee free eggs and meat sometimes is an excellent incentive to discourage employees from keeping a home flock of their own.

Within the poultry operation itself, movement of employees outside of their area of work responsibility should be restricted. For example, brooder house personnel should never move into the laying units or into other areas of the production unit. Some large units have used color-coded clothes as a means of identifying employees so those that wander may be easily detected. One of the best control measures for transmission of disease by visitors as well as employees is a strict sanitation program that starts with a shower and a change of clothes for each person entering the premises or area of work. This should include a head cover and sanitized boots that are maintained in the work area. Strict enforcement of such regulations is one of the first lines of defense in a disease-control program.

Trucks and automobiles are another means of transmitting microorganisms. A drive-through sanitizing bath for the wheels and undercarriage of a vehicle that utilizes a good sanitizing agent and necessitates at least one full rotation of the wheels, preferably to the hub caps, and a spray wash of the body of the vehicle is highly recommended. The driver should not leave the vehicle; all operations required from outside the truck should be performed by an employee of the poultry unit. Salespeople as well as service personnel that travel among farms must follow the same procedures as visitors if they are to enter the poultry units. If they are present for the purpose of discussion only, they should use a disinfectant foot bath for shoes and their visit should be limited to an office or room not commonly utilized by farm employees having contact with the birds.

A strict sanitary code as outlined should be closely adhered to with no exceptions. Although people may express their impatience and disagreement with such strict procedures, a well-planned sanitation program that is followed will prevent outbreaks of disease that could have a devastating effect on an otherwise successful business.

Outbreaks of disease may be attributed in general to three major factors (Figure 8–2) which interact: (1) degree of resistance of the bird, (2) numbers of microorganisms present, and (3) virulence of the microorganisms. Resistance of the bird is established through a vaccination program and/or natural exposure to pathogens as well as through good nutrition and management factors favorable to the well-being of the birds. Factors such as overcrowding, overheating, and other stressful situations may reduce the resistance of the birds. An outbreak of one disease may sufficiently reduce the resistance of the birds to allow introduction of a second infection more serious than the first. An example exists in virus

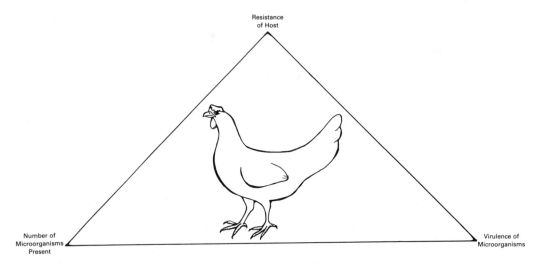

Resistance
of Host

Number of
Microorganisms
Present

Virulence of
Microorganisms

FIGURE 8–2
Factors determining disease outbreak.

infections. A virus disease outbreak may be treated with antibiotics that are generally ineffective against viruses because specific antibiotics provide protection against possible secondary invaders. Bacterial "opportunists" can take advantage of the weakened condition of the host brought about by the primary infection, the virus. Therefore, as a result of the protection provided through the antibiotic, the bird may more effectively utilize its body defense mechanisms against the virus.

Control of the numbers of microorganisms present is a management challenge that involves long-range care of the premises and birds, as well as reaction to short-term stresses. For example, a flock may be provided all the basic safeguards for control of multiplication of microorganisms utilizing good sanitation procedures, vaccination programs, and continued surveillance for symptoms of disease. However, a problem may arise to upset the balance. A water fount may overflow and flood a portion of one building or a fan may quit in a specified section of a building. Such occurrences may result in some birds being exposed to undue stress. Any one of these occurrences can upset the bird sufficiently to allow disruption of the body defense mechanisms, resulting in the rapid multiplication of pathogenic microorganisms within the bird, or provide a medium in the environment favorable for the rapid multiplication of microorganisms. Weak or injured birds will also provide a susceptible host for multiplication of disease microorganisms that can rapidly spread to healthy birds throughout the flock. Thus continued surveillance and removal of weak, injured, or sick birds is recommended.

Virulence of the pathogenic microorganism refers to its ability to produce a disease; its strength to overcome the defense mechanisms of the body and cause infection. Virulence of the pathogens may be increased by many factors that enhance the rapid multiplication of microorganisms. Indiscriminate use of antibiotics and certain other medications allows a genetic antibiotic resistance to develop in the microorganism. Many microorganisms predominate in a given environment or host on the basis of survival of the fittest, resulting in the microorganism gaining in virulence with each multiplication.

Many pathogenic microorganisms are present to a limited degree under most management conditions. If conditions favorable for multiplication of the specific pathogen exist, an active disease outbreak may occur in apparently healthy flocks. Constant surveillance is therefore necessary, and optimal management practices must be followed at all times. Although a pathogen may be airborne on dust particles or arrive with a visitor or through some other vector or vehicle, chances are that the disease-causing microorganism was already present and for one reason or another was given the opportunity to thrive. Many "surprise" disease outbreaks develop because somewhere in the management program a "link" broke and weakened the "chain" of defense. Many dollars are spent on medications, antibiotics, and vaccinations when economic advantage could be realized through following a sound disease-prevention management program.

Disease outbreaks usually are accompanied by sufficient mortality to cause significant economic problems. Other serious problems may be loss in production, such as slower growth rate and low rate of reproduction, which result specifically in a decrease in egg production, rate of gain, and egg and meat quality. These problems are sometimes referred to as morbidity losses. In total they can cause economic losses far exceeding those experienced from mortality, since removed dead birds require no more expense input. Resumption of the growth process, egg production, and fertility or hatchability may prove to be very difficult to regain after a disease outbreak, and the effect on the total marketing scheme of an organization usually is disruptive and costly.

An early indication of disease may be a drop in feed consumption. Therefore, measurement of daily feed intake may signal a problem in time to head off a serious outbreak. Since a flock may drop slightly in feed consumption for reasons other than a threat of a disease outbreak, other management problems as well as potential disease problems should always be suspected. For example, interruption of water service will seriously curtail feed consumption. Without water, birds will not eat. This problem could hit a whole house or be localized to specific areas of a building. A new batch of feed, with a diet change planned or unplanned, may result in the birds not eating. A case of someone in the feed mill forgetting to add the salt or adding too much salt has been demonstrated to upset feed intake. Careful analysis of all factors is necessary when a problem is suspected, and diagnostic procedures must be immediately employed to minimize losses.

Routine checks on flock health are highly recommended. Monitor the flock through periodic observation of the birds. In a floor house sit down for an hour at a time, minimize disturbing movement, and watch the birds. Much can be learned about birds' habits and problems and some good ideas on management may develop. In cage units, routine observation of the birds is also recommended as is inspection of various sections of the house for unique problems. In a flock of birds where feather picking, cannabilism, or egg eating occurs, the problem may be eliminated in the early stages by careful observation of the birds to determine the individuals that are causing the problem. Blood or egg on the beak are principal indicators, and careful observation will reveal the participants. Specific management techniques, such as more frequent gathering of eggs, reducing the intensity of the light, rearrangement of equipment, and use of blinders on the birds, may be employed.

Many other conditions may be discovered by routine flock observation and a keen sensitivity to the birds' needs and health. Although the practice may appear to be a waste of time, the immediate benefits to the long-term welfare of the flock will be obvious. Scheduled or unscheduled noise, such as the clatter of a water line or the rattle of a loose roof panel or an unsecured door or window, may upset a flock causing egg shell problems or piling of birds in floor pens and cages. These disturbances may not be recognized as a problem by humans, particularly when someone is moving about the house. Their occurrence during a quiet period can be most disruptive to the birds. The desire of top management to minimize costs, the concern of middle management to keep pace with the production schedule, and the demands on the time of the caretaker often do not provide the time that should be taken to observe the birds and attend to necessary details that are the foundation of successful management. Instead, there may be a disproportionate urge to produce more per square foot, per man hour, or per dollar invested—worthy objectives to be sure—but often to the detriment of the birds' welfare. Through proper management a balance should be attained.

Removal of sample birds for routine laboratory analysis is highly recommended for disease surveillance as this will provide a good picture of the general condition of large flocks. Some form of random selection is preferred, a method by which a truly average bird may be selected as opposed to a weaker bird, which would not present a true picture of the situation. In some pullet flocks a few cockerels will be allowed to roam among the pullets during the developing period for the purpose of providing the sample, thus potentially valuable birds will not have to be sacrificed. In addition, some managers believe that the cockerels add stability to the pullet flock and have a calming influence to control flightiness. Sample birds may be removed from floor flocks by use of a foot or leg hook so birds can be easily snared with minimal disturbance to the flock.

Disease in poultry should be looked upon as a flock problem. Individual birds are generally not treated in sick pens. Unthrifty and sick individuals should be removed from the flock and disposed of in a sanitary way. Dead-bird disposal must be carried out through burning, burying, or by some other means by which the pathogens are destroyed and the potential for their spread is eliminated (Figure 8–3). No contact with other animals, rodents, flies or insects can be tolerated, and by no means should uncooked carcasses be fed to other animals. Professional advice on disease control in a flock should be obtained by a reputable laboratory's diagnosis of a representative sample of at least six birds from the diseased

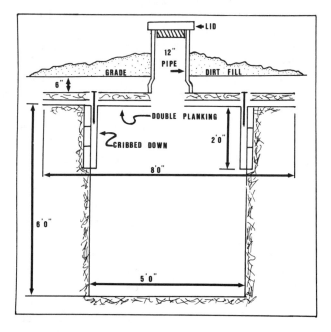

FIGURE 8–3
Design of a dead bird disposal pit.

flock. Constant monitoring of other flocks on the premises is essential so that disease problems may be anticipated and a sound program of prevention followed.

A predetermined vaccination schedule should be established for poultry flocks and must be designed to meet the needs of a specific area. A vaccination schedule is only a guide. It must be adjusted to be applicable to a specific poultry operation in order to develop maximum effectiveness. A qualified avian pathologist should be consulted for aid in disease control and treatment. Although many poultry managers are knowledgeable of disease problems, consulting with a professional pathologist might save time and money in deciding on effective disease-control programs.

Vaccination procedures are as important as the actual vaccination program. Select one person to do all vaccinations whether or not there is one house, one farm, or an organization with many farms and locations. This person should be trained in vaccination techniques and methods and must keep up with the latest information on disease outbreaks in the area. Sanitation precautions should be followed among flocks and among farms. Service vehicles should be kept clean and sanitized. Before entering any poultry house, clean coveralls, sanitized rubber boots and a disposable paper cap should be put on.

Review flock history prior to vaccinating, and do not vaccinate a flock that is sick or experiencing stress caused by debeaking, moving, and so forth. Stress conditions may limit the effectiveness of the vaccine. Records should be kept on each flock showing the name of the vaccine manufacturer, type, serial number, expiration date of vaccine, method of vaccination used, date vaccine was administered, name of person that administered vaccine, and method, including temperature of vaccine storage.

In vaccine preparation and administration, the following are recommended. Be sure the vaccine is not outdated and keep all vaccines refrigerated as recommended. Withhold sanitizers from the drinking water three days prior to administering a live-virus vaccine by the water method. Do not try to stretch vaccine dosages to make the vaccine go further; doses are accurately calculated. Water vaccines should be prepared according to directions and used within 30 minutes from the time the vaccine and diluent are mixed. Remove drinking water from the flock for a period of one hour prior to vaccination with water vaccine in order to encourage increased water consumption following the introduction of the vaccine. Wash all drinkers with a brush and clean water before administering water vaccine. However, do not use sanitizer or soap compounds at this time as they reduce the effectiveness of the vaccines. Keep vaccines away from heat and direct sunlight as this also reduces their effectiveness. All vaccines are designed for a specific application. Follow the directions and make sure each bird will receive the proper dose of vaccine recommended by the manufacturer. Powdered skim milk should be added to all water-type virus vaccines. Milk proteins neutralize the small amounts of sanitizer that may be present in the water. Powdered skim milk is premixed at a level of 85 g (3 ounce) pack per 38 l (10 gal.) of clean water using a clean container. Vaccine is premixed as directed, and then the premixed vaccine and water with skim milk are combined and thoroughly mixed. The vaccine is then administered immediately. A suggested program to follow is shown in Table 8–1.

Breeder flocks should be revaccinated every 45 days with Newcastle and bronchitis vaccines if the dust or spray methods are used or every 10 weeks with water vaccine. Laryngotracheitis vaccination should be used only when the disease is prevalent in the area. Vaccinate with a modified, low virulence, eye-drop vaccine. The vent-brush technique is not acceptable in some states; therefore, it is advisable to check before using this technique. Fowl Cholera Bacterin is generally not recommended for chickens and turkeys unless a serious problem exists. Also infectious coryza vaccine is not generally recommended unless there has been a problem. Marek's vaccine is available commercially; follow the directions of the manufacturers. Following all vaccinations, burn or disinfect all used and opened containers to prevent accidental spread of a disease.

All vaccination programs should be tailored to the needs of a particular farm, considering such factors as the diseases present in an area as well as the purpose for which the flock is being raised. Consultation with a knowledgeable poultry pathologist is recommended prior to administration of any vaccine.

Everyone in the poultry business should be aware of the potential threat of exotic Newcastle disease and a number of other infectious dis-

TABLE 8–1

A Suggested Vaccination Program for Chickens

Age	Vaccine	Method
7–12 days	Combination Newcastle Disease and Infectious Bronchitis	Water
32–37 days	Newcastle	Dust or Spray
10–12 weeks	Fowl Pox	Wing Web (Mild Strain)
12–14 weeks	Avian Encephalomyelitis	Water
16 weeks	Newcastle and Infectious Bronchitis	Dust or Spray
18–20 months (First Molt)	Newcastle and Infectious Bronchitis	Water, Dust or Spray

eases carried by pet birds that are illegally brought into the United States. There have been numerous annual cases of the disease that have been traced to illegally imported pet birds for sale in pet shops. One of these diseases, psittacosis (parrot fever), can be contracted by humans and can be fatal if not recognized promptly and properly treated.

There are many other diseases of poultry not described in this chapter. Those presented here represent examples of some commercially important diseases that respond to control by the flock-management practices discussed. Poultry producers do not need to be familiar with all avian diseases if they follow sound management and disease-control practices that will assure healthy flocks and a successful enterprise.

CHAPTER 9

FOOD EGGS
AND
EGG PRODUCTS

One of nature's most perfect foods, the bird's egg, has long provided humans a nearly complete balance of vital nutrients, and
today, economically provides a high quality, wholesome, delicious, and versatile food widely used througout the world. Factors
related to egg quality, its determination, and preservation are discussed.

Everyone should be familiar with the chicken egg as a food item. The
average person in the United States consumes over 270 chicken eggs per
year, somewhat more than a single hen's production in one year. However, there are more hens in the United States than there are people, since
the average egg production per hen per year is about 245 eggs. There are
also hens that produce fertile eggs for hatching both meat type and egg
type chickens. The egg is the only food product consumed by humans
that is derived from an animal, prepackaged and ready to cook, natural
with no artificial additives.

White-shell chicken eggs are preferred by most consumers in the
United States and are the only color eggs available at most supermarkets.
However, brown-shell chicken eggs are preferred by consumers in the
northeastern states and in many other parts of the world. Many people
who have dual-purpose American breeds of chickens on their own farms
have probably developed a preference for brown-shell eggs. It seems consumers attach importance to visual characteristics of products, particu-

larly color, whether they be food or nonfood, plant or animal. Shell color has never been shown to be correlated with the quality of the food egg inside or its nutritional value.

Eggs are most commonly considered a breakfast entree. However, eggs can be used as major constituents of many appetizing and nutritious food dishes. The egg in its own natural package is easy to transport to such remote areas as the shore of a mountain lake—far from the chicken that produced it—where it easily provides appetizing, nourishing food for humans. Two eggs provide a convenient and nutritious meal in a shell and cost much less than a can of soft drink. A large egg has fewer than 80 calories and contains more protein per calorie than most meat and dairy products. Chicken eggs provide the highest quality (most complete) protein, containing essential amino acids for humans, all necessary vitamins except vitamin C, and 13 mineral elements.

White-shell eggs are produced commercially by the Single Comb White Leghorn chicken, which has been bred for high production and efficient feed conversion. It requires only about three kilograms of feed to produce one kilogram of egg. Hens start laying at about 22 weeks of age. A good laying hen may lay as many as 270 eggs during the first laying year, and in a second laying year she could conceivably approach that number again. A chicken, during her commercially productive life, produces many times her body weight in human food (eggs) (Figure 9–1).

FIGURE 9–1
Single Comb White Leghorn contemplating the amount of eggs she is expected to produce in two years. (Photograph by Stewart Drake.)

EGG QUALITY

The ultimate objective in marketing eggs for human food is to supply the consumer with eggs that have retained their original high quality. Quality may be thought of as the total inherent characteristics of the egg, which determine its degree of acceptability. Egg quality includes the visible physical characteristics as well as flavor and odor. Very few commercially produced eggs are of poor quality when they are laid; eggs freshly laid are of the highest quality, with few exceptions. The main problem concerned with egg quality is its maintenance in market channels. There are a number of ways to retain egg quality so it can be passed on to the consumer. Providing the consumer with higher quality not only increases the demand for eggs, but aids the producer in obtaining the highest market grade and price. Therefore, knowledge of proper production and marketing procedures and methods of measuring egg quality are very important to the egg producer.

Egg quality is determined by a number of exterior and interior factors. Nutritional value, flavor, odor, yolk color, taste, and appearance are quality factors that are not easily determined. Although there is a difference in appearance and taste between a fresh egg and a stale egg, no nutritional differences between the two have been demonstrated. There are at least five factors that influence the quality of eggs before they are laid.

1. There are breed, strain, family, and individual differences in eggshell color, size, shape, and texture and in albumen and yolk quality, as well as in the presence of blood or meat spots. These quality characteristics are inherent in the dam, but they may also be influenced by environmental factors.

2. Ration fed to layers influences the quality and to some extent the nutritional value of the eggs. Calcium, phosphorus, manganese, and vitamin D influence shell quality; yellow-pigmented feed influences yolk color; and many feed constituents can influence the flavor of eggs. Eggs may acquire undesirable flavors from certain ingredients. Fish products, for example, in excessive quantities can impart an undesirable taste to eggs. Concentration of a nutrient such as a vitamin in the feed influences the concentration of that nutrient in the egg. Increased intake of protein results in large eggs, but this effect does not occur if the diet is low in energy, since protein would then be utilized for energy rather than in synthesis of egg material. Defects in eggs from nutritional influences appear frequently as a problem in large numbers of eggs within a production unit. One of the most frequent and noticeable defects is blood spots, which economically cause a significant loss to the industry. Their direct cause may be due to factors other than dietary, however excessively high levels have been traced to the diet. A blood spot is basically a clot of blood formed in close conjunction to the egg yolk and can usually be detected in candling. Vitamin A or vitamin K deficiency has been known to increase the incidence of blood spots. Yolk changes, mottling, and discoloration may result from the inclusion of certain drugs in the diet, usually as a contaminant, however certain drugs used as coccidiostats or for worming have been reported to be detrimental to yolk color. Most common causes of yolk mottling have been cottonseed meal and oil, which have been shown to cause pink discoloration in egg whites as well. Excessive amounts of riboflavin in the diet sometimes result in the albumen appearing slightly yellow-green. "Blond" or "platinum" yolks sometimes appear in eggs where low levels of xanthophyll pigments are encountered.

3. Disease can have a devastating effect on egg production. Newcastle disease, infectious hepatitis, or infectious bronchitis can cause abnormally shaped shells. Many can cause physiological disturbances that will result in yolk mottling, thin albumen, and decreased egg size. Hens with heavy worm infestation may, in rare instances, "package" a worm in the egg.

4. Age of the hen influences egg quality. The quality of albumen declines throughout the normal egg production cycle. Shell quality declines after the first few months of laying and in subsequent production years.

5. Environment will affect egg quality. High temperature in the laying house will result in lower albumen quality, reduced shell strength, and decreased thickness of the shell. This may be due in part to decreased feed consumption in hot weather. Egg size will decrease at temperatures above 29°C (85°F).

Management plays an important role in controlling all of these factors to produce eggs of high quality. A great deal of time, money, and effort is expended toward controlling these factors. To assure the production of high quality eggs on the farm before the eggs are laid, one should select a strain of birds known to produce eggs of good quality, since egg quality is a heritable characteristic. Also, enough cage space should be provided. Prolonged periods of temperatures above 30°C (86°F) in the laying house should be avoided; a range of 20°C–30°C (68°F–86°F) is generally recommended. Feed should be formulated to produce eggs of high market quality and good nutritional value. Necessary steps to prevent disease and other physiological disturbances in the flock should be practiced. The time pullets start to lay can be regulated by controlling feed and light in a planned program. Since egg quality decreases as the age of the hen increases, the number of years to keep a hen should be considered in relationship to all factors of the production plan.

Eggs are perishable and will deteriorate in quality unless properly handled. From the time the egg is laid through processing and marketing, the major objective is to preserve as much of the original quality as possible until it reaches the point of consumer use. Proper home storage by the consumer after the egg leaves the food market is vital also. A major quality change is the result of moisture loss through the pores of the shell by evaporation, resulting directly in an increase in air cell size. Evaporation of moisture depends on the environment in which the egg is stored, the temperature, relative humidity, and ventilation. In addition, the porosity of the shell determines rate of moisture loss into the environment. Eggs should be cooled quickly after laying and be stored at 10°C–13°C (50°F–55°F). In order to retard moisture loss, relative humidity should be maintained between 70% and 85%. If the holding room temperature is colder than 10°C (50°F), moisture may condense on the shell at this high humidity.

Thinning of the albumen is a sign of quality loss. Thinning depends on high temperature, which enhances chemical and physical reactions, resulting in a breakdown of the protein structure of the thick albumen. The higher the temperature of egg storage, the more rapidly the albumen breaks down with the greatest rate of decline occurring during the first two days following lay. Enzymes act on proteins in the albumen and hydrolyze the amino-acid chains destroying the protein structure and releasing water bound by the large protein molecules. The water in the thin albumen passes across the vitelline membrane by osmosis into the yolk, which contains less water. Extra water in the yolk causes it to enlarge, resulting in weakening of the vitelline membrane. This results in the yolk appearing enlarged and flattened, particularly when the egg is broken out onto a flat surface (Figure 9–2). When the vitelline membrane becomes stretched and weakened, albumen can pass through the weakened vitelline membrane into the yolk causing the yolk to appear mottled.

A freshly laid egg contains about 0.5% carbon dioxide. Loss of carbon dioxide during holding results in a change in flavor of the egg, which is related to an increase in alkalinity from pH 7.6 to pH 9.5.

Most eggs are clean at the time they are laid, but they can become contaminated with manure and nest and cage debris after they are laid. There are many places in the world where eggs are sold unwashed and unrefrigerated in the open marketplace (Figure 9–3). In the United States and some other countries where sanitation is stressed in food production,

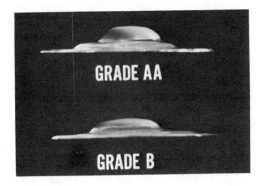

FIGURE 9–2
Quality deterioration is noticeable in a broken out
egg by the enlarged and flattened yolk.

FIGURE 9–3
Eggs sold unwashed and unrefrigerated in the open marketplace. (Photograph by Bonnie Bechtold.)

an egg with manure on the shell is not marketable. Therefore, the producer must prevent or minimize the soiling of eggs. Eggs from caged hens are easier to keep clean since the eggs roll away from the bird when laid. Birds in floor pens should be provided clean nests and nesting materials. Eggs should be gathered frequently and placed in clean egg flats. Cracked eggs should be refrigerated at all times and should not be sold retail. Any eggs leaking their contents are considered unfit for human consumption and should be disposed of or used as pet food.

There are several recommended practices to assure maintenance of the quality of eggs after they are laid. Eggs should be gathered frequently, two or three times per day, if possible. Clean eggs should be segregated from dirty, cracked, or leaking eggs. Collected eggs should be refrigerated immediately at 10°C–13°C (50°F–55°F) and at 70%–85% relative humidity. Eggs should be at this storage-room temperature prior to packaging. Eggs are properly washed in water that is warmer than the temperature of the egg. If eggs are washed in water that is cooler than the temperature of the egg, it will cause the contents of the egg to contract, producing a partial vacuum inside of the shell that will draw dirty water through the pores of the shell, contaminating the interior contents with bacteria. If the wash water is warmer than the temperature of the egg it will cause the contents of the egg to expand slightly, producing a positive pressure that prevents dirty water on the shell from entering the egg through the pores. It is safer not to wash the eggs at all, rather than wash them in water cooler than the egg. For this same reason it is important that the temperature and relative humidity of the holding-room environment be regulated to prevent moisture from condensing on the outside of the egg shell, which could be drawn into the egg as the egg cools. Since washing removes the protective natural shell cuticle, it must be replaced by applying a paraffin-base mineral oil to the washed egg shell. This effectively closes the shell pores and retards moisture evaporation during storage. Eggs should be air dried before packaging. Eggs should be graded at cool room temperature and packed in clean, single-service containers. Packaged eggs should be stored in humidified coolers at 10°C–13°C (50°F–55°F), 70%–85% relative humidity, and marketed at least once a week. Eggs should be transported in refrigerated or insulated trucks, depending on the distance and time involved. Eggs should be refrigerated during wholesale and retail marketing and in the home. Although eggs are the only animal agricultural food product produced by the animal, prepackaged and ready to cook, there are a few things that are done commercially before selling them to the consumer.

Egg grading is the method used commercially to determine the quality of eggs. The grading of shell eggs involves classifying individual eggs according to established standards. United States standards for quality of individual shell eggs have been developed on the basis of:

Interior Quality Factors

albumen thickness

condition of yolk

size and condition of air cell

abnormalities, such as blood spots and meat spots

Exterior Quality Factors

cleanliness of shell

soundness of shell (checks, cracks, texture)

color

shape

Eggs are also classified according to weight (or size) expressed in minimum:

	Net Weight Per Dozen (grams/ounces)	Weight for Individual Eggs (grams/ounces)
Jumbo	851/30	68.5/2.4
Extra large	766/27	61.4/2.2
Large	681/24	54.3/1.9
Medium	596/21	47.2/1.7
Small	511/18	40.2/1.4
Peewee	426/15	

Egg grading is the sorting of eggs into groups having similar characteristics in quality and weight (which are not related).

Exterior quality factors are apparent from external observation or candling. Interior quality factors must be determined by candling or by a flock-selection method where small numbers of eggs from each flock are broken out and examined. United States standards for quality of individual shell eggs based on candled appearance may be used to classify eggs as: AA quality, A quality, B quality, dirty, check, or leaker. Tables 9–1 and 9–2 summarize United States standards for quality of individual shell eggs. The quality of shell eggs is determined by a number of factors, but the final quality score (grade) can be no higher than the lowest score given to any one of the quality factors.

Shells that are unusual in shape, such as those having ridges, rough areas, or thin spots and those that are long and narrow or spherical, cannot be placed in Grades AA or A. "Body checks" are eggs with shells that have been cracked while still in the uterus of the hen and have had a layer of calcium deposited over the crack before the egg is laid. Body checks sometimes appear as ridges on the shell, but can easily be detected by candling. Depending upon the extent and severity of the ridge, body checks may be classified as B quality. These shells are usually weaker than normal shells and are more likely to break in shipment, and they lack consumer appeal.

Eggs are hand candled by two eggs being held in each hand. The uppermost egg in the right hand is examined first, then the uppermost egg in the left hand. The position of the eggs is changed in one hand while one of the eggs held in the other hand is being candled. The hand that holds the egg to be viewed arrives at a point near the candling light palm down (Figure 9–4). When the hand is turned with a snap of the wrist in

TABLE 9–1
Exterior Egg Quality Factors

1. *Shell shape and texture:*
   a) practically normal—A shell that approximates the usual shape and that is sound and free from thin spots. Ridges and rough areas that do not materially affect the shape and strength of the shell are permitted. (AA or A Quality).
   b) abnormal—A shell that may be somewhat unusual, or decidedly misshapen, or faulty in soundness or strength, or may show pronounced ridges or thin spots. (B Quality).

2. *Soundness of shell:*
   a) sound—An egg whose shell is unbroken.
   b) check (or cracked)—An egg that has a broken shell or crack in the shell but with its shell membranes intact and contents that do not leak. Checks may range from a very fine hair-like crack (blind check) that is discernible only by candling to obvious dented checks. Blind checks will not keep well or stand even moderately rough handling, and so should be used immediately.
   c) smashed—An egg whose shell is crushed or shattered.
   d) leaker—An egg that has a crack or break in the shell and shell membranes to the extent that the egg contents are exuding or free to exude through the shell.

3. *Shell cleanliness:*
   a) clean—A shell that is free from foreign material and from stains or discolorations that are readily visible. An egg may be considered clean if it has only very small specks, stains, or cage marks—if such specks, stains, or cage marks are not of sufficient number or intensity to detract from the generally clean appearance of the egg. (AA and A Quality).
   b) moderately stained—A shell that is free from prominent stains and adhering dirt, but which has moderate stains that do not cover more than $\frac{1}{32}$ of the shell surface if localized, or $\frac{1}{16}$ of the shell surface if scattered. (B Quality).

TABLE 9–2
Interior Egg Quality Factors

1. *Air cell:*
   a) practically regular—Air cell maintains a practically fixed position with an even outline as the egg is rotated. (AA and A quality).
   b) free air cell—An air cell that moves freely between the intact membranes toward the uppermost point of the egg, as it is rotated. (B quality).
   c) bubbly air cell—A ruptured air cell resulting in one or more small separate air bubbles usually floating beneath the main air cell. (B quality).

   d) | Size-Quality | Maximum Depth |
   |---|---|
   | AA | 0.3 cm ($\frac{1}{8}$ in.) |
   | A | 0.5 cm ($\frac{3}{16}$ in.) |
   | B | may be over 0.5 cm ($\frac{3}{16}$ in.) |

2. *Yolk:*
   The yolk shadow outline from egg candling is defined as:
   a) outline slightly defined—The yolk outline is indistinctly indicated and appears to blend into the surrounding white as the egg is twirled. (AA quality).
   b) outline fairly well-defined—The yolk outline is discernible but not clearly outlined as the egg is twirled. (A quality).
   c) outline plainly visible—The yolk outline is clearly visible as a dark shadow when the egg is twirled. (B quality).

   The yolk size and shape determined by egg candling is defined as:
   a) enlarged and flattened—A yolk in which the yolk membranes and tissues have weakened and/or moisture has been absorbed from the white to such an extent that the yolk appears definitely enlarged and flat. (B quality).

   The terms used to describe yolk defects are:
   a) practically free from defects—The yolk shows no blastoderm development but may show other very slight defects on its surface. (AA and A quality).
   b) serious defects—The yolk may show well-developed spots or areas and other serious defects that do not render the egg inedible. (B Quality).
   c) clearly visible germ development—Development of the blastoderm on the yolk that has progressed to the point where it is plainly visible as a circular area or spot on the yolk with no blood in evidence. (B Quality).
   d) blood due to germ development—Blood caused by development of the blastoderm in a fertile egg to a point where it is visible as definite lines or as a blood ring. (inedible).

3. *White:*
   The condition of the white is determined by candling as follows:
   a) clear—The white is free from discolorations or foreign bodies floating in it. Prominent chalazas should not be confused with blood spots or meat spots. (AA quality).
   b) thickness—see yolk shadow outline.
   c) meat spots and blood spots—May be on the surface of the yolk or floating in the white; dark gray and brilliant red respectively—less than 0.3 cm ($\frac{1}{8}$ in.) diameter (B Quality), greater than 0.3 cm ($\frac{1}{8}$ in.) diameter. (inedible).
   d) bloody white—Blood has diffused through the white. (inedible).

(a)

(b)

FIGURE 9–4
Hand candling of eggs: (a) Egg placed at candling
light with palm of hand down, (b) Hand turned with
a snap of the wrist to cause egg contents to move
within the shell.

an arc of 180°, the shell contents will move within the shell. The long axis of the egg should be at about a 45° angle to the candling aperture. The thumb and index finger should be on opposite sides of the shell. An efficient grader will be able to grade 7,200 eggs per day by hand candling. Commercial egg processors use mass candling equipment that automatically turns many eggs simultaneously over a large area of light, allowing rapid candling of many more eggs by a single egg candler (Figure 9–5).

Albumen thickness is determined by the shadow the yolk casts upon the shell when candled. The thinner the albumen, the closer the yolk will be to the shell when the egg is twirled, due to the centrifugal force. The yolk shadow is more distinctly projected onto the shell when it is close to the shell than when it is closer to the center of the egg. Although appearance of the yolk is dependent on the condition of the albumen, shape and size of the yolk itself can be determined by candling.

Blood spots result from hemorrhage of a small blood vessel in the ovary or oviduct. If it is on the yolk it indicates the hemorrhage was in the ovary or infundibulum; the follicle probably did not rupture along the stigma where there are no blood vessels. If the spot is in the albumen it indicates a hemorrhage in the wall of the oviduct. Meat spots are degenerated blood spots or loose pieces of oviduct tissue in the albumen. Blood spots and meat spots that are in the albumen appear to move more rapidly

FIGURE 9–5
Mass candling of eggs. (Photograph by Marty Traynor.)

FIGURE 9–6
Whole egg weight determined on a balance for use in
Haugh unit calculation.

on candling than the chalazae, which may be mistaken for meat spots, and they are most easily detected if the eggs are stored for at least 24 hours prior to candling. They will appear as rather distinct spots that move rapidly past the candlelight.

"Haugh unit" is used as a measure of egg quality. The individual whole egg is weighed on a sensitive balance (Figure 9–6). It is then broken out on a smooth, level surface (Figure 9–7). The albumen height in millimeters is measured with a micrometer, midway between the edge of the yolk and the outer edge of the thick albumen. The chalaza is avoided. Conversion tables or Haugh unit calculators (Figure 9–8) are available to convert albumen height and egg weight to Haugh unit value. A high Haugh unit value indicates high quality and relates to egg grade, other factors being normal. It is used in research as a measure of interior egg quality and to assist in diagnosing quality problems in commercial egg production. "Yolk index" is a measure of the standing-up quality of the yolk. The yolk index equals yolk height divided by average yolk diameter. "Albumen score" equals thick albumen height divided by diameter.

A freshly laid, intact shell egg from a healthy hen is usually sterile on the inside and is naturally protected, physically as well as chemically, from bacterial invasion. However, when subjected to improper washing and/or storage temperatures, particularly if moisture has condensed on the shell, bacteria may pass through the pores of the shell and through the shell membranes and albumen, thus overcoming the egg's natural defense mechanisms. Although the albumen contains antibacterial substances, improper storage conditions resulting in decreased albumen viscosity allows the yolk to float close to the shell membranes, thus facilitating bacterial invasion of the yolk. Once bacteria have penetrated the shell membrane and vitelline membrane, the nutrient materials in the egg yolk are excellent for supporting bacterial growth and multiplication. At room temperature to over 38°C (100°F), bacteria within the yolk will multiply and cause the egg to rapidly decompose, often producing undesirable by-products.

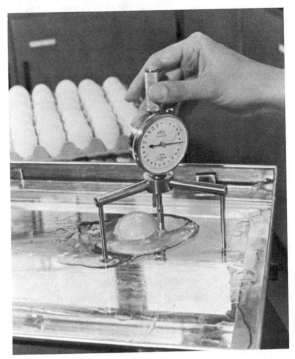

FIGURE 9–7
Albumen height determined with a micrometer for use in Haugh unit calculation.

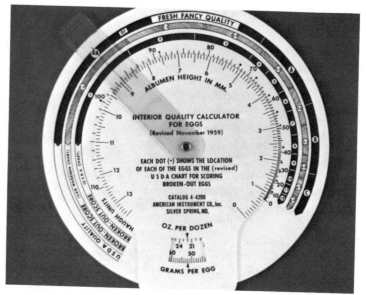

FIGURE 9–8
Haugh unit calculator to convert albumen height and egg weight to Haugh unit value.

The United States Department of Agriculture Egg Grading Manual[1] defines the following conditions as constituting "inedible eggs." "Sour egg," caused by *Pseudomonas* bacteria, may show a weak white and murky shadow around an off-center and swollen yolk. These bacteria produce a material that fluoresces, appearing as a green sheen when the egg is candled with an ultraviolet light (black light). "Green whites" in eggs are also caused by *Pseudomonas* bacteria. They will also fluoresce under ultraviolet light when broken out but may or may not have a sour odor. A mixed bacterial contamination may cause a condition known as "white rot." This will cause thread-like shadows in the thin albumen progressing to a severely blemished yolk detectable by candling. When broken out the yolk will appear crusted and the contents will have a fruity odor. Multiplication of *Proteus* bacteria in the egg contents causes a brown to black color and produces a putrid odor. This condition is known as "black rot" and can also be detected on candling by the dark opaque color of the egg contents.

Eggs will easily pick up musty odors from a variety of environmental

[1] Agricultural Marketing Service. 1977. Egg Grading Manual. Agricultural Handbook No. 75. U.S. Department of Agriculture, Washington, D.C.

materials or directly from bacteria contaminating the shell. This condition, known as "musty eggs," is impossible to detect by visual examination since the eggs can appear clear and free of foreign material when candled, and therefore, must be detected by the odor from the case and packing material that is noticed immediately upon opening the cases of eggs. Mold may be present on or in eggs even when a moldy or musty odor is not present. This condition, known as "moldy eggs," is best detected by visual observation of mold spots on the shell, or mold growth in checks or cracks in the shell, or by mold growth inside the egg, which can be detected by candling. Washing eggs in dirty water, applying dirty mineral oil cooler than the egg, or storing of eggs in a high humidity atmosphere encourages contamination of the egg by mold and subsequent growth and penetration of the mold through the shell. As mold growth continues inside of the egg, it may produce a darkening of the contents, which is noticeable on candling.

Commercially, shell eggs produced by hens kept in cages are automatically or hand collected (Figures 9–9, 9–10), refrigerated (Figure 9–11); and automatically washed (Figure 9–12), dried, oiled, mass candled (Figure 9–5), weighed (Figure 9–13), and packaged (Figure 9–14). Refrigerated shell eggs are rapidly marketed through various wholesale and retail channels (Figure 9–15), usually reaching the consumer only a few

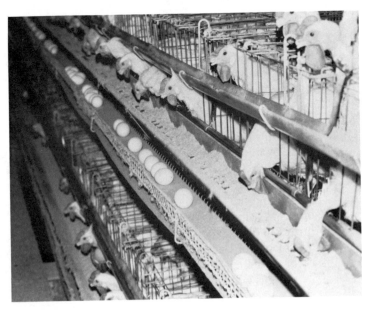

FIGURE 9–9
Automatic egg collection from caged laying hens. (Photograph by Marty Traynor.)

FIGURE 9–10
Eggs moved on conveyor belt from laying house to refrigeration prior to processing. (Photograph by Marty Traynor.)

FIGURE 9–11
Overnight refrigerated storage of eggs prior to washing, candling and packaging.

FIGURE 9–12
Automatic egg washing machine. (Photograph by Nancy Nydegger.)

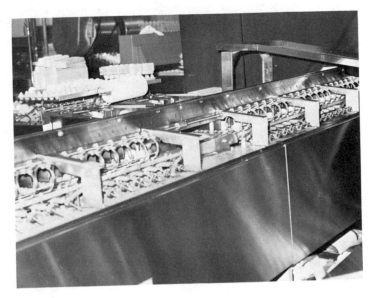

FIGURE 9–13
Automatic egg weighing machine. (Photograph by Marty Traynor.)

274

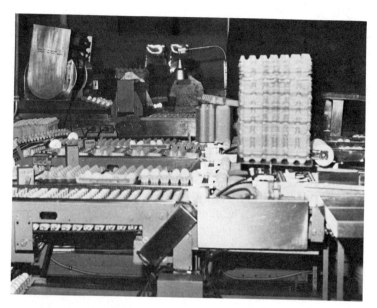

FIGURE 9–14
Automatic egg packaging machine. (Photograph by Marty Traynor.)

FIGURE 9–15
Packaged eggs loaded into refrigerated trucks for direct retail distribution.
(Photograph by Marty Traynor.)

days from the time they were produced by the hens. With controlled environment, confinement housing of laying hens, there is essentially no seasonal cycle of egg production and no need for storing shell eggs, as was done in the past.

EGG PRODUCTS AND MARKETING

Traditionally, the further processing of shell eggs has primarily been to make them frozen pasteurized liquid egg and dried egg. This involves special processing plants with automatic egg breaking and separation equipment. The liquid egg or egg components must then be pasteurized at 60°C (140°F) for 3.5 minutes prior to packaging. Pasteurized liquid egg is blast-frozen in metal containers and sold to bakeries or other food processing plants for use as an ingredient in a variety of fabricated food products. Pasteurized liquid egg may be dried by special equipment designed to spray it, in small droplets, into a hot-air chamber, which produces a fine dry powder. The dried egg powder is packaged and sold to food manufacturers for use as an ingredient in such foods as cake mixes, pasta, and candy.

Further processing of fresh shell eggs into a variety of fresh and frozen egg products and food products containing egg significantly increases the total demand for shell eggs as well as the profit margin to the egg producer-processor. As the profit margin on production of food eggs is reduced in the face of increased production costs and, if the consumer is willing to pay more for further processed convenience foods, development of further processed, convenient, egg food products will be expanded. Food processing technology allows the production of cooked, prepackaged, and frozen egg products that have consumer acceptability and that can be conveniently prepared at home by boiling them in the package or heating them in a microwave oven. Some egg products already developed for this market include fried egg, scrambled egg, smoked egg, crepes, omelets, souffles, quiche, French toast, egg sandwich, liquid egg for scrambling in retail size containers, and hard-cooked eggrolls. The consumer is willing to pay for the convenience provided by these products as long as the taste and appearance of the products are acceptable. This interest in paying for the time provided by convenience-food products increases the per capita consumption of eggs and creates a demand for further processing of eggs. This, in turn, will increase the total demand for eggs produced and improve the profit margin at both the production and processing stages.

One significant factor that could increase the per-capita consumption of eggs is the increased use of eggs in fast food operations. The successful introduction of a popular egg sandwich or breakfast into a large fast food chain can have a significant impact on the total additional eggs consumed per year on a nationwide basis.

The trend toward more meals being consumed outside of the home, the increased promotion of the nutritional and health benefits of eggs, the development of new, appetizing egg dishes that can be conveniently prepared in the home, and the introduction of commercially further processed eggs seem to indicate an expanding egg market. The advertising of eggs by the American Egg Board is a relatively new concept that seems to be having a positive effect on food egg consumption and will probably continue (Figure 9–16). The "incredible edible egg" has long been one of humanity's most economical, nutritious, safe, and reliable sources of food, and it appears it will continue to be an essential food of the future.

Marketing outlets for eggs are generally very good. Egg prices to the consumer have normally cycled on about a three-year frequency. Overproduction when egg prices are high very rapidly drives the prices down, which necessitates cuts in production before eggs start to increase

FIGURE 9–16
American Egg Board poster advertising the attributes of eggs.

in price. Price fluctuations have had little effect on egg consumption patterns.

Purchase, Preparation, and Consumption of Eggs

Retail markets in the United States do not sell eggs graded lower than US Grade B. Look on the egg carton for the USDA grade shield (Figure 9–17). It will read "USDA AA GRADE," "USDA A GRADE," or "USDA B GRADE." This grade shield not only indicates the quality of the eggs, but that they have been certified for quality under USDA supervision and graded and packaged in a plant that meets USDA sanitation requirements. Such grading service is provided by the USDA as well as by the state agencies and is available on a voluntary basis for a fee to those companies that request it.

The US Grade AA and A eggs are best to buy for table use since they produce a better-appearing cooked meal entree than a US Grade B egg, which may have thinner albumen. Most egg producers do not package Grade B eggs because they do not have any eggs that have been stored long enough to grade lower than A. Therefore, most retail markets do not have Grade B eggs available unless they package their higher grade eggs as Grade B to meet a specific market demand. Even truly Grade B eggs are as nutritious as higher grade eggs. They are sold at a reduced price, sometimes as "generic eggs," and are entirely satisfactory for baking, scrambling, or other cooking uses where best appearance is not essential.

Properly refrigerated shell eggs stored in their carton in a home refrigerator will change from AA-grade to A-grade in about one week and from A-grade to B-grade in about five weeks. However, a properly han-

FIGURE 9–17
United States Department of Agriculture egg quality grade shield.

FIGURE 9–18
United States Department of Agriculture
egg grade shield, indicating quality, as
well as size, of eggs.

dled and refrigerated intact shell egg will retain its nutritional value and
wholesomeness for considerably longer time.

Egg sizes will be indicated on the carton label, occasionally within
the grade shield (Figure 9–18). Eggs within a carton vary somewhat in
size because the United States weight classes indicate the minimum required weight per dozen eggs, rather than the actual size of each egg. The
minimum weight per dozen for "Extra Large" eggs is 766 g (27 ounces),
for "Large" eggs is 681 g (24 ounces), and for "Medium" eggs is 596 g
(21 ounces). Also, there is a maximum tolerance of 5% per case for individual eggs in the next lower weight class.

Eggs within a carton may vary in grade, may be "checked," or be
lower than the indicated grade. Refrigerated storage for about one week
will cause a Grade AA egg to change to a Grade A. This could conceivably
happen in the home refrigerator as well as in the retail store. Egg quality
will decrease much more rapidly if eggs are not refrigerated and if they
are allowed to become very warm for even short periods of time. There
is a maximum tolerance allowed by the USDA at destination in a carton
of 12: US Grade AA eggs—3 Grade A or B eggs and 1 Check egg; US
Grade A eggs—2 Grade B eggs and 1 Check egg; and US Grade B eggs—
2 Check eggs. Individual states, however, may require lower tolerances.

Prices of eggs vary among grades and sizes. Price per dozen for eggs
is determined by supply and demand for the various sizes and grades.
Eggs of different weight classes will not always be the same price per
kilogram or pound. Therefore, the best value can be determined by cal-
culating the price per kilogram or pound for each weight class of eggs in
the store of a given quality grade.

Eggs should be one of the last items picked up from the retail market
prior to checking out and should be promptly transported to the home

and refrigerated immediately upon arrival. Eggs are best stored large end up in their original carton on an upper shelf in the refrigerator. Eggs should not be stored in the indented egg cups in the special shelf in the door provided in many refrigerators. Here they will be exposed to air drafts and physical shock every time the refrigerator door is opened and closed, which will hasten their loss of quality.

It is safe to consume raw eggs in uncooked or slightly cooked meal items such as home-made egg nog or milk shakes, only if the eggs are fresh and clean, have unbroken shells, and have been commercially washed, graded, and packaged. Ungraded "farm" eggs, even from your own chicken flock, cannot be depended upon to be properly cleaned and handled to assure safety from the bacterial contamination that could cause food poisoning. Ungraded eggs from small local flocks or any soiled or cracked eggs should be carefully opened, so as to minimize contamination of the contents, and thoroughly cooked prior to eating.

When cooking eggs or foods consisting primarily of eggs, low-to-moderate heat gives best results. Overcooking eggs at high temperatures will toughen egg yolks and brown albumin. Older eggs are recommended for hard-boiling as they will be easier to peel than fresh eggs. This is because the air cell that forms between the inner and outer shell membranes as moisture evaporates from the egg during storage and the concurrent loss of carbon dioxide from the albumin prevents the cooked albumin from adhering tightly to the shell membranes. Eggs that have been stored for a few days will, when cooked in the shell, peel more easily than freshly laid eggs. To prevent fresh shell eggs from cracking during cooking in water and to make subsequent peeling easier, a small puncture in the large end of the shell should be made using a thumb tack. Eggs should not be placed directly into boiling water, but immersed in cold water and brought up to boiling. Then the pan should be immediately removed from heat and eggs allowed to sit in hot water for 15 minutes. Hard-boiled eggs should be cooled immediately under running cold water as the shell is cracked and peeled away starting from the large end. This method will also prevent the egg yolks from having a greenish color on their cooked surface, which is caused by the formation of sulfur and iron compounds when the egg is cooked too long at too high a temperature. Should this green color appear on hard-cooked eggs, it will not affect the taste and the eggs will still be safe and nutritious.

It is beyond the scope of this book to present recipes and various procedures for cooking the many delicious meal items that can be prepared using eggs. Ideas and information should not be limited to basic general cookbooks, but cookbooks and recipe pamphlets dealing only with egg dishes should be sought out. A good source of such information is the American Egg Board.[2] However, don't limit imaginative ideas to any of these cookbooks and pamphlets.

The versatility of eggs makes possible their being prepared and consumed for breakfast, brunch, lunch, supper, dinner, or dessert, or even between meals. Eggs can be fried, poached, soft-cooked, hard-cooked, scrambled, baked, or microwave cooked; they can be made into omelets, crepes, pancakes, waffles, French toast, popovers, and muffins. Eggs can be used in a variety of sandwiches such as egg salad, fried egg, and scrambled egg, or combined with sausage or other meat and cheese, and they can be used in preparing appetizers such as deviled eggs, pickled eggs, dip, and canapes. Eggs are used in salads such as chef's, chicken and turkey, tuna, gelatin, or almost any type. Eggs may be included as an important part of many entrees such as quiche, lasagna, tacos, enchiladas, egg foo yung, fondue, rarebit, casseroles, creamed egg and meat, poached or fried egg with hash, eggs Benedict, and meat loaf, to mention only a few possibilities. Eggs can be used in beverages such as egg nog, milk shakes, and any high nutrient breakfast drink. Eggs can be used as ingredients in desserts such as meringue topping, custards, cream puffs, a variety of pies and puddings, souffles, homemade ice cream, and a variety of cakes, cookies, and pastries. Imaginative ideas should not be limited; and many more uses for eggs can be developed.

Eggs are one of the few foods that not only taste good but are also of highest nutritional quality. Chicken eggs are the most complete and nourishing of natural human foods available. This fact should not be surprising since eggs completely support the early growth and development of life in the embryonic chick. Milk is another very complete human food, as it also must completely support the early growth of newly born mammals. Since eggs contain all essential amino acids required by humans, and all necessary vitamins, except vitamin C, and many useful minerals, they are very completely utilized by the human; that is, they are efficiently metabolized into human tissue and are, therefore, retained in the human body. Therefore, eggs have a relatively high "biological value," which is the percent of the food that is retained in the body and metabolized into tissue. Chicken eggs with a biological value of 96% are second only to human milk at 98% in biological value to humans. Cow's milk follows closely at 94%. Meats, grains, and legumes are considerably lower in biological value than milk and eggs.

The retail price of eggs has traditionally been based on the dozen rather than on unit weight. Since a dozen large eggs weigh $1\frac{1}{2}$ pounds, the retail price of eggs cannot be readily compared on an equal basis with

---

[2] American Egg Board, 1460 Renaissance Drive, Park Ridge, Illinois, 60068.

the price per pound for most other food items. Therefore, it is important for the consumer to be able to easily convert egg price per dozen to price per pound for value comparisons. Since a large egg weighs two ounces, a dozen large eggs weigh 24 ounces, which is $1\frac{1}{2}$ pounds. If eggs cost $1.00 per dozen, it is $1.00 per $1\frac{1}{2}$ pounds, or 66 cents per pound. A retail price for eggs of 66 cents per pound is quite reasonable compared to most other foods sold retail, particularly since eggs have a much higher food value than the other retail foods. Some meats and cereal products may cost $2.00–$4.00 per pound and are considerably lower in biological value or actual usefulness in human nutrition. When egg prices are compared on an equal basis with other food prices per pound, eggs are found to be one of the most inexpensive foods on the market. Since they are the most complete and nourishing food, they are the best food value. Eggs are an excellent and inexpensive source of vitamins A, B_1, B_2, B_{12}, D, E, niacin, and riboflavin. Eggs supply many minerals required by humans including iron, phosphorus, iodine, and calcium. Eggs provide the least expensive source of at least 45 nutrients necessary for optimal health.

Eggs also provide humans the nutrient cholesterol; and herein lies a well-recognized and continuing controversy. Cholesterol is a nutrient that is utilized in, necessary for, and even synthesized in the human body. Cholesterol is a necessary chemical precursor to the synthesis in the human body of hormones. Also, cholesterol is a necessary constituent of skin cell membranes; it makes skin resistant to absorption and evaporation of water.

Cholesterol is also a significant component of plaque formation in the wall of diseased (hardened) arteries of patients with atherosclerosis. Since cholesterol is present in the plaque formations, it has been hypothesized that cholesterol in the blood may be the cause of plaque formation. There are a number of theories proposed to explain the cause and mechanism of plaque formation in atherosclerosis, only one which proposes that cholesterol is the cause of plaque formation. It still remains a viable hypothesis that, rather than being the cause of plaque formation, cholesterol may actually be the result of plaque formation caused by some other agent.

If a person tends to believe the questionable theory that cholesterol in the blood causes plaque formation and they are aware of the fact that the yolks of eggs contain much more cholesterol than any other common food, then they may readily jump to the conclusion that eating eggs regularly will cause athersclerosis (hardening of the arteries) and eventual death from a heart attack. Although possible, that reasoning is a little far-fetched when one considers that any healthy human will maintain a relatively steady level of cholesterol content in their body, including in their blood where it is usually measured. This level varies among humans and is partially an inherent characteristic of any one person. Although the cholesterol level in a person's diet may temporarily cause blood-level cholesterol to fluctuate, the body will not absorb an unlimited amount from the intestine. There is a feedback mechanism involved that will turn off additional absorption of cholesterol from the intestine once a certain blood level is reached. Also, there is a continuous synthesis of cholesterol in the liver that speeds up or slows down depending upon the body's need for more cholesterol and the fluctuation of blood-level cholesterol.

All of the cholesterol from a person's diet does not pass into the blood system, and it is highly questionable that cholesterol in the blood system causes plaque to form on artery walls. However, both eggs and plaque do contain significant amounts of cholesterol. It has not been proven that any number of eggs in a human's diet causes heart disease over any length of time; and it has not been proven that eggs don't. The controversy continues since there is no quick and simple answer. Yet there are many inadequately informed people today in positions of authority—including physicians, politicians, journalists, food producers and manufacturers, and college professors—who are giving quick and simple answers to the very complex questions food consumers are asking.

"Should I not eat eggs because they are high in cholesterol?", is one of those complex questions that humans ask their physicians; or seek the answer to in books, magazines, and newspapers; or ask their college professors. It is a good question, but without a simple, unqualified answer. Study, in some detail, both sides of this controversial issue, as well as the etiology of the disease, atherosclerosis; and then decide for yourself whether or not the known benefits derived from eating eggs outweigh the questionable risks. For healthy and physically active people, and with all other factors considered, eating two or three eggs per day will probably prolong rather than shorten life and will as conveniently and inexpensively as possible provide many of the essential nutrients the body needs for optimal health. This safety question cannot be answered in quick, simple, and sensational words that people like to hear and read; and the answer may not be the same for all people.

However, there are certain facts to remember about eggs. Eggs are versatile and can be used in many ways. Eggs come in their own natural, easy-open package. Eggs are high in protein and necessary vitamins and minerals. Eggs provide more usable nutrients per dollar spent than any other food. Eggs are good to eat, not only at breakfast, but anytime, anyplace. On a per unit of usable nutrient basis, there simply is not available a less expensive, higher quality food than the "incredible, edible egg."

CHAPTER 10

POULTRY MEAT AND MEAT PRODUCTS

Poultry meats have become inexpensive, wholesome, and nutritious animal-protein sources. The versatility of poultry meat, allowing development of innovative further-processed products, has resulted in a new market for poultry. The expansion of further processing of economically produced turkey and chicken meat exemplifies the potential for poultry as the meat of the future.

Poultry meat is produced commercially in many parts of the world from chickens, turkeys, ducks, geese, pigeons, and guinea fowl. Broiler (or fryer) chickens and turkeys provide most of the total world production of poultry meat, with roaster chickens, ducks, geese, pigeons, guinea fowl, and mature laying hens providing a relatively small percentage of the total. Ducks, geese, and guinea fowl provide a significant portion of total poultry meat consumed in localized high consumption areas of the world. Mature egg-laying hens, sometimes called spent hens after their productive life, are processed for use in poultry–meat-containing foods.

Broiler (fryer) chickens are usually processed between 6 and 8 weeks of age, or even up to 13 weeks of age, and can be of either sex. Being young, immature birds, their meat is characteristically tender and their skin is soft, smooth, and pliable. The breastbone has not completely calcified and consists of cartilage at the posterior end. Older, immature chickens between three and five months of age, of either sex, with similar meat and skin characteristics are known as roasters. Commercially, the roaster may not simply be a broiler grown to three months of age but may be from distinctly different breeding stock. Although the same basic breed cross may be used for the roaster, specific lines are selected for producing offspring with distinctly different production characteristics from those of the broiler. These birds also provide the basic stock for a highly specialized product, the capon. Mature hens (fowl or stewing chickens) is the classification usually applied to the egg-laying hens after they complete one or two years of egg production. These birds yield less meat than the broilers or roasters, and the meat is less tender.

Turkeys are usually processed commercially between 20 and 30 weeks of age, although male turkeys may be grown to 40 weeks of age and slaughtered for use in deboned, further-processed meat products. Sold as whole carcass "young turkey," female turkeys will usually be slaughtered at 16–18 weeks of age and males at 22–24 weeks of age. A fryer-roaster turkey is an immature turkey of either sex, usually slaughtered at less than 16 weeks of age.

Ducks are usually processed commercially as broiler-fryer "ducklings," which are of either sex and less than eight weeks of age. Geese may be processed commercially at any age, usually about 26 weeks, depending on other use of live geese and local demand for the meat.

An important additional use of ducks and geese in some areas of the world is for feather and down production. Most land fowl do not produce good quality down. The best quality down comes from older birds; often breeder geese are used. When the geese are out of egg production, they can be plucked by hand every six weeks. Down and feathers are separated by machine and washed and dried. North America is the world's largest importer of raw feathers and down; most of which comes from China, France, Switzerland, Poland, Taiwan, Romania, Czechoslovakia, Hungary, and Yugoslavia. The United States' duck and goose industry is much too small to supply enough feathers and down for clothing manufacturers. Also, ducks and geese are slaughtered too young in the United States to be a source of good-quality down. It takes a little more than four ducks to produce one pound of feather and down mixture, 15% of which is down. Three geese will yield a one-pound mixture, 20%–25% being down.

A delicious, gourmet, poultry-meat product *foie gras* has been popular in European countries. It is a canned, cooked, goose-liver product made from enlarged livers of force-fed geese. Whole or ground, precooked, moistened corn is force-fed to geese three times a day for four to eight weeks, producing enlarged fatty livers (Figure 10–1). When the geese are processed, the livers are canned. They are usually consumed cold in small slices as hors d'oeuvres or as garnish to other foods. *Foie gras* has a smooth, silky texture, is light in color, and has a very distinctive taste.

FIGURE 10–1
Enlarged, fatty goose livers, the meat ingredient for production of *foie gras,* a gourmet food product. (Photograph by Al Hollister.)

Guinea fowl may be processed commercially at almost any age. They are good producers of meat, and some strains may be excellent for egg production. They are of particular commercial importance in France. Squab is a young, immature pigeon of either sex that is slaughtered commercially where demand for this poultry meat product exists.

A gradual, but far-reaching change has been taking place over the past three decades in the processing and marketing, as well as the production, of poultry meat. The United States has led this change, which now is being evidenced in many other areas of the world. Local production, distribution, and consumption of poultry meat are no longer characteristic of the industry. Today, large quantities of poultry meat can be processed in a single facility and safely transported under refrigeration for marketing not only nationwide, but worldwide. As poultry production has become less seasonal due to the development of controlled environment and confinement rearing for breeders as well as meat production birds, the marketing of fresh poultry meat has become possible on a year-round basis. Even in some areas today where production still remains somewhat seasonal, the growing season has been lengthened and production concentrated to produce more meat yield per unit area. This increased total production of meat, along with the use of frozen storage, has allowed marketing of freshly frozen poultry meat on a year-round basis.

The processing and marketing phase is of equal importance to the production phase. Some producers sell their animals and never know the market grade or understand the grading system. It is important for the poultry producer to have some knowledge of the proper procedures used in processing and marketing and to understand the grading system.

The poultry-meat industry is vertically integrated to varying degrees, but typically the company that owns the processing plant will also own some other phases of the total production, for example, hatcheries, feed-mills, and growout farms. However, often the growing of production birds is contracted to independent farmers. Broiler- and turkey-processing plants are usually located within 160 km (100 miles)—and often within 80 km (50 miles)—of all growing farms, to minimize weight loss and mortality, which can result from transporting live poultry by truck.

PROCESSING POULTRY MEAT

Feed should be removed from the birds at least four and not more than ten hours prior to scheduled arrival at the processing plant. This allows the feed to pass through the crop and intestinal contents to be reduced, thus reducing the chance for contamination of the carcass during evisceration and minimizing processing weight loss. The live birds are typically hand transferred from the growing facility to wooden or plastic crates or metal cages that are loaded by use of a forklift onto a flatbed semitrailer for transport to the processing plant (Figure 10–2). Mechanical live-bird loading systems in the process of development must prove to be nonstressful to the birds and cost effective. Catching is usually done during the dark of the early morning when the birds are at rest, so as to cause the least possible amount of trauma, anxiety, and stress to them. The birds are scheduled to arrive at the processing plant in time for the first morning shift. However, since many trucks may be coming in from various locations, the birds may need to wait in the crates or cages on the truck for hours prior to being moved into the processing plant. For that reason, the trucks are required to pull under a cover with open sides equipped with adequate ventilation fans to circulate fresh air to the birds on the truck (Figure 10–3).

The birds will be moved to the processing plant in turn (Figure 10–4). Here they are unloaded and individually hung by their feet (shanks) on shackles (Figure 10–5). The shackles are attached to a moving conveyor, which takes each bird into the processing plant and through the

FIGURE 10–2
Turkeys loaded into metal cages on truck providing adequate space to minimize stress and prevent piling, assuring a high quality meat product. (Photograph by Marty Traynor.)

various steps of slaughter and disassembly (Figure 10–6). Poultry-processing plants will vary in the extent of automation as well as in the procedure used in specific processing steps, depending upon the type and quantity of poultry processed. All commercial poultry-processing plants in the United States are required to meet or exceed United States Department of Agriculture (USDA) requirements related to adequate facilities, equipment, and procedure, and must have adequate sanitation in all aspects of the processing operation.

Once the live poultry is shackled and moves into the processing plant it will undergo at least eight major processing steps: stunning, bleeding, scalding, picking, eviscerating, chilling, grading, and packaging and labeling.

Live poultry is usually stunned prior to slaughter by an electrical

FIGURE 10–3
Open-sided, fan-ventilated cover for turkeys on transport trucks, providing birds shade and fresh air prior to unloading at the processing plant. (Photograph by Marty Traynor.)

FIGURE 10–4
Turkeys on truck being moved to the processing plant. (Photograph by Nancy Nydegger.)

FIGURE 10–5
Turkeys unloaded from truck and secured by their
shanks on shackles. (Photograph by Marty Traynor.)

FIGURE 10–6
Turkeys secured by shackles on moving conveyor being
slaughtered directly following electrical stunning. (Photograph by John Ryan.)

conductor that imparts an electrical shock. This is done after the birds have been shackled to conveyors. This process renders the birds unconscious during the slaughter and bleeding, reducing stress. It is considered humane. Stunning also relaxes the dermal muscles, which hold the feathers, making picking more efficient. Stunning cannot electrocute the birds, since it is required by the USDA that they die by bleeding. The heart must be beating during slaughter so the carcass will bleed out properly and completely. Birds, if electrocuted by the stunning procedure, would be condemned by the USDA as "cadavers" and not be allowed to continue through the processing line into the human food supply.

Bleeding can be accomplished by several techniques that sever the left jugular vein. The skin is grasped at the back of the head with the thumb and first finger to pull the skin tight over the left side of the lower mandible (Figure 10–7). The jugular vein passes through this area very close to the skin. With a sharp knife a small incision is made through the tightly pulled skin in the soft area just posterior to the lower mandible. About a one-to-two centimeter cut (one-half to three-fourth inch) is made, and the grasp on the skin is released to allow the bird to bleed completely. Bleeding takes less than a minute for small birds and up to two minutes or more for large turkeys or geese (Figure 10–8). Broilers should bleed completely in 1½ minutes. If properly slaughtered, blood should flow from the severed jugular vein in a steady stream. If blood only drips slowly from the incision, the knife probably failed to completely sever the jugular vein. If the bird is not stunned prior to slaughter, it will rapidly be rendered unconscious after slaughter, due to rapid loss of blood from the brain. One variation on this method of slaughter is to hold the head by the thumb

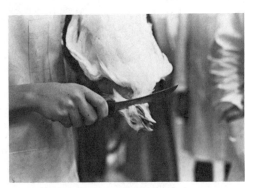

FIGURE 10–7
Broiler slaughtering procedure requiring a small incision below the lower mandible to sever the jugular vein. (Photograph by Colleen Coyle.)

FIGURE 10–8
Complete bleeding of slaughtered turkeys prior to scalding.

and first finger and insert the knife down the throat to make a cut diagonally across the blood vessels. By this method the bird will bleed through the mouth.

A bird that has been incompletely bled will have a noticeable reddish carcass after feather removal and will be condemned by the USDA inspector. Poultry must be completely bled and have stopped breathing prior to entering scald water. This prevents entry and circulation of contaminated scald water through the circulatory and respiratory systems, which can result in contamination of meat.

In commercial processing plants, birds are scalded immediately following bleeding while still hanging on the continuously moving conveyor, which carries them through a long tank of hot scald water (Figure 10–9) or through a scald tunnel (Figure 10–10). Speed of the conveyor and length of the scald tank or tunnel determine total exposure to the scald medium. Birds are scalded by immersion in or spraying with hot water in order to facilitate removal of feathers. The heat relaxes the dermal muscles around the feather follicles, loosening the feathers and allowing them to be picked more easily. Different types and sizes of birds require different temperatures of water and times of exposure. Older birds and waterfowl require a higher temperature and longer exposure. If the water is too cool, feathers will pull out with difficulty. If the water is too hot, feathers will come out

FIGURE 10–9
Broilers immersed in tank of hot water while hanging from shackles on
conveyor moving to allow required scald exposure.

very easily; however, the skin will appear pink and blemished due to
partial or complete removal of the outer epidermal layer. Over scalding
will also cause the skin to have a sticky feeling after picking and may
result in a shorter shelf-life for the meat. Surface agents, such as food-
grade detergent, may be added to the scald water to reduce the surface
tension of the feathers and thus facilitate water penetration to the skin
surface. Surface agents are particularly useful in scalding waterfowl on
whose oily feathers would otherwise tend to prevent penetration of the
hot water.

Although higher temperatures may be used, semi-scalding in water
at 50.5°C–54°C (123°F–128°F) for 1½–2 minutes will generally be adequate
for land fowl and will yield an attractive carcass. When scalding individual
poultry carcasses by hand, hold the feet of the bird, one in each hand,
and agitate the bird up and down in the scald water (Figure 10–11). The
bird must be immersed below the hock joint to facilitate removal of all
leg feathers plus the skin layer covering the hock joint. The minimum
necessary scald time can be determined by pulling on leg feathers; when
they pull out easily the bird has been adequately scalded.

Feather removal or "picking" is done commercially by a machine
through which the scalded birds pass, still shackled to the continuously

FIGURE 10–10
Bled turkeys entering scald tunnel while hanging from shackles on conveyor moving to allow required scald exposure. (Photograph by Marty Traynor.)

FIGURE 10–11
Hand-scalding broiler carcass. (Photograph by Colleen Coyle.)

moving conveyor (Figure 10–12). These machines have rotating drums or spinning wheels to which are attached rubber "fingers" (Figure 10–13). The wheels are adjusted so these rapidly moving fingers contact every part of the carcasses on the shackles as they pass through. The moving fingers will pull off almost all the feathers, leaving the carcasses with very few, if any, feathers or pinfeathers that need to be removed by hand. If the semi-scald method is used, the picking machine causes very little, if any, damage to the skin and of course no bruising since the blood has already been removed.

When processing just a few birds it is not difficult to hand-pick carcasses if they have been properly scalded. The wing and tail feathers should be removed first; the breast and back feathers should be removed in small bunches to avoid skin tears. This procedure may be aided by the use of a motor-powered spin (Figure 10–14) or revolving drum picking machine (Figure 10–15). Placing the carcass in contact with the moving

FIGURE 10–12
Turkeys on shackles moving out of feather-picking machine.

FIGURE 10–13
Rubber "fingers" mounted on wheels that are used in picking machines
to remove body feathers.

FIGURE 10–14
Motor-powered spin-picking machine. (Photograph by Al Hollister.)

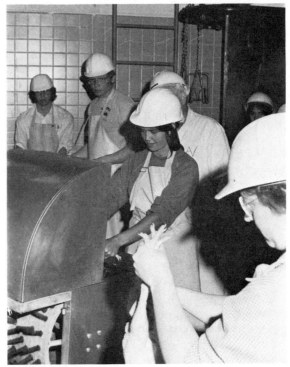

FIGURE 10–15
Motor-powered, revolving drum picking machine. (Colorado State University photograph.)

rubber fingers (Figure 10–16) will greatly aid feather removal and is particularly useful if more than a few birds are to be processed. Mechanically picked birds may need to have some pinfeathers removed by hand. This can be done by placing a flat knife under the pinfeather with the thumb on top and pulling the feather out of the follicle.

The "hairs" that appear along the back of picked poultry carcasses are actually a specialized type of feather known as a filoplume. These feathers lack most of the barbs along the rachis and therefore appear to be small hairs. Since they may be objectionable to some consumers, they are usually removed by singeing. The carcass is passed momentarily through a gas flame long enough to burn off filoplumes, but without heating the wet skin (Figure 10–17).

Waterfowl may be dipped in melted wax following scalding and picking. The wax is chilled and peeled off, taking with it the small feathers

FIGURE 10–16
Feather picking a broiler carcass using small revolving
drum picking machine. (Photograph by Colleen Coyle.)

FIGURE 10–17
Gas flame singeing of hair-like feathers (filoplumes) on the backs of picked
broiler carcasses.

and down, thus facilitating the otherwise difficult task of removing down, pinfeathers, and filoplumes from ducks and geese.

At this point in processing, the birds are sprayed with water to remove any adhering blood, feathers, or other contamination. "New York Dressed" poultry was at one time sold retail with the viscera, feet, and head still intact. These birds were ice packed in barrels, the head perhaps wrapped in paper. The entire carcass would be unpackaged and hung by the feet in the butcher shop, usually unrefrigerated. The butcher in the shop, or the customer in the home, would remove the head, feet, and viscera prior to cooking. Older people still recall stories of young, inexperienced, urban homemakers who unthinkingly roasted their first Thanksgiving turkey with the viscera left inside. Even when the viscera were removed in the home, there was danger of cutting the intestines and contaminating the meat and utensils with foul smelling, bacteria-laden feces. At best, there was potential for billions of bacteria multiplying rapidly on the carcass surfaces by the time the meat was ready to cook. This poultry would have a strong odor and would need to be prepared, cooked, and consumed in a short period of time, since even its refrigerated shelf-line was very short. The cooked meat could easily be recontaminated with bacteria on unwashed kitchen equipment prior to consumption, and probably was the cause of many an undiagnosed stomach ache that people attributed to "flu." Today the shelf-life of fresh poultry is considerably longer, and food poisonings from poultry meat are extremely rare. This is directly attributable to highly improved methods of evisceration, marketing, and preparation of poultry meat.

Evisceration is the removal from the dressed carcass of the preen (oil) gland, feet, head, lungs, and viscera; saving the liver, gizzard, and heart to be sold with the edible carcass as "giblets." This procedure of evisceration used to be referred to as "drawing" the dressed carcass. Thus, poultry that is "eviscerated" or "drawn" is completely cleaned with head and feet off and viscera removed.

For evisceration the carcasses are rehung on the shackles by the head (Figure 10–18). First the feet, including the shanks, are removed at the hock joint. Skin and tendons are cut at the hock joint until the feet can be pulled away. The bone should not be cut through as this leaves an unacceptable sharp edge or pointed splinter. Next, the preen gland at the base of the tail on the back side is first removed by cutting through the skin anterior to the gland and then continuing to cut under it and scooping it out, carefully so as not to cut into the gland itself. The neck skin may optionally be cut now or later on the dorsal side from skull to shoulder and then removed from the neck, leaving it attached to the body, but disattached from the head (Figure 10–19). The trachea and esophagus should remain attached to the neck skin at this point. Next, the birds are

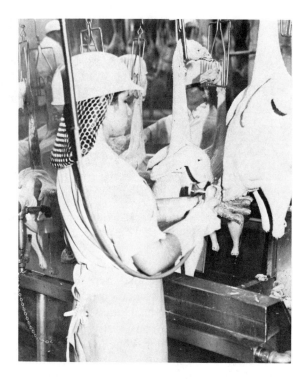

FIGURE 10–18
Turkey carcasses rehung on shackles by head for re-
moval of feet and preen gland. (Photograph by Marty
Traynor.)

rehung in the shackles by the hock joint (Figure 10–20) or transferred to
other shackles for passage into the evisceration room. The head remains
in the center part of the shackle, placing the carcass in the "three-point
suspension," which raises the abdominal area for easy access and allows
water and viscera to fall down away from the carcass.

It is important in commercial processing plants that further evisceration be in a different room, isolated from the slaughter, scalding, and
picking area, and that separate equipment and personnel be used for this
phase of processing. It is at this point that the product ceases being raw
material and becomes meat, which should not become cross-contaminated
with any removed part of the once live bird or with anything that contacted
that live bird or recently killed bird.

Although specific details of the proper evisceration procedure will
differ somewhat depending on the particular class of poultry, the following

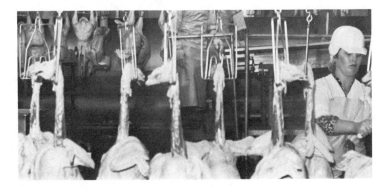

FIGURE 10–19
Skin removed from necks of turkey carcasses, leaving it attached. (Photograph by Marty Traynor.)

are generally recommended steps for eviscerating all classes of poultry and preparing a ready-to-cook product for packaging. Commercial poultry processing plants in the United States must meet very specific USDA regulations related to construction and proper operation of facilities and equipment and procedures of evisceration. These required procedures are frequently changed and should be determined by consulting the latest USDA regulations. However, most of the following steps will be generally

FIGURE 10–20
Turkey carcasses rehung in shackles by hock joints. (Photograph by Nancy Nydegger.)

applicable to most classes of poultry and are based on USDA required procedures to assure proper sanitation and a wholesome meat product.

1. Clean the cloacal region with water. Allow the water to flow away from, rather than over, the carcass.

2. Grasp the vent between thumb and forefinger with thumb covering opening. Pull vent up and make a half-circle cut around the posterior side of the vent, inserting the knife point into the body cavity toward the dorsal side. Do not cut the skin in the abdomen anterior to the vent since the large intestine lies close to the skin in this area and it must not be cut.

3. Still holding the vent, cover opening with thumb and insert other forefinger into the incision and tear the two ureters attached to the dorsal side of the cloaca. Also loosen any other tissue attached to the cloaca.

4. Pass forefinger over the large intestine and withdraw a 5 to 8 centimeter (2 to 3 in.) loop of intestine (Figure 10–21).

5. Carefully insert knife through the loop and with the blade turned up toward the vent, cut the abdominal skin anterior to the vent, allowing the vent, cloaca, and 10–15 cm (4–6 in.) of large intestine to hang down away from the carcass (Figure 10–22).

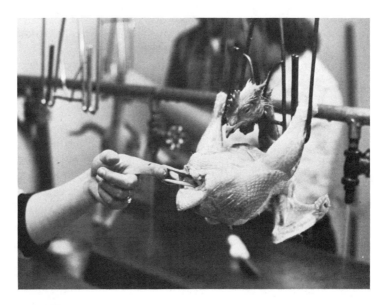

FIGURE 10–21
Withdrawing loop of large intestine from broiler carcass with half-circle cut around posterior side of vent.

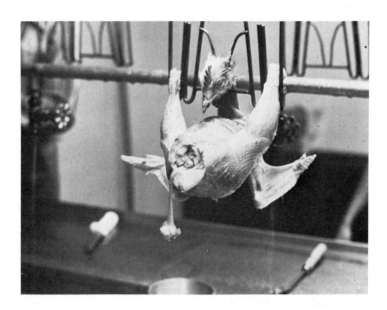

FIGURE 10–22
Vent, cloaca, and large intestine of broiler carcass hanging down, after
cutting abdomen skin anterior to the vent.

6. Strip any fecal material out of this protruding section of large
intestine by running it through two fingers under cold water spray so that
no fecal material contaminates the inside or outside of the carcass. If any
intestinal contents contaminate the carcass, rinse it immediately and then
trim away the contaminated tissue. Clean and sanitize contaminated utensils and equipment before proceeding.

Steps 2 through 6 are accomplished in commercial poultry processing plants with an air-powered, vent-cutting tool (Figure 10–23). This
tool has a cylindrical cutting blade which, when triggered to spin, makes
a clean cut around the vent and cloaca. A vacuum valve allows it to
simultaneously suck out any waste matter as it forms a suction hold on
the cloaca. After withdrawal of the cloaca with part of the large intestine,
the suction hold on the cloaca is released, waste matter is ejected, and
the tool is automatically washed before being used on another carcass
(Figure 10–24).

7. Enlarge the abdominal opening, as required, to accommodate the
hand. With broilers make a vertical cut from the original abdominal opening to the posterior tip of the sternum. For turkeys and geese, a horizontal
"bar cut" may be made in the abdominal skin about 4–5 cm (1½–2 in.)
from the abdominal opening, being careful not to cut intestines (Figure

FIGURE 10–23
Turkey carcasses in the "three-point suspension" from shackles, which raises the abdominal area for opening body cavity with a specialized vent cutting tool. (Photograph by Marty Traynor.)

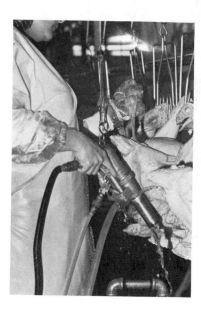

FIGURE 10–24
Vent cutting tool being rinsed between use on turkey carcasses. (Photograph by Nancy Nydegger.)

10–25). This second cut should be large enough to accommodate one hand, to permit removal of the viscera. This strap of skin will be used after evisceration to truss the legs prior to packaging.

8. Reach into the body cavity with your hand and loosen any tissues attaching the viscera to the body cavity wall, particularly in the anterior part of the cavity (Figure 10–26).

9. Grasp the gizzard in the palm of one hand and, with the proventriculus extending between the first and middle fingers, carefully but steadily pull the gizzard out of the body cavity. Most of the viscera will come out with the gizzard at this time. Viscera are left attached to the carcass and hanging down away from the carcass for postmortem inspection (Figure 10–27).

10. On postmortem inspection the USDA inspector observes all internal organs and membranes, inspects the entire carcass, and may palpate liver and spleen to detect lesions and other symptoms of systemic

FIGURE 10–25
Horizontal "bar cut" made in the abdominal skin of a turkey carcass to facilitate removal of viscera.

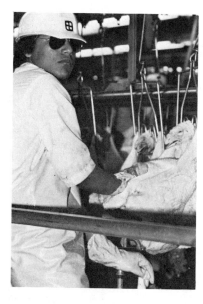

FIGURE 10–26
Loosening viscera prior to removal from a turkey carcass. (Photograph by Nancy Nydegger.)

disease (Figure 10–28). Adequate lighting of uniform intensity is required at this inspection point. The inspector may stop the process at this point and may remove any carcass or portion there of that fails to meet inspection requirements. Such a carcass or part would be condemned for human food and denatured and so identified prior to disposal.

11. After inspection, remove the liver from the viscera by holding

FIGURE 10–27
Viscera removed from a broiler carcass, left attached for post-mortem inspection. (Photograph by Colleen Coyle.)

FIGURE 10–28
Post-mortem inspection of viscera and carcass of broiler. (Photograph by Colleen Coyle.)

FIGURE 10–29
Separation of gallbladder, spleen, and intestines from liver held in palm of one hand.

the liver in the palm of one hand with the green gallbladder and intestines hanging down through the fingers (Figure 10–29). Detach the liver by pulling gallbladder down and away with the intestines. Thus, if the gallbladder should break, its contents (bile) would not contaminate the liver or carcass.

12. Detach the gizzard and intestines by cutting the esophagus $1–2\frac{1}{2}$ cm (0.5–1 in.) anterior to the proventriculus (Figure 10–30), after using two fingers to strip any contents into the proventriculus. Then trim away the small intestine at the posterior end of the gizzard and proventriculus, allowing both to drop down and away from the gizzard into the offal disposal container.

13. Carefully cut around the equator of gizzard muscle until the knife just contacts the inner pouch lining (Figure 10–31). This inner lining should not be cut. It will have a distinctly different texture and consistency and will appear yellowish in color compared to the dark purple gizzard

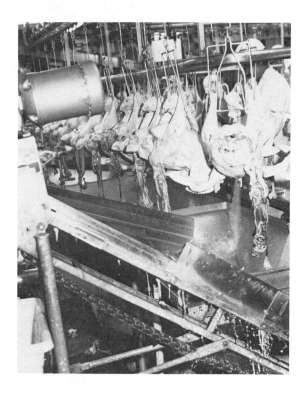

FIGURE 10–30
Intestines, gizzard, and proventriculus ready to be detached from inspected turkey carcasses. (Photograph by Marty Traynor.)

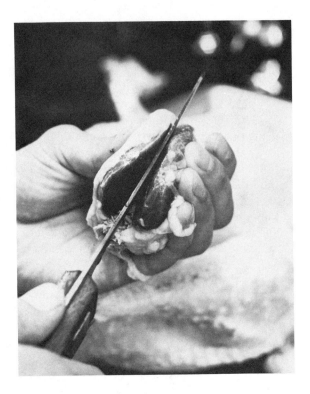

FIGURE 10–31
Cutting turkey gizzard muscle to remove intact inner pouch.

muscle. After exposing two or three centimeters (one inch) of the pouch along the equator, tear the gizzard muscle away from the pouch using both thumbs, being careful not to rupture the feed-filled pouch in the process (Figure 10–32). If the pouch ruptures before removal from the gizzard, carefully turn it and the gizzard inside out allowing the contents of the pouch to be rinsed away from the gizzard and attached fat. Then separate the pouch from the gizzard and rinse the gizzard well. Any portion of the gizzard or attached fat contaminated with contents of pouch, proventriculus, or intestine must be trimmed away.

14. The heart will usually not come out of the body cavity with the viscera. Remove it separately with the fingers. Remove the pericardium and cut off atria and attached blood vessels (Figure 10–33). Wash away any clotted blood from the chambers.

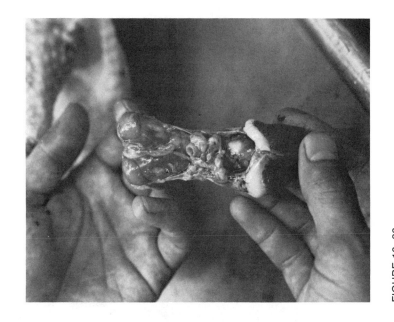

FIGURE 10–33
Removing pericardium of turkey heart prior to trimming atria and attached blood vessels.

FIGURE 10–32
Separating cut turkey gizzard muscle from intact feed-filled pouch.

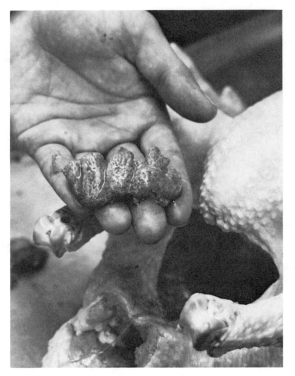

FIGURE 10–34
Turkey lung removed from rib cage by fingers.

15. Place the liver, gizzard, and heart in ice to cool prior to packaging.

16. The lungs will remain firmly attached to the rib cage in the thoracic cavity. Remove lungs with the fingers (Figure 10–34) or a special lung-removal tool (Figure 10–35). Care should be taken not to fragment the lungs, which would cause preventable bacterial contamination of the body cavity. Commercial processing plants often use a vacuum tube, which is inserted into the thoracic cavity and effectively removes the lungs by suction as the carcass moves along the conveyor line after evisceration (Figure 10–36). The kidneys can be removed from the dorsal wall by this means also. It is better to leave the kidneys in than to fragment them by instrument removal.

FIGURE 10-36
Turkey lung removal in a commercial processing plant, using a lung evacuator with vacuum tube inserted into thoracic cavity. (Photograph by Marty Traynor.)

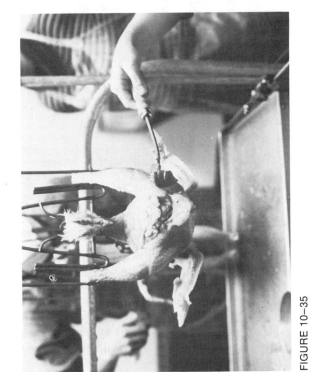

FIGURE 10-35
Broiler lung removed from rib cage by lung removal tool.

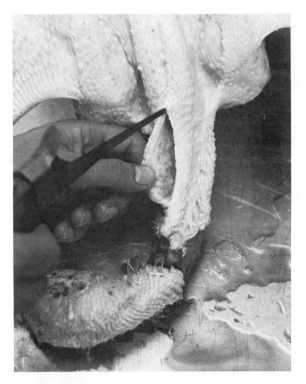

FIGURE 10–37
Turkey neck skin cut along groove on dorsal side from
head to base of neck.

17. If neck skin was not removed before opening the body cavity, unhook the head from the center of the shackle and cut the neck skin along the groove on the dorsal side from the head to base of the neck (Figure 10–37). Loosen skin and other tissue from the entire neck area (Figure 10–38).

18. Carefully loosen trachea from the neck skin and pull it out of the thoracic cavity, leaving the anterior end attached to head.

19. The crop will be firmly imbedded in the neck skin and must be separated. Locate the esophagus posterior to the crop and loosen it from the neck skin (Figure 10–39). While holding the esophagus and closing it off with one hand, work the fingers of the other hand down between the

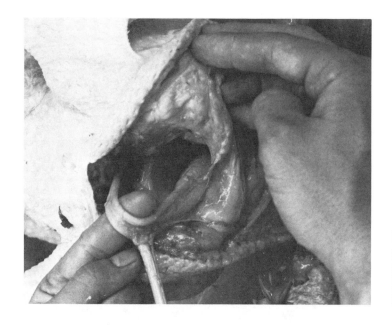

FIGURE 10–39
Locating and loosening turkey esophagus posterior to crop.

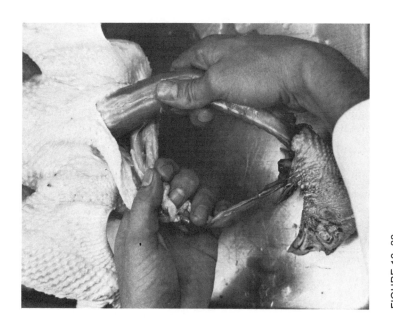

FIGURE 10–38
Skin, esophagus, and trachea loosened from neck of turkey carcass.

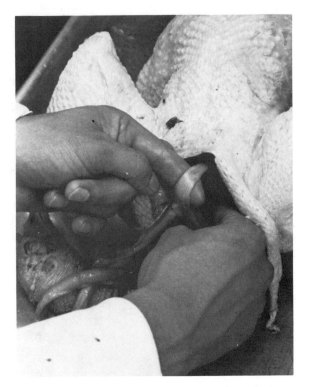

FIGURE 10–40
Loosening crop of turkey carcass from neck skin with fingers.

crop and the neck skin, carefully pulling it loose from attached tissues (Figure 10–40). Finally, separate the esophagus anterior to the crop from the attached tissues, leaving this end attached to the head (Figure 10–41).

20. If not done previously, cut the neck skin from the head as close to the skull as possible, avoiding any undesirable skin blemishes.

21. Cut the head, with attached trachea and esophagus, from the neck as close to the skull as possible and discard. Cut through muscle tissue and snap skull off at the first cervical vertebra.

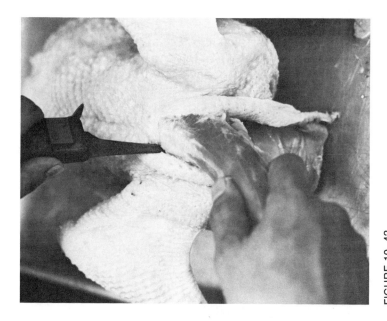

FIGURE 10–42
Cutting muscle on side of neck deep into shoulder groove of turkey carcass.

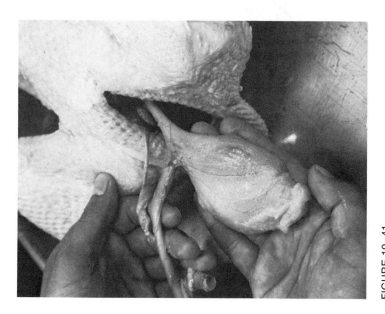

FIGURE 10–41
Turkey crop and esophagus separated from neck skin.

22. Make a cut through the muscle (not bone) on either side of the neck at its base, angling the knife deep into the shoulder groove as close to body as possible (Figure 10–42). Grasp the neck firmly in one hand and twist it while snapping it back and off (Figure 10–43). Cut any remaining tissues or tendons and separate the neck from the carcass. Place it in ice to cool prior to packaging.

23. Flush out body and crop cavities with a spray of clean, cold tap water and spray wash the entire outer carcass surface to remove any

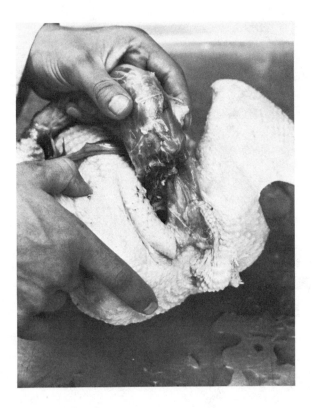

FIGURE 10–43
Removing neck from turkey carcass by twisting to separate vertebrae.

FIGURE 10–44
Eviscerated and rinsed turkey carcasses being drained of
excess water while being conveyed into further processing facility. (Photograph by Marty Traynor.)

adhering blood or loose tissues. Washed carcasses should be drained of
excess water prior to packaging or further processing (Figure 10–44).

24. If the bar cut was used for larger poultry, the carcass may be
"trussed" at this time before rigor mortis sets in. Place the end of legs
under the strap of skin just below the abdominal opening (Figure 10–45).

25. Poultry carcasses and parts must be rapidly chilled in ice water
to remove body heat. Internal muscle temperature of the carcasses and
parts must be less than 4.4°C (40°F) within four to eight hours, depending
on the weight of the carcass. Carcasses and parts should not remain in

ice water for more than 24 hours. Large commercial processing plants will generally use continuous in-line chilling machines that agitate the carcasses in ice water as they pass along the length of the line. When they come out after about 30 minutes they are adequately cooled to less than 4.4°C (40°F).

26. Carcasses may be weighed prior to packaging or in bulk after packaging.

27. Poultry may be cut into parts prior to packaging (Figure 10–46).

28. Poultry may be marketed either ice-packed, dry chill-packed, or vaccum-packed frozen. "Ice packed" whole carcasses are placed with crushed ice in waxed–paper-lined wooden boxes (Figure 10–47) or waxed

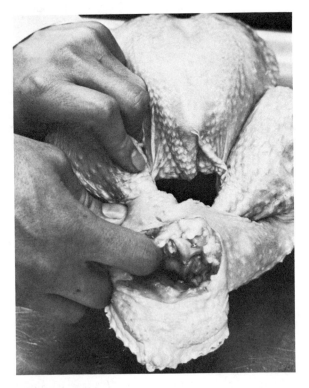

FIGURE 10–45
Trussing eviscerated and rinsed whole turkey carcass by placing legs under skin strap posterior to abdominal opening.

FIGURE 10–46
Turkey carcass cut into various retail parts: breast, back,
wings, legs ("drumsticks"), thighs, neck, and giblets (liver,
heart, and gizzard).

cardboard boxes for transport to retail markets. They will then be cut
into retail portions at the market and repackaged for display in the refrigerated meat counters. Alternatively, the carcass may be cut into portions at the processing plant and packaged for retail sale in plastic wrapped
meat trays containing an absorbant pad (Figure 10–48). These retail packages are then passed briefly through a blast freezer that rapidly lowers
the meat temperature before its transfer to a refrigerator where it equi-
librates to between −2.2°C and −1.1°C (28°F–30°F). Poultry meat remains unfrozen at −2.2°C (28°F) and is kept refrigerated through transportation and retail marketing. The meat absorbs less moisture than when
packed in ice, and is referred to as "dry chill-packed." Poultry meat may
instead be vacuum packed in plastic bags at the processing plant and
placed in a blast freezer until meat is completely frozen. It is then stored,

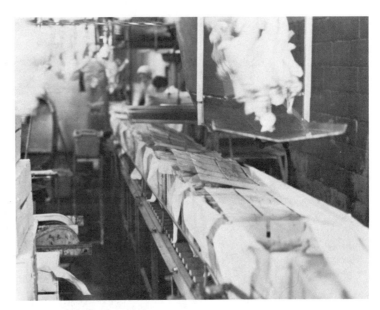

FIGURE 10–47
Whole broiler carcasses packed with crushed ice in waxed-paper-lined wooden boxes.

FIGURE 10–48
Broiler carcass parts packaged in plastic-wrapped meat trays.

FIGURE 10–49
Refrigerated turkey meat products being transported in refrigerated truck to distribution outlets. (Photograph courtesy of Longmont Foods Company, Inc., Longmont, Colorado.)

transported, and marketed as vacuum-packed frozen. All poultry meat is transported to distributors and retail markets in refrigerated trucks (Figure 10–49) designed to maintain its storage temperature.

GOVERNMENT REGULATION OF POULTRY PROCESSING

It was not until the 1920s that poultry production was done on an industrial scale. Poultry would be transported live by railroad from producing areas to distribution areas often many miles away. New York City was one of the larger distribution points. It was in the New York Central Railroad Yards on Manhattan Island, New York City, in 1924, that an outbreak of fowl plague occurred in a large shipment of poultry. This had a serious temporary effect on the New York City poultry supply, which demonstrated the need for a live-poultry inspection program. The New York Live Poultry Commission Association organized such an inspection program. In 1926, this program was taken over by the United States Department of Agriculture. In 1928, this live-poultry inspection program was enlarged to include the inspection of dressed poultry and edible products for their condition and wholesomeness. In 1927, the USDA offered poultry inspection service to cover exports to Canada. Soon other cities passed ordinances that prevented sale of poultry and poultry products that had not been inspected and passed under this USDA program. Any poultry producers or processors who wanted to ship their products into these cities for sale requested USDA inspection service. This inspection service was voluntary in that it was not required by federal law in order to ship poultry interstate, but it was required by many of the large poultry distribution cities. In the late 1940s there were approximately 150 poultry processing plants voluntarily under the USDA inspection program. In about five years this number doubled. Beginning in 1946, voluntary inspection service was provided under the authority of the Agricultural Marketing Act, and the cost of this service was paid by the poultry-processing establishment.

About this time (early 1950s) the public desire for compulsory USDA inspection of all poultry processors shipping interstate was evidenced by the many bills introduced to the 84th Congress favoring such legislation. In the Record of the United States Senate on July 27, 1956, Senator Wayne Morse, of Oregon, proposed and urged legislation for the compulsory inspection of poultry. He cited a psittacosis epidemic in Oregon in which the disease was transmitted to humans from turkeys, involving 64 people, 2 of whom died, and a salmonellosis outbreak in Michigan traced to poultry. He pointed out that there were 26 diseases transmissible from poultry to humans and that many food poisoning outbreaks each year were traced to poultry. He also pointed out that future disease outbreaks traced to poultry would severely hurt the poultry industry, which already had received much bad publicity, resulting in a decrease in consumer confidence and embargos by certain states. He cited various public health groups, women's organizations, consumer groups, farm organizations (National Farmer's Union), and labor unions (AFL-CIO, Amalgamated Meat Cutters, and Butcher Workmen) which not only supported, but actively campaigned for compulsory poultry inspection. On August 28, 1957, President Dwight D. Eisenhower signed an act that provided for the compulsory inspection by the United States Department of Agriculture of poultry and poultry products moving in interstate or foreign commerce. It was known as the Poultry Products Inspection Act.

The Poultry Products Inspection Act of 1957 requires that all poultry slaughtered for human food that travels in interstate commerce be inspected for wholesomeness by the USDA. In 1968, President Lyndon B. Johnson signed into federal law the Wholesome Poultry Products Act, which authorizes federal help to states to assure that poultry-processing plants selling their product only within the state meet or exceed USDA inspection requirements. This law effectively put out of business all small poultry processing plants that could not afford to redesign their facilities and purchase new equipment required by federal regulations. This, howeve, had no significant effect on total poultry meat production in the United States, since the new law coincided in time with the inevitable concentration of poultry-meat production into fewer but much larger integrated companies, with greatly increased total production.

In the United States, over 90% of commercially processed poultry meat is inspected for wholesomeness by the United States Department of Agriculture. The USDA poultry inspector is trained to diagnose avian diseases and either is, or is under the direct supervision of, a doctor of veterinary medicine (DVM). The USDA inspector determines the safety of the processed poultry meat and assures that it came from birds that were not diseased. He also determines that it was processed under sanitary conditions.

The USDA poultry inspector conducts "ante-mortem inspection" of poultry at rest in crates prior to their entry into the processing plant. Although each individual bird is not examined at this time, an attempt is made to detect any dead, diseased, injured, or otherwise unfit birds. Such birds would be condemned and destroyed and not allowed to enter the processing plant.

The USDA poultry inspector conducts "post-mortem inspection" of each individual carcass on the processing ling, including its organs and other viscera. These are examined for evidence of avian diseases, improper bleeding, and contamination with feces or foreign material. Avian diseases may be indicated by lesions, tumors, cysts, or other pathological conditions of the viscera or air sacs. All carcasses and parts and meat products found to be adulterated or unwholesome are condemned and destroyed under supervision of an inspector, unless they are made wholesome and unadulterated by reprocessing. Some meat condemned for human food may be heat processed and then used in animal feed.

The USDA inspector will assure that the plant premises, facilities, and equipment and its operation and plant personnel meet established sanitary requirements, in order for poultry to be processed under USDA inspection. If a poultry-processing plant fails to meet USDA requirements of sanitation and proper food processing technology, the company cannot sell its product for human consumption, since it will not be allowed to bear the official USDA or state "Inspected for Wholesomeness" seal (Figure 10–50).

The USDA provides a voluntary poultry meat grading service at cost to processing plants. Most commercial poultry processors subscribe to this service since they can sell higher quality Grade-A poultry for a higher price than nongraded meat. The USDA consumer quality grades of ready-to-cook poultry are: US Grade A, US Grade B, and US Grade

C (Figure 10–51). The major factors determining quality grade are: conformation (shape), fleshing (amount of meat), fat covering (amount of fat under skin), pinfeathers (amount), exposed flesh (amount and location), discolorations (size), disjointed bones (amount), broken bones (amount), missing parts (location), and freezing defects (amount). Grading is based on these quality factors, is voluntary, and is not related to inspection for wholesomeness (healthiness), which is required.

It was the American consumers' demand for wholesome, standardized, and graded meat that resulted in the development of federal inspection and grading services and the meat and poultry inspection laws. These laws tend to eliminate unfair competition, result in a more uniform price structure, and increase consumer confidence in the food. Sanitary processing, inspection for wholesomeness, and grading for quality all play an important role in the development of a sound marketing program for poultry meat. These programs enable the producer to receive a greater return for better quality and allow the consumer to compare prices in relation to quality. The consumer has a poultry meat inspection law in the United States that assures that the poultry meat product bearing the official USDA inspection seal has been properly prepared from healthy poultry and is truthfully labeled. We have this law because the consumer wanted it.

The poultry industry is in business for and because of the consumer, and most industries realize this. Ultimately control of profit or loss is with

FIGURE 10–50
Official United States Department of Agriculture seal indicating poultry meat product has been inspected for wholesomeness.

FIGURE 10–51
Official United States Department of Agriculture shield indicating quality grade of ready-to-cook poultry.

the consumer who decides whether or not one company's product is better than that of its competitors. Consumers today are too intelligent and aware to be deceived, and they have too much power to be cheated. They want government regulation so they won't need to worry about the quality and safety of the food they have had no hand in producing or processing. Government regulation of the food industry is, in fact, consumer regulation. Sometimes people in the food industry believe government regulatory agencies are not always completely aware of the realities of industrial food production, even though the regulatory agency's representatives may have good motives and legitimate concerns about food safety and quality. However, when government regulation is comprised of realistic, common sense procedures, which should be followed whether required or not, this does not place an unreasonable burden on industry. In fact, as a result of intense competition in the poultry industry today, most companies set and maintain higher quality and safety standards than the minimum required by government regulations.

FURTHER PROCESSING

The poultry industry in recent years has attempted to broaden the market and increase per capita consumption of poultry meat through development of convenience items for the consumer. The whole, oven-ready carcass has long been the most familiar poultry meat item (Figure 10–52). Now, however, raw and/or precooked carcass parts, boneless roasts, ground poultry meat, sausage products, hams and other cured items, and any lunch-meat product, including frankfurters, are made with turkey or chicken meat (Figure 10–53). Also, poultry meat is being used increasingly as an ingredient in other fabricated foods such as soups, pot pies, and frozen combination dinners.

"Further processing," then, is the cutting of the whole poultry carcass into smaller parts for specific uses in development of more convenient food products to increase consumer demand. Further processing is being increasingly employed in the commercial turkey, chicken, duck, and goose industries to varying degrees. However, it is being applied most extensively in turkey processing. Most of the meat is cut from the skeletons (racks) of the hanging carcasses as they move on a conveyer line past the meat cutters (Figure 10–54). Major muscles are formed into roasts, which are wrapped in aluminum foil for cooking (Figure 10–55) prior to being repackaged in plastic bags for institutional and retail marketing. The rack (bones) with adhering meat is finely ground in a deboning machine which extrudes flexible meat particles through very small holes in the sides of a metal cylinder and retains larger hard bone particles

FIGURE 10–52
Whole oven-ready turkey carcass.

FIGURE 10–53
A variety of further-processed turkey meat products available to the consumer. (Photograph courtesy of Longmont Foods Company, Inc., Longmont, Colorado.)

which will not fit through the holes. Figure 10–56 shows the extruded meat particles being collected in the hopper nearest the machine and the larger bone particles being forced out the smaller tube in the center and collecting in the other hopper. The finely comminuted meat, separated from most of the bone, contains less than the maximum allowable concentration of calcium and is used in a variety of further-processed meat emulsion-type products.

Turkeys are the most efficient source of animal protein to use in further-processed meat products. At a feed-to-live-weight ratio of about 3:1, they are more efficient in producing meat than any red meat animal. Although broiler chickens have a better feed conversion ratio (2:1) during growth, it takes about as much labor to cut and debone a broiler carcass as it does a large whole turkey carcass, which yields much more further

FIGURE 10–54
Removal of turkey meat from whole carcasses moving on a conveyer
line past meat cutters. (Photograph by Marty Traynor.)

processed me a oduct. Also, a large male turkey will yield 90% of its
live weight in whole carcass, compared to about 75% for a broiler chicken
and increasingly less for swine, cattle, and sheep. The turkey industry is
the further-processed meat industry of the future, although this trend toward more further-processed meat will continue with other types of poultry as well as pork and beef.

It is becoming less important to the consumer to think of meat in
terms of animal species or even the anatomical part of the animal; but
rather, in terms of further-processed meat product. This further-processed
product will be identified to the consumer by its distinctive appearance
and taste; that is, ham, frankfurters, bologna, or sausage, rather than by
the animal species from which it was derived. Perhaps meat from more
than one animal species will be combined to produce a meat product with
the desired characteristics, which, because of flavors added, does not
taste like either beef, pork, or poultry. The modern animal producer today
is looking toward the future of producing meat protein as efficiently as
possible for further processing into cooked meat products, which will
return a larger price per pound of product than the whole carcass or
selected raw cuts. The poultry industry will lead animal agriculture in this
expanding area of further-processed meat because the product made from

poultry meat is equally desirable in taste, is less expensive to produce, has fewer calories and fat, and is equal or better in nutritional value when compared to its red meat counterpart. The poultry industry is the meat industry of the future and is already taking the lead in many areas of the world.

Further-processed poultry meat products are being increasingly used in food-service establishments, particularly fast-food restaurants. This trend will likely increase in the future as consumers develop an awareness of the taste, nutritional value, and relatively low cost of new poultry-meat products. Such further-processed poultry products lend themselves well to the changing life-style of the consumer who is eating more meals away from home and spending less time at home preparing meals.

Although commercial further processing provides convenience for the consumer, whole poultry carcasses at a greatly reduced price per pound are the better buy, and the meat can be further processed in the

FIGURE 10–55
Boneless breast of turkey wrapped in aluminum foil for oven roasting. (Photograph by Marty Traynor.)

FIGURE 10-56
Deboning machine extruding ground turkey meat particles into hopper nearest machine and ground bone
particle from center tube into other hopper.

home. A whole poultry carcass may be cut at home into typical retail
cuts, at a considerable saving in cost, by the procedure in Appendix 6.
The procedure is best applied to broiler chicken or other poultry carcasses
of a similar size, such as ducks; but may it also be used on larger carcasses,
such as turkeys or geese. Alternatively, a whole poultry carcass may be
deboned at home for use of the meat in a variety of further-processed
products by the procedure noted in Appendix 7. This procedure is best
applied to large turkey carcasses, but may also be used on smaller carcasses such as chickens or ducks.

Deboned poultry meat may be used in a number of further-processed
meat products. Although the following products were specifically developed for utilization of deboned turkey meat, any type of deboned poultry
meat could be used. However, other types of poultry will yield less meat
than turkey.

The supracoracoideus muscle can be easily pulled apart from the large outer breast muscle (pectoralis) (Figure 10–57). This smaller, inner muscle is very tender and can be dipped in egg batter and breaded prior to freezing and/or cooking. A boneless rolled roast can be made from the larger breast muscle and thigh meat. Place one side of the breast meat in the forming funnel making sure the skin is toward the outside and the neck skin is forward. Then place both thighs on top of the breast meat with the skin on the outside. Place the neck skin attached to the breast up over the thighs. Place elastic meat netting on the funnel and, using a plunger, gradually force the meat through the funnel into the tight-fitting, cylindrical meat netting (Figure 10–58). Place the meat roll, in its elastic netting, into a plastic bag, vacuum-seal, heat-shrink it if possible, and rapidly freeze. The meat should be thawed and the plastic bag then removed before cooking. Place the roll in a pan, cover with foil, and bake at 163°C (325°F) until an internal muscle temperature of 80°C (175°F) is reached. Then remove from the oven, slice, and serve.

Deboned poultry meat with adhering skin and fat may be ground in a meat grinder, packaged, and frozen. This product can be formed into patties for frying or barbecuing burgers, or can be used in meat loaf or in any dishes requiring ground meat.

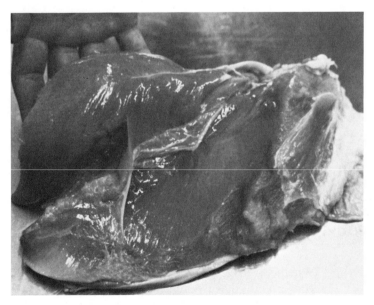

FIGURE 10–57
Supracoracoideus muscle separated from large outer breast muscle for fabrication of turkey meat products.

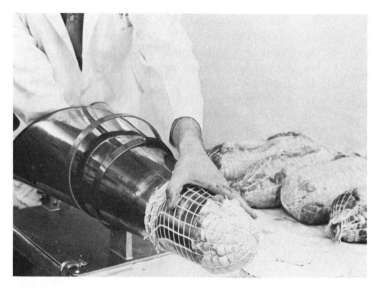

FIGURE 10–58
Raw boneless turkey breast and thigh meat being forced through forming funnel into meat netting.

Prior to freezing, ground poultry meat may be used to prepare sausage. If there is not enough skin and adhering fat, beef tallow may be added up to 15% of the mixture to facilitate cooking. However, if leaner meat is preferred do not add beef fat. There are many different sausage recipes readily available to suit specific tastes.

Whole poultry carcasses or any poultry meat may be smoked during cooking. This requires soaking the meat in a special brine prior to cooking and smoking. Turkey is the most comonly smoked poultry meat. However, chicken and other poultry may also be successfully smoked.

PURCHASE, PREPARATION, AND CONSUMPTION OF POULTRY MEAT

Whether refrigerated or frozen, ready-to-cook chicken, turkey, duck, goose, and guinea purchased in the United States as whole carcass or parts should have a package label or wing tag displaying the USDA grade shield (Figure 10–51). This shield is the designation of quality and certifies that the meat product has been evaluated for quality by a USDA poultry grader. The highest quality is designated "US Grade A" for poultry carcasses that are well-fleshed and meaty, and well-finished and attractive in appearance (Figure 10–59). "US Grade B" poultry carcasses may be slightly lacking in meatiness, have less fat covering under the skin and be slightly less attractive in appearance. US Grade B poultry carcasses are seldom found in the retail markets since they will usually be further processed into other meat products. "US Grade C" poultry carcasses are sometimes sold in retail markets at a reduced price per pound and may be marketed under a generic label, often downgraded only because of skin or wing removal. They may have the finish and meatiness of a US Grade A carcass with excellent cooking quality and thus provide a wise economical purchase.

Before poultry meat can be graded for quality by the USDA, it must be inspected for wholesomeness. The inspection mark and the grade shield (Figures 10–50 and 10–51) may be displayed together on the label or wing tag, which must also indicate the class of poultry in the package. The age class of the poultry indicates the tenderness of the meat. Poultry meat from young birds will be more tender than that from older birds. Young chickens may be labeled: young chicken, Rock Cornish game hen, broiler, fryer, roaster, or capon. Mature chickens may be labeled: mature chicken, old chicken, hen, stewing chicken, or fowl. Young turkeys may be labeled: young turkey, fryer-roaster, young hen, or young tom. Mature turkeys may be labeled: mature turkey, yearling turkey, or old turkey. Young ducks may be labeled: duckling, young duckling, broiler duckling, fryer duckling, or roaster duckling. Mature ducks, geese, and guineas may be

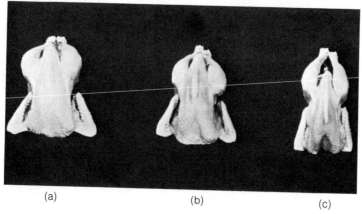

(a)   (b)   (c)

FIGURE 10–59
Ready-to-cook whole broiler carcasses: (a) US Grade A; (b) US Grade B; (c) US Grade C.

labeled: mature or old. Since the young age classes of poultry have very tender meat they are best purchased for barbecuing, frying, broiling, or roasting. The mature, less tender classes of poultry are better used for stewing, baking, and as an ingredient in other dishes and fabricated foods.

In the United States, chicken meat is usually marketed fresh, that is, not frozen; whereas turkey meat is usually marketed frozen. Turkey meat is frozen rapidly immediately after processing and is seldom held in frozen storage more than a few months before it is sold. However, around the holiday seasons, fresh, unfrozen, whole turkey carcasses will often be available.

All poultry meat is perishable and must be kept refrigerated or hard frozen prior to cooking. Therefore, select poultry meat items just before leaving the supermarket. Assure that the packages are not torn or damaged. Have all frozen and refrigerated meats wrapped together in the same bag. Transport these perishable meat products rapidly and immediately place them in the refrigerator. Poultry should not be exposed to periods of high temperatures, such as sitting in a warm car for an extended length of time. Cook refrigerated unfrozen poultry meat within one or two days of purchase. When freezing previously unfrozen poultry meat in the home you should wrap it tightly in aluminum foil or freezer paper or leave it in its retail plastic package. Store frozen meat in a home freezer at a temperature of $-18°C$ ($0°F$). Unfrozen poultry meat should be kept in the coldest part of the refrigerator. The special meat drawer in the refrigerator is generally satisfactory. The temperature of the refrigerator should be between $2°C$ and $4.5°C$ ($35°F$ and $40°F$). Poultry meat may be kept properly frozen for 6–12 months. However, fresh or thawed, it should only be refrigerated for up to two days before being cooked. Thawed poultry meat may be refrozen if it contains ice crystals or is still cold and has not been held in the refrigerator for longer than one or two days. Refreezing, however, may reduce the quality of the meat.

Thawing of poultry meat is most safely done in the refrigerator, where the food temperature cannot exceed the refrigerator temperature. However, this method requires advanced planning, for a frozen 9 Kg (20 pound) turkey carcass requires three or more days to thaw by this method. A faster, yet acceptable thawing method is to immerse the tightly wrapped frozen poultry meat in cold running water in the sink. The water need only flow at a slow rate. The sink must be cleaned before and after this method is used in order to reduce the risk of cross contamination. The microwave oven has brought the food handler a new method of thawing smaller pieces of frozen meat. Most microwave units have a defrost cycle that can be used effectively for thawing poultry meat immediately prior to cooking. It is not recommended to thaw frozen poultry meat at room temperature. If it is necessary to thaw large frozen pieces of poultry meat or whole carcasses at room temperature, use the following procedure: Place the wrapped frozen package in a paper grocery bag of approximately the same size, and slip a second paper grocery bag over the opening of the first. This will provide insulation from room heat and a cooler environment immediately surrounding the surface of the frozen meat, which will thaw first. Thus, the entire package of meat will thaw more uniformly, and the surface should not be at a dangerously high temperature while the center thaws. Do not thaw frozen poultry meat on surfaces or trays where other foods are kept and don't let moisture from the thawed package drip into other foods on lower shelves.

Poultry meat should be rinsed under cold running prior to preparation for cooking. Appropriate equipment, such as ovens and appliances, must function properly and reach the proper temperature so recommended cooking times can be safely employed. Poultry meat must be cooked thoroughly for the proper length of time to achieve the proper internal muscle temperature. Cook poultry meat to a required internal muscle temperature as measured by an accurately calibrated meat thermometer. Chicken should be cooked to an internal muscle temperature of 74°C–77°C (165°F–170°F). Turkey should be cooked to an internal muscle temperature of 82°C–85°C (180°F–185°F). Boneless poultry roasts should be cooked to an internal muscle temperature of 77°C–79.5°C (170°F–175°F). Stuffing in a turkey carcass should reach a temperature in all parts of 74°C (165°F). Frozen poultry takes about one and a half times as long to cook thoroughly as the same weight and size of unfrozen poultry. In using the meat thermometer for accurate measurement of internal muscle temperature, be sure the tip of the thermometer is immersed in the deep muscle but not touching bone or fat. In a poultry carcass, insert the meat thermometer into the center of the thigh muscle on the inside toward the body of the carcass. Poultry meat and juices must be thoroughly cooked and not appear pink. Estimate the proper time for cooking based on the size of the piece of meat so that it is completely cooked and can be served immediately after cooking. Poultry meat should never be partially cooked prior to storage.

When stuffing raw poultry carcasses with dressing, you should not refrigerate or freeze the bird prior to cooking, but should cook it immediately. Stuffed frozen poultry purchased retail should be cooked without thawing. Any frozen, combination poultry-meat dishes should be cooked without thawing. Follow specific cooking instructions on the labels of all processed poultry meat products.

It is important in preparing poultry meat not to cross contaminate the cooked meat or other food, and not to cross contaminate any food that will not be cooked, with the raw poultry meat. For example: In the process of cutting and proportioning raw poultry meat, the table, cutting board, and your hands should be thoroughly washed before contacting other food. Failure to do this will contaminate other food that comes in contact with your hands and the work surfaces.

Serve poultry meat as soon as possible after cooking. It should not cool to below 60°C (140°F) prior to being served. Leftover cooked poultry, broth, stuffing, and gravy should be placed in separate containers, loosely covered, and immediately refrigerated; or frozen if not to be used within one or two days. Cooked poultry meat may be stored frozen for up to six months. Meat should be cooled at no higher than 7°C (45°F) in a refrigerator in containers no deeper than four inches. The wings, thighs, and drumsticks should be separated and removed from the poultry carcass, wrapped loosely in aluminum foil, and immediately refrigerated. Large pieces of meat should be cut into smaller pieces before refrigerating to facilitate adequate rapid cooling. Gravy may be cooled before freezing by agitating it for several minutes in containers held in cold water to decrease total cooling time.

Following these common-sense recommendations in the handling and preparation of poultry meat will assure maximum benefit from the highly nutritious, delicious tasting, and wholesome product. Numerous recipes are available for preparing and cooking poultry meat in a great variety of ways, either by itself or in combination with other foods. However, one excellent method of preparing poultry meat is barbecuing.

A poultry barbecue is a traditional American pastime that to most people is synonymous with lots of fun, food, friendly people, and delicious chicken or turkey. A poultry barbecue can be a small family affair in the backyard, a reunion of all the relatives, a gathering of a few families in a backyard or park, or a much larger gathering of hundreds of people. Student clubs and other organizations can put on poultry barbecues as a means of making money. Barbecued poultry meat will practically sell itself as the aroma from the barbecue pit drifts out over the surrounding area. A little help from some homemade signs and a few enthusiastic promoters will bring in all the customers. By the second barbecue, promotion will be easier since many previous customers will return. Although barbecued poultry meat will just about sell itself, it doesn't prepare itself. Barbecuing poultry is not difficult but there are some specific procedures that must be followed to do it successfully.

A poultry barbecue, properly planned and conducted by knowledgeable and concerned people working together as a team, can be an extremely enjoyable and satisfying experience for guests as well as for those who host it. Many compliments will be received on a delicious meal highlighted by the main entree of barbecued chicken or turkey. Once you are involved in the preparation, it will be easier and even more fun the second time. Once people taste delicious, barbecued poultry meat they will return again many times to enjoy this excellent food cooked to a taste simply not achieved by any other method of cooking.

The comparative value of available meats should be of interest to anyone who purchases, prepares, and/or consumes meat. Agricultural animals differ greatly in their efficiency of converting feed into meat. This comparison can be looked at in a number of different ways.

Feed conversion ratio is the number of kilograms/pounds of feed per kilogram/pound of live weight during growth of an animal to market (slaughter) weight. Feed conversion values for meat producing animals are:

sheep*	7–8
cattle*	7–8
swine	3.0–3.5
turkeys	3.0–3.5
chickens (broilers)	2

* Grown in feed lot on a concentrated ration.

As can be seen, broiler chickens are the most efficient converters of feed to live, ready-to-slaughter agricultural animals. Turkeys and swine are also relatively efficient converters of feed to live weight, compared to cattle and sheep. However, this isn't the only factor to be considered.

Eviscerated yield in whole carcass is the percent weight of uncut carcass and edible organs (minus blood, feathers, hair, hide, head, feet, and inedible viscera and organs) of live market weight just prior to slaughter. Eviscerated yield values for meat producing animals are:

sheep	55%
cattle	50%–62%
swine	72%
turkeys	80%–90%
chickens (broilers)	75%

So it appears that the more efficient feed converters also have a higher yield of carcass from live weight. For poultry, the larger the bird, the greater the eviscerated yield. Large male turkeys will frequently yield a carcass over 90% of live weight, whereas smaller hen turkeys will yield closer to 80%, and even smaller broiler chickens about 75%. This difference between turkeys and broilers in carcass yield makes the difference of one pound in feed-conversion ratio less significant.

Let's carry this comparison even further, since we don't actually eat the entire carcass, which contains bone and a variable amount of fat, tendons, and cartilage. Percent edible raw meat of carcass weight includes fat normally adhering to uncooked retail cuts or forms of red meat and skin and underlying fat of poultry, but does not include any bone or fat trimmed prior to retail sale. Percent edible raw meat of carcass weight values for meats are:

lamb	64%
beef	62%
pork	67%
turkey	75%
broiler	68%

A related statistic for comparison is percent edible raw meat of live ready-for-market (slaughter) weight:

lamb	35%
beef	38%
pork	48%
turkey	64%
broiler	51%

One reason poultry yields a much higher percent edible raw meat from either carcass weight or live weight is its relatively lighter weight bones. Most avian bones are hollow and therefore contribute considerably less to the weight of the carcass and live animal than do the bones of red-meat animals, which are more dense and filled with marrow. Turkey has considerably more musculature in relation to bone mass than lamb, beef, or pork. The difference between turkeys and broilers in percent edible raw meet also makes the difference of one pound in feed coversion even less of an advantage, if any, for broilers.

To carry this comparison a step further, one should realize two additional factors concerning retail cuts of meat. The retail weight of raw meat purchased by the consumer includes a certain percent that is not eaten after cooking, such as bone, cartilage, tendons, fat, and moisture, as well as fat lost during cooking. The retail price per pound of raw poultry is considerably less than any of the red meats. In 1983, an average retail price per pound for meats was:

beef (choice)	over $2.50
pork	over 1.50
turkey	less than .80
broiler	less than .60

Therefore, it is meaningful to compare meats on the basis of cost per pound of cooked edible portion, that is, what you pay per pound for what you actually put in your mouth and swallow. This calculated statistic will vary for any meat as the retail price per pound of the raw ready-to-cook meat changes. The values in Table 10–1 were calculated using actual retail prices per pound in 1983 for the meats compared. Thus, considering the cost per pound of the meat actually eaten, chicken and turkey are by far the most economical retail meat buys.

One of the most important items in any consumer's budget is food. Today, with costs of all foods increasing and awareness and concern for good nutritional diets also increasing, most consumers are looking for ways to stretch their food budget further and allot a larger portion of it to improved nutrition. Many food shoppers try to seek out least-cost items on the supermarket shelf. Unfortunately, however, nutritional information related to cost is not readily illustrated on the food package. Even with nutritional labeling, cost per unit of a given nutrient, such as protein, is not readily apparent. Food shoppers, in attempting to be economical, often compare food values on the basis of cost per package or individual

TABLE 10–1
Meat Costs Per Pound of Cooked Edible Portion

Meat (ready-to-cook)	Percent Edible Portion after Cooking	Retail Price Per Pound[1]	Cost Per Pound of Cooked Edible Portion
Beef: chuck roast	39.2	$1.85	$4.72
round roast	56.0	2.95	5.27
Pork: rib and loin chops	37.6	1.47	3.91
Turkey: whole carcass	58.7	.79	1.35
Broiler: whole carcass	50.2	.54	1.08

[1] In 1983, Denver, Colorado

serving, rather than cost per unit of a major nutrient such as protein. Here is where true value comparisons should be made. Foods should not be evaluated by comparing package or even serving prices, but rather by comparing costs for the food that actually enters the body and stays there to nourish it. The following cost analysis (Table 10–2) should help in planning meals that are highly nutritious as well as economical. It is evident from this cost analysis that eggs and poultry meat are the least expensive sources of high quality animal protein.

Since meat is largely protein with a relatively small amount of fat and an insignificant source of dietary carbohydrate, it is reasonable to compare meats based on cost per pound of protein. Meats are good sources of high quality protein (containing all essential amino acids) in the human diet, and nutritionally, meat is eaten to supply dietary requirements for protein. But when people eat steak, frankfurters, or even turkey and chicken, they are not thinking primarily of supplying their dietary requirements for protein or essential amino acids. Foods are eaten primarily for their taste and the enjoyment they provide. People in affluent

TABLE 10–2
Cost Per Pound of Protein in Various Meats

Meat (ready-to-cook)	Percent Protein in Uncooked Edible Portion[1]	Retail Price Per Pound[2]	Cost Per Pound of Protein
Bacon (sliced)	8.4	$ 1.79	$ 21.31
Lamb chops	13.0	4.39	33.77
T-bone steak	14.7	3.49	23.75
Beef rib steak	16.9	3.59	21.25
Frankfurters (hot dogs)	12.5	1.57	12.56
Ham	15.9	2.19	13.78
Pork chops	17.1	1.39	8.13
Beef roast (chuck)	18.7	1.85	9.90
Hamburger (beef)	17.9	1.69	9.45
Eggs (chicken)	12.9	.54	4.19
Ground turkey	32.4	1.19	3.68
Turkey, whole carcass	21.4	.79	3.70
Broiler, whole carcass	18.6	.54	2.90

[1] Watt, B. K. and A. L. Merrill. 1963. Composition of Foods. Agricultural Handbook No. 8. United States Department of Agriculture, Washington, D.C.

[2] In 1983, Denver, Colorado.

societies in many areas of the world buy steak at over three dollars per half kilogram (pound) and frankfurters and bacon at over one dollar per half kilogram (pound) because they enjoy the taste; not realizing the fact that cost may be over $23, $12, and $21 per half kilogram (pound), respectively, for the nutrient, protein.

Many people mistakenly think that because they are on a tight budget, they are economically forced to eat lots of hamburger and frankfurters. Actually, hamburger and frankfurters, which may have a relatively low retail price per package, are two of the more expensive foods in cost per pound of protein; much more expensive than ground turkey, eggs, or chicken. Eggs and poultry meat are the most economical sources of high quality animal protein. For this reason, poultry meat and eggs will be a major source of food animal protein in most developing as well as developed countries in the world in future years.

CHAPTER 11

AGRICULTURAL ANIMAL WELFARE

Poultry is produced commercially only for the purpose of providing food for humans. However, humane treatment of the birds, adapted to live in confinement and be cared for by humans, is essential; not only for the comfort and welfare of the birds, but also for realizing their maximum potential for efficient food production.

Animal husbandry, now an outdated term, generally applied to the caring for domesticated animals. However, although the term is outdated the basic objectives of husbandry have not changed. Although humans eat plants and animals for nourishment, up until about 10,000 years ago they obtained this food only by gathering, scavenging, and hunting. The domestication of animals probably originated with humans caring for the abandoned young of certain animals. This led to the realization that animals could be cultured just as could plants; and as villages developed, this procedure proved a more reliable and easier method of feeding large populations than gathering, scavenging, and hunting. Culturing animals required care, housing, feeding, and protection. As a result, some animals reproduced readily and grew well. Obviously wild animals needed to adapt psychologically, as well as physiologically, to captivity. Thus, genetic selection in this new environment resulted in propagation of those animals that, through adaptation to confinement, reproduced and grew well in captivity. Animals not adapting to domestication did not reproduce in confinement and were therefore never domesticated.

ANIMAL CARE

Over the course of time, humans began to apply artificial selection in breeding domesticated animals, and they developed breeds within species that had characteristics humans desired in food-producing animals. By selecting for these food-producing characteristics, humans often caused animals to lose many of their natural survival characteristics, which required humans to provide additional protection from the environment. Increasing the level of confinement of domestic animals most easily provided them protection from their environment. This change saw a gradual development of confinement from open range, to fenced range, to outdoor pens, to fenced range shelters, to complete confinement in "houses." Increasing the extent of confinement of domesticated animals made it easier for humans to provide necessary protection from predators, unfavorable weather, and temperature extremes.

As more confined animals rapidly consumed available natural food, humans fed them. This was not an insurmountable task since humans were culturing and harvesting surplus quantities of plant materials that could be fed to the confined animals. The labor involved in animal agriculture consisted of providing feed and water for the confined animals and harvesting the food products (meat, eggs, and milk) produced. Development of sophisticated equipment for use in the confinement units, such as automatic feeders, waterers, and egg collectors, reduced some labor. Also, it became obvious that less total labor was required when additional animals were concentrated in a given confinement unit, rather than the alternative of building additional units for additional animals at the same concentration levels. Food production per animal was not severely reduced by placing two, three, or even four times as many animals in a given confinement unit; thus, total labor decreased as yield per unit increased.

The increased concentration of confined animals did have inherent problems, such as the need for increased ventilation, waste removal, and control of communicable disease and animal hostility. These problems were readily controlled by concurrent advancements in mechanical equipment, animal health, and animal breeding, thus meeting the basic biological needs of the animals.

Advances in the sciences of nutrition and genetics since 1900 were then easily applied to the confined agricultural animals, further increasing their yield and efficiency. They were fed a scientifically determined, computer calculated, optimal diet, rather than being allowed to choose what to eat, and were bred for most economical and rapid production of meat, eggs, or milk. To most efficiently convert feed into animal tissue (meat, eggs, or milk), movement of the animals, which required energy from the feed, was minimized, further curtailing the animals' natural freedom. The animals were now penned or caged. This change was necessary because the new, rapidly growing breeds soon became too heavy for their immature bones to support, and leg problems developed, preventing unlimited movement. Flying for poultry became virtually impossible. Although agricultural animals still maintained the natural instinct to breed in captivity, turkeys became too large and clumsy to mate successfully enough to supply the yield in offspring that humans now required. This problem was solved by utilizing artificial insemination. Although in many animals natural mating occurred only in the spring, artificial insemination allowed year-round breeding, further increasing total productive yield. Light and temperature were controlled artificially in the confinement units to make the animals receptive to reproduction at any time of the year.

Thus over many generations, humans have changed these domesticated animals biologically from what their wild ancestors were to the relatively efficient food production "machines" of modern animal agriculture. There are additional gains planned for feed conversion efficiency that will necessitate further biological change in these animals. These biological changes in the animal are of benefit to humans in terms of yielding more food more efficiently, but they have correlatively produced biologically weaker animals in terms of their ability to survive and reproduce in the "natural" or wild environment. These changes necessitate an increased reliance of the agricultural animal on humans to provide protection from the environment, in which they would otherwise suffer, perish, and/or fail to reproduce.

There are two opposing viewpoints that can be looked at in this historical development of animal agriculture. The remarkable progress humans have made since they gained dominion over animals, particularly during the last century, may be considered favorable to the well being of these animals, as well as to humans. By using our superior intelligence to manipulate animal biology and care for the altered animal produced, we have caused these animals to efficiently provide an abundance of high quality, nutritious, good tasting food. Animal agriculture, led by the poultry industry, is truly a modern day miracle of the agricultural revolution, benefiting many humans. However, one could instead consider that humans treat agricultural animals inhumanely. Are agricultural animals' "rights" being violated when poultry are confined in high density populations, debeaked, caponized, comb-dubbed, force molted, desnooded, toe-clipped, and finally when they are killed for use as human food? Are they being physically and even psychologically abused because they may appear to be either uncomfortable and/or unhappy under conditions of their confinement? Since humans can exist without animal food products, is it immoral and unjustified to subject agricultural animals to present production methods? Some feel that it is wrong to subject any animal life to the conditions to which agricultural animals are exposed. The controversial issue is "animal rights," related to animal agriculture.

ANIMAL RIGHTS

The issue of animal rights is no longer academic or hypothetical. It has become a hotly contested issue involving two opposing factions sometimes referred to as "animal rights supporters" and the "agricultural animal producers." Concerned individuals studying the issue will be positioned philosophically somewhere on a continuum at or between the extremes of these two opposing factions. Some serious, open-minded study of the issue is necessary before a decision may be reached between these two extremes. Currently too few people on either side of this issue have done enough study on the philosophies underlying the opposite ends of the continuum.

There is an entire spectrum of positions espoused by those concerned with animal welfare issues. On one end of the continuum there is extreme "anthropomorphism" that ascribes human characteristics, behavior, and motivation to animals or inanimate objects (Figure 11–1). This term has also been referred to as "Bambiism," symbolic of the many storybook animals that take on human characteristics and behaviors. Peter Rabbit, Uncle Wiggley, Mickey Mouse, Bugs Bunny, Smokey Bear, Winnie the Pooh, Morris the Cat, Snoopy, and Garfield the Cat are just a few of many such fictitious animals we love for their human behaviors. By his "humanization" of animals, Walt Disney has probably influenced countless people in the direction of anthropomorphism by directing their early thought processes relative to animals. Although there were others before and after Walt Disney who literally breathed human life, not only into animals but also into inanimate objects such as cars, trucks, trains, boats, planes, houses, and so forth; the most famous of these characters and the most beloved rodent in the world has to be Mickey Mouse. Therefore, how could anyone kill a mouse? But let's get more personal; what about Chicken Little, Donald Duck, and Big Bird? Who would ever want to kill a chicken? Also on this end of the continuum is "animism," a belief that animate and inanimate things possess an innate soul.

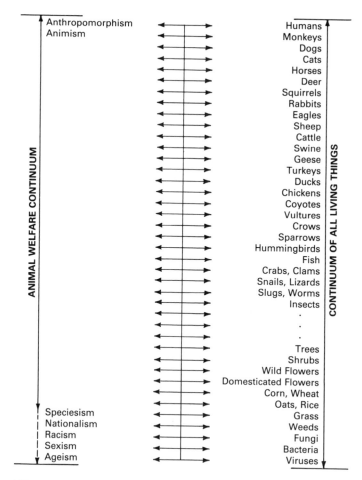

FIGURE 11–1
Continua related to the animal welfare issue.

On the opposite end of the animal welfare continuum we have what has been called "speciesism", a prejudice against the interests of members of other species and an attitude of bias for the interests of one's own species (Figure 11–1). Speciesism contends that humans can do anything they want to exploit animals of another species since these other animals are not human, do not reason, are less intelligent, and do not have a soul. However, this end of the continuum could conceivably be stretched out even farther to include nationalism, racism, sexism, and ageism, thus justifying one's exploitation of humans of another nation, race, sex, or age group.

A further question complicates the animal welfare issue: Which animals are worthy of having "rights" necessitating human concern? A separate but parallel continuum of all living things (Figure 11–1) may place humans at one end; and, along this continuum, in the following order, might be placed: monkeys, dogs, cats, horses, deer, squirrels, rabbits, eagles, sheep, cattle, swine, geese, turkeys, ducks, chickens, coyotes, vultures, crows, sparrows, hummingbirds, fish, crabs, clams, snails, lizards, slugs, worms, grasshoppers, moths, wasps, cockroaches, ants, flies, ticks, mosquitos, giant redwood trees, pine trees, oak trees, cherry trees, shrubs, wild flowers, domesticated flowers, corn, wheat, oats, rice, grass, weeds, mushrooms, mildew, bread mold other fungi, beneficial bacteria, pathogenic bacteria, and viruses. Start with this continuum and decide where you fit in; that is, which of these forms of life do you believe humans are morally justified in killing for their benefit? Which are humans morally justified in abusing or causing to suffer? Which forms of life can experience pain and discomfort? Does an axe cut in the side of a tree hurt? Is it all right to step on an ant; or swat a fly; or squash a mosquito; or poison a rat or cockroach; or cook or poison bacteria or molds; or pick flowers; or cut grass; or poison weeds; or cut wheat; or kill coyotes; or slaughter chickens, swine, cattle, or sheep; or hunt pheasant or deer; or kill horses, eagles, cats, dogs, monkeys, or humans? Where should the line be drawn? Is it uncomfortable for four adult chickens to live in a small cage? Are they suffering? Is it uncomfortable for four or more adult humans to live together in a small apartment in a high-rise building in New York City? Are they suffering? How should suffering be defined?

Positions taken on either continuum depend largely on experience and association with these various philosophies and forms of life. For example, consider a person of any age who has had almost daily exposure to the caring for and loving a pet cat, but has rarely seen or even heard much about his own cousin. Both the cat and cousin die a slow and painful death from cancer. The person cares lovingly for the cat during its illness prior to death; but does not witness the long illness of the cousin who lives thousands of miles away. This person could very conceivably feel much more grief and sorrow over the death of the pet cat than over the human cousin. If a person's only exposure to mice is in children's books they would rank mice higher on the value of life continuum than would someone who has lived in mice-infested housing. Thus, exposure to philosophies and life forms may profoundly influence one's evaluation of the controversial animal rights issue.

Chicken houses are environmentally regulated for temperature, humidity, and odor control and provide protection of birds from weather (Figure 11–2). More study, research, money, and technology have gone into determining and providing an optimal, nutritious diet for the chicken

FIGURE 11–2
Environmentally controlled chicken house for regulation of temperature,
humidity, and ventilation and to provide protection of birds from weather.
(Photograph by Marty Traynor.)

than for any other animal, including humans. Humans are not nearly as
well-fed as commercial chickens, because humans eat what they want to
rather than what is good for them. Commercial chickens receive much
better care and diet than do barnyard chickens. Why do humans treat
commercial chickens so much better than they do rats, cockroaches, and
often many humans? Because the chickens are to be killed and eaten.
And comfort, protection, and optimal diet are the most economical ways
to produce high quality chickens for human consumption. Basically there
are no stronger moral feelings about chickens than rats or cockroaches;
it's just that chickens can serve human needs better than many other forms
of life, so therefore they are exploited for their potential use. The question
remains: Is that immoral? This is a difficult question that cannot be answered without serious consideration of philosophical thought along the
entire animal welfare continuum previously defined and by scientific study
of evidence related to animal suffering.

Considerable recent interest in the animal welfare issue has
prompted written expression of philosophical thought on animal rights
from what appears to be an increasing number of authors. Notable out-
spoken authors on the topic have included Michael Fox, James Mason,

Peter Singer, and Bernard Rollin. They have brought the issue to the forefront and have provided other authors a basis for expansion or challenge of their philosophies. They have encouraged people to raise questions about the ethics of commercial animal production management practices. The resultant necessity for animal producers to think about ethical implications of these practices will enhance their ability to make intelligent decisions either to alter, or not alter, any of their own animal management practices.

Are agricultural animals justifiably worthy of moral concern by human beings? If you say, "No," why not? Perhaps because they do not possess an immortal soul, as humans do? But, do we know they don't? Rollin suggests that it doesn't really matter whether or not animals possess an immortal soul, since having a soul is irrelevant to deserving moral consideration.[1] This implies that any metaphysical or practical difference between humans and other animals does not provide sufficient grounds for excluding animals from moral concern. The argument is, if there are no morally relevant differences between animals and humans and if morality does apply to humans, then rationally we should include all animals within our scope of moral concern. He also questions why humans' language and ability to reason is considered morally relevant. Since animals can feel pain and pleasure and since they apparently anticipate, remember, and love, they should be allowed "entrance into the moral arena."[2] Although these characteristics of animals do not in themselves justify moral concern for animals, the presence of either needs, desires, goals, aims, wants, or interests—which humans can help, ignore, or hinder— do justify moral concern. Even without language, higher animals can communicate these needs and interests to humans. Rollin further suggests we should broaden the scope of moral concern beyond the ability of an animal to experience pleasure and pain to what may be considered the essential characteristics of life itself and a conscious awareness of this life. That is, we should regard all higher forms of life as worthy of considered thought, prior to making moral decisions concerning human control of their lives. In animal production we should be aware of, and provide for, the needs that an animal has an "interest" in and would consciously miss if absent. Rollin concludes that animals have the "right to be dealt with or considered as moral objects by any person who has moral principles, regardless of what those moral principles may be."[3] If humans recognize

---

[1] Rollin, B. E. 1981. Animal Rights and Human Mortality. Prometheus Books, Buffalo, N.Y.

[2] Ibid.

[3] Ibid.

this right, they must look at agricultural animals as having more than economic value.

Although any animal's "right to life" is not absolute, Rollin contends that to take the life of any animal for food, we need to identify strong, morally relevant reasons that outweigh the animal's presumptive right to life.[4] He also suggests that agricultural animals have the "right to the kind of life which (their) nature dictates."[5] The genetic code determines not only an animal's physical nature, but also its behavioral, psychological, and social nature. To understand an animal's nature one must observe the animal's life and activities. The nature of farm animals has been and continues to be "molded by human beings" through many years of artificial selection. Although humans have drastically modified the nature of domestic animals to serve their needs, the original nature of the animals is still genetically encoded and deserves moral concern. This animal behavior should be studied to help determine the proper way to care for agricultural animals so as not to violate their nature. The animal producer should have a "willingness to see" the animal's behavior and have "good reason" for all management practices based on observations of the animal's behavior. Rollin suggested that each case of a life form be evaluated independently in light of all circumstances before a decision on life, death, or treatment be made; but that the case must be evaluated by moral humans. Thus, we can't draw an absolute unchanging line on the continuum of life forms that will apply to all situations. He concludes by showing that his theory must serve only as an ideal and "that we must be prepared to accept less than the ideal when seeking the intersection between pure theory and the pressures of reality, in order to achieve anything at all."[6]

The current state of poultry science and the poultry industry is evidence of agreement philosophically with most of the high science, high technology practices of modern agribusiness as they relate to the rights and welfare of agricultural animals. Many look with pride and moral gratification at the world poultry industry as a leader in the production of nutritious, high quality, inexpensive food for the welfare of millions of humans. Illustrations presented in previous chapters clearly exemplify the application of science and technology to the business of food production through poultry. The poultry industry is a modern, dynamic, and vital segment of agriculture with excellent career opportunities for properly educated and trained people. The poultry industry is an example of one of human beings' successful attempts to supply an increasing demand

---

[4] Ibid.

[5] Ibid.

[6] Ibid.

for food through application of scientific knowledge. Today, poultry leads in the science of food production. In the future, poultry will continue to economically provide high quality, appetizing food for an expanding human world population.

Worldwide, most of the commercial poultry production practices are justified on the basis of the fact that the birds have been genetically changed through years of natural and artificial selection to the point that they require the protection we provide them. The birds' freedom to roam has been replaced by security necessary for survival and comfort. This appears to be a beneficial trade-off, particularly for the birds that have never known freedom and would quickly perish if released into the natural environment of its ancient ancestors: an environment in which it is incapable of living comfortably and one that it has never experienced.

Commercial management practices, for the most part, enhance the birds' welfare providing comfort, protection, and food with minimum effort expended by the birds (Figure 11–3). They, in turn, yield maximum growth (meat) or eggs, both extremely sensitive indicators of their well-being. Much thought, research, and effort has gone into eliminating the birds' stress in commercial poultry production, as stress due to suboptimal conditions has a rapid and severe negative effect on growth and egg production. Such a reduction in meat and egg yield would eliminate profit and put a poultry producer out of business fast. Although the motive is based on economics rather than ethics related to animal welfare, the welfare of commercial poultry is provided for under current production technology. However, productivity of an entire poultry operation cannot be

FIGURE 11–3
Inside of environmentally controlled chicken house for regulation of temperature, humidity, and ventilation.

used as the only measure of the welfare of individual birds since less production per bird due to increasing housing density could still result in greater yield per production unit. Nevertheless, as a group, poultry are possibly the best provided for animals on earth: receiving better care, a more comfortable environment, and a better, more consistant supply of food than many pets and humans. As humans, we value our freedom over this type of security; but possibly animals don't have this same value system. Perhaps, as long as chickens get plenty of food to eat and water to drink, and are not too hot or too cold, and are among thousands of other chickens with which they don't need to compete for the basic needs of life, they may prefer not to be set free into the cruel world of competition and survival. They certainly are not fit for this level of competition, and inevitably they would endure much suffering prior to an agonizing conscious death. In a processing plant, commercial poultry are rendered unconscious prior to slaughter and thus have no pain or awareness of their death by bleeding through a small incision of the jugular vein. Very few humans die this painlessly and without prior anxiety of their inevitable mortality. One could argue that commercial poultry live and die more humanely than many humans. But again, we warn against applying human values to animals, and vice versa.

As avian scientists we are basically biologists in our training and education. As biologists, life is studied in many forms, from viruses and bacteria, to plants, and to small and large animals; from single cells, to tissues, to organs, to complex living organisms. As students and teachers of biology, we have developed an intense love for and appreciation of "life" and all living things. Agriculture is applied biology, the study of living things applied to the production of food. Many plants and animals have served humans very well by supplying necessary quantities of nutritious, palatable food. We can and should exploit these few species of plants and animals that have proven to adapt well to the culturing systems of domestication, since they are necessary to efficiently convert the sun's energy into plant and animal tissue that humans conveniently consume to maintain what is considered the highest form of life. Agricultural animals, however, should not be made or allowed to suffer under uninformed, uneducated, and/or unconcerned managers who do not listen to, or who do not allow themselves to be questioned by, "animal rights supporters" and who will not seek feasible changes that would further enhance the welfare of their agricultural animals.

Modern poultry scientists and commercial poultry producers should react to the "animal welfare" issue with serious concern about the welfare of all live poultry. Any unnecessary suffering should be eliminated and optimal care for the birds emphasized. Well-designed research should be conducted to determine the effects not only of confinement and lack thereof but also of "factory farming" technology on the health, emotional status, and well-being of agricultural animals, as it relates to: (1) reproduction and production as affected by stress, and (2) adaptability of animals to confinement in a controlled environment. Poultry scientists and producers should modify negative thinking on the issue of animal welfare and maintain a dialogue with animal rights supporters as well as with government representatives who will make the ultimate legal decisions on the issue. The public should be educated relative to the problems and other realities involved in mass food production and to the consequences of possible legislative actions on the cost and availability of food for feeding massive populations.

The animal rights issue points up the necessity for a good basic education in the humanities and social sciences, in verbal and written communication skills, and in business principles, as well as in basic and applied science. A study of agricultural animal science is pursued by many because they like animals and appreciate their ultimate worth to humans. However, agricultural animal scientists and business people must be prepared to deal morally and effectively with more than just the physical, physiological, biochemical, pathological, and mechanical characteristics of animals. They are morally and professionally obligated to consider them in a philosophical, psychological, and sociological context. Professionals in poultry production careers will be better business managers if they broaden their considerations of the animals' welfare in the many decisions they make. If they seriously consider the welfare of the animal and balance that against related human welfare prior to making management decisions, such as the optimal number of laying hens per cage, the decisions made will be defensible, ethically justified, and accepted by rationally thinking people, even those who may disagree with the decisions. The important point is that the animals' welfare is considered and an educated, humane decision is reached based on deliberate thought and a consideration of all available knowledge.

As poultry scientists and producers we learn in the classroom and on the job the science and technology of producing animals for human food. Along with this knowledge, we should learn to understand the lives upon which our actions have a profound and considerable effect; for only through such understanding can we respect the rights of, and live in harmony with, our fellow humans . . . and animals.

CHAPTER 12

PLANNING AND MANAGING A POULTRY ENTERPRISE

A well-planned poultry enterprise should be located near sources of supply as well as markets, and the design of the facilities must take account of many factors that are associated with efficient production. Management decisions should be based on a least-cost systems approach incorporating all aspects of production and marketing. Planned production should be effectively managed to realize the maximum potential for income.

HATCHERY OPERATION MANAGEMENT AND DESIGN

Commercial hatcheries in the United States have been decreasing in number since 1945. However, the hatching capacity has increased substantially. Now, larger hatcheries, operating on a year-round basis, supply the needs of the poultry industry that has changed from seasonal operation to continuous operation. Hatcheries with a million-chick capacity utilize multiple units of incubators and hatchers at a ratio of three incubators to one hatcher. Large hatcheries are located close to the production areas so that chicks are shipped relatively short distances in special vans and buses that are climate controlled.

The hatchery business has developed into a highly specialized endeavor. Highly sophisticated hatcheries with mechanical equipment provide many services in addition to the hatching of chickens and turkeys (Figure 12–1). These services include sexing (Figure 12–2), debeaking,

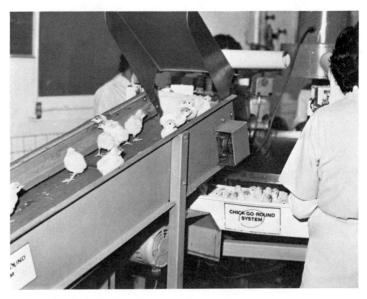

FIGURE 12–1
Hatched poults being conveyed from plastic boxes to service table. (Photograph by Marty Traynor.)

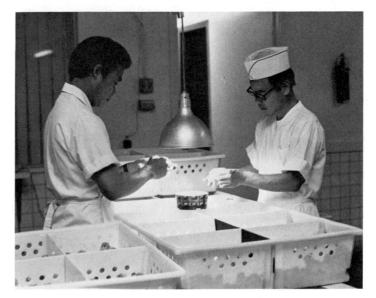

FIGURE 12–2
Sexing turkey poults shortly after hatching by cloacal examination ("vent sexing"). (Photograph by Marty Traynor.)

(Figure 12–3), wing notching, wing clipping, toe clipping (Figure 12–4), antibiotic-vitamin injection (Figure 12–5), and many specialized procedures requested by the customer. Young birds are frequently shipped from the hatchery to the customer by air or in special climate-controlled vans (Figure 12–6) for shorter distances. Very few are shipped by postal service, although this means may be used for small orders by mail-order type businesses. There are about ten large commercial incubator manufacturers in the world. Many smaller companies cater to the smaller as well as the specialized game bird and waterfowl markets. The large machines available to the commercial hatcheries have a capacity of 60,000 eggs. Hatchery buildings, designed expressly for the purpose to which they are intended, provide optimal efficiency of operation and disease control. They are located close to poultry-producing areas in an attempt to minimize distance for the shipping in of hatching eggs and the transportation of the birds produced. A flow-through system is employed in which eggs

FIGURE 12–3
Trimming beak ("debeaking") of turkey poults to control cannibalism during the growing period. (Photograph by Marty Traynor.)

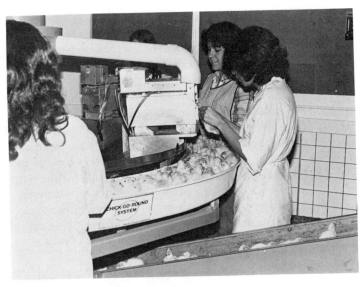

FIGURE 12–4
Trimming toes ("toe clipping") of turkey poults to control carcass skin tears and scratches during the growing period. (Photograph by Marty Traynor.)

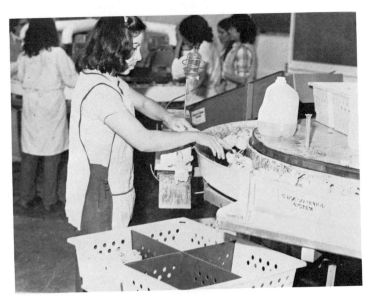

FIGURE 12–5
Injecting turkey poults with antibiotic-vitamin supplement to enhance growth and disease resistance. (Photograph by Marty Traynor.)

FIGURE 12–6
Serviced turkey poults in plastic shipping boxes loaded into climate-controlled van for transportation to nearby brooder houses. (Photograph by Marty Traynor.)

coming into the building and the birds produced do not cross paths, and employees of the various areas are not interchanged without careful sanitation precautions followed. The hatchery should be a model for cleanliness and sanitation. Many procedures and precautions are followed, from blood-testing egg supply flocks to the treatment of eggs by fumigation or egg dipping, all under strict management control. Standby electric generators (Figure 12–7) provide insurance against power interruption, which, even for short periods of time will cause embryonic mortality.

The National Poultry Improvement Plan is a voluntary, state-federal cooperative program for the control of certain egg-transmitted, hatchery-disseminated diseases of poultry. The plan became operative in 1935 when the United States poultry industry was starting to expand into the giant agricultural enterprise that it is today. At that time, a bacterial disease of poultry known as pullorum disease was quite rampant in the industry. This disease, caused by *Salmonella pullorum* would cause mortality of 60%–80% of the baby chicks that were hatched from eggs produced by infected breeding flocks. If the industry were to expand, this disease had to be conquered. Thus, the plan was established, with the United States Department of Agriculture being the coordinating agency and with an agency within each state being responsible for carrying out the provisions of the program within the industry.

The original program was limited to the blood testing of breeding stock to determine whether or not they were infected with *S. pullorum* and identifying those flocks that were negative. This procedure, coupled with improved sanitation practices at the flock and hatchery levels has nearly eradicated pullorum disease from United States' poultry flocks. During the 1950s, the antigen used in the blood test was modified to permit *Salmonella gallinarum* to also be detected. This microorganism, which causes fowl typhoid in poultry, has been nearly eliminated, also. During the 1960s and 1970s, other programs were added to the plan that provided for blood tests for some of the mycoplasma microorganisms. These microorganisms cause chronic respiratory disease and other maladies in poultry, which result in economic losses through morbidity, loss of feed conversion and egg production, and condemnation of carcasses at the processing plant. Blood tests and subsequent certification of breeding flocks which are free of *Mycoplasma gallisepticum* and *Mycoplasma syn-*

FIGURE 12–7
Standby electric generator to provide emergency power for hatchery.
(Photograph by Marty Traynor.)

FIGURE 12–8
Turkey hatching eggs from breeding stock tested and determined to be pullorum-typhoid clean, under the direction of the National Poultry Improvement Plan. (Photograph by Marty Traynor.)

oviae are now an important part of the National Poultry Improvement Plan. It is anticipated that a program for the control of *Mycoplasma meleagridis* in turkey breeding flocks will be started in 1983.

Approximately 90% of all United States poultry breeding stock is classified under the National Poultry Improvement Plan (Figure 12–8). For the year ended June 30, 1981, this included classification of the following numbers of breeding birds in the United States as to their freedom from the diseases indicated:

Free from:
Pullorum Disease and Fowl Typhoid

Chickens: 35.7 million breeders in 6,723 flocks
Turkeys: 3.2 million breeders in 669 flocks

Mycoplasma gallisepticum

Chickens: 12.9 million breeders in 1,332 flocks
Turkeys: 3.1 million breeders in 652 flocks

Mycoplasma synoviae

Chickens: 12.4 million breeders in 1,254 flocks
Turkeys: (no official program available)

PLANNING

In the process of reaching a decision to enter into poultry production careful consideration must be given to the product to be produced, types of markets available, the demand for the product in the area to be serviced, and the scope of the production unit planned. There are many areas of production through which one may enter the poultry business: rearing pullets for sale to egg production farms; market egg production; breeder hens to supply eggs to a hatchery; broilers, roaster, or capon production; or some comparable phase of the turkey business. Specialized fowl such as ducks, geese, and the domestically reared game birds, squab and guinea fowl, may also be considered if a market is available or can be established.

There are a number of levels at which one may enter into the poultry business, whether contracting with established companies or starting a small business. In a small business operation some unique means of marketing specialty products may provide a necessary advantage in competing with larger companies offering more standard products. Offering smoked meat, a barbecue service for special picnics and social events, farm fresh brown-shell eggs, and custom growing birds raised without antibiotic or other feed additives for health food or special allergy customers are just a few ideas. Before entering the business as a private venture you should gain some experience by working for an established poultry operation. This will provide valuable basic information as well as applied experience related to management of birds, people, and finances.

The potential market for the product should be a primary concern in planning a poultry business. Seasonal fluctuations in market must be considered along with the cycles of production. The methods of marketing that may be available should be carefully evaluated. A processing plant satisfactory to meet marketing requirements should be located within a one-hour drive from the point of production. In the United States, inspected products are the only food items of processed poultry that may be marketed through retail outlets. Established requirements should serve as guidelines to evaluate potential locations of a production unit and the capital equipment costs. For example, the location should provide isolation from other birds and people, but must provide accessibility to supply sources and to the market. A feasibility study of the proposed unit must be carefully planned before any steps are taken toward site selection and building construction. The need to project market demand is of prime importance. Financial stability must be established based upon potential price for products produced, realistic financing, and production risks that may modify income and cash flow.

Market goals and projections should be outlined as a primary step in planning. In an egg-production business, methods of marketing provide a number of options to the producer. The producer may market directly to the consumer through a store or a delivery route or directly from the farm. To do this, in most states, a candling license is required. A second option to the egg producer is to sell shell eggs to a processor who, through a series of contracts with stores, restaurants, and other commercial users, markets the eggs. In contract marketing a specified number of eggs of desired size and grade are delivered by the producer to the distributor at regularly scheduled times. A brand name often attracts consumers to continue to purchase a particular brand. Eggs are traditionally packed in one-dozen cartons although other marketing innovations may be successfully promoted. Eggs are marketed wholesale in case units of 30 dozen eggs. Surplus eggs, which result from overproduction, as well as offsize or misshapen eggs and body check eggs, can be broken out and marketed to bakeries or other institutional outlets as frozen liquid egg or dried egg. This requires adherence to specific standards, inspection, additional equipment, and labor that can be provided by specialized breaking plants.

Seasonal fluctuations in market demand as well as in production provide surplus eggs that may necessitate some ingenuity in moving them through the market channels to prevent oversupply that could result in depressed prices. Surplus eggs are shipped out of some areas into other markets outside of the area of influence of the primary market. These eggs, although sometimes sold at a loss, provide a means of stabilizing the local market price. Egg market prices are sensitive, fluctuating in response to relatively few surplus or deficit eggs on the market at any given time. Easter, for example, provides a stimulus increasing price, but immediately following this holiday there can be a serious price slump.

Broiler production in the United States is done primarily by contract growers marketing with large corporate integrator-processors. Broiler marketing is almost entirely by contract from integrator-processor to distributors or from distributors direct to retail outlets. Turkey production and marketing is handled similarly. Roasting chickens, geese, ducks, and capons are marketed as specialized products. Marketing may utilize special processing techniques such as deboning and providing cut up parts and precooked meals. Special packaging may be used providing a means by which the product becomes more visible and attractive to the consumer. Contracts with restaurants and other food service establishments that utilize poultry meat have resulted in increased consumption. Substituting poultry meat for other meats, mainly beef and pork in processed meat products such as hot dogs, luncheon meats, and other fabricated meat products, has provided a relatively new market outlet for turkey and chicken, significantly increasing consumption.

Production goals should be determined at the marketplace. The market potential for a particular product, whether it be eggs or poultry meat, must be carefully evaluated based upon immediate potential as well as future market development. Seasonal trends in production and consumption as well as variations in production over a particular period of time should be carefully considered. In an egg-production business, for example, a decision to recycle year-old layers for a second year or a third year of production usually will be critical to the overall operational plan. Whether or not to recycle layers must be a decision considered relative to the season of the year, the price of replacement pullets, and the level of production of birds to be recycled. The numbers of birds necessary to produce eggs to meet specific market demands must be accurately determined and a plan covering at least a one-year to two-year demand should be developed. Therefore, planning for housing, equipment, and the source of replacement stock should be done well in advance of the initiation of production. In broiler and other meat-producing poultry units a suitable contract with an integrated company must be negotiated prior to initiation of production. The integrator will usually require the grower to have suitable housing and utilities, and will provide feed and medication, advice, and processing.

Availability of supporting resources must be considered. Potable water must be available in adequate supply. Potable water may be obtained from a well, a river, or from municipal water lines that deliver directly to the poultry unit. Electricity, natural gas, or other sources of power must be available. Construction materials for physical facilities and equipment availability must be evaluated. Location of the poultry enterprise and processing units must be reasonably near the potential market, as well as close to the supply of materials and services such as a hatchery and feed and equipment distributors.

In locating the poultry unit, soil types, topography of the land, and drainage of the land must be considered. Water runoff can be a significant factor where heavy rains occur. Water runoff from roofs of buildings as well as from the surrounding lands and drainage from neighboring areas must be diverted so that buildings and grounds will not be subject to flooding. It is preferable to locate poultry units on hillsides where air movement is obtained without exposure to excessive winds, rather than in flat land areas having little air movement.

The availability of building materials is a consideration that should not be overlooked. In some areas lumber may provide the best material to use, although many poultry units today are constructed from prefabricated metal. Shipping costs and product availability, as well as lowered maintenance expense once the building is constructed, are important considerations, particularly in areas relatively isolated from services and suppliers. The availability of carpenters, electricians, plumbers, roofers, and engineers is required for proper design and construction of suitable facilities. The layout of buildings, roads, and on-site services that will comprise the total operation should be considered in the design of any part. Laying houses, pullet growing houses, and brooder houses must be adequately separated so cross air flow as well as cross traffic patterns are avoided. Strict isolation among the various units is necessary to prevent cross contamination from older birds to the younger growing stock.

Many poultry businesses integrate feed mixing as part of the operation to save money and increase efficiency. Adequate storage facilities will allow for purchase of ingredients during favorable price periods. Considerable savings can result through purchase of ingredients on the futures market. Close proximity to areas of grain and other feed-ingredient production with relatively low transportation costs may make it advantageous to integrate feed mixing into the poultry enterprise, rather than purchasing mixed feed. Adequate storage facilities for finished feed should be provided so the unit may operate with at least one week's supply of feed on hand at all times and to minimize the possibility of running out of feed during storms, floods, and strikes. A rodent-proof building should be provided for dry storage of basic nutrient ingredients obtained in sacked form, such as meat scrap, vitamin supplements, mineral supplements, and other feed products that are not normally marketed in bulk. Scales for proper weighing of ingredients and recording feed consumption are necessary.

Many poultry production units include some type of processing and storage facilities, whether it be for egg production or poultry-meat processing. Refrigeration and freezing units as well as refrigerated storage facilities to provide flexibility for hedging against market surpluses at certain periods of the year will assist the marketing process.

Power requirements must be accurately estimated so that electricity and other fuel supplies are always available. Standby power generators should be provided to avoid power interruption, which could rapidly destroy entire flocks. Manure, feathers, and waste water from cleanup and processing must be adequately treated for disposal or utilization. This will involve local laws and zoning ordinances that should be studied thoroughly as plans are formulated.

Transportation for receiving raw products as well as to assure that finished products can be moved rapidly to the market in good condition is important. What transportation equipment to be purchased for the farm and what should be leased or rented should be determined on the basis of seasonal requirements within the production unit. Available housing for employees, either on the farm or in nearby towns or cities, is necessary in order to minimize travel time and increase operating efficiency. A central office for proper handling of business and production records should be located close to the main entrance of the premises, thus minimizing traffic of visitors and service vehicles throughout the production unit.

If a hatchery is to be included on the business unit, strict isolation from other segments of the enterprise is essential. A central egg-storage unit for the hatchery should be located to minimize cross contamination within the hatchery unit. Equipment should be provided for handling hatching eggs in the processes of fumigation, grading, sorting, and dipping. The source of hatching eggs should be planned to minimize transportation stresses to the eggs and to assure that fresh hatchable eggs are available to meet an established schedule.

In large poultry businesses a diagnostic and disease-control laboratory should be an integral part of the operation. Alternatively, this work may be contracted to a local laboratory that can provide prompt service and advice. All poultry production operations should have an incinerator or other proper sanitary disposal equipment for dead birds. Dead birds must not be buried or thrown in a pile allowing contamination and infection of rodents, flies, or other animals that may cause cross-infection of the flocks. Along with sanitation and disease-control planning, a flock vaccination program should be established to provide effective defense against potential disease outbreaks. An additional control of disease spread is to prevent employee movement among units.

Financial requirements should be thoroughly investigated. Initial investment as well as long-range funding requirements and the cash flow pattern of the unit should be considered along with the return on the total investment to the owner and investors. One of the major advantages of some types of poultry units is a relatively rapid turnover of cash. This cash flow can be very favorable if the market is good and may be a major determinant of the success or failure of a poultry business.

Thorough consideration should be given to selecting personnel for all levels of involvement in the operation, the managerial level as well as the operational. A financial manager may be required to assure proper handling of financial resources. The decision will have to be made whether to employ persons with required expertise or to hire consultants for specific expertise. Occasionally, specific advice is required by even the larger companies, where an outside expert can perhaps detect developing problems and provide advance advice appropriate to the problem.

MANAGEMENT

The design of a management program for a poultry flock should be based upon the efficiency of operation necessary to meet the production objectives of the unit. Efficient use of space, equipment, time, and employees' knowledge should combine with many other factors which must be applied toward the production goals of a specific program. Feed is one of the highest cost items in a production program. Feed efficiency, therefore, should be given top priority in most commercial units. Conversion of raw ingredients to the products of the poultry enterprise is of utmost importance and feed wastage must be minimized. Many large poultry companies provide salary bonus incentives to employees for favorable production efficiency ratios, resulting in higher economic returns for the business. Not only is this an important factor in the commercial operation, but feed wastage and other inefficiencies should be avoided in home poultry flocks too.

A poultry enterprise may be initiated in just about any of the many phases of the total, complex, poultry-production cycle. For example, in a laying operation one may begin by purchasing day-old chicks or started pullets ready to lay. In many poultry units, the brooding phase is the most logical starting point. Brooding should be planned to coordinate production of the end product for entry into other phases of the operation or market demand. Brooding and rearing facilities as required must be constructed and utilized in the proper sequence. Bird replacement should be planned so as to coordinate building management. A plan of development should direct expansion from a small unit to a larger unit, providing experience and allowing indicated necessary changes in equipment and building design prior to the completion of the total physical facility.

Uniformity is important, and building design and equipment changes should not be made unless there are serious problems with the initial plans. Staffing with personnel who are dedicated and interested is a key to success. An effort should be made to develop personnel for the job required. Personnel turnover should be minimized. Trained individuals that have developed the experience and ability to adapt to different phases of a poultry operation provide a valuable component necessary in an effectively managed business. Although previous experience is very important, it is advisable to carefully screen potential employees for other characteristics, such as their willingness to follow orders and to learn new procedures and techniques.

Money management is an intricate part of financial planning. Some source of credit is usually necessary, and cash flow provides the "circulatory system'' that is basic to the total function. Credit may be obtained from local lending institutions, although money for poultry enterprises may not be obtained easily from local banks and other financial sources that normally provide funds for other businesses. One of the biggest problems is short-term financing, where contracts must be renegotiated after relatively short periods of approximately three to five years. The poultry unit frequently is not in a position to pay off a loan or renegotiate in this short time period. Often financing is available through private investors or business associates, feed mills, equipment companies, and processing plants. One should be alert in negotiating a contract to insure that a minimum number of constraints on the management of the operation are incorporated. A realistic plan of the cash-flow pattern and the return on the investment should be carefully developed so that even a successful operation is not a disappointment because income may be below that which was expected or planned.

Least-cost production objectives should be based on total least cost, not merely on the capital outlay and isolated segments of the total program. Losses in efficiency and production are difficult to measure in some phases of the operation because there are no controls by which valid comparisons can be made.

Sound management programs should not only be based upon the desires of upper level of management, but should include all phases of personnel management involved in the operation. The animal caretakers are sometimes in the best position to help middle management and upper management discover some of the deficiencies of the operation. They are on the "front line" and observe birds more frequently than others involved. A good communication network involving all personnel is essential for effective management. It is advisable to provide all employees a certain amount of decision-making responsibility as well as routine jobs to challenge, stimulate, and motivate them, resulting in a better working environment for the total system. Profit-sharing plans and production incentive bonuses appear to sharpen observation and interest in flock welfare in situations where routine jobs may otherwise tend to become dull and uninteresting. A competitive situation among employees can stimulate aggressiveness and desire to meet and exceed production goals. Increased overall productivity and profits may be realized by providing these favorable personnel relationships. All of these factors will affect the entire operation of the business and provide the impetus necessary to improve the profit margin. Although mechanization is extensively utilized in the poultry industry today, the individual employee is still the key to management success. Individuals can and should be considered the basis of the operation since the complete success of a profitable poultry enterprise is dependent on the smooth functioning of all individuals.

Many poultry business enterprises depend upon professional accounting procedures to keep a record of financial activities, production in various laying or growing houses, medication applications, mortality, feed consumption, and other necessary information. The systematic recording of daily events is very useful in maintaining a record of operations that can provide essential information when the production results are reviewed and evaluated. Computers can quickly and effectively monitor and control processes as well as maintain records and recommend action.

Computers are being utilized more extensively in poultry businesses, not only in the accounting office or the feed mill, but in poultry houses, processing plants, hatcheries, and other aspects. Computer capability that in 1960 cost a million dollars can now be purchased for a fraction of that cost. A high degree of the efficiency to be gained in the industry in the next few years will be achieved through the use of computers. The application of computers to poultry production is limitless. Training materials for producers, from beginners to experts, on subjects ranging from managing to egg quality break-out analysis, and the monitoring of possible factors that affect carcass quality in the processing plant can be made immediately available on the computer. When problems arise, environmental conditions can be monitored and a summary of ventilation, lighting, feeding, and watering systems fed into a computer programmed to diagnose the cause. Managers will be in a position to vary production and processing decisions as cost and production factors change.

Communication with a computer is accomplished through programming materials, or software. This software is developed to meet the specific needs of a particular company program and requirements. Hardware refers to the computer itself. There are many types available at various prices based on their capacity to perform computations and store information, as well as other specific features. The main unit involved is the video display terminal and the "brain," called the central processing unit. This unit carries out all the computations and stores information in the "memory." Random access memory and read only memory are the two major types. The random access memory is most useful as it is the memory bank into which data, computer program, calculations, and results will be acted upon and stored by the central processing unit. The read only memory is also a memory bank, but here the information is placed permanently by the manufacturer of the program. The output should be attached to a printer to provide a permanent recording of the results on the video display terminal. Everyone involved in poultry management and decision making should become familiar with the potential capacity of the microcomputer and be able to apply it to the needs of a business.

CHICKEN BREEDS AND VARIETIES

BREEDS, VARIETIES, AND STRAINS[1]

Chickens exist in many colors, sizes and shapes. There are more than 350 combinations of physical features. In order to identify and classify each a system was established with designations: class, breed, and variety.

A class is a group of breeds originating in the same geographical area. The names themselves indicate the region where the breeds originated, such as Asiatic, Mediterranean, American, and English. The breeds of chickens are arranged first according to their class and then alphabetically by breed within each class. Other classes, breeds, and varieties are included at the end of this appendix.

A breed possesses a specific set of physical features, such as body shape or type, skin color, carriage or station, number of toes, and feathered or nonfeathered shanks. Individuals within a breed, when mated to its own kind, transmit these features to their offspring.

Variety is a subdivision of a breed. Differentiating characteristics include plumage color, comb type and presence of a beard and muffs. In Plymouth Rocks, for example, there are several colors, Barred, White,

---

[1] This entire section, authored by John Skinner, is reprinted with some editing and permission from the author: J. Skinner, *Chicken Breeds and Varieties* Bulletin A2880. (Madison, Wisc.: University of Wisconsin Extension, 1978).

Buff, Partridge, and so forth. Body shape and physical features, however, are identical. The color is the only difference, and each color is a separate variety. The Leghorn breed has many varieties in color, and most can be either single comb or rose comb, with all other features being identical.

Strains are families or breeding populations possessing common traits within a breed and variety. They may be subdivisions of a breed or variety or they may even be progeny of systematic crosses. However, a strain shows a relationship more exacting than that for others within the breed or variety of similar appearance. Strains are the products of one person's or one organization's breeding program. Many commercial strains exist. DeKalb, Hyline, Babcock, and Shaver are a few examples of organizations that have bred specific strains of chickens for specific purposes.

Most of the breeds and varieties we know in the United States today were developed between 1875 and 1925. During that time the emphasis throughout the poultry world was on breeds and varieties for show purposes. Success was measured in terms of the excellence of individual birds. As the commercial egg and poultry meat industries developed, the emphasis changed from the individual bird to the average for the entire flock. This caused some breeders to adopt intensive selection programs based on the performance of certain outstanding families while others worked with breed crosses and crosses of strains within a given breed. Today the commercial poultry industry is based primarily on strain crosses. However, foundation breeders are constantly looking for additional material for new gene pools. This must come from fanciers and hobbyists who maintain the various breeds for personal and esthetic reasons.

The American Poultry Association publishes a book: *The American Standard of Perfection*. This book contains a complete description of each of the more than 300 recognized breeds and varieties. Size, shape, color, and physical features are described and illustrated in detail. Excellent sources of detailed information on poultry breeds may be found in: *The American Standard of Perfection*, American Poultry Association, P. O. Box 70, Cushing, Oklahoma 70423; *The Bantam Standard*, American Bantam Association, P. O. Box 610, North Amherst, Massachusetts 01059.

AMERICAN CLASS

Jersey Giants

Varieties: Black, White.

Standard Weights: Cock—13 pounds; hen—10 pounds; cockerel—11 pounds; pullet—8 pounds.

FIGURE A1–1
Jersey Giants

Skin Color: Yellow.

Egg Shell Color: Brown.

Use: A very heavy meat-type fowl for heavy roaster and capon production. Fairly good layers. The dark colored pigment from the shanks tends to move up into the edible portion of the carcass, which has hurt the Jersey Giant in commercial circles.

Origin: Developed in New Jersey in the late 1800s, at which time there was a demand for heavy fowl for capon production, particularly for the New York market. Size was a prime consideration.

Characteristics: Jersey Giants are the largest breed in the American Class. They should be rugged, with an angular shape, single comb, and with black (with willowish tinge) shanks in the Black variety and dark willow shanks in the White variety (Figure A1-1). The Jersey Giant will go broody but is not the best choice for incubating and brooding because of their size. Their tendency to grow a big frame first and cover it with meat later make them a poor fit for today's conditions. The meat yield is disappointing until they are six months or older. No fowl with black plumage or dark or willow shanks has ever remained popular in this country for long, although they used to be more widespread. However, good specimens do have an appeal, mainly because of their size.

New Hampshire

Varieties: None.

Standard Weights: Cock—$8\frac{1}{2}$ pounds; hen—$6\frac{1}{2}$ pounds; cockerel—$7\frac{1}{2}$ pounds; pullet—$5\frac{1}{2}$ pounds.

Skin Color: Yellow.

Egg Shell Color: Brown.

Use: A dual purpose chicken, selected more for meat production than egg production. Medium heavy in weight, it dresses a nice, plump carcass as either a broiler or a roaster.

FIGURE A1–2
New Hampshire

Origin: New Hampshires (Figure A1-2) are a relatively new breed, having been admitted to the Standard in 1935. They represent a specialized selection out of the Rhode Island Red breed. By intensive selection for rapid growth, fast feathering, early maturity, and vigor, a different breed gradually emerged. This took place in the New England states—chiefly in Massachusetts and New Hampshire from which it takes its name.

Characteristics: They possess a deep, broad body, grow feathers very rapidly, are prone to go broody and make good mothers. Most pin feathers are a reddish buff in color and, therefore, do not detract from the carcass appearance very much. The color is a medium to light red and often fades in the sunshine. The comb is single and medium to large in size; in the females it often lops over a bit. These good, medium-sized meat chickens have fair egg-laying ability. Some strains lay eggs of a dark brown shell color. New Hampshires are competitive and aggressive. They were initially used in the "Chicken of Tomorrow" contests, which led the way for the modern broiler industry.

Plymouth Rocks

Varieties: Barred, White, Buff, Partridge, Silver Penciled, Blue, Columbian.

Standard Weights: Cock—9½ pounds; hen—7½ pounds; cockerel—8 pounds; pullet—6 pounds.

Skin Color: Yellow.

Egg Shell Color: Brown.

Use: Meat and eggs.

Origin: Developed in America in the mid-to-latter part of the 19th century. The barred variety was developed first (Figure A1-3). It was noted for its meaty back and birds with barred feathers brought a premium on many markets. The light and dark bars of the male are approximately equal while in the female the dark bars are approximately twice as wide as the light. Most of the other varieties were developed from crosses containing some of the same ancestral background as the barred variety. Early in its development the name Plymouth Rock implied a barred bird, but as more varieties were developed, it became the designation for the breed.

Characteristics: Plymouth Rocks are a good general farm chicken. They are docile; normally will show broodiness; possess a long, broad back; a moderately deep, full breast and a single comb of moderate size. Some strains are good layers while others are bred principally for meat. White Plymouth Rock females are used as the female side of most of the commercial broilers produced today. They usually make good mothers. Their feathers are fairly loosely held but not so long as to easily tangle. Generally, Plymouth Rocks are not extremely aggressive, and tame quite easily. Some males and hens are big and active enough to be quite a problem if they become aggressive. Breeders should be aware of the standard weights and not select small or narrow birds for the breeding pen. Also note the wide, straight back of the drawing. This is a definite breed characteristic and should be maintained. Common faults include shallow breast, high tails, narrow bodies, and small size.

FIGURE A1–3
Plymouth Rocks

FIGURE A1–4
Rhode Island Reds

Rhode Island Reds

Varieties: Single Comb, Rose Comb.

Standard Weights: Cock—$8\frac{1}{2}$ pounds; hen—$6\frac{1}{2}$ pounds; cockerel—$7\frac{1}{2}$ pounds; pullet—$5\frac{1}{2}$ pounds.

Skin Color: Yellow.

Egg Shell Color: Brown.

Use: A dual-purpose medium heavy fowl; used more for egg production than meat production because of its dark-colored pin feathers and its good rate of lay (Figure A1-4).

Origin: Developed in the New England states of Massachusetts and Rhode Island, early flocks often had both single and rose combed individuals because of the influence of Malay blood. It was from the Malay that the Rhode Island Red got its deep color, strong constitution and relatively hard feathers.

Characteristics: Rhode Island Reds are a good choice for the small flock owner. Relatively hardy, they are probably the best egg layers of the dual purpose breeds. Reds handle marginal diets and poor housing conditions better than other breeds and still continue to produce eggs. They are one of the breeds where exhibition qualities and production ability can be successfully combined in a single strain. Some "Red" males may be quite aggressive. They have rectangular, relatively long bodies, typically dark red in color. Avoid using medium or brick red females for breeding because this is not in keeping with the characteristics of the breed. Also, don't breed from undersized individuals or birds with black in their body feathers (called "smutt"). Black in the main tail and wing feathers is normal, however. Most Reds show broodiness, but this characteristic has been partially eliminated in some of the best egg-production strains. The Rose Comb variety tends to be smaller but should be the same size as the Single Comb variety. The red color fades after long exposure to the sun.

(A breed of similar size and type to that of the Rhode Island Red has been developed. It has pure white feathering and is known as Rhode Island White.)

Wyandottes

Varieties: White, Buff, Columbian, Golden Laced, Blue, Silver Laced, Silver Penciled, Partridge, Black.

Standard Weights: Cock—$8\frac{1}{2}$ pounds, hen—$6\frac{1}{2}$ pounds, cockerel—$7\frac{1}{2}$ pounds, pullet—$5\frac{1}{2}$ pounds.

Skin Color: Yellow.

Egg Shell Color: Brown.

Use: Meat or eggs.

Origin: America. The Silver Laced variety (Figure A1-5) was developed in New York State and the others in the north and northeastern states in the latter part of the 19th century and early 20th century.

Characteristics: Wyandottes are a good, medium-weight fowl for small family flocks kept under rugged conditions. Their rose combs do not freeze as easily as single combs and the hens make good mothers. Their attractive "curvy" shape, generally good disposition, and many attractive color patterns (varieties) make them a good choice for fanciers as well as farmers. Common faults include narrow backs, undersized individuals, and relatively poor hatches. Also, it is not uncommon to see single combed offspring come

FIGURE A1–5
Wyandottes

from rose combed parents. These single combed descendents of Wyandottes should not be kept as breeders.

Other Breeds in the American Class

Buckeyes: A dark red, muscular bird with pea comb, closely held feathers and broad shoulders. No varieties.

Chanteclers: Developed in Canada as a dual purpose farm chicken, they have muscular bodies, small combs (pea) and wattles, and lay brown eggs. Varieties: White, Partridge.

Delawares: A nearly white, rapid growing, dual purpose fowl developed to figure into broiler crosses, with single comb and brown egg shells. No varieties.

Dominiques: America's oldest breed. They are rather indefinitely barred—black and white, have rose combs, are relatively small, with tightly held feathers. No varieties.

Hollands: Developed in the 1930s and '40s in an attempt to provide a medium-sized fowl with good meat properties that laid white-shelled eggs. Varieties: Barred, White.

Javas: A medium-sized, angular bird which was a common farm chicken in the United States in the 19th century. Javas possess single combs. Varieties: Black, Mottled.

Lamonas: Lamonas have single combs, appear short legged, and are one of the few chickens with red ear lobes that lay white-shelled eggs. No varieties.

ASIATIC CLASS

Brahmas

Varieties: Light, Dark, Buff.

Standard Weights (Light): Cock—12 pounds; hen—$9\frac{1}{2}$ pounds; cockerel—10 pounds; pullet—8 pounds.

Standard Weights (Dark and Buff): Cock—11 pounds; hen—$8\frac{1}{2}$ pounds; cockerel—9 pounds; pullet—7 pounds.

Skin Color: Yellow.

Egg Shell Color: Brown.

Use: A very heavy fowl for the production of heavy roasters or capons. Fair egg layers.

Origin: The ancestry of the Brahma traces back to China although much of their development took place in the United States between 1850 and 1890.

Characteristics: Good Brahmas (Figure A1-6) are beautiful, stately birds. Their large size and gentle nature combined with intricate color patterns

FIGURE A1–6
Brahmas

makes them favorites for the country estate. The Brahmas' appearance in the showroom never fails to command the admiration of one and all. These qualities have made them a favorite with showmen and fanciers. Brahmas do go broody and are fairly good mothers. Their small comb and wattles, together with profuse feathering and well-feathered shanks and toes enable them to stand cold temperatures very well. The relatively slow rate of growth and long time required to reach maturity have caused Brahmas to be passed by as a commercial fowl.

Cochins

Varieties: White, Black, Buff, Partridge.

Standard Weights: Cock—11 pounds; hen—$8\frac{1}{2}$ pounds; cockerel—9 pounds; pullet—7 pounds.

Skin Color: Yellow.

Egg Shell Color: Brown.

Use: Mainly an ornamental fowl, but their ability as mothers is widely recognized, and Cochins (Figure A1-7) are frequently used as foster mothers for game birds and other species.

FIGURE A1–7
Cochins

Origin: Cochins came originally from China but underwent considerable development in the United States and now are found and admired in many parts of the world.

Characteristics: Cochins are literally big, fluffy balls of feathers. They are mainly kept as an ornamental fowl and are well-suited to close confinement. The profuse leg and foot feathering makes it desirable to confine Cochins on wet days and where yards become muddy to keep the birds from becoming mired or collecting balls of mud on their feet. They exhibit extremely persistent broodiness, are good mothers, and are intense layers for short periods of time. Because of their feathering, it is necessary to clip some of the feathers or resort to artificial insemination to obtain good rates of fertility.

Langshans

Varieties: Black and White.

Standard Weights: Cock—$9\frac{1}{2}$ pounds; hen—$7\frac{1}{2}$ pounds; cockerel—8 pounds; pullet—$6\frac{1}{2}$ pounds.

Skin Color: White.

Egg Shell Color: Brown.

Use: A general purpose fowl for the production of meat and eggs. The general shape of the Langshans (Figure A1-8) makes them better suited to roaster and capon use than fryer use.

Origins: Langshans originated in China and are considered one of our oldest breeds.

Characteristics: Langshans enjoyed considerable popularity in the United States during the latter part of the 19th century. However, today they are primarily an exhibition fowl. They appear to be very tall, with long legs and tails carried at a high angle. They are active and quick. The black variety has a deep greenish sheen when viewed in the proper light. Many other breeds were created using Langshan blood in the foundation matings. They are a good general breed; females go broody and make good mothers. Their

FIGURE A1-8
Langshans

feet and legs are feathered but not as fully as the Cochins or Brahmas. Long legs and narrow body conformation leave much to be desired as a meat bird by today's standards.

ENGLISH CLASS

Australorp

Variety: Black.

Standard Weights: Cock—$8\frac{1}{2}$ pounds; hen—$6\frac{1}{2}$ pounds; cockerel—$7\frac{1}{2}$ pounds; pullet—$5\frac{1}{2}$ pounds.

Skin Color: White.

Egg Shell Color: Brown.

Use: Generally a very good egg producer with a fairly meaty body of intermediate size.

Origin: The Australorp (Figure A1-9) was developed in Australia from Black Orpington stock. It is smaller than the Orpington with a trimmer appearance.

Characteristics: Australorps have intense beetle-green sheen on the black birds, dark eyes, deep bodies, and are very active. They are one of the best dual-purpose fowls, having gained attention in the 1930s and '40s by being one side of the successful Austa-White cross. This cross of Australorp x White Leghorn became the successor to purebred breeds on many Midwestern farms. Broodiness was a problem with the cross, and some markets discounted the tinted eggs they laid. Therefore, they soon fell victim to the inbred hybrid commercial crosses of "Hyline" and "DeKalb." Australorps are good egg producers and hold the world's record for egg production with one hen having laid 364 eggs in 365 days under official Australian trapnest testing.

FIGURE A1–9
Australorp

FIGURE A1–10
Cornish

Cornish

Varieties: Dark, White, White Laced Red, Buff.

Standard Weights: Cock—$10\frac{1}{2}$ pounds; hen—8 pounds; cockerel—$8\frac{1}{2}$ pounds; pullet—$6\frac{1}{2}$ pounds.

Skin Color: Yellow.

Egg Shell Color: Brown.

Use: Developed as the ultimate meat bird, the Cornish has contributed its genes to build the vast broiler industry of the world. Its muscle development and arrangement give excellent carcass shape.

Origin: Cornish were developed in the shire (county) of Cornwall, England where they were known as "Indian Games". They show the obvious influence of Malay and other oriental blood. They were prized for their large proportion of white meat and its fine texture.

Characteristics: The Cornish (Figure A1-10) has a broad well-muscled body. Its legs are of large diameter and widely spaced. The deep set eyes, projecting brows, and strong, slightly curved beak give the Cornish a rather cruel expression. Cornish males are often pugnacious, and the chicks tend to be more cannibalistic than some breeds. Good Cornish (Figure A1-11) are unique and impressive birds to view. The feathers are short and held closely to the body and may show exposed areas of skin. Cornish need adequate protection during very cold weather as their feathers offer less

FIGURE A1–11
Cornish

insulation than can be found on most other chickens. Because of their short feathers and wide compact bodies, Cornish are deceptively heavy. Due to their shape, good Cornish often experience poor fertility, and artificial mating is suggested. Cornish are movers and need space to exercise and develop their muscles. The old males get stiff in their legs if they do not receive sufficient exercise. The females normally go broody but because of their very minimal feathers can cover relatively fewer eggs. They are very protective mothers but are almost too active to be good brood hens.

Dorkings

Varieties: White, Silver Gray, Colored.

Standar Weights (White): Cock—$7\frac{1}{2}$ pounds; hen—6 pounds; cockerel—$6\frac{1}{2}$ pounds; pullet—5 pounds.

Standard Weights (Silver Gray and Colored): Cock—9 pounds; hen—7 pounds; cockerel—8 pounds; pullet—6 pounds.

Skin Color: White.

Egg Shell Color: White.

Use: A good, general purpose fowl for producing meat and eggs. It was developed for its especially fine quality meat.

Origin: The Dorking (Figure A1-12) is believed to have originated in Italy, since it was introduced into Great Britain at an early date by the Romans.

FIGURE A1–12
Dorkings

Much of its development took place in England where it gained much acclaim for its table qualities. The Dorking is one of our oldest breeds of chickens.

Characteristics: The Dorking has a rectangular body set on very short legs. It is five toed and has a relatively large comb, thus requiring protection in extremely cold weather. Dorkings are good layers; they are one of the few breeds with red earlobes that lay a white-shell egg. Most Dorking hens will go broody, make good mothers, and are quite docile. Because of their white skin, Dorkings are not as popular in the United States as in Europe.

Orpingtons

Varieties: Black, White, Buff, Blue.

Standard Weights: Cock—10 pounds; hen—8 pounds; cockerel—8½ pounds; pullet—7 pounds.

Skin Color: White.

Egg Shell Color: Brown.

Use: A heavy, dual-purpose fowl for the production of both meat and eggs.

Origin: Orpingtons were developed in England at the town of Orpington in County Kent during the 1880s. They were brought to America in the 1890s and gained popularity very rapidly, based on their excellence as a meat bird. As the commercial broiler and roaster market developed, the Orpington lost out partly because of its white skin.

Characteristics: Orpingtons (Figure A1-13) are heavily but loosely feathered, appearing massive. Their feathering allows them to endure cold temperatures better than some other breeds. They exist only in solid colors; are at home on free range or in relatively confined situations; and are docile. Hens exhibit broodiness and generally make good mothers. Chicks are not very aggressive and are often the underdogs when several breeds are brooded together. They are a good general use fowl.

FIGURE A1–13
Orpingtons

FIGURE A1–14
Sussex

Sussex

Varieties: Speckled, Red, Light.

Standard Weights: Cock—9 pounds; hen—7 pounds; cockerel—7½ pounds; pullet—6 pounds.

Skin Color: White.

Egg Shell Color: Brown.

Use: A general purpose breed for producing meat and/or eggs. One of the best of the dual-purpose chickens, a good all-around farm fowl.

Origin: Sussex originated in the county of Sussex, England where they were prized as a table fowl more than 100 years ago. They continue to be a popular fowl in Great Britain, and the light variety has figured prominently in the development of many of their commercial strains. Sussex is one of the oldest breeds that is still with us today in fair numbers.

Characteristics: Sussex (Figure A1-14) are alert, attractive, and good foragers. They have rectangular bodies; the speckled variety is especially attractive with its multi-colored plumage. Sussex go broody and make good mothers. They combine both exhibition and utility virtues but are more popular in Canada, England and other parts of the world than in the U.S.

Rare Breed in the English Class

Red Caps: A rare member of the English class, these are characterized by having a large rose comb. They are one of the few breeds with red earlobes that lay white-shelled eggs.

MEDITERRANEAN CLASS

Anconas

Varieties: Single Comb, Rose Comb.

Standard Weights: Cock—6 pounds; hen—$4\frac{1}{2}$ pounds; cockerel—5 pounds; pullet—4 pounds.

Use: A small fowl that lays a fair number of rather small eggs.

Origin: Anconas take their name from the port city of Ancona, Italy, where they are said to have originated.

Characteristics: Anconas (Figure A1-15) resemble Leghorns in shape and size. They are small, active, alert, and black with white-tipped feathers evenly distributed. Anconas are noisy, good foragers, and considered non-broody. They were once a prime egg-producing breed, but today are mainly kept as an ornamental fowl.

FIGURE A1–15
Anconas

Blue Andalusians

Varieties: None.

Standard Weights: Cock—7 pounds; hen—$5\frac{1}{2}$ pounds; cockerel—6 pounds; pullet—$4\frac{1}{2}$ pounds.

Skin Color: White.

Egg Shell Color: White.

Use: An ornamental fowl with fairly good egg production potential.

Origin: Developed initially in Spain, the breed has undergone considerable development in England and the United States.

Characteristics: Andalusians (Figure A1-16) are small, active, closely feathered birds that tend to be noisy and rarely go broody. Andalusians are a typical example of the unstable blue color we see in the poultry industry. It is the result of a cross of black and white. When two blues are mated, they produce offspring in the ratio of one black, two blues, and one white. When mated together these whites and blacks produce mainly blues. Andalusians are beautiful when good, but the percentage of really good ones runs low in many flocks because of this color segregation. Hence, they are not widely bred and never in large numbers.

FIGURE A1–16
Blue Andalusians

Leghorns

Varieties: Single Comb Dark Brown, Single Comb Light Brown, Rose Comb Dark Brown, Rose Comb Light Brown, Single Comb White, Rose Comb White, Single Comb Buff, Single Comb Black, Single Comb Silver, Single Comb Red, Single Comb Black Tailed Red, Single Comb Columbian.

Standard Weights: Cock—6 pounds; hen—$4\frac{1}{2}$ pounds; cockerel—5 pounds; pullet—4 pounds.

Skin Color: Yellow.

Egg Shell Color: White

Use: An egg-type chicken, Leghorns figured in the development of most of our modern egg-type strains.

Origin: Leghorns take their name from the city of Leghorn, Italy, where they are considered to have originated.

Characteristics: A small, spritely, noisy bird with great style, Leghorns (Figures A1-17, A1-18) like to move about. They are good foragers and can

FIGURE A1–17
Leghorns

FIGURE A1–18
Leghorns

often glean much of their diet from ranging over fields and barnyards. Leghorns are capable of considerable flight and often roost in trees if given the opportunity. Leghorns and their descendants are the most numerous breed we have in America today. The Leghorn has relatively large head furnishings (comb and wattles) and is noted for egg production. Leghorns rarely go broody.

Minorcas

Varieties: Single Comb Black, Rose Comb Black, Single Comb White, Rose Comb White, Single Comb Buff.

Standard Weights: Single Comb Black: Cock—9 pounds; hen—$7\frac{1}{2}$ pounds; cockerel—$7\frac{1}{2}$ pounds; pullet—$6\frac{1}{2}$ pounds. All others: Cock—8 pounds; hen—$6\frac{1}{2}$ pounds; cockerel—$6\frac{1}{2}$ pounds; pullet—$5\frac{1}{2}$ pounds.

Skin Color: White.

Egg Shell Color: White.

Use: Developed for the production of very large chalk-white eggs, the Minorca (Figure A1-19) is today principally an exhibition fowl.

Origin: Developed in the Mediterranean area where they take their name from an island off the coast of Spain. Development may have been as an offshoot of the Spanish breed.

FIGURE A1–19
Minorcas

Characteristics: The largest of the Mediterranean breeds, they are long, angular birds that appear larger than they are. They have long tails and large wide feathers closely held to narrow bodies. Minorcas have relatively large combs and wattles. Good Minorcas are stately impressive birds and can give a fair return in eggs, although in recent years they have not been intensively selected for that purpose. They are rather poor meat fowl because of their narrow angular bodies and slow growth. Minorcas rarely go broody, are very alert, and fairly good foragers.

White Faced Black Spanish

Varieties: None.

Standard Weight: Cock—8 pounds; hen—$6\frac{1}{2}$ pounds; cockerel—$6\frac{1}{2}$ pounds; pullet—$5\frac{1}{2}$ pounds.

Skin Color: White.

Egg Shell Color: White.

Use: An egg-production type bird that has, in recent years, had very little selection for that purpose.

Origin: Coming from Spain, it arrived in the United States via the Caribbean Islands. Spanish are the oldest breed of chickens existent in the United States today. At one time known as "The Fowls of Seville", they were very popular in the South during the Colonial period.

Characteristics: The large area of snow white skin surrounding the face and wattles makes this breed unique (Figure A1-20). Actually this is an over-developed earlobe. Its color offers a marked contrast with the black plumage and the red comb and wattles. They are considered nonbroody and hold their feathers close to their body contours. Spanish are active and noisy. Many individuals are below recommended weight, and, at this time, most of the population is highly inbred.

FIGURE A1–20
White Faced Black Spanish

Other Breeds in the Mediterranean Class

Buttercups: A small, spritely breed from Sicily, their chief distinguishing feature is their cup-shaped comb. Buttercups are nonbroody, lay a fair number of small eggs, and are kept strictly as ornamental fowl.

Catalanas: The Buff Catalana is a medium-sized bird noted for its hardiness. It is not well-known in the United States but is widely distributed through South America. Catalanas come closer to being a dual-purpose breed than any of the other Mediterranean breeds.

GAMES CLASS

Old English Games

Varieties: Black Breasted Red, Brown Red, Golden Duckwing, Silver Duckwing, Red Pyle, White, Black, Spangled.

Standard Weights: Cock—5 pounds; hen—4 pounds; cockerel—4 pounds; pullet—$3\frac{1}{2}$ pounds.

Skin Color: White.

Egg Shell Color: White or light tint.

Use: Old English Games are strictly an ornamental fowl.

Origin: Old English Games are the modern-day descendants of the ancient fighting cocks. They are associated with England but their heritage is almost worldwide and they have changed little in shape or appearance in more than 1,000 years.

Characteristics: A small, tightly feathered bird, Old English Games (Figure A1-21) are very hardy, extremely active, and very noisy. Old English have figured in the development of many other breeds. The mature cocks should be dubbed (have the comb and wattles removed) with a characteristic cut. This is in keeping with their heritage. Old English hens usually show broodiness but are so small and aggressive as well as defensive that they are not always the best choice as mothers. Old English are capable of considerable

FIGURE A1–21
Old English Games

flight and may revert to a feral (wild) state in some areas. They are the domestic breed most like the wild jungle fowl in appearance.

Modern Games

Varieties: Black Breasted Red, Brown Red, Golden Duckwing, Silver Duckwing, Birchen, Red Pyle, Black, White.

Standard Weights: Cock—6 pounds; hen—4½ pounds; cockerel—5 pounds; pullet—4 pounds.

Skin Color: White.

Egg Shell Color: White or light tint.

Use: A strictly ornamental fowl.

Origin: Modern Games were developed in Great Britain.

Characteristics: A tightly feathered bird with long legs and neck, which give it a tall, slender appearance. The males of the Modern Games (Figure A1-22) should have their combs and wattles removed to enhance their long, slim shape. The feathers of Modern Games should be short hard and held very close to their bodies. They do not stand cold weather well because of their short feathers and need plenty of exercise to maintain muscle tone.

FIGURE A1–22
Modern Games

CONTINENTAL CLASS

Campines

Varieties: Golden, Silver. The campines (Figure A1-23) are a fairly small, closely feathered breed with solid colored hackles and barred bodies. They are chiefly an ornamental breed but will lay a fair number of white-shell eggs and are nonbroody. They are thought to have originated in Belgium.

FIGURE A1–23
Campines

Lakenvelders

An old German breed best known for its color pattern (black hackle and tail on a white body) (Figure A1-24). They are quite small, nonbroody, lay white-shell eggs and are rather wild and flighty.

FIGURE A1–24
Lakenvelders

FRENCH CLASS

Houdans

Varieties: Mottled, White.

Standard Weights: Cock—8 pounds; hen—6½ pounds; cockerel—7 pounds; pullet—5½ pounds.

Skin Color: White.

Egg Shell Color: White.

FIGURE A1–25
Houdans

Use: An ornamental fowl that is also a good egg producer and fairly good as a meat bird.

Origin: Houdans originated in France where they enjoy a good reputation as a high-class table fowl.

Characteristics: Houdans (Figure A1-25) possess a crest, beard, and muffs and have five toes on each foot. Their rectangular bodies are set on fairly short legs. They are one of the better ornamental breeds for general utility use. Because of their crest, they require plenty of space and feed and water containers that prevent them from getting the crest wet and dirty, especially in cold weather. Because of the fifth toe, baby Houdans often walk with a skipping gait.

Crevecoeurs

A very rare, crested breed, solid black in color, Crevecoeurs are strictly ornamental fowl.

Faverolles

An interesting breed that combines a beard and muffs with a single comb and feathered legs and feet (Figure A1-26). Faverolles are a medium-sized

FIGURE A1–26
Faverolles

breed and fairly loosely feathered, giving them a rather large appearance. They also have a fifth toe on each foot and, although chiefly ornamental, do possess some utility characteristics as well.

La Fleche

A very rare breed with a pair of spikes in place of a conventional comb. La Fleche are black, of medium size, and very active. They are strictly an ornamental fowl.

HAMBURG CLASS

Hamburgs

Varieties: Golden Spangled, Silver Spangled, Golden Penciled, Silver Penciled, Black, White.

Standard Weights: Cock—5 pounds; hen—4 pounds; cockerel—4 pounds; pullet—3½ pounds.

Skin Color: White.

Egg Shell Color: White.

Use: An ornamental fowl capable of laying fair numbers of relatively small eggs.

Origin: Hamburgs carry a German name, but are generally considered to have originated in Holland.

Characteristics: Hamburgs (Figure A1-27) are active, flighty birds. They are trim and stylish with delicate features, and wild in nature. They forage well and are capable of flying long distances. Although good egg producers, their eggs are often very small.

FIGURE A1–27
Hamburgs

ORIENTAL CLASS

Malays

Varieties: Black Breasted Red.

Standard Weights: Cock—9 pounds; hen—7 pounds; cockerel—7 pounds; pullet—5 pounds.

Skin Color: Yellow.

Egg Shell Color: Brown.

Use: Strictly an ornamental fowl.

Origin: A very old breed coming from Asia, they have changed little in modern times.

Characteristics: Malays (Figure A1-28) are very tall and appear bold and perhaps cruel due to their projecting eyebrows. They are closely feathered with short feathers and carry their bodies inclined upward with tail low or drooping. They are rugged and have a reputation for vigor and long life. They require exercise to maintain muscle tone and hardness of feather. Most hens will go broody but are not a good choice because their long legs don't fit easily in a nest.

FIGURE A1–28
Malays

Sumatras

Varieties: None.

Standard Weights: Cock—5 pounds; hen—4 pounds; cockerel—4 pounds; pullet—3½ pounds.

Skin Color: Yellow.

FIGURE A1-29
Sumatras

Egg Shell Color: White or light tint.

Use: Strictly an ornamental fowl.

Origin: Sumatras come from the island of Sumatra from which they take their name.

Characteristics: Sumatras (Figure A1-29) are a distinctive fowl that look less like domestic poultry than other chickens. They have rather long tails carried low enough to appear drooping. They have multiple spurs on each leg, dark purple faces, and a high degree of greenish luster on jet black plumage.

Cubalayas

A hardy bird developed in Cuba, they resemble a Sumatra in shape. Cubalayas exist in three varieties and should be considered a strictly ornamental fowl.

POLISH CLASS

Polish

Varieties: White Crested Black, Non-Bearded Golden, Non-Bearded Silver, Non-Bearded White, Non-Bearded Buff Laced, Bearded Golden, Bearded Silver, Bearded White, Bearded Buff Laced.

Standard Weights: Cock—6 pounds; hen—4½ pounds; cockerel—5 pounds; pullet—4 pounds.

Skin Color: White.

Egg Shell Color: White.

Use: A strictly ornamental fowl.

Origin: Probably eastern Europe, although they are so old that their history has been obscured.

FIGURE A1-30
Polish

Characteristics: Polish (Figure A1-30) are an unusual and beautiful breed. They have a crest (some also possess a beard and muffs), are small, tightly feathered birds, fairly active despite restricted vision due to their large "head gear." They need plenty of space to avoid damaging each other's crests by picking. Ice forming in their crests from drinking water can be a problem in cold weather. And sometimes their crests restrict vision and cause them to be easily frightened.

MISCELLANEOUS VARIETIES

Sultans

Sultans come to us from Turkey. They are strictly an ornamental fowl of very distinctive appearance. They have a large crest, muffs and beard, together with profuse feathering of the feet and legs.

Frizzles

While listed in the *Standard* as a breed, frizzling is a genetic modification that can be easily introduced into any population of chickens. It causes each feather to curl back toward the bird's head instead of lying naturally pointed toward the tail (Figure A1-31).

FIGURE A1-31
Frizzles

FIGURE A1–32
Turkens

Turkens

The Transylvania Naked Neck is often called Turken (Figure A1-32). Some people think it is a cross between a chicken and a turkey because of the unfeathered area on the neck. This skin turns red when exposed to the sun, further paralleling the turkey. However, this is actually the result of a single gene that affects the arrangement of feather-growing tracts over the chicken's body. It can be easily introduced into any breed. Turkens have no feathers on a broad band between the shoulders and the base of the skull. They also have a reduced number of feathers on their bodies, but this is not evident until the bird is handled. Turkens should be given protection from extremely cold temperatures as they have far less insulation than their normally feathered cousins. This characteristic is a novel feature that does not detract from the utility of the bird.

Araucanas

These fowls were discovered in South America. A few were brought to the United States but have been crossed with other chickens so much so that characteristics of size, shape, and so forth were dispersed. The trait of laying blue or greenish eggs persisted, and now breeders are attempting to standardize the physical makeup of the population and gain them recognition as a breed. Some of the Araucanas were rumpless and possessed some interesting ear tufts. Probably at some time in the future these fowls will be developed into an interesting breed with both economic and ornamental attributes.

FIGURE A1–33
Sebright

BANTAMS

Bantams are the miniatures of the poultry world. The word *bantam* is the overall term for the more than 350 kinds of true breeding miniature chickens. They exist in almost every breed and variety in which there are large chickens. In addition, there are some kinds of bantams that have no large counterpart. The term "Banty" or "Bantie" is often used to describe any nondescript, undersized chicken. This is misleading. Bantams are not unhealthy midgets or unproductive dwarfs. They are complete miniatures raised primarily for exhibition, a purpose for which they excel. The American Bantam Association issues standards for bantams and licenses persons qualified to judge at exhibitions. Bantams have the same requirements for shape, color, and physical features that the large fowl do (Figures A1-33, A1-34, A1-35, A1-36). They should weigh about one-fifth of their larger counterparts. They should be referred to by the name of their breed and variety plus the word bantam; for example, Buff Cochin

FIGURE A1–34
Antwerp Belgians

FIGURE A1–35
Silkies

Bantams. Bantams are kept for their beauty, exhibition, or as pets or companion animals. Their wide array of shapes, colors and personalities gives them broad appeal. However, they can be quite useful for the production of eggs and their meat is fine grained and nutritious. Often bantams can be kept in areas too small for regular chickens. They are, in fact, the "compacts" of the poultry business.

FIGURE A1–36
Japanese

PREPARING A SKELETON

When preparing a skeleton of a turkey or chicken, it is best to start with a live bird. A mature bird is needed so that all the bones are well calcified. If the bird is too young, some of the bones will still be in the cartilage stage. Bones not yet calcified won't make a rigid skeleton. Cartilage will cook away when the meat is cooked off the bones. It will also be cut easily if boning is done in place of cooking. A chicken should be at least 1 year old and a turkey should be at least 22 weeks of age.

Killing of the bird can be done by any method that does not injure, break, or destroy the bone structure. Recommended killing methods are: (1) asphyxiation by the use of ether or chloroform and (2) cutting the jugular vein at the throat. When cutting the throat it is best to run the knife parallel with the neck, cutting through the skin and into the jugular vein, making sure not to break the neck or to cut any bones.

The feathers should be removed by picking or skinning and the viscera should be removed. When cleaning the bird do not cut any bones and do not cut off the head or feet.

After this has been done the bird is ready to have the muscles and fat removed. There are two general methods. One is to bone the bird, or cut the meat off the bones. If this is done the meat can be saved for human consumption. The extremities can be removed in this process, but care must be exercised to remove them at the joints without breaking or cutting the bones. Remove the scales from the metatarsus and digits of the feet. The meat from the head and neck is best removed by cooking. A second method of removing the meat from the animal is by cooking the whole carcass. Fold the legs, wings, and neck along the body and tie with a string to make a small compact mass of intact skeleton. Place the bird in water at a low boil for 2½–3 hours. The legs and wings loosen from the body when sufficient time has elapsed. Meat should be cleaned off the carcass while it is still hot, as it comes off much easier. The bones will be soft and pliable when they are hot. Cool the cooked carcass and strip off remaining flesh. Scrub the bones clean with a toothbrush.

Following removal of the meat from the bones it is best to expose them to sunlight for at least two days. Place the bones in a wire container and expose them to the sun where they are not accessible to dogs, cats, or birds. After the skeleton has dried in the sun, at room temperature, or baked in oven at 93°C (200°F) for an hour, the bones can be bleached by placing them in a solution of 3% hydrogen peroxide or in a solution of 0.25 liters (1 cup) of chlorine bleach in 3.8 liters (4 quarts) of water for 24 hours. Following this procedure the bones are more rigid and white. Any remaining meat and tissue can now be removed by scraping carefully with a small knife.

The head, or skull, is a very delicate portion with which to work. It is made up of many small bones. If possible, it is best to remove the tissue from these bones without separating each small bone. There are two structures that can be easily overlooked when removing tissue and meat: (1) the hyoid apparatus, or the bone in the tongue, and (2) the sclerotic ring, made up of several small cartilage-connected bones inside the skull around the eye ball.

The head should be removed from the neck very carefully. A relatively firm wire such as a clothes hanger wire should be threaded through the neural canal of the vertebrae of the neck to keep the bones together and in proper sequence. Another wire should then be run through the opening in the bones of the back, through the vertebrae, and partially into the lower back. This keeps the bones in the proper order and in line allowing for easier cementing when assembling the skeleton and makes the structure more rigid.

The skeletal body should be put together first using an appropriate quick-drying adhesive cement, according to the directions to insure the proper use of the cement. The wire should be extended from the backbone when assembling the skeleton. Suspend or brace the skeletal body while assembling bones. Cotton or cloth can also be used inside the body cavity to keep the rib cage rigid and avoid its collapse. When assembly of the skeletal body is complete, the cloth or cotton should be removed.

Remove the neck vertebrae from the original supporting wire and keeping them in order, place them on the wire extending from the backbone. This wire can be shaped to hold the bones in the desired position. The vertebrae should be cemented together to keep them from turning freely on the wire. The head, or skull, can be placed on the end of the wire and glued to the first neck vertebra. The wire should be cut off to enable the skull to fit close to the vertebra of the neck; 0.6–1.3 cm (0.25 to 0.5 in.) of wire extending from the vertebra is sufficient.

The lower jaw (mandible) can be cemented or wired at the point of contact with the quadrate. The hyoid apparatus which supports the tongue can be put in place and cemented or supported by cemented thread. If the strain is not great, the thread works well and is hardly noticeable. The sclerotic rings may be suspended in place by cemented thread. Alternatively, the sclerotic rings and hyoid bone may be fastened to the mounting base, since they may be difficult to place in their original positions on the skeleton.

The bones of the wings, legs, and feet should all be wired or cemented together in their proper position prior to their attachment to the skeletal body. Care must be exercised so the bones are properly located on the correct side of the skeleton. It is best for the wings to be attached before the legs. This allows the carcass to be low and provides some support to be placed under the wings while the cement is setting.

Before attaching the legs to the skeletal body a hanger or support rod should be made. A wire coat hanger works very well for this purpose, shaped to make a loop that will extend from the tail region forward to the front of the body cavity and back again. The wire should then be extended downward and through the wooden base on which the bird is to be mounted and then fastened underneath. To hold up the front portion of the body the wire can be shaped and placed under the neck vertebrae. This wire should also go straight down and be fastened underneath the wooden base. Before fastening the supporting wire to the mounting base the skeleton should be level and at the proper height for the legs to be cemented to the skeletal body.

The mounting base can be made from whatever materials are available. A piece of 2 cm ($\frac{3}{4}$ in.) plywood 18 cm $\times$ 30 cm (7 in. by 12 in.) is satisfactory or perhaps a rock or log would be more desirable. Supports of some type on each corner of the base are needed to keep the board level because the wire extending through the bottom may cause it to be unsteady. These should be put on before the skeleton is placed on the base.

The femur bones of the legs must be inserted into the acetabula (cavities) of the pelvic girdle. Insert a pin of medium-size wire extending from one femur through the acetabula cavities to the second femur. Make the holes in the femur bones for this pin with a small drill. After attaching the legs to the pelvic girdle as described above, determine the length of the support rod or wire. Cut the rod or wire the necessary length to support the skeleton in an upright position and anchor it to the base.

When the skeleton is in its final position, retouch joints with quick-drying cement. Then spray the skeleton with clear plastic or brush it with a thin coat of varnish, for preservation.[1]

---

[1] Geiger, G. S. et al. The Chicken Skeleton: How to prepare it and mount it. Science Studies in Poultry Biology, 1974. *Poultry Science* 53:455–503.

MEASURING SPECIFIC GRAVITY OF EGGS

Measuring the specific gravity of eggs requires nine basins for holding the water and salt solutions in which the eggs are immersed, several baskets for holding the eggs as they are passed from basin to basin, a hydrometer, salt, a balance or scale for weighing the salt, and a graduated cylinder for measuring water. Prepare nine salt solutions ranging from 1.060 to 1.100 in specific gravity at intervals of .005. To three liters of water add the following amount of salt: 276 g for 1.060 specific gravity, 298 g for 1.065, 320 g for 1.070, 342 g for 1.075, 365 g for 1.080, 390 g for 1.085, 414 g for 1.090, 438 g for 1.095, and 462 g for 1.100 specific gravity. Specific gravity solutions should be verified with a hydrometer, and water or salt should be added as required. Maintain salt solutions at room temperature.

Eggs should first be immersed in a basin of water just prior to measurement for specific gravity. This will eliminate much of the absorption of the first salt solution. Immerse eggs in each salt solution, starting with solution number one with the lowest specific gravity, and document for each egg the salt solution number in which it first floats. Any score above four indicates good shell quality. Practically, only solutions three, four, and five may be needed. This measurement is accurate only if eggs have very small air cells, that is, only with fresh eggs.

POULTRY FEED INGREDIENT ANALYSIS TABLE

Values shown are conservative estimates to provide a margin of safety in the calculation of feed formulas.

A series of dashes (———) indicates that the amount present is negligible.

A question mark (?) indicates that there is no reliable data available.[1]

INGREDIENTS	Dry Matter %	Protein %	Fat %	Fiber %	Calcium %	Phosphorus %	Ash %	Xanthophyll mg/lb	M.E.[2] Cal/lb	M.E.[3] Cal/kg
Alfalfa meal, dehydrated, 20%	93	20	3.5	21	1.5	0.27	10.5	150	755	1661
Alfalfa meal, dehydrated, 17%	93	17.3	2.5	24.5	1.35	0.22	10	120	740	1628
Alfalfa meal, suncured	90	15	1.6	30	1.35	0.2	9	70	300	660
Bakery product, dried	92.5	10	12	1	0.1	0.25	5	6.2	1770	3894
Barley	89	11.5	1.9	6	0.06	0.37	3	———	1200	2640
Barley, West Coast	88	9.5	2	6.5	0.06	0.35	2.5	———	1150	2530
Blood Meal, flash dried	91	85	1	1	0.28	0.22	4.4	———	1250	2750
Brewers dried grains	93	27	7	12	0.27	0.55	3.8	———	1140	2508
Brewers dried yeast	93	45	1	2.8	0.1	1.4	6.5	———	1000	2200
Corn, yellow	87	9	3.8	2.8	0.02	0.25	1.5	10	1560	3432
Corn and cob meal	86	7.5	3.3	9.5	0.04	0.22	1.5	5	1280	2816
Corn gluten feed	89	21.5	2	10	0.35	0.85	7.8	———	820	1807
Corn gluten meal, 42%	91	42	2	4.2	0.1	0.6	4.5	60	1250	2750
Corn gluten meal, 60%	91	61	2.5	1.2	0.02	0.6	1	106	1650	3637
Cottonseed meal, solvent, 41%	93	41	1.5	12.4	0.15	0.98	6.3	———	950	2090
Cottonseed meal, solvent, 44%	91	44	1.2	11	0.15	1.2	6.3	———	935	2057
Cottonseed meal, solvent, 50%	89	50	1	8	0.2	1.4	7	———	1010	2222
Crab meal	94	35.5	3.6	10.5	13	1.75	40	———	850	1870
Distillers dried grains (corn)	92	27	7.6	12.8	0.08	0.37	2.3	1	740	1628
Dist. dried grains w/solubles (corn)	92	27	8	8.5	0.35	0.95	4.5	1	1190	2618
Distillers dried solubles (corn)	92	28	9	4	0.3	1.6	8.1	1	1250	2750
Fat, animal	99.5	———	99	———	———	———	———	———	3490	7678
Fat, animal—vegetable (hydrolyzed)	99.5	———	99	———	———	———	———	———	3700	8140
Fat, poultry	98	———	98	———	———	———	———	———	3720	8184
Feather meal	93	85	2.5	1.5	0.2	0.75	3.5	———	1035	2277

Fish meal (Menhaden)	92	60.5	10	0.9	5.2	2.75	19	—	1360	3000
Fish meal (Anchovy)	92	64.5	8.9	0.6	4	2.6	15.5	—	1330	2926
Fish meal (Herring)	93	72	8.5	1	2.7	2	10.4	—	1365	3003
Fish solubles, condensed, 50% solids	50	32	8.9	0.5	0.1	0.5	10	—	710	1562
Hominy, yellow	91	10.7	5	4	0.02	0.5	2.7	1.6	1365	3003
Linseed meal, hydraulic or expeller	91	32	4.7	9	0.39	0.87	5.7	?	700	1540
Linseed meal, solvent	91	33	1.5	9.3	0.38	0.86	5.9	?	640	1408
Meat and bone scrap, 45%	92	45	8.5	2.2	11	5.8	35	—	800	1760
Meat and bone scrap, 50%	94	50	9	2.4	11.1	5.2	28.8	—	1000	2200
Meat scrap, 55%	93	55	7	2.4	7.5	4	25	—	1050	2310
Molasses, cane	73	3	—	—	0.75	0.08	8.5	—	890	1958
Oats	89	11.5	4.6	11	0.09	0.43	3.5	—	1260	2772
Oats, west coast	90	9	5.1	11	0.1	0.35	3.8	—	1140	2508
Oat mill by-product	91	5.6	2	27	0.16	0.19	5.9	—	270	594
Peanut meal, solvent	92	50	1.3	3.9	0.2	0.6	5.5	—	1150	2530
Peas, cull	91	23	1	6.1	0.18	0.3	3	—	1180	2596
Poultry by-product meal	95	65	12.8	2.3	3.3	1.75	20	—	1365	3003
Poultry offal meal	83	60	19	1.8	2.3	1.2	12.1	—	1512	3326
Rice (rough)	89	8	1.7	9	0.09	0.36	4.5	—	1215	2673
Rice bran	91	13	13.3	12.9	0.06	1.43	12	—	1000	2200
Rice polishings	90	11.8	12.5	3.4	0.04	1.42	7.2	—	1300	2860
Safflower meal, solvent	91	21	0.5	37	0.25	0.65	6	—	530	1166
Safflower meal, solvent-dehulled	90	42	1.5	14	0.4	1	8	—	920	2024
Skimmilk, dried	94	33	0.9	0.1	1.25	1	8	—	1000	2508
Sorghum grains (milo)	89	9	2.9	2.1	0.03	0.28	2.1	—	1500	3300
Soybeans, full fat	90	36.7	18	5	0.25	0.6	5	—	1500	3300
Soybean meal, solvent	89	44	1	7	0.25	0.6	5.7	—	1000	2200
Soybean meal, solvent-dehulled	90	48.5	1	3.2	0.2	0.65	6	—	1100	2420
Soybean mill feed	90	12.5	2	36	0.59	0.17	4.5	—	460	1012
Sunflower seed meal	93	46.8	2.5	11	0.3	1	7.7	—	1000	2200
Tankage, 60%	92	60	7.8	2.2	5.5	3.1	21	—	1200	2640

INGREDIENTS	Dry Matter %	Protein %	Fat %	Fiber %	Calcium %	Phosphorus %	Ash %	Xanthophyll mg/lb	M.E.[2] Cal/lb	M.E.[3] Cal/kg
Wheat, hard	89	12.5	1.8	2.7	0.05	0.4	2	----	1360	2992
Wheat, soft	89	10.2	1.7	2.3	0.09	0.3	1.8	----	1400	3080
Wheat bran	89	15	2.7	11	0.14	1.17	6	----	575	1265
Wheat germ meal	88	25	7.5	3.3	0.07	0.8	5.3	----	900	1980
Wheat middlings, flour	90	18	4.6	4.9	0.07	0.65	3.9	----	1200	2640
Wheat middlings, standard	90	16	4.5	7	0.1	0.78	5	----	890	1958
Wheat millrun	89	15	4	8	0.1	0.9	5	----	800	1540
Wheat mixed feed	89	16	4.3	7.8	0.1	1	4.8	----	800	1760
Whey, dried	93	12	0.5	----	0.8	0.75	9.8	----	870	1914
Curacao Island phosphate 14%	99	----	----	----	34	14	91	----	----	----
Defluorinated rock phosphate	99	----	----	----	32	18	98	----	----	----
Dicalcium phosphate	98	----	----	----	22	18.5	78	----	----	----
Limestone or oyster shell	98	----	----	----	38	----	95.8	----	----	----
Steamed bone meal	95	12	1.2	1.4	26	13	70	----	400	880
Yeast, Torula*	93	48	5.1	2	0.55	1.6	5.8	----	845	1859
Corn, high lysine*	92	10.8	4	3.8	0.02	0.2	1.9	10	1560	3432
Rapeseed meal*, expeller	92	35	7	12.1	0.85	1.1	9.1	----	1025	2255
Triticale*	90	15	1.15	5	0.05	0.3	3	----	1460	3212

INGREDIENTS	Linoleic Acid %	Riboflavin PPM[4]	Panthothenic Acid PPM[4]	Choline PPM[4]	Arginine %	Isoleucine %	Lysine %	Methionine %	Cystine %	Threonine %	Tryptophan %
									Amino Acids		
Alfalfa meal, dehydrated, 20%	0.52	16	33	1600	0.97	0.9	0.8	0.3	0.22	0.81	0.42
Alfalfa meal, dehydrated, 17%	0.4	15	29	1550	0.6	0.65	0.6	0.23	0.14	0.58	0.35
Alfalfa meal, suncured	0.3	11	22	1000	0.63	0.6	0.6	0.2	0.13	0.6	0.25
Bakery product, dried	0.1	2	4	1000	0.61	0.54	0.31	0.23	0.16	0.59	0.04
Barley	0.85	2	7	1050	0.55	0.45	0.4	0.17	0.29	0.35	0.13
Barley, West Coast	0.85	2	7	990	0.43	0.35	0.3	0.12	0.22	0.3	0.1

Blood Meal, flash dried	0.02	2	1	750	2.35	0.62	4.5	0.65	1	3.38	0.72
Brewers dried grains	3	1	9	2050	1.3	1.56	0.9	0.45	0.35	0.9	0.4
Brewers dried yeast	0.05	33	110	3850	2.2	2.22	3	0.7	0.45	2.3	0.5
Corn, yellow	1.9	1	6	550	0.4	0.4	0.24	0.19	0.15	0.35	0.09
Corn and cob meal	1.5	1	4	350	0.35	0.19	0.18	0.14	0.12	0.36	0.06
Corn gluten feed	1	2	17	1430	0.75	0.6	0.5	0.35	0.4	0.42	0.1
Corn gluten meal, 42%	1.2	2	10	330	1.2	—	0.6	1	0.6	1.17	0.19
Corn gluten meal, 60%	1.5	2	9	435	2	2.29	0.72	1.73	0.89	2.1	0.31
Cottonseed meal, solvent, 41%	0.5	4	14	2800	4.19	1.2	1.58	0.46	0.56	1.21	0.47
Cottonseed meal, solvent, 44%	0.8	5	18	2900	4.9	1.45	1.86	0.54	0.72	1.09	0.53
Cottonseed meal, solvent, 50%	0.8	5	18	3200	5.57	1.65	2.11	0.61	0.73	1.39	0.61
Crab meal	0.33	6	7	1980	1.88	1.2	1.31	0.82	0.09	1.2	0.3
Distillers dried grains (corn)	4.5	3	6	1850	0.77	0.7	0.42	0.35	0.14	0.63	0.14
Dist. dried grains w/ solubles (corn)	4.5	8	11	2500	0.92	0.92	0.5	0.59	0.37	0.87	0.18
Distillers dried solubles (corn)	4.6	13	21	4900	1.15	1.25	0.95	0.5	0.4	0.98	0.3
Fat, animal	2.5	—	—	—	—	—	—	—	—	—	—
Fat, animal—vegetable (hydrolyzed)	12	—	—	—	—	—	—	—	—	—	—
Fat, poultry	22	—	—	—	—	—	—	—	—	—	—
Feather meal	—	2	10	880	3.9	2.66	1.05	0.35	2	2.8	0.4
Fish meal (Menhaden)	0.12	5	9	3050	3.23	2.2	4.25	1.68	0.9	2.25	0.61
Fish meal (Anchovy)	0.06	9	11	3600	3.3	2.7	4.4	2.11	0.53	2.4	0.67
Fish meal (Herring)	0.15	9	11	5100	4.28	2.86	5.59	2.51	0.68	3	0.92

INGREDIENTS	Linoleic Acid %	Riboflavin PPM[4]	Panthothenic Acid PPM[4]	Choline PPM[4]	Amino Acids						
					Arginine %	Isoleucine %	Lysine %	Methionine %	Cystine %	Threonine %	Tryptophan %
Fish solubles, condensed, 50% solids	0.12	13	35	3800	1.3	0.6	1.46	0.5	0.18	0.7	0.11
Hominy, yellow	3.3	2	8	960	0.46	0.37	0.31	0.14	0.11	0.37	0.12
Linseed meal, hydraulic or expeller	0.75	4	13	1700	2.74	1.7	1.12	0.81	0.63	1.1	0.55
Linseed meal, solvent	0.16	3	14	1440	2.7	1.8	1.1	0.84	0.66	1.2	0.56
Meat and bone scrap, 45%	0.4	4	3	1770	2.7	1.38	2.2	0.53	0.30	1.33	0.2
Meat and bone scrap, 50%	0.34	4	4	1920	3.08	1.5	2.5	0.6	0.55	1.45	0.3
Meat scrap, 55%	0.29	5	5	2000	3.6	1.78	2.65	0.7	0.66	1.73	0.33
Molasses, cane	—	2	37	785	—	—	—	—	—	—	—
Oats	1.5	2	15	1070	0.8	0.53	0.5	0.18	0.22	0.44	0.16
Oats, west coast	1.4	1	12	910	0.53	0.44	0.31	0.13	0.17	0.37	0.11
Oat mill by-product	0.7	2	33	380	0.14	0.14	0.14	0.07	0.06	0.13	0.07
Peanut meal, solvent	0.38	11	53	1790	5	1.81	1.73	0.44	0.72	1.1	0.49
Peas, cull	0.3	—	—	650	1.4	1.13	1.6	0.31	0.17	0.94	0.24
Poultry by-product meal	2.2	9	9	5985	4.2	2.15	2.44	1.28	1	2.1	0.49
Poultry offal meal	3.3	6	8	3582	3.4	2.03	1.76	0.66	1.18	1.81	0.38
Rice (rough)	0.65	1	5	920	0.7	0.38	0.3	0.17	0.1	0.31	0.12
Rice bran	3.6	3	23	1200	0.99	0.56	0.54	0.22	0.09	0.5	0.22
Rice polishings	3.6	2	11	1229	0.5	0.3	0.5	0.2	0.1	0.3	0.1
Safflower meal, solvent	1.1	2	33	1200	1.7	0.8	0.59	0.33	0.25	0.64	0.26
Safflower meal, solvent-dehulled	1.1	2	40	3260	3.7	1.7	1.3	0.69	0.7	1.35	0.6
Skimmilk, dried	0.01	20	3	1400	1.1	2.1	2.3	0.98	0.42	1.75	0.45
Sorghum grains (milo)	1.1	1	13	688	0.29	0.41	0.2	0.12	0.14	0.32	0.1
Soybeans, full fat	9	3	15	2670	2.8	1.97	2.4	0.55	0.54	1.5	0.54
Soybean meal, solvent	0.4	2	15	2600	3.37	2.38	2.84	0.65	0.67	1.79	0.66

Ingredient											
Soybean meal, solvent-dehulled	0.4	3	13	2761	3	2.35	3	0.7	0.7	2.2	0.7
Soybean mill feed	0.7	4	13	596	0.57	0.4	0.48	0.1	0.11	0.3	0.11
Sunflower seed meal	1.7	3	41	4260	3	1.64	1.52	1.35	0.71	1.52	0.51
Tankage, 60%	0.33	2	2	2185	3.4	1.8	3.8	0.72	0.35	2.4	0.59
Wheat, hard	0.6	1	14	900	0.6	0.53	0.4	0.17	0.22	0.28	0.16
Wheat, soft	0.6	1	13	860	0.47	0.40	0.32	0.13	0.18	0.28	0.13
Wheat bran	1.7	3	29	1004	0.62	0.39	0.37	0.11	0.15	0.23	0.17
Wheat germ meal	3.8	5	12	3250	1.6	1.2	1.6	0.3	0.5	0.8	0.3
Wheat middlings, flour	1.7	2	18	990	0.95	0.7	0.67	0.17	0.18	0.48	0.18
Wheat middlings, standard	1.9	2	20	1100	0.81	0.64	0.57	0.15	0.16	0.43	0.16
Wheat millrun	1.7	2	21	990	1	0.65	0.5	0.25	0.3	0.26	0.26
Wheat mixed feed	1.7	2	13	990	0.9	—	0.5	0.4	0.2	0.35	0.2
Whey, dried	0.1	30	48	1875	0.3	0.72	0.9	0.15	0.31	0.7	0.15
Curacao Island phosphate 14%	—	—	—	—	—	—	—	—	—	—	—
Defluorinated rock phosphate	—	—	—	—	—	—	—	—	—	—	—
Dicalcium phosphate	—	—	—	—	—	—	—	—	—	—	—
Limestone or oyster shell	—	—	—	—	—	—	—	—	—	—	—
Steamed bone meal	0.02	2	2	220	1.7	—	0.9	0.2	0.1	—	0.05
Yeast, Torula*	0.25	44	84	2875	2.6	—	3.8	0.78	0.61	2.6	0.1
Corn, high lysine*	1.9	1	5	528	0.67	0.34	0.35	0.13	0.16	0.39	0.12
Rapeseed meal*, expeller	1	4	9	650	2	1.35	1.9	0.66	0.52	1.5	0.45
Triticale*	0.55	—	—	463	0.7	0.48	0.4	0.14	0.16	0.37	0.14

* These ingredients are now being used in certain local areas. They exhibit a high degree of location variability.

[1] Information in this table was provided by Nutrius Inc., Cleveland, Ohio.

[2] Metabolizable energy (per pound) for poultry diets.

[3] Metabolizable energy (per kilogram) for poultry diets.

[4] PPM—Parts per million. To convert PPM to mg/lb divide by 2.2.

Vitamin premixes, choline chloride, DL-methionine, Nopgro (enzymes), UNF–40.

TYPICAL POULTRY RATIONS

Chick Starter and Developer Rations[1]

Ingredients	0–8 Weeks Starter (20% protein)	8–20 Weeks Developer (16% Protein)
Wheat bran[2]	——	10.00
Ground corn	30.50	20.00
Ground milo	34.00	45.70
Soybean meal (44% protein)	27.00	16.00
Fish meal (70% protein)	2.50	——
Meat and bone meal (50% protein)	——	2.50
Dehydrated alfalfa (17% protein)	2.50	2.50
Ground limestone	1.20	1.30
Phosphate supp. (P = 18 Ca = 24)	1.50	1.20
Salt	0.50	0.50
Vitamin mix*	0.25	0.25
Trace mineral mix**	0.05	0.05
DL Methionine	0.125	0.04
Total	100.	100.

*Vitamin mix supplies per pound of ration:

Vitamin A	2400	IU	2400	IU
Vitamin D	400	ICU	400	ICU

417

Chick Starter and Developer Rations[1] (*Continued*)

Ingredients	0–8 Weeks Starter (20% protein)		8–20 Weeks Developer (16% Protein)	
Vitamin K	.15	mg	.15	mg
Riboflavin	2	mg	2	mg
Niacin	10	mg	10	mg
Pantothenic acid	2	mg	2	mg
Choline	148	mg	148	mg

** Trace mineral mix supplies: Mn 50 ppm; Fe 50 ppm; Cu 5.0 ppm; Co 0.5 ppm; I 1.5 ppm, and Zn 50 ppm.

Calculated Analysis:

Protein, %	20.1	16.1
Fat, %	2.6	2.6
Fiber, %	3.8	4.3
Calcium, %	1.0	1.1
Phosphorus (Total)	0.68	0.72
Phosphorus (Available)	0.44	0.47
Lysine, %	1.12	0.78
Methionine and Cystine, %	0.73	0.55
Energy Calories/lb:		
Productive	961.0	932.0
C:P ratio	48:1	58:1
Metabolizable	1301.0	1236.0
C:P ratio	65:1	77:1

[1] Colorado State University standard ration.
[2] Wheat bran or standard middlings may be interchanged depending on availability.

Layer Rations[1]

Ingredients	18% Protein	17% Protein	16% Protein
Ground yellow corn	58.52	29.21	29.56
Ground milo	——	32.50	35.00
Brewers dried grains	5.00	5.00	5.00
Soybean oil meal (44% protein)	22.82	19.63	16.78
Meat and bone meal (50% protein)	2.50	2.50	2.50
Dehydrated alfalfa (17% protein)	2.50	2.50	2.50
Ground limestone	6.40	6.40	6.40
Dicalcium phosphate	1.50	1.50	1.50
Salt	0.50	0.50	0.50
Vitamin mix*	0.05	0.05	0.05

Layer Rations[1] (*Continued*)

Ingredients	18% Protein	17% Protein	16% Protein
Trace mineral mix**	0.05	0.05	0.05
Choline (25%)	0.13	0.13	0.13
Methionine	0.03	0.03	0.03
Total	100.	100.	100.

* Vitamin mix supplies per pound of ration:

Vitamin A	2250	IU
Vitamin D$_3$	750	ICU
Vitamin E	1	IU
Niacin	10	mg
Pantothenic acid	3.0	mg
Vitamin B$_{12}$	4.0	mcg
Riboflavin	2.0	mg
Vitamin K	.50	mg

** Trace mineral mix supplies: Mn 50 ppm; Fe 50 ppm; Cu 5 ppm; Cu 5 ppm; Co 0.5 ppm; I 1.5 ppm, and Zn 50 ppm.

Calculated Analysis:

	18% Protein	17% Protein	16% Protein
Protein, %	18.00	17.00	16.00
Energy Calories/lb:			
Metabolizable	1236	1270	1240
C:P ratio	69:1	75:1	78:1
Productive	904	906	916
C:P ratio	51:1	53:1	57:1
Calcium, %	3.16	3.15	3.20
Phosphorus (Total)	.73	.73	.78
Methionine, %	.319	.298	.306
Cystine, %	.291	.280	.264
Methionine and Cystine, %	.610	.578	.570
Fat, %	2.82	2.60	2.70
Fiber, %	4.00	4.00	3.90

[1] Colorado State University standard ration.

Turkey Rations[1]

Ingredients	Starter (28% Protein)	Grower (19% Protein)	Finisher (14.6% Protein)
Ground yellow corn	19.28	32.02	38.33
Ground milo	24.00	34.50	40.00
Soybean oil meal (44% protein)	44.90	22.75	11.93

Turkey Rations[1] (*Continued*)

Ingredients	Starter (28% Protein)	Grower (19% Protein)	Finisher (14.6% Protein)
Fish meal (70% protein)	5.00	——	1.00
Meat and bone (50% protein)	——	5.00	2.50
Dehydrated alfalfa (17% protein)	2.50	2.50	2.50
Ground limestone	0.60	——	0.50
Dicalcium phosphate	3.00	2.50	2.50
Salt	0.30	0.30	0.50
Vitamin mix*	0.05	0.05	0.05
Trace mineral mix**	0.05	0.05	0.05
Coccidiostat or histostat***	0.05	0.05	0.05
Methionine	——	0.10	——
Choline chloride (25%)	0.27	0.18	0.09
Total	100.	100.	100.

* Vitamin mix supplies per pound of ration:

Vitamin A	3000	3000	1500	IU
Vitamin D_3	1000	800	500	IU
Vitamin E	5	2.5	2.5	IU
Vitamin B_{12}	5	5	1	mcg
Niacin	30	15	10	mg
Riboflavin	2	2	1	mg
D-Pantothenic acid (pure)	3	1	——	mg
Folic acid	.25	——	——	mg

** Trace mineral mix supplies: Mn 50 ppm; Fe 50 ppm; Zn 50 ppm; Ca 45 ppm; Cu 5 ppm; I 1.5 ppm; Co 0.5 ppm.
*** Coccidiostat for first 8 weeks, then discontinued.
　　Blackhead (Hepzide) control from 8 weeks to market, in lieu of Amprolium.

Calculated Analysis:

Crude Protein, %	28.00	19.00	14.6
Fat, %	2.5	2.6	2.9
Fiber, %	2.4	2.9	2.9
Calcium, %	1.31	1.25	1.2
Phosphorus (Total)	1.10	1.04	0.92
Phosphorus (Available)	0.85	0.87	0.84
Lysine, %	1.77	0.95	0.70
Methionine and Cystine, %	0.93	0.69	0.50
Productive Calories/lb	906	966	1009
Metabolizable Calories/lb	1270	1338	1378

[1] Colorado State University standard ration.

CUTTING A POULTRY CARCASS

The following procedure may be used in the home for cutting a whole poultry carcass into typical retail cuts. The procedure is best applied to broiler chicken or other poultry carcasses of a similar size such as ducks, but may also be used on larger carcasses such as turkeys or geese. Never use a cleaver for cutting up poultry as bones easily splinter and are dangerous to the consumer; use a sharp knife.

1. Remove giblets and neck from body cavity or crop cavity.
2. Holding carcass by wing, cut off each wing at the joint (Figure A6-1). Bend wing into triangle by forcing wing tip under humerus bone.
3. Cut leg skin between thigh and abdomen (Figure A6-2).
4. Bend legs back, popping femur bone out of socket (Figure A6-3).
5. Cut thigh away from back around and including gluteal muscle (Figure A6-4).
6. Repeat with other leg.
7. Cut along white fat line on inside of leg at joint where drumstick attaches to thigh (Figure A6-5). It is easy to cut through the joint at this point by rocking the knife gently as it finds its own way through the joint (Figure A6-6). Then cut skin and remaining tissue from other side (Figure A6-7).
8. Repeat with other leg.
9. Cut above lateral caudal process of sternum and through ribs at cartilage joint up to shoulder area, on both sides (Figure A6-8).

10. Separate back from breast by snapping bones back (Figure A6-9) and cutting through extra tissue in the shoulder area (Figure A6-10).

11. Cut or break back just posterior to ribs.

12. Break fused backbone longitudinally on each side of the spinal column, so that the posterior back piece will lay flat.

13. Cut through the white cartilage portion of the ribs where they connect to the backbone.

14. Break the ribs back so the anterior back piece will lay flat.

15. Cut the breast piece longitudinally in halves along keel, or transversely at front of keel, break and cut.

16. When packaged for retail purposes, the meat is placed in tray with wings, back, neck, and giblets on bottom and drums, thighs and breast on top for an attractive display.

FIGURES A6–1   through A6–10
Cutting a turkey carcass.

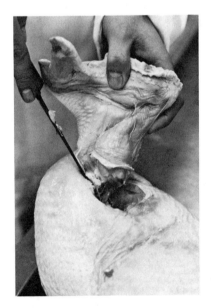

FIGURE A6–1

FIGURE A6–2

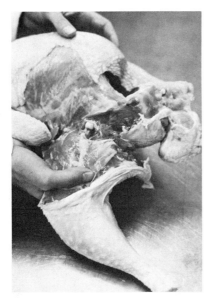

FIGURE A6–3

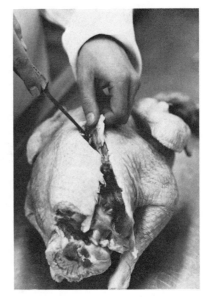

FIGURE A6–4

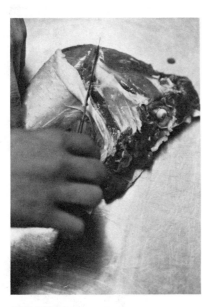

FIGURE A6–5

FIGURE A6–6

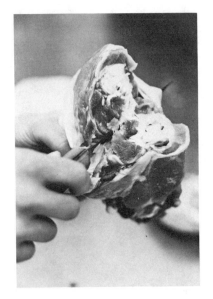

FIGURE A6–7

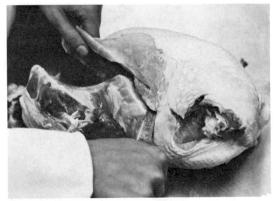

FIGURE A6–8

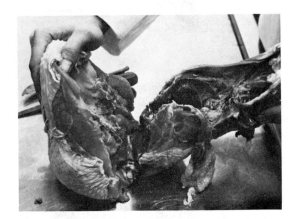

FIGURE A6–9

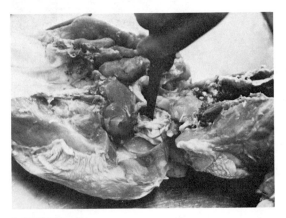

FIGURE A6–10

DEBONING A POULTRY CARCASS

The following procedure may be used in the home for deboning a whole poultry carcass, to obtain meat for use in a variety of further processed products. The procedure is best applied to large turkey carcasses, but may also be used on smaller carcasses such as chickens and ducks.

1. Remove giblets and neck from crop cavity or body cavity.

2. Remove and separate wings, thighs, and drumsticks as previously described for cutting a poultry carcass (steps 2 through 8).

3. Remove femur bone from thighs by making a longitudinal cut exposing the bone. Then cut meat away close to the bone while turning the muscle inside out with the other hand; remove the bone (Figure A7-1).

4. Cut skin down the back from tail to neck. Loosen skin and peel it away from backbone using a knife where necessary.

5. Cutting anterior to the gluteal muscle cavity, separate breast meat with attached skin from bone by cutting it away close to the bone on both sides to keel (Figure A7-2).

6. Cut through cartilage in the shoulder area and remove both sides of the breast meat in one piece with skin attached (Figure A7-3).

7. The remainder of the skeleton may now be trimmed as time and patience allow (Figure A7-4). The wings and drumsticks are generally not deboned. However, the humerus of the wing may be separated from the forepart of the wing at the joint and cooked as a "small drumstick" (Figure A7-5).

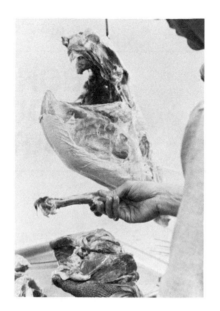

FIGURE A7–1

FIGURE A7–2

FIGURES A7–1 through A7–5
Deboning a turkey carcass.

FIGURE A7–3

FIGURE A7–4

FIGURE A7–5

GLOSSARY

Brailing   A technique used to prevent birds from flying. This may be accomplished by tying one wing in a closed position with a bandage type material. For more permanent results primary flight feathers on one wing may be clipped, the distal wing section may be removed or the tendon to that section may be severed.

Breed   Birds having a common origin with specific characteristics, such as body shape, that distinguish them from other groups within the same species.

Broiler   A young bird of either sex, up to eight to ten weeks of age and weighing three to six pounds, usually of the meat-type breeds. The term is used inerchangeably with the term *fryer*.

Brooder   A heat source for the period of growth from day of hatch to approximately five weeks of age. The heat source generally has a large reflector (hover) under which the birds may gather and where the heat is captured.

Brooding   The period of growth in the life of a young bird where it must be provided a source of heat in addition to that generated by its own body.

Broody   The condition of a hen when she is prepared to sit on eggs for the purpose of incubation and when she becomes receptive to caring for the young. Both physiological and psychological changes have taken place in the hen's body and she ceases to lay eggs during this period.

Candling   The process of examining an intact egg to determine interior quality, shell soundness, or stage of embryonic development. This is accomplished in a dark room by holding the egg in front of a strong beam of light and reciprocally turning the egg.

Capon   Castrated male chicken, chickens are usually caponized (castrated) between three and four weeks of age.

Caruncle   The red and blue fleshy unfeathered area of skin on the upper region of the neck of a turkey.

Chick   A young chicken, pheasant, or other gamebird from one day to about five to six weeks of age, either male or female.

Cock   Mature male chicken (rooster).

Cockerel   A young male chicken from day of hatch to approximately one year of age.

Comb   A fleshy outgrowth on the top of the head of a chicken, generally red in color and of various types and shapes.

Confinement   Practice of rearing birds completely housed so they spend their total time indoors.

Crumble   A physical condition of feed prepared at the mill by pelleting of the mixed ingredients and then crushing the pellet to a consistency coarser than mash.

Debeaking   (*Beak Trimming*) Trimming of the beak involving removal of the upper one-third to one-half of the mandible in growing and mature birds or about one-fourth of both mandibles in day-old chicks and poults, to prevent cannibalism.

Dew Drop Waterer   Equipment for providing drinking water to birds in cages, basically consisting of a pipe with a ball-bearing-type valve activated by the bird as it pecks at the valve, releasing drops of water.

Egg Dipping   The process of submerging eggs in an antibiotic solution under specific conditions of time and temperature. The purpose is to reduce or eliminate certain microorganisms on or within the egg.

Down   Soft fluffy type of feather located under the contour feathers and serving the bird as an insulating material.

Drake   Mature male duck.

Dubbing   Comb removal, usually in single comb type birds; may sometimes include removal of wattles. This is usually performed in young birds from day of hatch to five or six weeks by the use of a scissor, with minimal bleeding if trimmed close to head. In older birds the operation should not be performed due to more serious hemorrhage potential.

Duck   Mature female duck.

Duckling   Young duck, either sex, from day of hatch to about six weeks of age.

Earlobe A rounded, sometimes pigmented area of skin below the external ear canal of chickens.

Egg Eating A habit which, once it gets started, is difficult to contain in flock houses and usually is associated with overcrowding or thin-shelled eggs. Birds will eat their own eggs and those of other hens when eggs become broken in the nest or on the floor and will even proceed to break the shells and eat eggs once the habit is started.

Gander Mature male goose.

Goose Mature female goose.

Gossling Young goose, either sex, from day of hatch to about eight to ten weeks of age.

Gynandromorph Both male and female plumage on the same bird; a sex mosaic, one side (right) having male characteristics and plumage and the other side (left) having female characteristics and plumage.

Hatcher A machine or that portion of the incubator that is used for the last two or three days of incubation and hatching of the eggs. No turning of the eggs is required and the eggs are allowed to hatch in flat bottom trays.

Hatching The process by which the fully developed fetus (chick) leaves the protected environment of the egg and emerges into the world, *birth*.

Incubator A machine developed to provide the proper environment for the development of the fertile egg and embryo into a chick or poult.

Leg Band Aluminum or plastic bands that may be placed around the shanks of birds for the purpose of identification. The bands can be obtained in various colors and may be numbered.

Mash A form of a complete feed that is finely ground and mixed so that birds cannot easily separate out ingredients; each mouthful provides a well-balanced diet.

Ovotestis Development of tissue on the inner right dorsal wall of the female fowl, which normally only has one functional ovary on the left side. If the left ovary is destroyed, the right side may develop this organ.

Pellet A form of a complete feed that is compacted and extruded to about $\frac{1}{8}$ inch in diameter and $\frac{1}{4}$ inch long, usually fed to mature poultry.

Pinioning Amputating the last joint of one wing.

Potentiation Process used to increase blood levels of specific antibiotics generally by temporarily decreasing dietary calcium intake.

Poularde A bird that has had the ovary removed or destroyed and as a result acquires male-type plumage. This may occur at the time of molt, and if the ovary is reactivated the cock-like bird could lay eggs.

Poult   A young turkey, either sex, from day of hatch to eight to ten weeks of age.

Poultry   Domestic birds generally adapted to rearing in confinement for their eggs or meat production. This includes all chickens, turkeys, ducks, and geese, as well as swans, guineas, pigeons, peafowl, pheasants, and ostriches.

Pullet   A young female chicken from day of hatch through onset of egg production to one year of age; sometimes the term is applied through the first laying year.

Range   A large fenced area planted in alfalfa or some grass or small grain crop in which birds are allowed to roam and supplement their regular diet.

Setter   A separate machine or that portion of an incubator utilized for eggs from the onset of the incubation process to approximately two to three days prior to hatching.

Tenectomy   Cutting the tendon that controls wing movement. The cut is made on the front side of the wing where it crosses the last joint.

Wing Band   Aluminum or plastic bands that are placed in the wing web area of the bird at day one of age. These may be of various colors and may be numbered. They must be placed to hang over the front of the wing. It is important that they do not hang over the back of the wing as they will restrict bone development. A second type is a "wing badge" that is used on mature birds and which completely, but loosely, surrounds the upper wing (humerus) in the shoulder area.

INDEX

Abdominal air sacs, 66
Absorption, 219–22
Accounting procedures, 371
Adenine, 87, 88, 224, 226
Adrenal glands, 79, 80
Adrenalin, 80
Agricultural Marketing Act of 1946, 324
Agriculture, 8–13
Agriculture Department (see United States Department of Agriculture)
Air sacs, 65–68
Albumen, 71, 72, 78
  bacterial contamination of, 270–72
  height measurement of, 269–71
  quality factors, 266
  thinning of, 261
Albumen score, 270
Allantois, 140, 142
Alveoli, 66
American Bantam Association, 25, 402
American Class Chickens, 21, 22, 374–80
American Egg Board, 281
American Poultry Association, 374
American Standard of Perfection, The, 19, 25, 26, 28, 40, 41, 374
Amino acids, 211
  metabolism of, 220–32
  release of, 217, 218
  requirement for, 205–6
Ammonia, 222
Amnion, 139, 140
Anatomy, 47–84
  cardiorespiratory system, 65–70
  digestive system, 60–64
  endocrine system, 79–84
  feathers, 48–51
  muscular system, 56–60
  nervous system, 81–84
  reproductive system and the egg, 70–79
  skeletal system, 52–56
  skin, 48–50, 52
  urinary system, 64–65
Ancona chickens, 24, 388
Androgens, 80–81
Animal by-products (tankage), 207
Animal husbandry, 345
Animal welfare, 345–56
  care, 346–48
  rights, 348–56
Animism, 348
Ante-mortem inspection, 325
Antibiotics:
  dietary, 211
  dips, 155
Aortic rupture, 245
Araucana chickens, 400–401
Archaeopleryx, 16
Area opaca, 136, 138
Area pellucida, 136
Artificial incubation, 145–61
Artificial insemination, 106, 107, 120–34
  of chickens, 120–25
  equipment, 130–31
  of geese, 126–30
  low fertility following, 117–18
  spermatogenesis and semen, 131–34
  of turkeys, 120–27

Asiatic class chickens, 21, 22, 380–83
Atherosclerosis, 282–83
Atlas, 53, 54
Auger feeding systems, 166, 168, 182, 183
Australorp chickens, 23, 383
Avian anatomy (see Anatomy)
A vitamin, 208–9, 246, 282
Axial feathers, 37

Bacillary white diarrhea, 240–41
Bacterial contamination of eggs, 270–71
Bacterial diseases, 237, 240–43
Bambiism, 348
Bantams, 21, 25, 401–2
Bantam Standard, The 374
Barbecues, 338–39
Barbicels, 51
Barbs, 49–51
Barbules, 51
Bar cut, 304, 306
Barred feather color pattern, inheritance of, 91–93
Barred Plymouth Rock chickens, 95
Basal metabolic rate (BMR), 232
Bausch and Lomb spectronic "20," 133
Beak, 35
  anatomy of, 53–54
  debeaking, 359
  digestive system and, 60–61
  egg production and condition of, 110
Bean, 39, 40
Beard, 38, 39
Bile, 62
Bile ducts, 62, 63
Bill, 39–40
Blackhead, 244
Black Minorcas, 95
Black turkeys, 96–97
Blastoderm, 136, 138
Blastodisc, 77
Bleeding, 292–93
Blond yolks, 260
Blood, 69–70
Blood circulatory system, 68–70
Blood flow, 68
Blood islands, 138
Blood spots, 72, 260, 266
Bloom, 73, 76–77
Blue Andalusian chickens, 24, 388–89
Bluecomb disease, 246–47
Blue turkeys, 96
Body temperature, 68, 175
Bone meal, 207, 208
Bones, 52–56
Botulism, 242
Bourbon Red turkeys, 96, 97
Brahma chickens, 23, 380–81
Brazil, 5
Breast blisters, 247
Breast muscle, 56–59
Breed, defined, 373
Breeder flocks, 201
Breeding:
  genetics and, 85–100
  practices, 100–107
  selection, 113–14

Breeds, 15
  chicken, 21–24, 373–402
  development of, 16–21
  identification of, 21–33
Broad Breasted Bronze turkeys, 25
Broad White turkeys, 25–26
Broiler chickens, 3, 5, 6, 192–93, 285, 365
Bronchi, 65–67, 69
Bronchitis, 239–40
Bronze turkeys, 96, 97
Brooders, 165, 166
Brooding, 165–74
  broilers, 192–93
  capons, 194
  ducks, 197
  geese, 197
  pullets, 199
  roasters, 194
  turkeys, 196–97
Brown Leghorns, 95
Brown-shell eggs, 257
Bryan, William Jennings, 12
Buckeye chickens, 23, 380
Buff turkeys, 96
Building materials, 366–67
Bumblefoot, 247
Bursa of Fabricius, 84
Buttercup chickens, 24, 392
Buttercup comb, 36
B vitamins, 209–10, 282

"Cadavers," 292
Cage layer fatigue, 247
Cages, 111, 177–86, 193, 200–201
Calcium, 207, 208, 211, 230, 259, 282
Calcium carbonate, 72
Campine chickens, 393–94
Candling, 264–69
Cannibalism, 179, 195, 247–48
Capillaries, 66, 68
Caponettes, 195
Capons, 38, 194–95
Carbohydrates:
  absorption of, 219–21
  digestion of, 213–19
  metabolism of, 220, 221
  requirement for, 207–8
Carbon dioxide loss, 261
Carcasses:
  cutting, 421–24
  deboning, 425–27
Cardiorespiratory system, 65–70
Care of animals, 346–48
Carotene, 78
Catalana chickens, 24, 392
Ceca, 60–62
Cell differentiation, 135–38
Cell division, 87, 89, 135–37
Cells, 222–23
Cervical air sacs, 65, 66
Cervical vertebrae, 53, 54
Chain-drag feeders, 182, 183
Chalazae, 72, 78
Chalaziferous layer, 78
Chantecler chickens, 23, 380
Cheesecloth method of fumigation, 153–54

Chick, 38
Chicken eggs (*see* Eggs)
Chicken industry, 1–6
Chicken meat (*see* Poultry meat)
Chicken production (*see* Poultry production)
Chickens, 2–3
  age of, at processing, 285–86
  anatomical features, nomenclature of, 33–38
  anatomy of (*see* Anatomy)
  artificial incubation requirements for, 145
  artificial insemination of, 120–25
  breed identification and classification, 21–25, 373–402
  breeding (*see* Breeding)
  culling, 107–13
  cutting, 421–24
  deboning, 425–27
  domestication of, 16–19
  eggs of (*see* Food eggs)
  production of (*see* Poultry production)
  reproduction in (*see* Reproduction)
  showing of, 40–46
Chick starter and developer rations, 417–18
Chilling, 319–20
Cholera, 242
Cholesterol, 282–83
Chorioallantois, 142
Chorion, 140–42
Chromosomes, 86–94
Chronic respiratory disease (CRD), 238–39
Class, defined, 373
Classification, 15–40
  breed identification, 21–33, 373–402
  domestication and development of breeds, 16–21
  nomenclature, 33–40
Cleaning eggs (*see* Washing)
Cloaca, 60, 61, 63, 64, 71, 74, 116
Clostridium botulinum, 242
Cochin chickens, 23, 381–82
Cock, 38
Cockerel, 38
Cockfighting, 18, 19
Codon, 224
Coefficient of inbreeding, 102
Collection of eggs, 186, 263, 272
Combinability, 101
Combs, 34–36, 38, 44, 52, 109, 110
Comb type traits, 90, 91
Complete dominance, 90
Computers, 371
Confinement rings, 170, 171
Continental Class chickens, 393–94
Contour feathers, 48–51
Contract growers, 365
Cooking:
  eggs, 280–81
  poultry meat, 337–38
Coops, for showing, 41
Copper, 208
Copulation, 74–75, 116–17
Coracoid, 53, 54, 67
Cornish chickens, 21, 23, 384–85
Coryza, 243
Cottonseed meal, 206–7

Crevecoeur chickens, 395
Crop, 60, 61
  removal of, 314–17
Crossbreeding, 101
Crossing inbred lines, 103–4
Cubalaya chickens, 398
Culling, 107–14
Cup watering systems, 166, 167, 182, 185
Cushion comb, 36
Cuticle, 73, 76–77
Cutting carcasses, 421–24
Cytosine, 87, 88, 224

Dark meat, 56
Dark muscles, 56–59
Dead-bird disposal, 253
Debeaking, 359
Deboned poultry meat, 332–33
Deboning carcasses, 425–27
Defluorinated rock phosphate, 207, 208
Dehydration, 173
Delaware chickens, 23, 380
Deoxyribonucleic acid (DNA), 86–88, 223–27
Dewlap, 39, 40
Diets (*see* Nutrition)
Digestion, 213–19
Digestive system, 60–64
Diseases, 235–56
  abnormal conditions, 247–48
  bacterial, 237, 240–43
  egg production and, 260
  fungal, 237, 245
  genetic resistance to, 99–100
  miscellaneous, 245–47
  parasitic, 237, 244–45
  prevention and control of, 248–56
  protozoan, 237, 243–44
  viral, 237–40
Dissecting aneurysm, 245
Doctor of veterinary medicine (DVM), 325
Domestication, 16–21, 163–64, 345–46
Dominant genes, 90–95
Dominique chickens, 22, 380
Dorking chickens, 23, 385–86
Down production, 286
Drake, 40
Drum picking machines, 296, 298, 299
Duckling, 40
Duck production, 197, 199
  (*See also* Poultry production)
Ducks, 2, 285
  age of, at processing, 286
  anatomical features, nomenclature of, 39–40
  anatomy of (*see* Anatomy)
  artificial incubation requirements for, 145
  breed identification and classification of, 26–28
  cutting, 421–24
  deboning, 425–27
  domestication of, 20
  reproduction in (*see* Reproduction)
Duodenal loop, 62, 63
D vitamin, 209, 246, 259, 282

Earlobes, 35, 52, 110
Ectoderm, 136, 137

Egg industry, 3–4, 6, 12, 13
Egg production, 365
  characteristics of good and poor layers, 108–13
  fertility, basis of, 115–19
  food eggs (*see* Food eggs)
  housing, 164, 174–86
Egg products, 276
Eggs, 2–6
  anatomy and physiology of, 75–79
  artificial incubation of, 145–61
  breeding techniques and, 19
  collection of, 186, 263, 272
  food (*see* Food eggs)
  formation of, 72–73, 81–82
  measuring specific gravity of, 407
  natural incubation of, 137–46
  oviposition, 73, 82–84
  shells of (*see* shells)
  washing of, 186, 263, 274
Egg tooth, 143
Eimeria, 243–44
Eisenhower, Dwight D., 324
Ejaculation of semen, 116–17, 122, 127–28
Embden geese, 29
Embryonic development, 118, 134–46
Encephalomyelitis, 239
Endocrine system, 79–84
Energy, nutrition and, 228–32
English Class chickens, 21, 22, 383–87
Enteritis, 239, 243
Enterprise planning and management (*see* Poultry enterprises)
Entoderm, 136, 137
Environment-genetic interaction, 94, 99
Epidemic tremor, 239
Epididymis, 131
Erysipelas, 242–43
Erythrocytes, 69, 70
Escherichia coli, 242
Esophagus, 60, 61
  removal of, 314–17
Essential amino acids, 227
Estrogen, 81
Ethics (*see* Animal welfare)
Eviscerated yield in whole carcass, 339
Evisceration, 300–323
E vitamin, 209, 210, 246, 282
Excretory system, 64–65
Extraembryonic membranes, 139, 140
Eye ring chicken, 35, 109, 110
Eyes, 109, 110

Fabre, J. Henri, 9
Family farms, 5–6
Farmers, American, 11
Farm prices and profits, impact on food prices, 11
Fast feathering, 105
Fats:
  absorption of, 219–21
  digestion of, 213–19
  metabolism of, 220, 221
  requirement for, 207, 208
Faverolle chickens, 395–96
Feasibility study, 364–65
Feather follicle, 48–50

Feathers:
  anatomy of, 48–51
  color inheritance in, 90–92, 94–98
  egg production and condition of,
    108–10
  laying ability and condition of, 108–10,
    112–13
  production of, 286
  removal of, 294–99
  sex determination and growth of, 105
Feather tracts, 53
Fecal wastes, 64, 65
Feed conversion ratio, 339
Feeders, 165–68, 172–173, 177, 181–86
Feed formulation, 228–34, 259, 260
Feed grains, 5, 9, 11
Feed ingredient analysis table, 410–15
Feed intake, disease and, 251–52
Feed rations, 417–20
Femur, 53, 55
Fertile eggs, 117
Fertility, basis of, 115–19
Fertilization, 72, 116–17, 135
Fiber requirement, 210
Fibrinogen, 70
Fibula, 53, 55
Filoplume, 48, 298, 299
Financial requirements, 368
Flight muscles, 57–59
Flock mating, 105–7
Floor-reared poultry, 177, 182, 184
Floor space, 172, 177
Flow-through system, 359–60
Fluff, 50
Foie gras, 286–87
Follicle-stimulating hormone (FSH), 81
Food bills, 10
Food eggs, 257–83
  albumen height measurement, 269–71
  candling of, 264–69
  cholesterol and, 282–83
  cleaning of, 263, 274
  collection of, 263, 272
  consumption of, 276–78, 280, 282–83
  distribution of, 263, 275
  exterior quality factors, 264–65
  factors influencing quality of, before
    laying, 259–60
  grading of, 263–65, 278–79
  inedible, conditions constituting,
    271–72
  interior quality factors, 264, 266
  marketing of, 276–78
  nutritional quality of, 281
  packaging of, 275
  preparation of, 280–81
  prices of, 279, 281–82
  products made from, 276
  purchase of, 278
  shells of (*see* Shells)
  size of, 279
  storage of, 261, 263, 269, 273, 278–80
  unwashed and unrefrigerated, 261, 262
  weighing of, 269–71
Forced feeding, 173
Fowl, 286
Fowl cholera, 242
Fowl plague, 240
Fowl pox, 239

Fowl typhoid, 241–42
Fox, Michael, 351–52
French Class chickens, 394–96
Frizzle chickens, 399
Frozen poultry meat, 336–37
Fumigation of eggs, 152–55
Fungal diseases, 237, 245
Further-processed poultry products,
  327–34

Gall bladder, 62, 63
  removal of, 308, 309
Gallus, 17–18
Gallus bankiva (Red Jungle Fowl), 16,
  17, 18
Games Class chickens, 392–93
Gander, 40
Gas flame brooders, 165, 166
Gastrulation, 136
Geese, 2, 285
  age of, at processing, 286
  anatomical features, nomenclature of,
    39, 40
  anatomy of (*see* Anatomy)
  artificial incubation requirements for,
    145
  artificial insemination of, 126–30
  breed identification and classification,
    28–29
  domestication of, 20–21
  production of (*see* Poultry production)
  reproduction in (*see* Reproduction)
Generic eggs, 278
Genes, 86–98
Genetic code, 87
Genetics, 85–100
Genotype, 90–92
Giblets, 300
Gizzard, removal of, 306, 309–11
Glottis, 65, 69
Glucose, 217, 220, 221
Gosypol, 206–7
Government regulation of poultry meat
  processing, 323–27
Grading:
  eggs, 263–64, 278–79
  poultry meat, 322–23, 355–36
Gravity ventilation systems, 187
Green whites, 271
Growth hormones, 211
Guanine, 87, 88, 224, 226
Guinea fowl, 2, 21, 285
  age of, at processing, 287
  anatomy of (*see* Anatomy)
  artificial incubation requirements for,
    145
  breed identification and classification,
    29–30
  reproduction in (*see* Reproduction)
Guinea fowl production (*see* Poultry
  production)
Gumboro disease, 238

Hackles, 34, 35
Haemocytometer, 132
Hamburg chickens, 396
Hamburg Class chickens, 396
Hamuli, 51

Hanging bell waterers, 166, 169
Hardware cloth, 170, 196, 198
Hatchability, 148, 158
Hatchers, 152–53
Hatchery operation management and
  design, 357–64
Hatching record sheet, 156–57
Haugh unit, 269
Hausser and Levy-Hausser "Hy-Lite
  Corpuscle Counting Chamber,"
  132–33
Heart, 68, 69
  development of, 138–39
  removal of, 310
Hemoglobin, 69
Hens, 38, 39, 107–13
Heritability, 100
Heterozygous genes, 90–94, 101, 102
High-altitude incubation, 157–61
Histomonas meleagridis, 244
Histomoniasis, 244
Hock joint, 34, 35, 55, 59
Holland chickens, 23, 380
Homozygous genes, 90–94, 102
Hormone secretion, 79–84
Houdan chickens, 394–95
Housing, 164, 174–201, 350–51
Humerus, 53, 54
Humidity:
  housing, 172, 176–77, 261
  incubation, 145, 149–51
Hybrid, 100, 103
Hybridization, 103
Hybrid vigor, 100
Hydrolysis, 217–19
Hy-Lite Corpuscle Counting Chamber,
  132–33
Hyoid bone, 54, 61
Hypothalamus, 82
Hypoxia, chronic, 157
Hypoxic stress, 159

Immunity, 236–37
Inbred, 100
Inbred line, 100, 102–4
Inbreeding, 101–5
Incomplete dominance, 90, 94–95
Incubation:
  artificial, 145–61
  natural, 137–46
Incubators, 146, 148–52
Inedible eggs, conditions constituting,
  271–72
Infection, 236
Infectious bronchitis (IB), 239–40
Infectious bursal disease (IBD), 238
Infection coryza, 243
Infectious laryngotracheitis (LT), 240
Infertility, 117–19
Influenza, 240
Infundibulum of oviduct, 71, 72
Inheritance, 86–100
Insecticide, 41
Insemination (*see* Artificial insemination)
Inspected for Wholesomeness seal, 321,
  327
Inspection, 316–24
Insulation, 190
Insulin, 80

Integrated broiler production units, 6
Interclavicular air sac, 65, 66
Intercrossing, systematic, 101–4
Internal layering, 248
Intestines, 60–63
  removal of, 303–9
Iodine, 282
Iron, 208, 282
Islets of Langerhaus, 80
Isthmus of oviduct, 71, 72

Java chickens, 22, 380
Jersey Giant chickens, 22, 374–75
Johnson, Lyndon B., 324
Jugular vein, severing of, 292–93

Keel, 108, 110
Khaki Campbell duck, 26–28
Kidneys, 64
Kilocalories, 231
Knob, 39, 40
K vitamin, 209

La Fleche chickens, 396
Lakenvelder chickens, 394
Lamona chickens, 22, 380
Langshan chickens, 23, 382–83
Large intestine, 60–63
Laryngotracheitis, 240
Larynx, 65, 69
Latebra, 77
Layers, characteristics of, 107–13
Least-cost production, 232, 370
Leghorn chickens, 21, 24, 42, 95, 176,
  258, 389–90
Leg muscle, 56–60
Legs:
  anatomy of, 53, 55–60
  egg production and condition of, 108,
    110
Leucocytes, 69–70
Leucosis, 210
Lice, 244
Light:
  four housing, 170, 186, 199–200
  ovulation and, 83–84
  reproduction and, 119–20
Limestone, 207, 208
Litter, 170, 177, 193, 245
Liver, 62, 64
  removal of, 307–9
Lumbar vertebrae, 53, 54
Lungs, removal of, 312–13
Luteinizing hormone (LH), 81
Lymphoid leukosis, 238
Lysine, 206

Magnum of oviduct, 71, 72
Malay chickens, 397
Male process, 73
Management of poultry enterprises,
  369–71
Mandible, 53, 54
Manganese, 207, 208, 259
Manure, 190–92
Manure handling, 178, 179
Marek's disease, 210, 238

Market demand, 365
Market goals and projections, 365
Market potential, 364, 366
Mason, James, 351–52
Mating, 73–74, 105–7, 118
Mediterranean Class chickens, 21, 23,
  388–92
Mesoderm, 137
Messenger RNA, 223–27
Metabolism, 222–32
Metabolizable energy, 231
Metatarsus, 55, 56
Methionine, 206
Microvilli, 215–17, 219
Milking bench, 121
Minerals:
  absorption of, 62
  egg quality and, 259
  in eggs, 282
  metabolism and, 222
  requirements for, 207, 208
Minorca chickens, 24, 95, 390–91
Mites, 244
Modern Game chickens, 393
Mold, 245
Moldy eggs, 272
Molting, 109, 110, 112–13
Money management, 369–70
Monosaccharides, 217–20
Morse, Wayne, 324
Mosaic hybrid turkeys, 98
Muscovy ducks, 26, 145
Muscular system, 56–60
Musty eggs, 272
Mycoplasma, 238–39, 362–64

Narragansett turkeys, 96, 97
National Poultry Improvement Plan,
  361–63
Neck, removal of, 314–18
Negative pressure ventilation systems,
  188–90
Nervous system, 81–84
Neural groove, 137–38
Newcastle disease, 210, 240, 255–56
New Hampshire chickens, 22, 41, 43,
  375–76
New York Dressed Poultry, 6–7, 300
New York Live Poultry Commission
  Association, 323
Nomenclature, 33–40
Nonessential amino acids, 227
Nutrient composition table, 230
Nutrients, required, 204–11
Nutrition, 203–34, 351
  absorption, 219–21
  digestion, 60–64, 213–19
  feed formulation, 228–34
  metabolism, 220–32
  required nutrients, feed ingredients,
    and additives, 204–11
Nutritional influences on eggs, 259–60
Nutritional quality of eggs, 281

Oil meals, 206
Oil requirement, 207, 208
Old English Game chickens, 392–93
Omphalitis, 247

Oriental Class chickens, 397–98
Orpington chickens, 23, 386
Ovarian follicle, 81
Ovary, 70–73
Oviduct, 71, 72, 81, 175, 248
Oviposition, 73, 82–84
Ovulation, 81, 82, 83
Ovum, 71–72, 88, 91–92, 135
Oxygen, 158, 159
Oxytocin, 82–83
Oyster shells, 207, 208

Packaging:
  eggs, 275
  poultry meat, 314–15, 326
Panting, 68
Pan-type waterers, 166, 168
Papillae, 73, 74
  copulation and, 116
  stimulation of, for semen collection,
    121–22, 127–28
Parabronchi, 66–68
Parasitic diseases, 237, 244–45
Parathyroid glands, 79, 80, 81
Paratyphoid infection, 243
Pasteurella multocide, 242
Patella, 53, 55
Pea comb, 35, 36
Peafowl, 21, 30, 32
  anatomy of (*see* Anatomy)
  artificial incubation requirements for,
    145
  reproduction in (*see* Reproduction)
Peafowl production (*see* Poultry
  production)
Pectoral girdle, 53, 54, 55
Pectoralis major, 59
Pendulous crop, 247
Pen mating, 105–7
Percent edible raw meat of carcass
  weight, 340, 341
Percent edible raw meat of live ready-
  for-market weight, 340–41
Perosis, 245–46
Personnel management, 248–49, 370
Personnel selection, 368
Pheasant production (*see* Poultry
  production)
Pheasants, 21
  anatomy of (*see* Anatomy)
  artificial incubation requirements for,
    145
  reproduction in (*see* Reproduction)
  variety identification and classification,
    30, 32
Phenotype, 90, 94–95, 101
Phosphorus, 207, 208, 211, 259, 282
Physical characteristics, inherited, 94
Picking, 294, 296–99
Pigeon milk, 83
Pigeons (squab), 2, 29, 30
Pituitary glands, 79–81
Planning of poultry enterprises, 364–69
Platinum yolks, 260
Plumal feathers, 48, 51
Plymouth Rock chickens, 22, 42–43, 95,
  376–77
Polish chickens, 398–99
Polish Class Chickens, 398–99

Posing, 41
Positive pressure ventilation systems, 187–89
Post-mortem inspection, 306–8, 325
Potassium permanganate method of fumigation, 154
Poult, 39
Poultry barbecue, 338–39
Poultry classification (*see* Classification)
Poultry enterprises, 357–71
  hatchery operation management and design, 357–64
  management, 369–71
  planning, 364–69
Poultry industry, 1–13
  as American agricultural enterprise, 8–13
  poultry development as industry, 1–8
Poultry meat, 2–8, 10, 285–343
  comparative value of available meats vs., 339–43
  muscle anatomy and, 56
  preparation of, 337–39
  price of, 3, 4, 340–42
  processing of (*see* Poultry meat processing)
  purchase of, 334–35
  storage of, 335–36
Poultry meat processing, 285–334
  age of bird at, 285–87
  bleeding, 292–93
  chilling, 319–20
  evisceration, 300–323
  government regulation of, 323–27
  grading of, 322–32, 335–36
  industry changes in, 287–88
  meat products, 325, 327–34
  packaging, 314–15, 326
  picking, 294, 296–99
  scalding, 293–95
  shackling, 288–89, 291
  stunning, 289, 292
  transport to processing plant, 288–91
Poultry nomenclature, 33–40
Poultry production:
  animal welfare (*see* Animal welfare)
  artificial incubation, 145–61
  breeder flocks, 201
  breeding (*see* Breeding)
  broilers, 192–93
  brooding, 165–74, 192–94, 196–97, 199
  capons, 194–95
  diseases (*see* Diseases)
  ducks, 197, 199
  eggs (*see* Eggs; Food eggs)
  feeding, 228–33
  geese, 197, 199
  housing, 164, 174–201, 350–51
  nutrition (*see* Nutrition)
  poultry enterprise planning and management (*see* Poultry enterprise planning and management)
  poultry meat (*see* Poultry meat)
  pullets, 199–201
  roasters, 193–94
  turkeys, 196–98
Poultry Products Inspection Act of 1957, 324–25
Power requirements, 367

Preen gland, 52
Prices:
  egg, 277–79, 281–82
  poultry meat, 3, 4, 340–42
Primary coverts, 37
Primitive streak, 137
Prolactin, 83
Prolapse, 248
Protein, 5
  absorption of, 219–21
  concentration of, in conversion of poultry feed to poultry carcass, 228
  cost per pound of, 340–43
  digestion of, 213–19
  metabolism of, 220–32
  requirement for, 205–7
Proteus, 271
Protozoan diseases, 237, 243–44
Proventriculus, 60–62
Pseudomonas, 271
Pterylae, 52
Pubic bones, 53, 55, 109, 110
Pullet, 38
Pullet disease, 246–47
Pullet production, 199–201
Pullorum disease, 240, 361–63
Pygostyle, 53, 55

Quail disease, 243
Quill feathers, 48, 49, 51

Rations, 417–20
Rearing, 165–75
Recessive genes, 90–95
Red blood cells, 69, 70
Red cap chickens, 23, 387
Red Jungle Fowl, 16, 17, 18
Refrigerated trucking, 6
Reproduction, 115–34
  age and, 119
  artificial insemination (*see* Artificial insemination)
  breeding (*see* Breeding)
  embronic development, 118, 134–46
  fertility, basis of, 115–19
  incubation, 145–61
  light and, 119–20
  selection and, 120
Reproductive system, 70–79
Resistance to disease, 249–50
Respiratory disease chronic (CRD), 238–39
Respiratory system, 65–69
Retail price per pound of raw poultry 341, 342
Rhode Island Red chickens, 22, 41–43, 378–79
Rhode Island White chickens, 22, 95
Rib cage, 53, 55
Ribonucleic acid (RNA), 224–27
Ribosomes, 222–27
Ribs, 53, 55, 67
Rickets, 246
Rights of animals, 348–56
Roaster chickens, 193–94, 285–86
Rollin, Bernard, 352–53
Rooster, 38
Roosts, 177

Rose comb, 35, 36
Rouen ducks, 26
Roup, 243
Runner ducks, 26
Rusty Black turkeys, 97

Salivary glands, 61
Salmonella gallinarum, 241
Salmonella pullorum, 240–41, 361–62
Salt requirement, 207, 208
Sanitation program, employee, 249
Sanitizing bath, drive-through, 249
Scalding, 293–95
Scald tunnel, 293, 295
Scapula, 53, 54, 67
Secondary coverts, 37
Secretory goblet cells, 215
Selection, 113–14
Semen, 73, 75
  collection of (*see* Semen collection)
  composition of, 131
  ejaculation of, 116–17, 122, 127–28
  evaluation of, 132–34
  production of, 118–20
  quality of, 122–23
  sperm concentration in, 132, 133
  variations from normal, 131–32
Semen collection:
  geese, 127–29
  receptacles for, 130
  roosters, 120–24
  turkeys, 120–24
Seminiferous tubules, 73, 75, 131
Sertoli cells, 131
Sex cells, 131
Sex chromosomes, 87–89, 91–94
Sex determination, 88–89, 94, 104–5
Sex hormones, 80–81
Sex linkage, 91–93, 104–5
Sexual dimorphism, 34, 38
Shackling, 288–89, 291
Shanks, 34, 35, 45, 52, 55, 110
Shells, 71–73, 76–79
  color of, 257–58
  membranes of, 72, 76, 77
  moisture loss through, 261
  quality of, 148, 264, 265
  thickness of, 77
Showing poultry, 18–19, 40–46
Singeing of filoplumes, 298, 299
Singer, Peter, 352
Single comb, 35
Single Comb White Leghorn chickens, 258
Skeleton, preparation of, 403–6
Skin:
  anatomy of, 48–50, 52
  egg production and condition and pigmentation of, 109–11
Skull, 53, 54
Slate turkeys, 96
Slipped tendon, 245–46
Slow feathering, 105
Small intestines, 60–62
Smith, S. B., 146
Snood, 38, 39
Somatic cells, 87
Sour egg, 271
Soybean oil meal, 206, 233–34

Speciesism, 349
Specific gravity of eggs, measuring, 407
Spent hens, 285
Sperm, 73, 75, 76, 88, 116, 117
  avian vs. mammalian, 117
  concentration of, 132, 133
  counting, 132–33
  in fertilization, 117, 135
  inadequate numbers of, 118
  motility of, 133, 134
Spermatids, 131
Spermatocytes, 75, 131
Spermatogenesis, 73, 75, 131
Spermatozoa (*See* Sperm)
Spin-picking machine, 26, 297
Spur, 55–56
Starve outs, 73
Sternum, 53, 55, 67
Stewing chickens, 286
Stigma, 72
Storage:
  eggs, 149, 150, 261, 263, 270, 272,
    278–80
  poultry meat, 336–37
Strains, 15, 21, 119
Strawberry comb, 35–36
Stunning, 289, 292
Sultan chickens, 399
Sumatra chickens, 397–98
Summer disease, 246–47
Supporting resources, availability of, 366
Supracopacoideus muscle, 59, 333
Sussex chickens, 23, 387
Swans, 33
Syrinx, 65, 69
Systematic intercrossing, 101–4

Tankage, 207
Temperament, egg production and,
  108–10
Temperature:
  artificial incubation and, 145, 150
  body, 68, 175
  egg quality and, 260, 261, 263
  energy requirement and, 230
  housing, 171–76, 260
  poultry meat storage and, 336–37
  of scalding water, 293–94
  vitamins and, 210
Tendons, 58–60
Testes, 73, 74, 80–81, 116
  surgical removal of, 194–95
Testosterone, 80–81
Thawing of poultry meat, 336–37
Thigh muscle, 35, 56–57
Thoracic air sacs, 66
Thoracic vertebrae, 53, 54
Thymine, 87, 89, 224, 226
Thymus, 79, 80
Thyroid glands, 79, 80, 83
Tibia, 53, 55
Toe clipping, 360
Toes, 34, 40, 45, 52, 53, 55, 58, 60

Tom, 39
Tongue, 61
Toulouse geese, 29
Trachea, 65, 66, 67, 69
  removal of, 314–15
Transfer RNA, 224–27
Transportation, 288–91, 323, 367–68
Transylvania Naked Neck chickens, 400
Triglycerides, 217–19
Trough feeders, 165, 167, 182
Trough waterers, 166, 169, 182, 184
Tube feeders, 165, 167
Tumors, 238
Turken chickens, 400
Turkey industry, 1, 4, 6–8
Turkey meat (*see* Poultry meat)
Turkey production (*see* Poultry
  production)
Turkey rations, 419–20
Turkeys, 2, 3
  age of, at processing, 286
  anatomical features, nomenclature of,
    38–39
  anatomy of (*see* Anatomy)
  artificial incubation requirements for,
    145
  artificial insemination of, 120–27
  cutting, 421–24
  deboning, 425–27
  domestication of, 20
  feather color, inheritance in, 96–98
  reproduction in (*see* Reproduction)
  variety identification and classification,
    25–26
  wild, 20
Typhoid, 241–42

Ulcerative enteritis, 243
United States Agriculture Department
  (USDA):
  egg grade shields of, 278, 279
  Egg Grading Manual of, 271–72
  poultry meat grade shields of, 326–27
  poultry meat grading by, 326–27,
    334–35
  poultry meat inspections by, 324–27,
    335
  poultry meat requirements of, 289,
    292, 302–3
Uracil, 224, 226
Ureters, 64
Urinary system, 64–65
Urine, 64–65
Uterus, 71–72

Vaccination program, 254–55
Vagina, 71–73, 74
Vapor barrier, 190
Varieties, 21–24, 373–74
Vascular sac, 72
Vas deferens, 73, 74, 116, 131
Vent-cutting tool, 304, 305

Ventilation:
  housing, 164–65, 172, 187–90
  incubator, 151–52
Vent picking, 248
Vertebrae, 53, 54
Viral diseases, 237–40
Virulence of microorganisms, 250, 251
Vitamins:
  absorption of, 62
  deficiency of, 208–9, 246
  in eggs, 282
  metabolism and, 222
  requirements for, 207–10
Vitellus (*see* Yolk)
V-shaped comb, 36

Warm-room brooding, 173
Washing:
  eggs, 186, 263, 274
  show birds, 43–44
Waste disposal and utilization, 190–92
Waterers, 166, 168–70, 173, 182, 184–85,
  205
Water requirement, 205
Wattles, 35, 52, 109, 110
Web surface, 50, 51
Weighing of eggs, 269–71
White blood cells, 69–70
White Faced Black Spanish chickens,
  390, 391
White feather color inheritance, 95
White Leghorn chickens, 95
White meat, 56
White Pekin ducks, 26, 27
White Plymouth Rock chickens, 95
White rot, 271
White-shell eggs, 257, 258
White turkeys, 96
Wild chickens, 17
Wild turkeys, 20
Windpuffs, 195
Wing bow, 36–37
Wing coverts, 37
Wing feathers, 36–37
Wing front, 36, 37
Wing shoulder, 36–37
Worms, 245
Wright, Sewell, 102
Wyandotte chickens, 22, 42, 379–80

Yellow pigment and egg production,
  109–11
Yellow skin chickens, 52
Yolk, 71, 72, 77–78
  bacterial contamination of, 270–71
  development of, 135–143
  quality factors, 260, 266
Yolk index, 269
Yolk sac, 139, 143
Yolk stalk, 139, 140

Zinc, 207, 208
Zygotes, 89, 135–36